FINANCIAL CRISIS, CONTAGION, AND CONTAINMENT

FINANCIAL CRISIS, CONTAGION, AND CONTAINMENT

FROM ASIA TO ARGENTINA

Padma Desai

PRINCETON UNIVERSITY PRESS   PRINCETON AND OXFORD

Published by Princeton University Press, 41 William Street,
Princeton, New Jersey 08540
In the United Kingdom: Princeton University Press, 3 Market Place,
Woodstock, Oxfordshire OX20 1SY

Library of Congress Cataloging-in-Publication Data

Desai, Padma.
Financial crisis, contagion, and containment : from Asia to
Argentina / Padma Desai.
p. cm.
Includes bibliographical references and index.
ISBN 0-691-11392-0 (alk. paper)
1. Financial crises. 2. Economic stabilization. I. Title.
HB3722 .D47 2003
332'.042—dc21   2002031745

British Library Cataloging-in-Publication Data is available

This book has been composed in Sabon

Printed on acid-free paper. ∞

www.pupress.princeton.edu

Printed in the United States of America

10 9 8 7 6 5 4 3 2

For
TN
ācharyah pūrva-rūpam, antevāsy uttara-rūpam, vidyā samdhih
(Taittirīya Upaniṣad, 1.3.3)

Contents

Preface

THE BORROWING BINGE of the eighties and the nineties was a pervasive phenomenon in the global economy. Japanese businesses borrowed heavily and invested unwisely in the eighties. U.S. households went overboard in stretching their finances in the second half of the nineties. Businesses, banks, and several governments in emerging market economies accumulated unsustainable foreign debt obligations.

There was however a difference in the process in the developed group at the center and the vulnerable economies at the periphery of the international financial system. Borrowers in the developed market economies managed their debt burden, by source and duration, of their free will. Their policy makers undertook homegrown measures for battling the consequences of the resulting economic booms. By contrast, the emerging market economies analyzed in this book invited financial and currency crises in their economies from destabilizing foreign capital flows. These flows resulted from a premature opening of their financial systems in an environment of hothouse pressure that emanated from private and institutional lenders in the U.S.-led developed center. From Asia in 1997 to Argentina in 2002, these countries struggled with the consequences of externally imposed financial crises and International Monetary Fund (IMF)-led policy prescriptions that they did not own.

I adopt this comparative center-periphery framework in the book for tracing the origins and spread of financial crises. I also employ it for arguing that emerging market economies with weak institutions and political maneuverability cannot be expected to grow crisis-free in a world of unrestricted capital mobility and floating exchange rates which are the latest magic bullets uncovered by the IMF. Even the U.S., eurozone, and Japan, advanced market systems with institutional capabilities and open economy adaptability face problems, which I analyze, in implementing successful policies in pursuit of stable growth.

The book also provides simple analytical models grounded in step-by-step empirical evidence in the crisis-swept countries for isolating the impact of volatile short-term capital flows in initiating financial crises and spreading them across countries. My policy judgments flow from relevant facts and unfolding events rather than from esoteric conceptualizing or random stone throwing. I also keep away from an all-embracing treatment of globalization issues and focus on financial crises with an eye on the IMF, its dubious record in rescuing crisis-ridden economies, and its unfolding policy agenda with uncertain promise for preempting future crises. The IMF, I feel, is neither good nor bad; it is simply incorrigible.

I would like to thank Manmohan Agarwal for commenting on a draft, Emil Czechowski for designing the maps and charts, tracking data sources, and providing creative research input on Argentina and Turkey, Bikas Joshi for locating the chronology and the cartoons relating to the Asian financial crisis, and Nyree Hartman and Nelly Nyambi for providing information on Brazil. The book has grown over the years from my continuing association with students at Columbia University and interaction with participants from the world of business and finance at conferences around the world. I have written it in the hope of convincing students and non-students alike that financial globalization is a complex process and can be destructive. A sensible approach with alternative possibilities, which I suggest, is in order so that lenders from the developed countries at the center of the world economy and borrowers at its periphery can benefit from the collective gains of global capital flows.

Padma Desai
New York, 2002

FINANCIAL CRISIS, CONTAGION, AND CONTAINMENT

Asian crisis
- Premature opening to foreign inflows pushed by IMF

- Recession: IMF forced contractionary measures
   - CA

1

Introduction

THE GLOBAL ECONOMY experienced extraordinary changes in the nineties that affected the economic prospects of both developed and less developed countries when the decade ended.

One of its alarming features was the widespread and massive borrowing in both groups. In the U.S., the government budget deficit was being energetically brought down during the Clinton administration, but American households and businesses borrowed freely during the unprecedented economic boom of the second half of the decade. Japanese corporate and financial sectors borrowed heavily and invested unwisely in land and real estate, burdening Japanese banks with a mountain of nonperforming loans when the unsustainable expansion of the eighties ended. In that regard, investors in the European Monetary Union (EMU), latecomers on the scene with its formation in 1998, were an exception. They took advantage of the expanded bond market defined in the single currency euro and invested in U.S. industry and financial activities.

Countries of the less developed group did not lag behind as borrowers. In the East Asian cluster of Indonesia, Malaysia, Philippines, South Korea, and Thailand analyzed in this book, government finances were in balance but businesses and banks borrowed on short term in foreign currency and invested long term in dubious domestic assets. Governments in Russia, Brazil, Argentina, and Turkey accumulated a significant foreign debt burden without concern or ability to meet their repayment obligations via export earnings.

A major difference in the borrowing activities of the two groups arose from the decision-making process. Borrowers, public and private, in the three dominating zones—the U.S., the eurozone, and Japan included in this book—were free agents unencumbered by external pressures in their decisions to borrow and pay up their debts. By contrast, the economies in the second group analyzed here invited financial and currency crises from the borrowing binge facilitated by a premature opening up of their capital markets to free entry of short-term, speculative funds. Preferences of developed country lenders, private and institutional, played a role in the hasty liberalization of their economies' financial and capital account transactions involving foreign exchange.

A difference in the policy responses between the two sets of countries was also apparent when the debt-led expansion came to a halt. It ended in Japan in 1990 and in the U.S. in mid-2000. The East Asian economies were swept in a capital-outflow led financial and currency crisis that began in Thailand in mid-1997. Currencies tumbled at varying rates in Russia in August 1998, Brazil in January 1999, Turkey in early 2001, and Argentina in December 2001. Policy decisions to promote stable growth in Japan (marked by failure) and the U.S. (significantly on track despite the negative impact of the terrorist attacks of September 11, 2001) were domestically driven. By contrast, the crisis-ridden economies lost their decision-making initiatives under International Monetary Fund (IMF) bailouts, which consisted of extreme monetary and fiscal discipline and unrealistic triple-policy arrangements of floating exchange rates, free capital mobility, and a presumed monetary policy autonomy. The IMF sought to resolve an externally imposed crisis by subjecting these recession-prone economies to severe contractionary regimens, which would have been unthinkable in a developed economy in the midst of an economic downturn. None of these countries were adequately prepared for achieving postcrisis stable growth by implementing independent monetary policy in the midst of unrestricted capital flows and freely floating exchange rates. These triple-policy arrangements, preferred by the IMF, were more suited to the developed economies with flexible markets, robust institutions, and adequate supervision of their banking and financial sectors.

In this chapter, I introduce the book's theme of the contrasting interaction between the economic challenges and the policy responses of recent years in the developed center of the world economy and the less developed periphery. I begin with the former group.

The Developed Countries: Events and Outcomes

At the start of the new millennium, policy makers in the three dominant economies—the U.S., the eurozone, and Japan—were engaged in maintaining inflation-free, stable growth. The unprecedented expansion of the U.S. economy, marked by the stock market boom, ended in mid-2000, raising policy debates about a stimulus package aimed at arresting the economic slowdown that turned into a recession after the events of 9/11. Twelve of the fifteen European Union countries formed a monetary and economic union in May 1998, and surrendered their monetary policy autonomy to the European Central Bank by discarding their individual currencies and adopting the euro. The end of the Japanese investment boom of the eighties left a massive burden of bad loans with banks that posed formidable policy challenges for Japanese authorities in steering the economy to stable growth.

In 2002, the outcomes of the policy initiatives in each area varied significantly. The U.S. emerged in the first quarter out of a post-9/11 recession, which turned out to be short and shallow. The swift U.S. recovery was aided by the Federal Reserve's aggressive monetary easing and the government's budgetary stimulus. Continuing productivity growth added to the prospects of sustained growth in 2002. The eurozone's economic recovery lagged behind that of the U.S. as the European Central Bank fitfully implemented its mandate of achieving inflation-free growth for the zone in the midst of halting labor market liberalization and corporate sector deregulation reforms in member countries. The worst performer was Japan: a prolonged, on-again, off-again policy mix of monetary easing, tax reform, and clearing of bank debts failed to pull the economy out of the eventual malaise of declining prices. As a result, consumers postponed their spending and companies battled the impact of price deflation on their profitability and delayed capital spending. Japan's economic stagnation continued into 2002.

As I noted, the early years of the nineties were also marked by capital inflows into developing countries that abolished their capital account controls and liberalized their domestic credit and financial markets.

The Developing Countries: Premature Capital Mobility and Its Consequences

These inflows, pushed by determined Washington policy makers and supported by avid Wall Street financiers, were massively short term, speculative, and destabilizing. The banks and financial institutions of the borrowing countries were poorly supervised and their capital/asset ratios were inadequate Their lenders and borrowers were linked via special ties and traditional norms of financial practices. Risk management of portfolios was rudimentary. Short- term loans in hard currency were lent long term to domestic borrowers who invested the funds in real estate and businesses of questionable worth. As the highly leveraged borrowers missed debt payments and declared bankruptcies, foreign creditors withdrew funds aggravating the finances of these borrowers and dragging with them the values of the currencies they dumped. The 1997–98 financial crisis that spread from Bangkok to Brazil via Moscow became a currency crisis.

The nineties were thus marked by economic growth followed by severe downturn in several less developed countries of Asia as well. The East Asian economies of Indonesia, Malaysia, South Korea, and Thailand recorded high growth and low inflation rates and balanced government budgets in the decade leading to 1997. During this same period, the Philippine economy also steadily improved in terms of these norms. These five economies were hit by the financial and currency crisis that began with the collapse of the Thai currency in mid-1997 and spread to Russia and Brazil in 1998; they experienced severe recession from the IMF-imposed monetary and fiscal austerity measures calculated to restore currency stability and foreign investor confidence in their systems.

In contrast to the robust macroeconomic indicators in these East Asian economies in the pre-crisis decade, Russia's economic performance was shaky. The control of inflation from quadruple-digit levels of 1992 to low double-digit numbers thereafter was uncertain, budget deficit at 7 percent of gross domestic product (GDP) remained high, and economic growth in 1997 following a severe contraction of the economy (by half in domestic prices since 1991) was barely visible. In Brazil, the record of successful inflation control and positive economic growth following the adoption of the *Real* Plan in July 1994 was also handicapped by high budget deficits that spilled into current account deficits. As a latecomer attempting the painful transformation from a command to a market economy, the Russian economy in 1997 was far more deficient in its macroeconomic health than the Brazilian economy. It was also more vulnerable to the crisis contagion that spread from East Asia as foreign investors withdrew their ruble- and *real*-denominated assets. On August 17, 1998, the Russian authorities declared a unilateral default on the government's ruble debt, prohibited commercial banks from clearing their foreign liabilities, and devalued the ruble from 6 rubles to a dollar to 26 rubles. In response to a similar withdrawal of assets by nervous foreign investors in the final weeks of 1997, the Brazilian government cut back budget outlays by 2.5 percent of GDP, the central bank pushed up the basic lending rate to 43 1/2 percent, and finally allowed the *real* to float in January 1999.

The East Asian "Crisis Five" and Brazil revived at rates varying from 2 to 3 percent in 2000. More remarkable was the turnaround of the Russian economy at 8 percent, driven by a booming oil sector and the relative price advantage of a substantially devalued ruble in favor of domestic industry. While these economies put the symptoms of a recession behind them, fears arose in late 2000, in unrelated developments, about financial and currency turmoil in debt-ridden Argentina and Turkey. In Argentina, the peso's link to the strong dollar backed by a currency board type arrangement helped squeeze inflation and promote growth until 1998. Following the devaluation of the Brazilian *real* in January 1999, however, the link slowed export growth and set in motion a recession that affected tax revenue inflows resulting in persistent budget deficits. These escalating uncertainties raised foreign investor's fears about a debt default and a peso devaluation, both of which occurred in December 2001. The Turkish lira too came under pressure toward the end of 2000 as a result of endemic budget deficits and extreme inflation that remained at 60 percent in 2001. In 2002, Argentina's economic uncertainties, defying an early solution, threatened to spill into political chaos as well. Turkey's prospects for a steady, low inflation growth depended on its policy makers' ability to bring its budget deficits under control in the midst of contentious politics which worsened with the dissolution of the parliament in August 2002 and announcement of new elections. In Brazil, too, voters' preference in the public opinion polls in favor of a left-of-center presidential candidate in the October 2002 election raised fears of a reversal of pro-market reforms. The IMF sought to relieve the pressure on the *real* induced by capital flows with the announcement of a rescue package of $30 billion on August 7.

The performance and policy record of both groups of countries, in bouncing back from economic slowdown or recession following a boom (as in the U.S., Japan, and the East Asian "Crisis Five") or maintaining steady growth following quadruple-digit inflation (as in Russia, Brazil, and Argentina) or simply achieving stable growth with low inflation without having to overcome the consequences of an economic boom or extreme inflation (as in the eurozone and Turkey), had major differences.

The Differences: Center versus Periphery, and Endogenous versus Exogenous Disturbances

First, among the developed economies of the U.S., the eurozone, and Japan, the U.S. arrangements, despite recent corporate governance scandals, meet the demands of an open market economy. They are least handicapped by structural bottlenecks such as fragmented labor markets, an overly regulated corporate sector, or extravagant welfare benefits. They are endowed with a sophisticated network of financial institutions including commercial banks that are regulated by supervisory agencies. The rapid and extensive adoption of information technology has also kept the U.S. economy ahead in productivity performance. In practice and philosophy, it is relentlessly engaged in the process of Schumpeterian creative destruction, which is encouraged by the resilient responses of households and businesses to policy signals. Despite frequent differences on economic policy issues, the two-party system is committed to the advancement of the free enterprise system. Benefiting from the combined impact of these attributes, the U.S. is better equipped than the eurozone and Japan in overcoming economic fluctuations and maintaining inflation-free, stable growth. It can also readily function under the policy trinity of a floating dollar, free capital mobility, and pursuit of monetary easing or tightening by the independent Federal Reserve.

Mon flex. thanEU

Second, from a historical perspective, the developed group as a whole (including other member countries of the Organisation for Economic Co-operation & Development) is more advanced than the developing group (and others in that category excluded from this book's focus) in institutional capabilities, appropriate policy formulation, cohesive political decision making, and technological and managerial adaptability. It also has the maneuverability to battle the competitive pressures of an open global economy. The developed group belongs to the center of the world economic system not only because it has a dominant share of global income but also because it is better equipped to prevent the less developed group in the periphery from enlarging its share of the pie. This uneven playing field raises the issue of the speed with which the peripheral group can adopt the institutions and economic practices of the developed center and integrate with it in order for both to profit from capital flows from the developed center to the developing periphery. Ready or not for such integration, the less developed economies, which have opened their borders to capital flows, are called emerging market economies, a label I adopt for my analysis.

Third, the center-periphery inequitable relationship was brought into sharp focus in the nineties as the fast-paced and premature opening up of several emerging market economies to the free flow of capital threw them into economic turmoil in 1997, beginning with the East Asian crisis. Emerging market policy makers with few exceptions (in China and India) operated in a highly pressured environment in favor of such flows pushed from the advocates, official and private, of the U.S.-led center. The resulting economic and political destabilization in these economies in the nineties was thus imposed from outside, whereas the economic problems and acute challenges in the U.S., the eurozone, and Japan were endogenous.

Fourth, the exogenous-endogenous difference also extended to the policy measures that the crisis-swept economies were inevitably driven to implement under IMF rescue, which they sought. By contrast, the success (in the U.S.), the paralysis (in Japan), and the slowness (in the eurozone) resulted from policies that were domestically formulated and implemented. The countries that sought IMF bailout (with the sole exception of Malaysia which instead imposed capital account controls to moderate capital outflows) did not "own" their programs. The IMF fiscal and monetary austerity measures aimed at restoring investor confidence and arresting currency declines were severe because the financial support was inadequate to fill the liquidity crunch that resulted from the sudden and massive outflows of speculative funds. The IMF was also ideologically opposed to the adoption of market-based capital account controls in crisis-swept economies that sought its support, although such measures could have reduced the necessary funding. Again, the IMF failed to initiate timely and comprehensive debt restructuring for highly indebted recipients, such as Argentina, without which its budget deficit targets became irrelevant and its monetary tightening recipe ceased to be credible. Occasionally the size, timing, and frequency of support were influenced by the non-economic considerations signaled by the U.S.-led center. Far from being an objective and adequate lender of the last resort for emerging markets in financial crisis, the IMF in effect operated as a G-7–led institution, aggressively extending a mandate of irreversible capital mobility in inadequately prepared and therefore financially vulnerable emerging markets.

Based on these arguments, I adopt a comparative, center-periphery framework in this book. I lift the analysis beyond the narrow focus of crises origins, the contagion which may or may not spread, the factors leading to the relatively speedy revival of some emerging market economies in contrast to others, and the failure of IMF policy prescriptions. Some of this has been done before although I combine systematic empirical underpinning and analytical rigor in my comparative framework in order to reach policy judgments.

The Comparative Perspective

My broader, panoramic theme centers on four propositions. First, some economies even among the developed group are more geared toward bouncing back from a slowdown or a recession or a banking crisis than others. The U.S., for example, weathers economic ups and downs more resiliently and rapidly than other countries. Second, irrespective of the impact and duration, the economic malaise of the nineties in the developed center was homegrown and its resolution domestically driven. By contrast, the financial crises in the periphery were planted from outside. Third, the premature opening of peripheral economies to capital flows from the advanced center was based on the assumption that they were similar in their absorptive capacity to the robust performers in the center. The capital market globalizers overlooked the fact that the countries in the periphery lacked the necessary institutions and corporate practices enabling investors and borrowers to gain from capital flows. Finally, the IMF preference for capital flows into emerging markets, its standard prescriptions of fiscal and monetary austerity in crisis-swept economies, its lack of flexibility in initiating country-specific policy responses, such as preemptive debt restructuring, and its insistence on the triple arrangements of a floating exchange rate, free capital mobility, and monetary policy independence, create a less than benign view of its policy agenda with respect to capital account liberalization in emerging market economies. Specifically, this no-pain no-gain approach means that the recurring crises of recent years are the inevitable costs of the extension of financial globalization that the peripheral economies must undergo in order to reap financial globalization's eventual benefits.

The lack of institutional and structural readiness of the borrowing economies in the periphery for absorbing capital inflows can best be contrasted by examining the preparedness of the economies in the center for voluntarily attracting these flows and maintaining stable economic growth.

Policies and Performance in the Developed Center: The Contrasts

Of the three dominant global economies of the center, the U.S. (discussed in chapter 2) is more adept in overcoming economic fluctuations of internal origin via an interplay between institutional and structural underpinning and policy signals than the eurozone (discussed in chapter 3) and Japan (discussed in chapter 4). The U.S. free enterprise model, supported by the strength of its institutions and its technological innovativeness, and marked by the resilient responses of its businesses and households to appropriate policy signals, has been hard to implant in the eurozone and in Japan, even though both are market systems with institutional capabilities and open economy adaptability. In particular, the Federal Reserve has been more successful in implementing the policy trinity, also adopted by Japan and the eurozone, of a floating dollar, capital mobility, and monetary policy autonomy with a view to achieving inflation-free growth. Despite the continuing debates about the effectiveness of Federal Reserve policies, their timing and the lags, the conflicting signals about the economy's prospects of bouncing back in 2002 from the slowdown of early 2001 followed by the post-9/11 recession, the model's resilience backed by its upbeat productivity performance is incontrovertible. By contrast, the European Central Bank, reined in by a less integrated and deregulated eurozone and lower productivity growth, has continued battling the dilemma of economic growth and inflation control. EMU members have lagged behind in forging a unified free enterprise area, marked by reduced pension benefits and low budget deficits, unregulated labor markets, and low corporate taxes that can propel their corporations into high-productivity trajectories.

Despite this contrast, the economies in the center created their economic problems and "owned" their remedies. Emerging markets, on the other hand, experienced financial and currency turmoil associated with externally pressured opening up of their economies to short-term capital inflows and underwent IMF policy prescriptions that produced severe recessions.

Financial Crisis and Contagion

I analyze nine Asian borrowers (in chapter 5) from the perspective of their exposure to financial destabilization arising from short-term capital inflows. I divide them into three groups of crisis-prone (Indonesia, Malaysia, Philippines, South Korea, and Thailand), crisis-immune (China, Hong Kong, and Taiwan) and crisis-safe (Singapore). These three groups were similar in having strong macroeconomic fundamentals of high growth and low inflation rates, high saving and investment rates, and low to nil budget and current account deficits in the years before the onset of the crisis. The first group however was engulfed in the financial and currency turmoil of 1997–98 (which I narrate in chapter 6), precisely because its short-term capital inflows in relation to foreign exchange earnings were massive and resulted in excessive loans to domestic borrowers and money supply growth. The related collapse of the Russian ruble in August 1998 (discussed in chapter 7) and the sharp decline of the Brazilian *real* in January 1999 (discussed in chapter 8) also resulted from the panic-driven withdrawal of short-term funds, although the Brazilian economy's short-term exposure to foreign borrowing in relation to long-term foreign investment was less precarious.

The financial and currency problems of Turkey and Argentina (discussed in Chapter 9), that gathered speed toward the end of 2000, were unrelated to the Asian malaise, and provide a contrast to the problems relating to crisis management and post-crisis recovery. The emerging market economies of this book from Asia to Latin America had weak institutions, regulatory underpinning, and structural handicaps. However, the fundamentally strong Asian Crisis Five during the pre-crisis years had a greater potential for rapid economic recovery than Turkey, which was fiscally mismanaged and ran high double-digit inflation, and Argentina, which was burdened with the policy albatross of the peso's link with the strong dollar long after the arrangement had successfully squeezed quadruple-digit inflation from the economy. The declining Argentine economy in the end was left without resources for meeting its debt obligations or credible policy choices for initiating a quick recovery.

The 1997–99 contagion (analyzed in chapter 10), spreading from Bangkok to Brazil, was financial in its transmission mechanism, unlike the trade-linked contagion of the earlier decades. Such a financially transmitted global contagion did not transpire from the Argentine and Turkish crises of 2000–01 because quality-conscious, common lenders had kept away from investing in emerging markets except in China and Mexico, and had expected and adjusted to the Argentine debt default. The juxtaposition of these two contrasting contagion scenarios again highlights the role of short-term financial capital in triggering global contagion.

Having failed to plug capital outflows and stabilize their currencies, policy makers in the financially troubled economies, who turned to the IMF with a view to be 'rescued' or 'bailed out' from a desperate predicament, could not expect to 'own' the policy prescriptions. The lone exception was Malaysia, which resorted to capital account controls. The IMF imposed strict monetary control and fiscal discipline, and worked up detailed programs for structural and institutional reforms (as I discuss in chapter 11). Its funding was occasionally supplemented by bilateral credits and bolstered by intrusive performance criteria. The conditions required higher interest rates to stem capital outflows, sharp budget cutbacks and fiscal discipline to restore investor confidence, and a switch from fixed to floating exchange rates. (An exception to this occurred in Argentina until December 2001, when Argentine authorities were forced to free the peso from its link with the dollar in reaction to the IMF's refusal to extend a credit tranche.) The programs created severe recessions in most cases and intensified political uncertainties (in Indonesia) and investor nervousness about the prospective success of IMF bailout (in Russia and Argentina, and subsequently in Brazil in 2002).

The IMF to the Rescue: How Did It Fare?

The IMF's rescue packages were inadequate to meet the liquidity needs of recipients; its macroeconomic targets of budget deficits and inflation control failed to distinguish between feasible and desirable possibilities; and its role became increasingly controversial. A firm believer in global capital markets, it rejected policy deviations from its arsenal such as temporary, market-based controls on capital outflows that could soften the need for excessive fiscal and monetary austerity on a crisis-ridden economy. It also did not consider implementing timely and orderly debt restructuring, for example, in Argentina, with a view to equitably distribute the costs of such arrangements on foreign lenders, domestic borrowers, and local citizenry and pave the way for the removal of the fixed peg of the peso to the strong dollar. Requiring extensive restructuring of institutions and practices in borrowing members as part of its bailout, the IMF itself remained largely un-reconstructed. Having encouraged capital flows in economies unprepared for absorbing them successfully, it failed to monitor the extravagant borrowing of some members. Emerging market borrowers were badly hurt, their policy makers were removed from their jobs, advanced country lenders lost their shirts, but the IMF decision makers, in a business-as-usual mode, have stuck to their rigid, worn-out orthodoxy.

The IMF thus sought to resolve financial crises by imposing fiscal and monetary austerity in the troubled economies in order to stem capital outflows, exchange rate collapses, and inflation spirals. Over time, it drifted from its original mission of supporting members in temporary balance of payments difficulties and floated bailouts to pull them from financial collapses that resulted from the destabilizing capital inflows that it promoted. The recurring crises prompted calls for reforming the global financial arrangements (which I discuss in chapter 12).

Financial Architecture Reforms

These proposals ranged from the choice of an ideal exchange rate regime to stabilize currencies to the adoption of internationally sanctioned bankruptcy provisions for suspending debt payments by heavily indebted countries, and inclusion of collective action clauses in bond contracts to facilitate debt resolution. It is doubtful if the IMF's preference for the adoption of freely floating exchange rates (or hard pegs) in the midst of unrestricted capital flows will endow emerging market economies with monetary policy autonomy. The inclusion of bankruptcy-type provisions and collective action clauses in bond contracts will deter potential lenders from stepping into emerging markets. From the perspective of these economies, the proposals are directed at stabilizing the world financial system rather than providing them with stable long-term capital flows. As an alternative to its one-rule-fits-all-situations approach, the IMF would be better off applying its surveillance procedures vigilantly, ensuring that the borrowers' financial needs are met by long-term flows, encouraging market-based measures for the purpose, and stepping in with debt- restructuring initiatives on a case-by-case basis when the need arises. Such a middle-of-the-road, hands-on approach can convert the IMF into an effective lender of limited resort; otherwise its ideologically driven commitment to free capital mobility and floating exchange rates will confine it to the current controversial role of crisis management, large bailouts, intrusive conditionalities, and continuing criticism.

The misplaced zeal of the advanced market economy center policy aficionados in favor of free capital mobility in the unprepared emerging market periphery not only imposed massive recessionary costs on the affected economies, but also raised doubts about the *long-run* allocative efficiency of global financial markets in raising collective gains for borrowers and lenders. It damaged the prospects for the adoption of Anglo-

American–style institutions and corporate practices by emerging market economies. The resulting financial turmoil raised controversies over the wisdom of subjecting them to the free flow of capital. At the same time, it created interest among policy makers and analysts in a variety of conceptual and empirical issues which I address in the book.

Conceptual Conundrums and Empirical Issues in Financial Crisis

For example, what are fundamentals and what are structural problems? Was the Asian crisis an episode of over-investment or of unregulated, premature capital flows? Has Japan been a victimizer in East Asia? Did investors assume that the IMF would bail them out if their Asian investments went sour? In other words, did moral hazard calculations prompt investors to stretch their risk taking or were they driven by a herd instinct? Does corruption affect economic growth? How does one measure it? Can the Chilean inflow tax direct capital flows into long-term placements? How did India and China, two major mavericks of the East, only gradually liberalize their economies en route to full capital mobility while maintaining high growth rates exceeding 6 percent in the nineties and policy autonomy as sovereign states? I address these questions with a heavy dose of skepticism so that interested readers might critically assess the continuing financial crises in emerging market economies and form reasonable judgments about containing them in the future. Financial globalization is a complex process in which the animal spirits of risk-prone, return-savvy investors from the developed market economies with global, electronic reach collide with the weak financial institutions, traditional corporate practices, and vulnerable political arrangements of emerging market economies with disastrous consequences for the latter. A sensible approach with alternative possibilities is in order.

2

The U.S. Economy in Transition

DOMESTIC UPS AND downs of economic activity characterize the U.S. economy. It manages, however, to overcome these self-generated fluctuations via resilient responses of its households and businesses to policy signals. The special features of a highly mobile labor force, a less intrusive government, a weakening welfare system, increasingly deregulated markets, and the Schumpeterian drive of its corporate sector for creative destruction drive this process. The interaction between policy incentives and private sector behavior is not only facilitated by these structural features but also by the underlying institutions, which continuously renovate themselves. The U.S. financial institutions, including the banks and the stock market, react energetically to market data and information about the economy's health, and provide the necessary services to their customers under a regulatory environment that, despite the post-Enron accounting scandals, is quite robust. This maximally deregulated market economy supported by minimally necessary financial regulations has evolved under the political underpinning of a two-party system that despite occasional contentious posturing has contributed to its efficiency in a pragmatic, accommodating mode.

The policies driving the American economy flow from the triple arrangements of an independent central bank, an open capital market, and a floating dollar. For example, in its most recent policy record, the Federal Reserve (hereafter the Fed) brought down the benchmark federal funds rate through eleven successive reductions, from a high of 6.5 percent of January 2001 to a 40-year low of 1.75 percent by January 2002, on the basis of its judgment of the necessary monetary stimulus for reviving the economy without being encumbered by other considerations or extraneous pressures. The Fed is genuinely independent. Foreign funds continue flowing in the U.S. in search of high return assets. And the market forces of supply and demand determine the value of the dollar. This "possible policy trinity" of an independent monetary policy, capital mobility, and floating exchange rate however is not an exceptional U.S. feature. Among the developed market economies, Britain, Japan, and the eurozone have adopted it, although, as I argue later, the independence of the Japanese and eurozone central banks for pursuing an aggressive monetary policy remains severely tested.

What makes the U.S. market model unique even among the developed economies is the remarkable combination of this policy mix and the structural-institutional-political underpinning that continues promising high economic growth driven by labor productivity performance. By contrast, the eurozone is hobbled by its slow progress in removing a number of structural impediments and building the necessary institutions (which I discuss in chapter 3), and Japan remains paralyzed by its nonperforming bank loans and regulated markets (which I narrate in chapter 4). Significant as the asymmetry is between the U.S. model and these two large areas of the world economy, the distance between its resiliently functioning market system and the reality on ground in the emerging market economies analyzed here is even larger. Their politics is generally fragmented; their banks and stock markets are inadequately regulated; their tax collecting muscle is limited; their businesses tend to be integrated with each other via close ties that promote the survival of inefficient performers. These handicaps raise serious doubts about their ability to function crisis-free by embracing the currently favored International Monetary Fund (IMF) policy mix of free capital flows, a floating exchange rate, and an independent monetary policy. (I discuss the limitations of this policy approach for emerging market economies in chapter 12.)

By contrast, the U.S. economy during its unparalleled expansion of the nineties followed by the short post-9/11 recession provides clues about the functioning of a market model that is sufficiently healthy in terms of the interaction between policies and private sector respondents for overcoming cycles of economic activity. Notwithstanding the policy debates and the acute concerns among analysts and policy makers concerning specific features of the economy during this period stretching into late 2002 (which I highlight in the chapter), its systemic resilience is unique and difficult to replicate elsewhere.

The U.S. Expansion of the Nineties and Issues of Concern

The U.S. economy's unprecedented expansion in the nineties was marked toward the end of the decade by high growth and low unemployment rates. The devaluation of the Thai baht of mid-1997 followed by the Asian crisis and the collapse of the ruble in August 1998 left this expansion virtually unscathed. Three successive interest rate reductions by the Fed in the fall of 1998 restored investor confidence in the aftermath of the brief nosedive of the U.S. stock and bond markets and the collapse of the over-leveraged Long-Term Capital Management hedge fund. On June 1, 1998, the chairman of the Federal Reserve, Alan Greenspan, said glowingly: "The current economic performance, with its combination of strong growth and low inflation, is as impressive as any I have witnessed

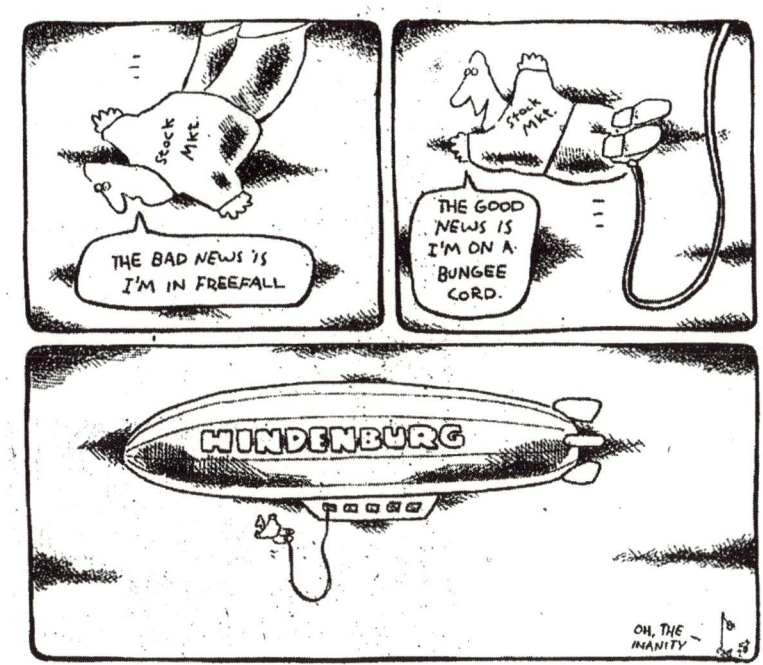

Source: The *New York Times, Week In Review,* April 16, 2000, p. 16.

in my near-half—century of daily observation of the American economy" (*Wall Street Journal,* January 18, 2001, p. A12). The continuing expansion, that turned into a slowdown by mid-2000 and a slower-than-expected recovery in 2002, raised concerns and debates.

First, was the high current account deficit stalking the strong economic fundamentals sustainable over the long haul? In particular, did the U.S. economy, marked by a high current account deficit and a booming and volatile stock market, resemble crisis-swept Thailand which had a similar current account deficit on the run-up to the Asian financial debacle?

Second, did the stock market boom accompanying the expansion represent a Hindenburg (see cartoon above) that could burst plunging the economy into a serious recession even before the events 9/11? Was the boom propelled by irrational exuberance or by shareholders' calculations of the returns they expected to receive? Did the widespread adoption of information technologies lift labor productivity and corporate returns in the economy promising a continuation of these gains in the future?

Third, did the Fed time and implement monetary policy effectively? Or did it bring about an undue expansion by lowering rates and later endanger a recession by raising them, too far and too long?

Fourth, did the heavy borrowing by the corporate sector and private households that accompanied the boom prolong the economy's subsequent downturn and drag it into a recession after 9/11? According to this view, business response through new investments to the interest rate cutting by the Fed that began on January 21, 2001 was delayed because of large capacity and inventory build-up during the expansion. Again, households anxious to repay excessive debts, spent less and frustrated the policy makers' intention of lifting the economy through consumer spending.

Finally, the 9/11 terrorist attacks spurred debates about the ideal combination of monetary and fiscal stimulus that would pull the U.S. economy out of the recession that was imposed on a slowing economy by the economic costs and uncertainties of the attacks and the military response to counter them.

I analyze these issues in this chapter beginning with a brief description of the performance of the U.S. economy in the nineties. Despite the concerns, I conclude that the interaction between Fed policy decisions and resilient responses by businesses and households, representing an exceptional feature of the U.S. economy, carried the prospects of converting the post-9/11 recession into a recovery in early 2002 and growth thereafter. Again, these debates steered clear of doubts about the independent policy stance of the Fed and the continuation of free capital mobility and a floating dollar. This policy mix, of frequent concern in emerging market economies, is, an enduring feature of the U.S. economy.

U.S. Economic Fundamentals

The real growth rate of the U.S. economy, shown in figure 2.1, averaged annual 4 percent in the eight years from 1992 to 1999, representing a juggernaut unmatched in its recorded history. At the same time, inflation measured in consumer prices, shown in figure 2.2, declined from 3 percent to a little under 2 percent, and unemployment (figure 2.3) dropped from 7 percent to 3.9 percent of the labor force, raising debates about the possible demise of the short-run Phillips curve. The long-term growth rate of the U.S. economy, that could be sustained without the economy experiencing an accelerating inflation or a recession, also became part of the intellectual debate and the policy-making agenda.

Aside from the unusual low inflation-low unemployment combination, the aforementioned issues of concern that sparked a lively discussion were the surging current account deficit and the booming and volatile stock market.

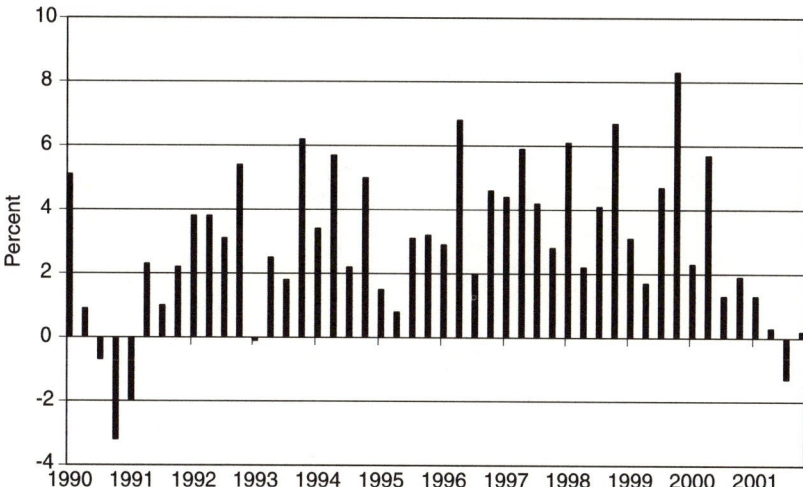

Figure 2.1. U.S. real gross domestic product (GDP). Annualized quarterly change in GDP based on chained 1996 dollars, January 1990–December 2001. *Source:* U.S. Department of Commerce, Bureau of Economic Analysis.

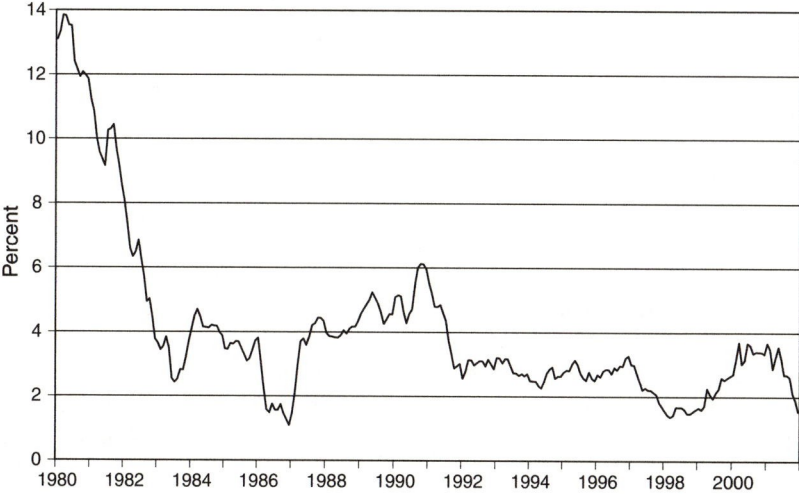

Figure 2.2. Inflation. Year-over-year percentage change in consumer prices, based on monthly consumer price index data, January 1980–December 2001. *Source:* U.S. Department of Labor.

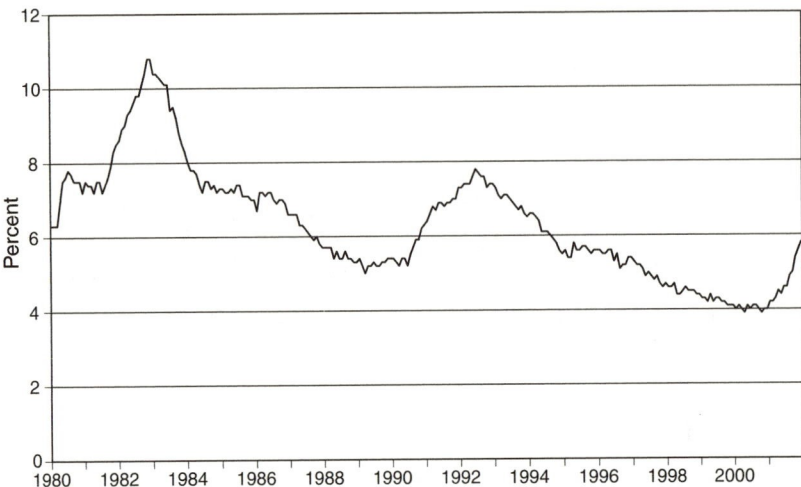

Figure 2.3. Unemployment rate. Recorded monthly unemployment as percentage of population over age 16. January 1980–December 2001. *Source:* U.S. Department of Labor.

Does the Current Account Deficit Present a Danger to the Dollar's Health?

The current account deficit depicted in figure 2.4 had moved up from a sustainable less than 1 percent of gross domestic product (GDP) in 1992 to a high 4.5 percent in 2000. During this period, a steady improvement in the public sector net balance was associated with a marked deterioration in the private sector net performance. In figure 2.5, the former had improved from a deficit of $300 billion in 1992 to a Congressional Budget Office estimated surplus of $250 billion in fiscal 2000, projected to reach $2.1 trillion in the decade ahead. This emerging budget surplus bonanza defined the major issues of the 2000 presidential campaign concerning the tradeoffs of using it for consolidating social security, or paying up part of the federal debt, or cutting taxes, or spending it for improving public education, extending health care, and upgrading the military. In contrast to the improved performance of the budget sector, American households came close to spending every dollar they earned as 1999 ended. The net deficit of the private sector, including businesses, had accelerated from 1992 to 2000, spilling in turn in the high current account deficit noted previously.

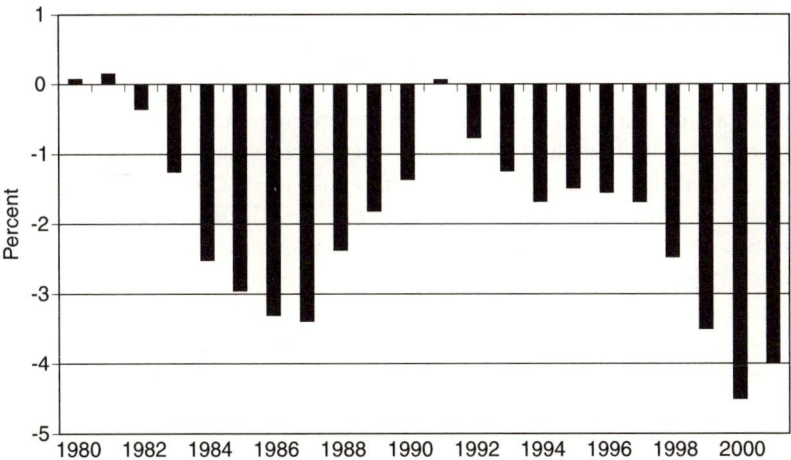

Figure 2.4. Current account balance as a percentage of gross domestic product. Data for 2001 are estimated. *Source:* Economist Intelligence Unit.

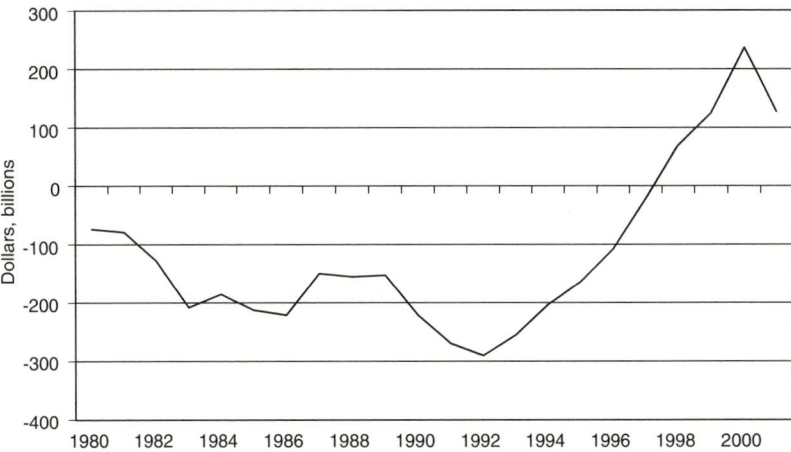

Figure 2.5. Federal budget balance. Federal government budget deficit or surplus, in billions of dollars. *Note:* Years are fiscal, ending October 1 of each year. Data are for the unified budget, including social security. *Source:* Congressional Budget Office.

However, the surge in the current account deficit to 4.5 percent of GDP in 2000 also represented the readiness of investors to hold dollar equities, nongovernment and government bonds, and direct investment, and did not threaten the value of the dollar. Currency traders and investors were skeptical about a rapid economic recovery in Japan and eurozone growth outstripping that in the U.S. Despite the uncertainty of the protracted presidential election and the court battles and the dive in the U.S. technology stocks that weakened the dollar temporarily, holders of dollars saw no reason to dump them and switch to yen or euro at the end of 2000. In the months leading to September 2001, however, the dollar weakened against the euro. As well, the U.S. economic slowdown heightened the risk of holding dollar assets, the Fed's successive monetary policy failed to deliver a visible economic turnaround, and the Republican administration's signals to lower taxes threatened the long-term survival of the budget surplus. In other words, the economic fundamentals worked against the greenback's health by signaling a weak earnings outlook in dollar assets breaking its ascent of 37 percent in trade-weighted real value index over five years ending in 2000. A similar market-determined weakening of the greenback, accentuated by corporate accounting scandals and stock market volatility, took place in 2002. At no stage, however, has the dollar's downward movement been worsened by a wholesale dumping of the currency resembling the collapse of the currencies that marked the Asian financial crisis in 1997–98 and the Russian woes of August 1998. The dollar has continued to be perceived as a safe investment haven for holders of dollar assets.

The dollar gained in strength from 1995 during the robust economic expansion but the accompanying unprecedented and volatile explosion of the U.S. stock market prompted debates about the factors contributing to its exceptional performance.

Why Did the Stock Market Bull Turn Suddenly into a Bear?

The stock market boom, represented in figure 2.6, is based on Standard & Poor's (S & P) composite stock price index in real terms and, as shown in figure 2.7, on the price-earnings ratios of these stocks derived by averaging the real earnings in the denominator over a period of ten years. Figure 2.6 shows, according to Robert Shiller, that "the market has been heading up fairly uniformly ever since it bottomed out in July 1982. It is clearly the most dramatic bull market in U.S. history. The spiking of prices in the years 1992 through 2000 has been most remarkable: the price index looks like a rocket taking off through the top of the chart! This largest stock market boom ever may be referred to as the millennium boom"

Figure 2.6. Stock prices and earnings, 1871–2000. Real (inflation-corrected) Standard & Poor's (upper series), and real S & P composite earnings (lower series), January 1871 to September 1999. *Source:* Shiller (2000), p. 6.

(Shiller, 2000, pp. 5–6). In figure 2.7, the price-earnings relationship shows "an enormous spike after 1997, when the ratio rises until it hits 44.3 by January 2000. Price-earnings ratios by this measure have never been so high. The closest parallel is September 1929, when the ratio hit 32.6" (ibid., pp.7–8). The price/earnings (P/E) ratio would undoubtedly fall as it did from its high points throughout U.S. stock market history in 1901, 1929, and 1966.

The speed and scale of the decline, however, depended on the factors that pushed share prices and the P/E ratios up in the nineties in the first place. Did irrational exuberance of speculative investors driven by a herd mentality boost share prices in the upswing or did rational calculations of expected business earnings arising from technology-led productivity gains drive stock prices up? More to the point, did the Fed's monetary stance aimed at curbing excess consumer outlays, flowing from the wealth effect of stock market affluence, moderate the growth and temper the fluctuations around a rising stock market?

The link between productivity growth and corporate earnings (which I analyze subsequently) and the impact of the continuing high earnings on stock prices provide an answer to these questions. The higher productivity of the U.S. since 1995 contributed to phenomenal across-the-board

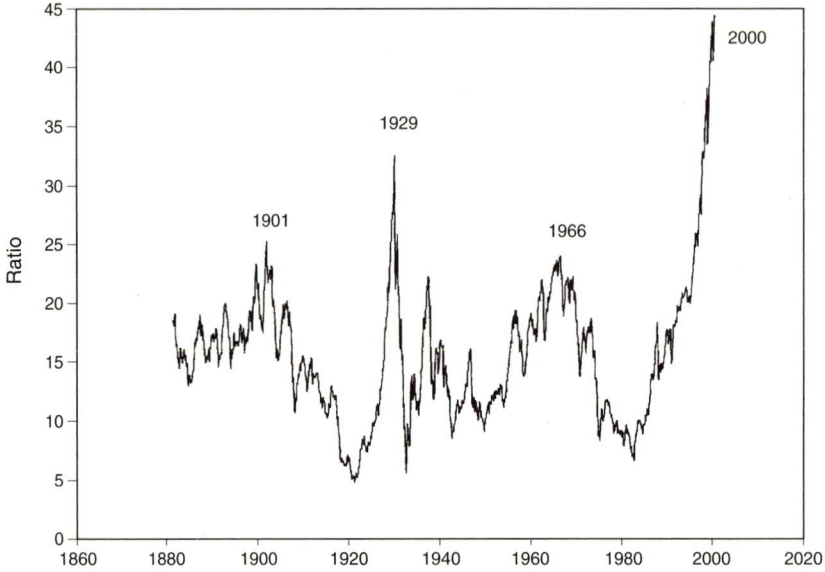

Figure 2.7. Price-earnings ratio, 1881–2000. Monthly, January 1881 to January 2000. *Notes:* Numerator: real (inflation-corrected) S & P composite stock price index. Denominator: moving average over preceding ten years of real S & P composite earnings. Years of peaks are indicated. *Source:* Shiller (2000), p. 8.

earnings of companies and soaring stock prices in anticipation of continuing economic growth and robust earnings of businesses. By mid-2000, however, successive monetary tightening by the Fed and the resulting slowdown in the economy and lower earnings expectations were set to turn the stock market into a bearish mode. Shifts in and out of stocks by smart risk calculators responding to changing relative valuations (to be distinguished from the irrational exuberance or despondence of speculative investors driven by a herd mentality) prevented the financial and stock markets from running out of control. A number of Internet companies folded in the process and several 20-year-old dot-com millionaires were reduced to living simply like 20-year-olds, presaging the market's collapse and the economy's plunge into a (pre-9/11) recession.

Irrational Exuberance versus Rational Choice: The Debate

Are stock market prices driven by corporate earnings? Peter Lynch, the investment analyst (cited in Shiller, 2000, p. 181), responds with a resounding thumbs up: "Despite 9 recessions since WWII, the stock market's up 63-fold because earnings are up 54-fold. Earnings drive the mar-

Source: The *Financial Times*, October 25, 2000, p. 7.

ket." According to Shiller, however, the link is not clear: the great bull market of 1920–29 showed a correspondence between stock prices and earnings but the succeeding ones from 1950–59 and from 1982–99 failed to reveal such correspondence (details are in Shiller, pp. 181–182).

By contrast, Robert Hall (2001, p. 24) suggests that "the enormous appreciation of market values in the 1990s is hardly a challenge in view of the consistently high rates of growth of cash flow [corporate after-tax profits plus interest payments] during the decade. And the reversal of that appreciation in 2000 appears to coincide with diminished cash flow growth, though it is too early to be confident on that point." Hall also provides cross-section evidence for the link. Technology users, such as insurance, banks, and business services, built enormous stocks of intangible wealth (measured by the market values of their securities) in recent years in contrast to utilities, oil and gas extraction, primary metals, and air travel, each of which had low levels of intangible wealth and large claims from other stakeholders (such as suppliers, workers, managers, and the government) on their corporate revenues. The former set of businesses accumulated intangibles during the nineties because they earned growing cash flows for their bond and equity holders. Both the timing and the indus-

Source: Roger Beale, in the *Financial Times Weekend*, April 14–15, 2001.

try distribution of financial intangibles measured by market valuations of corporate stocks therefore suggested a link between earnings and stock values and a strong association of these values with productivity-raising computers and software that accompanied the economic expansion.

Information Technology-Led Pickup in Productivity Growth Rate and Corporate Earnings: Analysis and Evidence

The U.S. economic expansion was propelled by a growth of labor productivity which picked up from a low annual 1.6 percent between 1990 and 1994 to a robust 2.4 percent since 1995. Extensive adoption of informa-

Source: *The New Yorker*, May 22, 2000.

tion technology contributed to a spurt in labor efficiency leading Robert Solow, the Nobel laureate, to switch from his earlier skepticism of 1987 to an affirmative stance in an interview with Louis Uchitelle, "You can now see computers in the productivity statistics" (*New York Times*, March 12, 2000, p. BU4).

Labor productivity normally gets a boost from higher and new vintage capital investment. According to Peter Hooper and Trevor Dinmore (2000, p. 5), investment by companies in constant dollars in 1998 and 1999 in computer systems went up on average by a huge 45 percent a year, in software adoption by 25 percent, and in communications equipment by 20 percent. These three components of information technology pushed their share in corporate fixed capital investment from 10 percent in 1996 to an estimated 14 percent in 2000. The authors put their contribution to output growth at 1 percent in 1997, 1.7 percent in 2000, and a projected 2 percent in 2001 (ibid., p. 6). The new economy pushed productivity growth via faster, cheaper computers, their rapid adoption by businesses, and network externalities: the adoption by one user added to gains for all users. Oliner and Sichel (2000) attributed the extra 1 percent productivity growth beginning in 1995 (on top of the lackluster 1.5 percent average from 1973 to 1994) to computer and semiconductor manufacturing at 25 percent, to information technology (defined previously) at 44 percent, and to other factors at 31 percent. The authors also concluded that "a sizable portion" of the productivity spurt flowing from these factors would persist in the years ahead.

Switching from labor productivity to total factor productivity (TFP), Jorgenson (2000, p. 3 and table 5) measured the contribution of information technology (investment by companies, households, and the government in computers, software, and communications equipment) to TFP growth of an annual average 0.75 percent in 1995–99 at a remarkable 0.50 percent. This is true even when it is considered that information technology's share in GDP was a mere 4.26 percent during the period. Investment in information technology during these years was boosted by the relentless decline in the prices of information technology equipment that, in turn, was prompted by developments in semiconductor technology. "A substantial acceleration in the IT price decline occurred in 1995, triggered by a much sharper acceleration in the decline of semiconductors in 1994" (ibid., p. 2). Semiconductor prices would continue declining as chip makers produced semiconductors on a quick cycle until 2003. Litan and Rivlin (2001) projected massive savings ranging from $100 billion to $230 billion in the next five years resulting from lower costs in insurance processing in health care, and efficient routing with fuller loads by the trucking industry. In an April 2001 announcement accompanying the lowering of the federal funds rate by 50 basis-points to 4.5 percent, the Federal Open Market Committee (FOMC) stated that "the impressive underlying rate of [productivity] increase that developed in recent years appears to be largely intact" (*Wall Street Journal*, April 19, 2001, p. A9). Defying these information technology-related, productivity-enhancement assessments and the bright prospects for its continuation, Robert Gordon (2000) suggested that the *traditional* mechanisms of higher corporate spending and harder effort by workers had lifted productivity since 1995. Historically, the railroads and electricity, in his view, generated larger productivity gains than did Internet technology in modern times.

Gordon's lone dissenting view belied the rapid and extensive adoption of information technology in American manufacturing and financial sectors and the resulting productivity lift (noted earlier). A global, business-to-business retail bazaar was launched in February 2000 when Sears and Carrefour, two retailers with annual purchases of $80 billion from 50,000 suppliers, hooked up with Oracle, the software company, to form Global-NetXchange enabling retailers to buy a variety of goods and services over the Internet. In early 2000, Ford, General Motors, and Daimler-Chrysler formed an online exchange for procuring their requirements. Manufacturers across the board from autos to cosmetics rolled out Web sites for dealers and retailers guaranteeing ready access to product features and

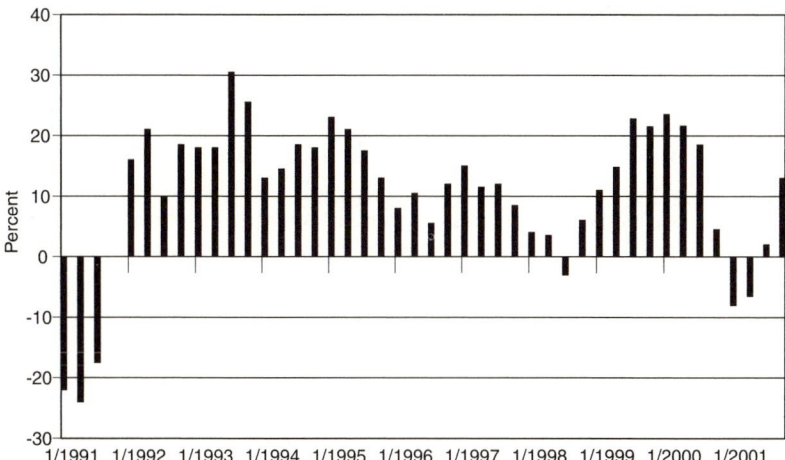

Figure 2.8. Company earnings. Year-to-year percentage change in the earnings of S & P 500 companies. *Note:* The figures for 2001 are forecasts. *Source: Wall Street Journal.*

related services. They not only provided better products from quieter washing machines and faster-cooking ovens to more versatile computers but also complemented them with solve-it-yourself, troubleshooting on-line services. The open economy competitive pressures accompanying the boom forced companies to downsize and cut costs and improve product quality. The adoption of technology-driven inventory control enabled companies to manage inventories without being burdened with shelves full of goods. High-tech reached agribusiness, too. Jimmy Harrell, a North Carolina potato farmer, made profits despite steady potato prices by investing in computerized bagging machines operated by fewer workers that added to savings in bulk shipments (*Wall Street Journal*, August 9, 2000, p. 2). Businesses also learned to anticipate Fed interest rate moves and absorb their impact. The eurozone, as I argue in the next chapter, lags substantially behind the U.S. in this productivity-enhancing, extensive adoption of information technology.

The expanding economy led by high productivity boosted corporate earnings of S & P 500 companies to unprecedented levels.

PHENOMENALLY HIGH CORPORATE EARNINGS IN THE UPSWING

Figure 2.8 shows how these quarterly, earnings averaging below 10 percent growth in 1996 and 1997 and stagnating at negative growth in the aftermath of the East Asian and Russian crises in 1998, picked up in 1999. In the first quarter of 2000, companies battling a tight labor market, higher energy costs, and interest hikes, nevertheless posted double-digit earnings growth exceeding the 18 percent growth rate for 1999. This performance, remarkable for an economy in the midst of continuing expansion, covered not only the high tech firms, but also the consumer goods sector and financial services. It was helped by soaring retail sales, "rising at an annual rate of 15.8% in the first quarter, the fastest pace since early 1983" (*New York Times*, April 20, 2000, p. A2).

By contrast, a slowing economy marked by sluggish consumer spending toward the late summer of 2000 signaled lower earnings expectations.

THE ECONOMY AND CORPORATE EARNINGS IN DECLINE

Lower anticipated earnings in the final quarter of 2000 dampened stock prices with varying impact, in turn, lowering their P/E ratios. Thus, in a single day, in anticipation of sluggish sales, Apple Computer share value dived by 52 percent on September 21; Home Depot by 29 percent on October 12; and Intel by 22 percent on September 22 (*New York Times*, November 5, 2000, p. BU13). Starbucks's losses in its Internet investment, which wiped out all its profits for the fiscal fourth quarter, depressed its stock prices. With declining share valuations, the P/E ratios tumbled. Big tech stocks in S & P 500 stock index traded at 83 times their earnings for the previous 12 months in March 2000; that ratio had more than halved to below 40. The average P/E ratio of these tech stocks, however, was almost twice the overall P/E of S & P 500 in the middle 20's (*Wall Street Journal*, November 27, 2000, p. C1).

Did the bull market tire in response to Fed policies? Indeed, were Fed policies aimed at deflating the bull market?

The Fed at Work: How Successful?

The Fed's mandate is to maintain full employment and stable prices without being encumbered by explicit targets of inflation or GDP growth rates or the value of the dollar. This broad mission endows with it a flexible approach perfected by Chairman Alan Greenspan into an *otoh-botoh* (on-the-one-hand-but-on-the-other-hand) art form. Excruciatingly ponderous, generally prescient, notoriously ambiguous, sufficiently fortunate, and ultimately successful, Greenspan has been perceived as a divine presence on the policy-making scene.

The pursuit of monetary policy, that would maintain a sustainable growth rate without pressure on wages and prices, required a calculated guess about the timing and impact of the new technology on labor productivity growth. A higher productivity resulting from accelerating business

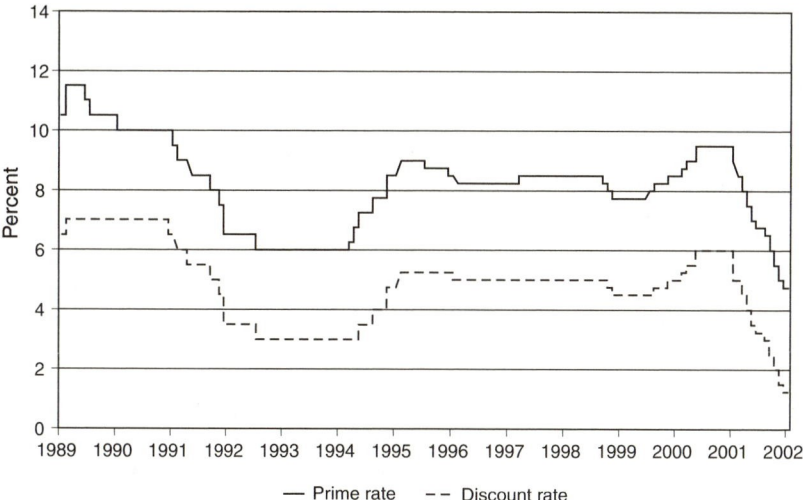

Figure 2.9. Federal Reserve interest rates. Federal Reserve Bank daily prime and discount rates. January 1989–January 2002. *Source:* Federal Reserve Bank.

investment in new technologies held the prospect of a higher noninflationary GDP growth rate. The corresponding level of unemployment was of concern to the Fed. The higher the labor productivity, the higher the nonaccelerating inflation rate of unemployment (Nairu according to Edmund Phelps, 1999). In the pre-new economy days, Nairu could be as high as 5 to 6 percent of the workforce because labor productivity growth was low at 1.5 percent. But a productivity performance that was almost twice as high could not only sustain a low unemployment rate, but it could also promote a robust GDP growth rate without generating a wage-price momentum. As argued earlier, rising productivity fed by rising investment in new technology, resulted in high-output growth combined with low unemployment and inflation rates until mid-2000.

In order to navigate the economy to such a benign scenario, the Fed raised interest rates six times between June 1999 and May 2000 (figure 2.9). Testifying before the Senate Banking Committee on February 22, 2000, the Fed chairman justified the rate increases for reining in excessive consumer spending on goods and services that ran ahead of the available supply. In his view, the excess demand, resulting from the "wealth effect" of a booming stock market, rendered an outbreak of inflation likely. The *Financial Times* reported, "Net household worth rose by $17,000bn in 1995–99; by $5,200bn, more than half US GDP, in 1999 alone. Americans have been spending their new wealth" (December 5, 2000, p. 18).

The Fed estimated the wealth effect, linking the gain—actual or antici-pated—in American household portfolios and their spending on goods and services, both domestic and imported: "2 to 4 cents out of every additional dollar of stock market wealth eventually is reflected in in-creased consumer purchases" (*New York Times*, February 24, 2000, p. B15). Rising stock prices over a period resulted in an imbalance between the supply and demand for goods and services through the wealth effect.[1] In late 1998 and early 1999, the imbalance between demand and supply was cushioned by surging imports into the U.S. from crisis-impaired East Asia and a weak Europe and by the available labor supply in the U.S. contributing to domestic supply. But in the final months of 1999 and early 2000, while reviving East Asian and European economies absorbed more at home, the U.S. labor market, having hit a 30-year low unemployment rate of 3.9 percent, was running out of surplus workers.

As for the productivity-led supply largesse, Greenspan was hesitant in acknowledging the impact of the technology-led new economy, but later gave a Greenspan-style thumbs-up signal in late August, 2000 by saying it was "still difficult to find credible evidence in the United States that the rate of structural productivity growth has stopped increasing" (*New York Times*, August 26, 2000, C1).

The Fed's policy moves raised debates about its intended target and doubts about the efficacy of monetary policy in controlling the economic expansion. Some analysts suggested that Greenspan couched his policy decisions in terms of balancing aggregate supply and demand but the real target was the booming stock market itself. Others doubted the impact of interest rate changes on economic activity.

How Effective Was the Fed?

The Fed signals interest rate changes by varying the federal funds rate on overnight loans between commercial banks and the discount rate at which it lends to banks rather than directly controlling the monetary base con-sisting of currency in circulation and commercial bank deposits with the Fed. The discount rate is less important in tailoring monetary policy be-cause most banks do not borrow from the Fed. Variations in these rates directly controlled by the Fed influence borrowing costs and therefore economic decisions by businesses and households. The FOMC reviews the economy every six weeks and makes appropriate monetary policy decisions unencumbered by legislative debate or approval.

The FOMC's policy prescription follows from evidence on the chang-ing state of the economy. The hard data relate to a series of items including corporate profits and spending, business inventories, consumer spending

and household asset portfolios, worker hiring and layoffs, and the unemployment rate.[2] If the evidence suggests that the economy is on the brink
of overheating or sliding into a recession, the Fed must forestall that outcome by pushing or releasing the monetary brake in time and in right
measure. It must not only sift the evidence in a changing economy but
make shrewd judgment calls, assess investor and consumer psychology,
and focus on its mandate of inflation-free stable growth.

Do the stock market ups and downs directly influence Fed monetary
policy decisions? The Fed chairman opened up this possibility when, in
1996, he famously referred to the "irrational exuberance" of market investors, evidently suggesting that the economy had become more sensitive
to stock market volatility. His references to the link between high stock
prices, the wealth effect, and consumer spending in the context of the
booming economy in late 1999 and early 2000 laid him open to the speculation that he was tailoring monetary policy with the stock market as his
target. Such speculation notwithstanding, promoting growth and stabilizing inflation remain the Fed's primary concern.

It is not surprising, that given the complexity of the task, the Fed invited
criticism from policy analysts and Wall Street players, big and small. In
principle, monetary policy promises to work by influencing consumer and
investment spending by changing the structure of interest rates; by influencing the exchanger rate of the dollar which will go up (down) with a
higher (lower) interest rate; and by influencing the corporate bond market
via lower or higher borrowing costs and through the wealth effect as
shareholders feel richer or poorer. Because it was offset by more powerful
forces in the economy, these three channels failed to work from January
to September 2001 in response to the sustained easing of monetary policy.
Consumers and investors had their balance sheets massively in the red as
a result of excessive borrowing of the late nineties; the equity market
failed to bounce up in response to monetary easing because of poor earnings prospects; and the dollar was caught in the conflicting pulls between
the failure of the monetary stimulus to work quickly (and therefore declined) and the better relative growth prospects of the U.S. economy, despite the slowdown, via-à-vis the eurozone and Japan.

As the millennium came to a close, the triple bliss of low inflation,
low unemployment, and high growth rate had ended, bringing in worries
about the slowdown accelerating into a recession.

Analysts and investors were concerned about the growth prospects of
the economy even before the terrorist attacks of September 11. They spec-
ulated in mid-2001 if the economy, aided by the four interest rate cuts
between January and mid-April, would move to a 1 to 1.5 percent annual
growth rate in the pre-9/11 period itself, or would descend into a recession
despite the monetary easing by the Fed. In other words, before the terror-

ist attacks on the U.S. on 9/11, there were as many arguments in favor of a soft landing as against a hard landing with a recession. The proponents of a soft landing marked by a swift recovery and a hard landing marked by a recession differed about the steps by which the economy would recover in reaction to the lower interest rates. These arguments became pronounced as the recession became a certainty after 9/11. Will the trajectory be a flat, protracted U or a small, sharp V? In the view of the U-proponents, the revival of consumer demand in reaction to the monetary stimulus would cut back business inventories to the levels below those desired by businesses who would then respond with increased production and spending to build new capacities. In the view of the latter, such a classic pull up in response to monetary policy easing was unlikely to work because American businesses had built massive capacities and consumers had borrowed heavily to finance their spending binge. Both needed an unusual balance sheet adjustment before they could activate the economy via rapid spending in response to monetary policy stimulus. In this view, therefore, a recession was unavoidable even before the terrorist attacks that made it inevitable after 9/11.

Additional problems arose from the difficulties associated with defining a recession.

When Is an Economy in Recession?

Recession popularly defined conjures bad times with many workers out of jobs and tough prospects for politicians seeking elective office. Accurately defined, a recession implies GDP decline in two consecutive quarters. Marking such a drop ahead of time, however, is difficult. The National Bureau of Economic Research (NBER), which keeps away from such forecasting, and pinpoints peaks and troughs of economic activity after the fact, has a flexible definition: a recession is "a recurring period of decline in total output, income, employment, and trade, usually lasting from six months to a year, and marked by widespread contractions in many sectors of the economy" (*Wall Street Journal*, January 10, 2001, p. A2).

In mid-April 2001, the economic outlook was mixed because the signals were confusing. Most consumers thought the economy was already in a recession although household spending held firm. The New York-based Conference Board saw no recession in sight whereas the Economic Cycle Research Institute (ECRI) declared that a recession was unavoidable. (Details are in note 2, at the end of the chapter.) Robert Hall, chairman of NBER's business cycle dating committee, saw no need to call a committee meeting because the drop in industrial production from September 2000 of 2 percent was below the size of decline typical in a reces-

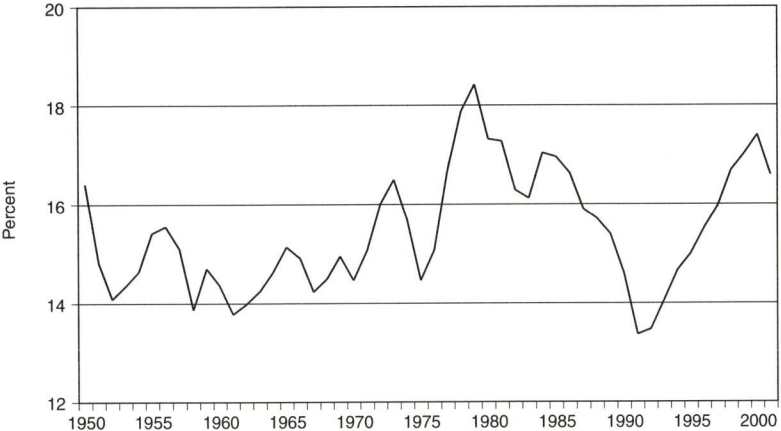

Figure 2.10. U.S. private fixed investment as percent of gross domestic product. Annual data, 1950–2001. *Source:* U.S. Department of Commerce, Bureau of Economic Analysis.

sion. Again, non-farm employees on payrolls dropped by 86,000 in March, but "the general trend over the previous 12 months was one of growth averaging 152,000 monthly" (*Wall Street Journal*, April 11, 2001, p. A2). The Fed forecast a growth slowdown in the first half of the year followed by a revival in the second half of the year.

Understandably, the debate before 9/11 involved as many arguments in favor of a recession-marked hard landing as those against it.

Why A Pre-9/11 Hard Landing?

The transition of the massive $10 trillion economy was beginning from a hyper-charged growth performance that had hit 6 percent in the first half of 2000. The economic expansion was also marked by low inflation averaging less than annual 2 percent and supported by productivity-enhancing investments in the second half of the nineties. The massive capacity expansion since 1995 in manufacturing, mining, and utilities to sustain this performance at an annual 5 percent, more than double the pace from 1980 through 1994, resulted from gross fixed investment exceeding 17 percent of GDP in 1999 (figure 2.10). Companies borrowed in the bond market, built excessive capacities, and created significant fixed costs. The stock market reflected and fed the investment boom. The S & P 500 stock index rose 200 percent between the end of 1994 and June 1999. The Nasdaq stock index surged 40 percent in 1998 and a dizzying 86 percent in 1999.

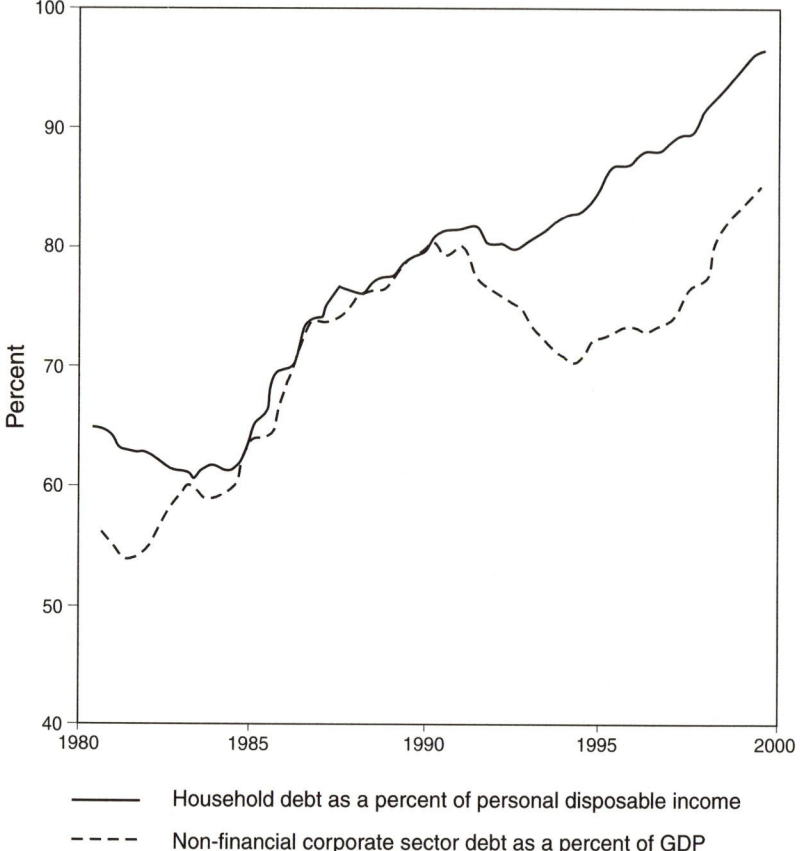

Figure 2.11. U.S. household debt as a percentage of personal disposable income and corporate debt as a percentage of gross domestic product. *Source:* U.S. Department of Commerce.

The Excess Capacity Hangover

In the eight years prior to 1999, the economy grew, created jobs, and spurred demand because companies could raise capital by borrowing in the bond market. Figure 2.11 shows how corporate debt had escalated since 1995, reaching 85 percent of GDP in 1999. Many companies borrowed excessively and created significant fixed costs that could not be rolled back as demand for their products fell in a softening economy. Companies with poor credit quality needed to borrow at high interest rates as they could not meet their interest payments and finance their current operations from dwindling cash flows. Nervous investors demanded higher rates from borrowers forcing them to issue high-yield corporate bonds. Such debt ballooned among companies in telecommunication, cable television, health care, and technology. In telecommunications and media services alone, such debt exploded to a total of $485 billion during 1996–2000 in sharp contrast to the total high-yield debt of $160 billion during 1983–90 (Details are in Gretchen Morgenson, "How Easy Cash Became Hard Debts," *New York Times*, November 19, 2000, p. BU13). With an increasing number of such deadbeat companies going belly up because of their inability to raise cash, the economy could move from a slowdown into an increasingly steep decline. The junk-bond default rate exceeding 5 percent was the highest in nearly a decade. At the end of March 2000, 3.3 percent of syndicated loans were considered problem-ridden, up from 1.3 percent two years earlier (*Wall Street Journal*, December 1, 2000, p. A1). These highly leveraged companies created financial risks for suppliers of equipment who had financed such sales to dot-com and telecommunication customers via loans. Lucent Technologies, Cisco Systems, Motorola, Oracle, and Hewlett-Packard faced poor earnings prospects as a result of their customers' bad debts and the slowdown in tech spending that left these giant hardware suppliers with bloated inventories and excess capacities.

Increasingly, small and medium businesses with healthy balance sheets found it difficult to raise new cash as banks demanded tighter repayment schedules. Even healthy companies faced higher borrowing costs. "When Citigroup Inc. issued $3 billion of 10-year bonds in early October [2000], it offered investors 1.47 percentage points more interest yield than comparable Treasury notes. Yesterday [November 30], the company sold $1.25 billion more of the same bond but had to pay about 1.89 percentage points over Treasurys, a huge increase for bonds with a strong single-A plus credit rating" (ibid.). In a speech on December 5 before New York City community bankers, Greenspan referred to banks' tightened lending standards and exhorted bankers to refrain from denying credits to creditworthy business clients.

Declining profits and tight credit availability threatened to affect new capital spending that could accentuate output decline further. In early 2001, business earnings were not only squeezed by interest charges on the borrowing binge but also wage costs that did not decline at the same rate as revenues. From 1993 to 2000, companies lowered wage costs from 66 percent of revenues to 62 percent from a combined impact of adopting efficient technologies, shifting location to China and Mexico, and offering workers stock options in return for accepting lower wages. These cost-reducing, output-lifting advantages had all but disappeared.

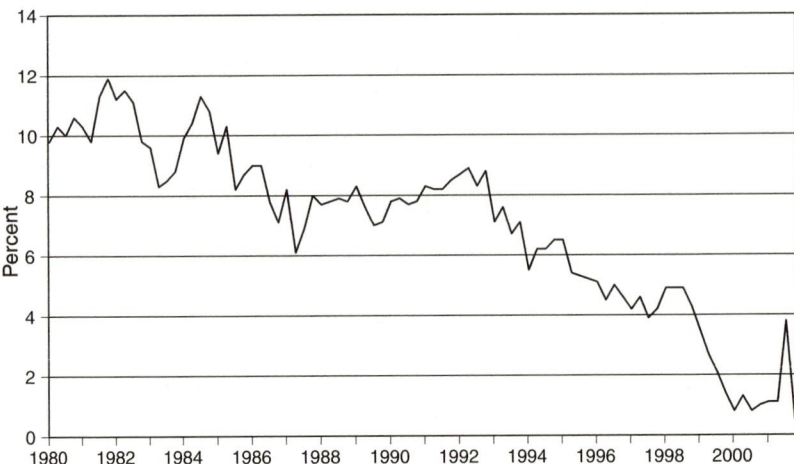

Figure 2.12. U.S. personal savings as a percent of personal disposable income. Quarterly data, January 1980–December 2001. *Source:* U.S. Department of Commerce, Bureau of Economic Analysis.

On the other hand, would increased household spending activated by lower borrowing costs rescue the economy from an impending recession?

The Hangover of Excessive Household Borrowing

In the first quarter of 2001, GDP grew by a 2 percent annualized rate and consumer spending by 3.1 percent, at a pace higher than the previous quarter offering hopes for activating the economy in response to lower interest charges. Pessimists cast doubts on the continuation of this positive scenario because households carried excessive debt liabilities at 98 percent of personal disposable income in 1999 (figure 2.11). At the end of the millennium, personal savings as a fraction of disposable income (figure 2.12) had dropped to a low 1 percent. As the stock market soared in the second half of the nineties, families, on average holding 60 percent of their savings in stock, felt richer, and bought homes, cars, and other durables that boosted manufacturing activity. The wealth effect from stock ownership prompted Americans to spend through borrowing (and avoid taxes on tax deductible interest payments) rather than sell their shares (and pay taxes on capital gains). As the economy slowed and worker layoffs increased, consumers were expected to ration their spending, perhaps start saving, thus accentuating the slowdown.

According to this scenario, therefore, the overhang of the symptoms of corporate and consumer overspending of the nineties, both financed by massive borrowing, would plunge the economy into a severe decline marked by accelerating rise in claims for unemployment benefits, plummeting household incomes and consumer confidence, and spending cutbacks. However, several features pointed toward a less turbulent outcome before the events of 9/11 converted the prospects of a slow-growth transition into a bona fide recession.

Why a Less Rocky Pre-9/11 Transition?

Despite the go-go features associated with the expansion, the economy had built-in prospects for a smooth transition. The situation differed from a pyramidal Ponzi scheme or the seventeenth-century Dutch tulip mania,[3] or the Japanese asset bubble of the eighties that plunged Japan into a deep recession. During the boom, American businesses borrowed massively, invested heavily, and hired excessive amounts of labor. But unlike in the boom economies of Asia and Japan, the extensive restructuring during the slowdown set the stage for recovery of profits and growth. A solid underpinning that sustained the economic expansion was the productivity growth rate between 1995–99 that kept unit labor cost down and inflation low at an annual 2.5 percent in 2000. The subsequent labor productivity estimates between 1.5 and 2 percent were lower than the rise in unit labor cost. Employers, however, countered the negative impact of the cost disadvantage on their earnings by cutting work hours, eliminating overtime, and shedding workers. With increasing labor layoffs and a softening labor market, an aggressive monetary policy shift to lower interest rates by the Fed in early January 2001 promised to soften the downturn and revive the economy, especially because inflation control was manageable.

It also started a slow process of corporate cleanup by prompting investors to seek out profitable takeover targets whose share prices had collapsed to bargain levels.

Corporate Shakeout via Leveraged Buyouts

Investors chastened by the relentless decline of the stock market, led by Nasdaq's 50 percent tumble since March 2000, shifted their strategies in the second half of the year from technology and telecommunication stocks to traditional varieties. The switch from "clicks to bricks" was also marked by strategic calculations of relative values away from stocks whose prices had dipped. Investors and buyout firms interested in capturing cheap companies concentrated on relative valuations which increasingly became the guiding mantra of strategic acquirers and leveraged buy-

"What was it this time, old economy or new economy?"

Source: *The New Yorker*, April 24 & May 1, 2000.

out firms that carefully weighed their opportunities among consumer products, basic industries, and financial companies.

Such deals proliferated. PepsiCo bought Quaker Oats for $13.4 billion, pushing up the share prices of both. Texas Instruments announced a cross-licensing agreement with a rival allowing each company to sell integrated circuits to customers without the rival suing for patent infringement. Warren Buffet, the old-fashioned valuation guru of Berkshire Hathaway, Inc., moved into bricks, carpet, paint, and boots. "If it is a nonglamorous business then there is a reasonable chance that the price will be right," said Buffet (*Wall Street Journal*, November 27, 2000, p. C1). Not to be left behind, rating agencies continuously monitored company fortunes and upgraded or downgraded units providing signals about their health to potential buyers. Hiring and firing of CEOs added to the shakeout. Some "wait-and-watch" players bought back their own shares, boosted their earnings per share in the process from less dividend outflows, and accumulated cash that could be invested in profitable ventures. Thus, the announcement by Compaq, the world's largest computer manufacturer, in early December, to buy back $1 billion of its shares lifted PC stocks in the entire sector, including Gateway's which had earlier announced lower revenues and profits. In late 2001, Hewlett-Packard mounted an aggressive, controversial move to acquire Compaq.

These cherry-picking activities, typical of the U.S. corporate and financial sectors during an economic downturn and less prevalent in other economies, continued sifting the winners from the losers at a measured pace in 2001 and demonstrated the economy's resilience at creating real value through such cleansing. Mergers were more pronounced in the energy and financial sectors to the exclusion of telecommunication, media, and technology sectors marked by sharp stock declines. Potential buyers and sellers, however, continued exploring opportunities for making deals and awaited their next chance of making a million or more as the economy revived. This American-style optimism in yet another opportunity was summed up by Elliot Rogers, who organized a conference of the leading who's who of technology investors and computer manufacturers in Scottsdale, Arizona in early December 2000. In an interview with the *New York Times*, Rogers stated, "There is a shortfall in demand, if not a serious growth deceleration. It's not just in computers. It's in everything. I've been through this many times before. It's called a cycle" (December 4, 2000, p. C4).

The boom therefore was not expected to lead into a recession before 9/11 because the Fed maintained the monetary easing stance in 2001 and cut interest rates further inducing families to purchase a new home or refinance an old mortgage, and businesses to capture a profitable stake in old-economy sectors.

Aggressive Monetary Easing to Head off a Recession before 9/11

The attention-grabbing, half-point slashing of the benchmark short-term interest rate on January 3, 2001 that launched three similar cutbacks in less than four months demonstrated Greenspan's resolve to head off a recession and avoid the mistake of late 1989 when, failing to see a recession, the Fed lowered interest rates in mini-steps as the slowdown turned into a full-blown recession in the summer of 1990. Three additional interest rate cuts slashing the benchmark interest rate by full 3 percentage points to 3.5 percent by September 2001 helped sustain the housing market, and support consumer spending. As mortgage rates declined, consumers took out a second mortgage, refinanced mortgages at lower rates, and took out bigger mortgages as housing prices soared. From the end of 1999 to March 2001, the *drop* in the value of shares owned by households of $3,600 billion outstripped the *rise* in equity value of houses of $800 billion. Yet there was no let up in consumer spending despite the negative wealth effect (*Financial Times*, August 17, 2001, p. 11).

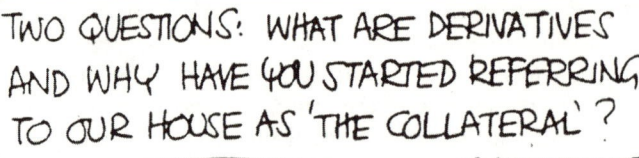

Source: "Home ownership and speculation," by Roger Beale. *Financial Times.*

But manufacturing production and fixed investment failed to pick up by mid-2001. Businesses had less incentive to upgrade equipment or expand capacities because of falling profit projections and weak economic prospects. However, in contrast to the second half of 2000, banks were healthier and companies relied less on short-term borrowing for fear of inviting a default, and turned instead to long-term borrowing at lower corporate bond rates. As a result, their balance sheets were better geared for investment as soon as economic prospects improved. By the end of August 2001, the automobile and durable goods industries were edging up in contrast to the declining outputs in the technology sector.

These nascent benefits of the aggressive monetary maneuvering aimed at moderating the slowdown were thrown off balance by the negative economic impact of the terrorist attacks, the uncertainties surrounding the length and intensity of the military action they called for, and the debates over the possible policy responses that could blunt the fallout.

Post-9/11 Policies and Prospects

The attacks shut down the New York Stock Exchange for almost two weeks, the first time in its 123-year history, severely disrupted air travel, hurting the fortunes of already struggling airlines, impaired consumer confidence, damaged business prospects further, and called for substantial new public spending combined with tax cuts that was bound to slash the Federal budget surplus and perhaps lead to fresh borrowing by the Federal government. Within six weeks of the attacks, the decline in capital spending had intensified, consumer confidence had plunged to its lowest levels in seven years, and mounting labor layoffs had pushed the October unemployment rate to 5.4 percent of the workforce.

The Policies and the Debates

The monetary policy response aimed at softening the negative impact on the economy was swift. The Fed immediately pumped up to $45 billion into the banking system to prevent a funding crisis by enabling big banks and securities firms to borrow for their day-to-day needs. Within three weeks, the Fed twice lowered the benchmark federal funds rates bringing it down by a total of 4 percentage points, since January, to 2.5 percent. Equally speedy was the emergency fiscal stimulus: Congress passed legislation approving $40 billion for disaster relief and $15 billion for rescuing the airlines The White House proposed an additional spending-plus- tax-cut-package designed to bring the total stimulus to $115 billion to $135 billion in fiscal 2002 at 1.1 to 1.3 percent of the GDP, the biggest such package since 1975.

The package was bound to whittle down the budget surplus already under increasing pressure from a slowing economy. The earlier hot-button issue of balancing the non-Social Security budget in fiscal 2002 was replaced by disturbing questions over the Treasury's likely need to borrow: How large will the borrowing be? Will it raise long-term interest rates? Will higher interest charges damage the health of the federal budget? Will higher long-term interest rates run counter to the Fed's purposive monetary easing of 2001 and defeat the stimulus it sought via lower interest rates? More to the point, in what proportion should fiscal stimulus to the economy combine higher spending and lower taxes? If the latter, should tax cuts drive consumption or investment or both in a suitable mix?

The size, timing, and type of the required fiscal stimulus fueled wide-spread debates in the media and in Congress with Democrats and their allies warning about the long-run economic costs of rushing into indis-criminate tax cut legislation favored by the Bush administration. Former Treasury Secretary Robert Rubin, a leading protagonist of fiscal discipline that had kept long- term interest rates down during the Clinton years, recommended a wait-and-watch approach. "Far more important to be right than quick," said Alan Greenspan who suggested a total stimulus package of $100 billion that would not undermine the government's long-run fiscal discipline. Nobel laureate Milton Friedman altogether ruled out the need for a fiscal stimulus that, in his view, would start working after the recession was over. The "quick shot of [monetary] adrenaline" in-jected by the Fed was bound to lift the economy after a lag obviating the need for "crude Keynesianism" (*Wall Street Journal*, October 10, 2001, p. A17). A broad consensus of voices pointed to the need for an optimum consumption-cum-investment–driven fiscal stimulus that would provide tax rebate for high spenders at the lowest income scale[4] and time-bound investment incentives for businesses. Spending increases and tax cuts that threatened to become permanent fixtures of the federal budget should be avoided because they could worsen the government's fiscal health by requiring it to borrow from the Social Security trust fund and the market. Besides, excessive government spending and tax relief could set the stage for the revival of inflation as the economy recovered.

The Bush administration's fiscal proposals bent these rules by bringing forward accelerated income tax breaks for higher income brackets and by repealing the corporate alternative minimum tax introduced in 1986 to prevent profitable corporations from using loopholes for tax evasion. Economist Paul Krugman wondered whether these proposals were de-signed to exploit the immediate difficulties of the economy for pursuing unrelated, long-run political goals. Asked policy watchdog Gretchen Morgenson in exasperation, had "self-interested corporate machina-tions" become de rigueur of the moment, war or peace?

The budget battles centered on hammering out a bipartisan compro-mise. These included Republican-led legislative proposals of $100 billion in the House tilted toward tax cuts and a Senate formula worked up by the Democratic majority favoring less tax relief for companies and more subsidized health care coverage and generous compensation for the unem-ployed. The fiscal stimulus combined with the continuing monetary eas-ing was set to revive the fourth quarter of 2001, which was marked by declining factory orders and business spending, mounting worker layoffs, and softening consumer demand.

How successful would the monetary-fiscal stimulus be in pulling the economy out of the post-9/11 recession and helping it grow significantly in 2002?

The Prospects for 2002

The post-9/11 turnaround began with a GDP growth rate of 0.2 percent (subsequently revised by the Commerce Department to 1.4 percent in March) in the last quarter of 2001 following a decline of 1.2 percent in the third quarter. The recession, it seemed, was short and shallow. On March 19, 2002, the FOMC kept the short-term benchmark interest rate unchanged at 1.75 percent from its level of January 30. It signaled a possible rate increase later, however, by suggesting that the risk between economic weakness (in view of an incipient recovery) and inflation (the result of a significant expansion) were evenly balanced. The subsequent data however revealed a tumbling of the GDP growth rate from an annualized 5 percent in the first quarter of 2002 to a meager 1.1 percent in the second quarter, raising the specter of a negative growth rate. The unemployment rate was stuck at a high 5.9 percent although inflation was low, annualized at less than 2 percent. Households continued responding to the Fed's low-rate policy by buying cars and homes, the former in response to zero-interest rate incentives and the latter to take advantage of lower mortgage rates. But confidence was low all around, casting a shadow on future retention of aggregate demand. Falling stock prices undermined household wealth, dented consumer confidence, and decreased consumer willingness to spend. The corporate accounting scandals led by Enron made investors risk-averse, squeezed credit in the bond market, and created difficulties for some companies in raising cash. The dollar became weak without providing timely relief to exporters.

In a testimony to Congress on July 16, Greenspan sounded optimistic. "The effects of the recent difficulties will linger for a bit longer but as they wear off . . . the U.S. economy is poised to resume a pattern of sustainable growth" (*Wall Street Journal*, August 14, 2002, p. A2). A month later, the FOMC panel was somber in its assessment and left the benchmark interest rate unchanged. ""The softening in aggregate demand . . . has been prolonged . . . by weakness in financial markets and heightened uncertainty related to problems in corporate reporting and governance" (ibid.) The FOMC also changed its policy tone. The Fed's policy tilt of the first half of the year was toward lifting interest rates from their 41-year low levels to prevent the economy from overheating. On August 13, the FOMC conveyed an opposite likely prospect for lower rates if the worsening persisted.

Thus several policy options were available. The Fed could still lower the benchmark interest rate on September 24 if warranted. The government could step up spending of the appropriated money to fill the gap created by lagging consumer and business spending. Most important, the economy's potential for high-productivity growth had scarcely diminished as a result of the 9/11 attacks. After a one-time decline in productivity resulting from the higher spending by businesses on security and computer backup systems, productivity growth rate was expected to pick up to rates higher than the annual 1.5 percent of 1972–95. A surprising contributory factor to the economic recovery in the final quarter of 2001 was the robust productivity growth rate of 3.5 percent, unusual in the midst of a recession during which output generally declines at a faster pace than employment. Indeed, the fears of a Japanese-style stagnation, a double-dip recession, a further unwinding of the bubble mentality on the stock market, or a eurozone-type struggle between maintaining growth rate and fighting inflation were misplaced. The remarkable combination of available policy alternatives and resilient responses by households and businesses in the midst of a market-oriented institutional environment and entrepreneurial drive promised to keep U.S. productivity and growth rates ahead of those in the eurozone and Japan. The triple arrangements of a floating exchange rate, free capital flow, and independent monetary policy were also set to remain firmly in place. Finally, as a contender to the greenback, the euro might rally now and then, but a sustained euro pickup resulting from massive unloading of the dollar in currency markets was unlikely in view of the uncertain relative growth and inflation control prospects in the eurozone. I turn to an analysis of these issues in the next chapter.

Notes

1. Such an ex post aggregate estimate averaged over a period is consistent with the absence of the wealth effect in sample surveys seeking to link consumer spending behavior with stock market fluctuations. Thus, in a Gallup poll of 1,000 Americans by Paine Webber in July 2000, 90 percent with stock market investment disclosed that "market *fluctuations* [emphasis added] made no difference" to their spending level (*Financial Times Weekend*, September 9/10, 2000, p. XXIV).

2. The New York-based Conference Board, to which the federal government handed over its leading indicator program in 1996, lists ten indicators in its forecasting index. It includes money supply, consumer expectations, manufacturers' orders for capital goods and materials, average weekly manufacturing hours, stock prices, vendor performance, weekly claims for unemployment insurance, building permits, interest rates, and manufacturers' orders for consumer goods. In contrast to the Conference Board's single index designed to forecast economic activity in the next three to six months, the Economic Cycle Research Institute (ECRI), a private group studying business cycles, constructs eleven leading indexes including one each for manufacturing, construction, finance and services, and for inflation, credit, trade, and employment for the coming six to twelve months. In mid-April 2001, the two agencies disagreed about the prospects for the economy.

In the next three to six months, the Conference Board suggested a slowdown whereas ECRI predicted an "unavoidable recession." (*Wall Street Journal*, April 19, 2001, p. A2.)

3. The Dutch tulip mania of 1636–37 represented a short-lived episode during which demand for the bulb soared to incredible heights representing a bubble that burst when the craze suddenly evaporated. The Dutch, prospering in a booming economy, found an outlet for their riches in new and exotic varieties of the tulip. At the height of the mania in 1636, people exchanged their assets including homes, farm animals, and gold for the bulbs. "One Viceroy tulip bulb . . . commanded a down payment of eight pigs, a dozen sheep, two oxheads of wine, four tons of butter, a thousand pounds of cheese, a bed, clothing, some wheat and rye, and a silver beaker." More details are in Kindelberger (2000), who turned ninety-one in 2002.

4. The Bush administration's mid-year tax rebate of $38 billion, part of the ten-year, $1.3 trillion tax cut, endowing every recipient with $300, was, however, counterproductive in stimulating consumption by the beneficiaries. Although a meager 0.5 percent of GDP, it raised personal disposable income more than spending in July, boosting household savings to 2.5 percent of disposable income, the highest in two years. Having brought their balance sheets to a sustainable plateau, the tax rebate recipients might however direct the additional rebates for household purchases.

3

The Euro: Teething Troubles and Faltering Responses

IN EARLY MAY 1998, eleven of the fifteen European Union (EU) member countries (figure 3.1), linked by common agricultural, trade, and environmental policies, agreed to take a giant step forward by forming an economic and monetary union and creating a single capital market. From its inception, however, it faced difficulties in functioning as a single unit, raising doubts about its potential to compete with U.S. growth performance and about the euro's rapid emergence as an effective rival to the dollar. These problems, which I analyze in this chapter, appeared from several directions. Trapped in structural bottlenecks, the eurozone trailed the U.S. in its adoption of information technology and productivity growth record. The European Central Bank (ECB), charged with a common monetary policy and excessively committed to a price stability mandate, generally opted for a stricter than desirable monetary stimulus for the entire zone. The budget management in individual members, signatories to the deficit norms of the Maastricht Treaty, lacked a counter-cyclical policy stance (for example, in favor of growth-promoting tax cuts when their economies faced a downturn). The euro's long-term prospects of emerging as a serious contender to the greenback depended on the speed with which the zone's members succeeded in forming a cohesive federal union as it continued expanding by admitting new members. In that regard it was held back by structural impediments; a corporate sector marked by interlocked arrangements, trade union activism, and high taxes; and nascent financial institutions battling the challenges of a common currency area. It lagged behind the U.S. economy whose market-friendly arrangements and institutions prompted interaction between job-oriented policies and resilient responses by businesses and households that I discussed in the previous chapter.

The Eurozone: Principal Features

The original signatories in 1998 were Austria, Belgium, Finland, France, Germany, Ireland, Italy, Luxembourg, the Netherlands, Portugal, and Spain. Britain, Denmark, and Sweden opted to stay out, and Greece, which did not fulfill the inflation and budget deficit ceiling requirements

Figure 3.1. Map of Europe. Distinguished by European Union (EU) and European and Monetary Unit (EMU) membership, and EU candidacy. *Source:* Emil Czechowski.

for membership, joined later, in 2000. As a first step, the members locked their exchange rates to one another on July 1 in preparation for the formal introduction of the common currency euro on January 1, 1999. In deciding to form a monetary union, they surrendered their sovereign right to issue and manage a currency to the ECB located in Frankfurt. Thus, they lost the power to vary their exchange or interest rates to stimulate or cool their economies. All national currencies, among them the Deutsche mark and French franc, the Finnish markka and the Italian lira, were targeted to be abolished by the spring of 2002. Following the announcement, member-country banks began processing transactions in double-entry book-keeping in the euro and local currencies, and large corporations like Daimler-Benz and Siemens prepared to replace local currencies.

The national governments however retained the right to pursue their budgetary and tax arrangements, and foreign policy. The impact of these discretionary powers on budget deficits, inflation rates, and government debts was however locked in a straightjacket by the European Union's 1992 Maastricht Treaty that set the ceilings on these three criteria. It required that the annual budget deficit be maintained by a member at 3 percent of gross domestic product (GDP) or less, the inflation rate at 2 percent, and the ratio of government debt to GDP at 60 percent or less, unless, according to Martin Wolf, it was "sufficiently diminishing and approaching the [target] value at a satisfactory pace" (*Financial Times*, February 10, 1998, p. 12). The inflation rate, to be measured in terms of the noncore price index, including the volatile energy, alcohol, food, and tobacco prices, sought to impose stricter discipline on members.

By 1997, the eleven eurozone members were close to fulfilling the inflation rate and budget deficit requirements as indicated in figures 3.2 and 3.3. Except in Greece, which was admitted to the zone in late 2000, annual inflation rate had settled more or less at 2 percent and the budget deficit at around 3 percent of GDP in all member countries. However, the debt-to-GDP ratio, as shown in figure 3.4, was higher than 60 percent for most, and had increased in 1997 as compared to 1991 for Austria, Germany, Italy, and Spain which were admitted to the zone. Belgium registered a slight decline but the ratio remained exorbitant at 124.5 percent. Italy's ratio had soared 22 percent to 122 percent.

Public indebtedness in relation to GDP thus posed a problem at the inception of the monetary union. More daunting however were the structural rigidities characterizing member countries' inflexible labor markets and trade union activism; their inherited tax systems with varying and generally high tax rates creating opportunities for intrabloc predatory competition; their entrenched welfare systems involving high pension payments; and significant unemployment compensations encouraging high unemployment levels. As the eurozone heralded a single capital market, doubts arose about its ability to evolve into an Anglo-American style shareholder capitalism in which capital moved in search of profits unencumbered by these structural roadblocks (which I discuss immediately below).

The Structural Problems

The switch to the euro called for a few minor adjustments. Parking lot machines needed to be fixed so that they could automatically take the new coins and issue tickets; telephone systems required adjustment so that

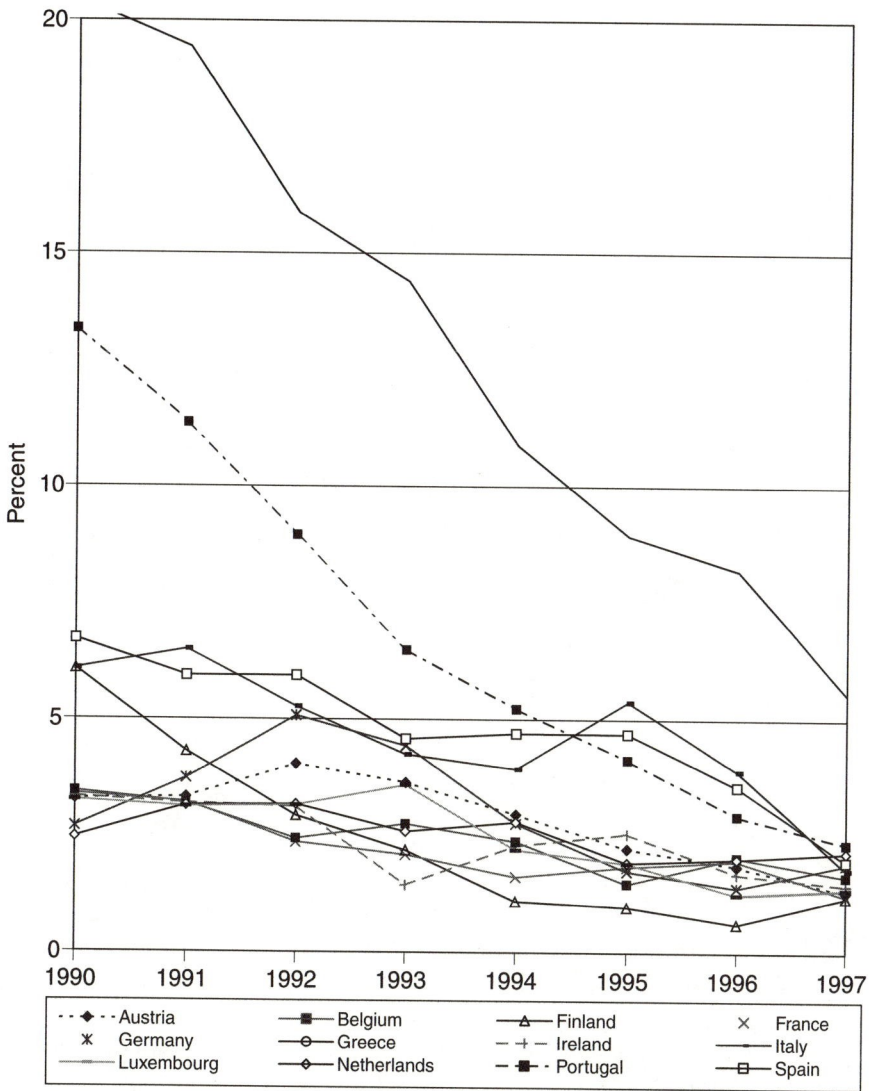

Figure 3.2. Inflation in eurozone countries. Annual percentage change in consumer price index, 1990–97. *Note:* 1990 value for Greece is 20.4 percent. *Source:* Economist Intelligence Unit.

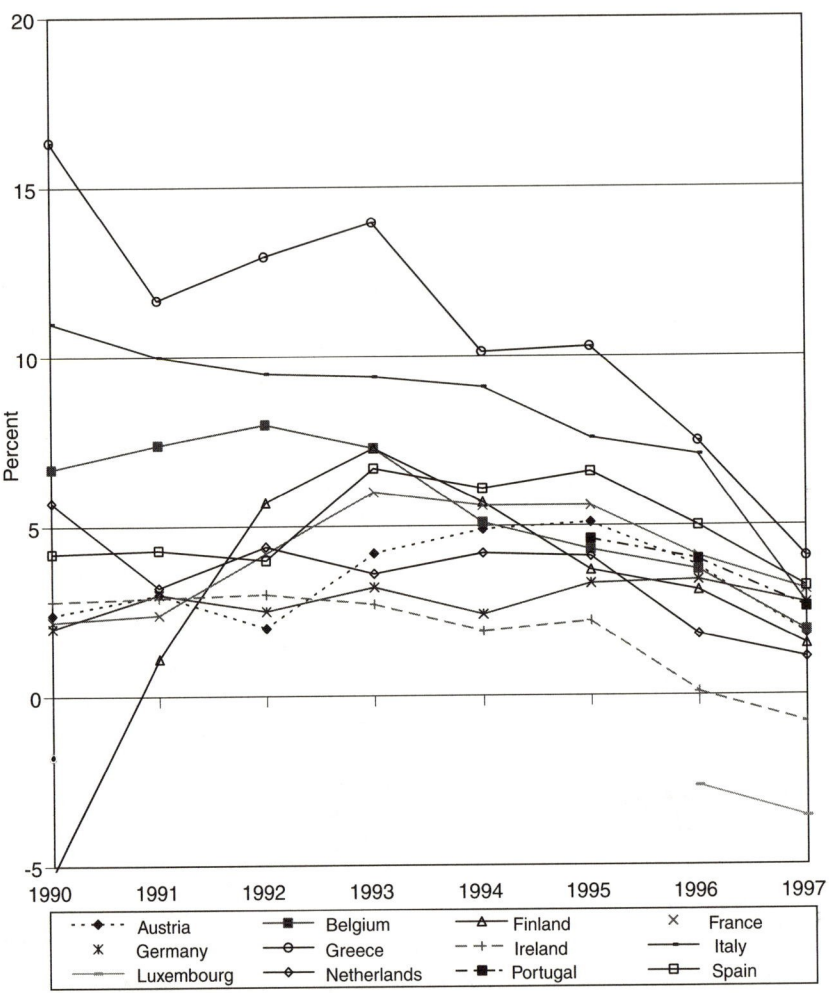

Figure 3.3. Budget deficit in eurozone countries. Budget deficit as a percentage of gross domestic product, 1990–97. Negative values denote budget surplus. *Source:* Economist Intelligence Unit.

they could operate with the new calling cards; and the new E-shaped euro symbol had to be added to computer keyboards alongside the dollar. The transition from the virtual to the real currency on January 1, 2002, when banks stopped issuing local currencies, took place without a glitch and temporarily lifted the euro's value against the dollar in reaction to the transaction demand for it. The conversion of hidden cash into euros by tax evaders and drug smugglers, especially the billions of German marks

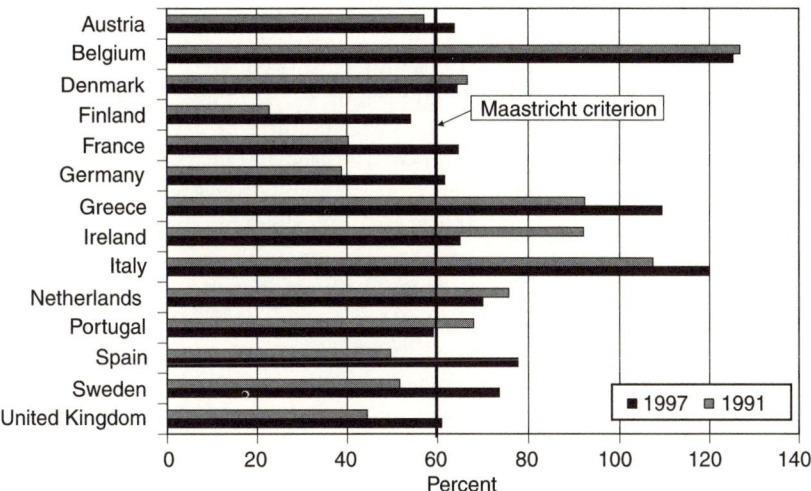

Figure 3.4. Gross public debt. Total debt (both local and foreign currency) owed by government to domestic residents, foreign nationals, and multilateral institutions, such as the International Monetary Fund, expressed as a percentage of gross domestic product. *Source:* Economist Intelligence Unit.

circulating outside Germany in central Europe, Turkey, and the Balkans, contributed to this pickup. By the end of March, retailers stopped accepting local currencies as legal tender. However, the major problems affecting the currency's health vis-à-vis the dollar even before its actual appearance were the regulated labor markets, the varied tax arrangements, the budget-busting pension payments, and the outdated practices of continental capitalism that held back the launching of a full-fledged market economy in the zone, and weakened its productivity growth rate in contrast to its sustained and superior performance in the U.S. economy.

Constrained by the budget deficit and inflation control rules, the center-left governments voted into power in France in 1997, in Germany in 1998, and in Italy in 1998 managed prudent macroeconomic policies. However, the record of eurozone policy makers in initiating structural reforms involving labor market deregulation, pension benefit cutbacks, and investor-friendly tax regimes was slow.

Regulated Labor Markets

In principle, restricted cross-border mobility in the eurozone could be compensated by resource transfer from Brussels to an area that was hit by a recession—a course of action that was ruled out because the Maastricht

Treaty did not provide for such emergency support. European cross-national worker movement failed to match American labor mobility practices because of language barriers and cultural preferences. However, labor turnover via occupational choices by workers and job hiring and firing by employers was limited *within* each country because of labor market regulations. Workers could not be released because of stringent job protection laws, which precluded American-style fixed term, negotiable contracts. Companies tended to hire fewer workers because of high minimum wages and employment taxes. The unemployed, for their part, lacked incentives to find work because of significant and ill-conceived unemployment compensations.

Labor market reforms, initiated by several eurozone countries in the eighties and continuing into the nineties, were pell-mell. France and Germany cut back unemployment compensation; Italy delinked wages from chasing inflation; Belgium, France, and Spain lowered minimum wages for the young. France, Italy, and Spain introduced flexible work contracts for part-time and temporary workers. But job security for the workforce remained largely intact and contributed to labor immobility. The center-left government of Chancellor Gerhard Schroeder extended the role of workers' councils in German factories and discouraged employers from hiring workers on American-style, fixed-term contracts. Voicing his opposition to flexible labor markets, the chancellor declared: "We don't want an American-style labour market because we believe a higher level of job security and certainty is right" (*Financial Times*, July 13, 2001, p. 2). France's Socialist-led government succumbed to union-led protests against job cuts by several companies and tightened job guarantees. These one-step-forward-two-steps-backward measures failed to significantly boost employment. If, for example, unemployment benefits were to be reduced, workers with given skill profiles, who were induced to seek work, could be hired at lower wages by firms if they could adjust their workforce by being allowed to release current, unwanted employees. According to David Coe and Dennis Snower (1997), the combination of unemployment compensation cutbacks and flexible hiring and voluntary choice firing by employers could generate more resources resulting in output and employment growth.

As the eurozone economies, initially stimulated by a sliding euro and growing exports, took off in 1999, the average unemployment rate in 1999 came down to 9 percent of the workforce from a high of over 12 percent. Individual economies also grew with the expansion of intra-eurozone trade aided by the fixed exchange rates of the eleven currencies and the resulting elimination of volatile currency risks. The higher growth, so far unaided by labor market deregulation, contributed to the adoption of flexible working hours, some labor mobility, and unemployment decline. In France, labor markets were freed via a combination of practices involving the adoption of a lower, 35-hour work week, part-time work, and more job opportunities in the service sector prompted by low interest rates. In Spain, the center-right government of Prime Minister José Maria Aznar effectively used its comfortable majority in the parliament to launch a radical liberalization package opening up the oil, gas, electricity, and telecommunications markets and limiting the role of state-controlled units. On balance, the pick up in growth rates supplemented by government-supported job creation measures and some easing of trade union opposition to labor market deregulation contributed to lower unemployment rates in the zone. In specific sectors, such as information technology in Germany and the Netherlands, the emerging labor shortages raised political issues relating to lowering of immigration barriers designed to alleviate such shortages. However, despite an impressive growth rate of 3.4 percent in 2000, unemployment in the zone remained high at 8.3 percent of the workforce; it was slated to grow from month to month in early 2002 after 9/11, as temporary workers were laid off across the zone in the midst of deteriorating business conditions and declining growth prospects.

Out-of-Control Pension Benefits

Retirement benefits in most industrialized countries, based on the pay-as-you-go arrangements, pay retirees out of earnings of current workers who contribute to pension funds. A smaller ratio of workers to retirees imposes a higher burden on the treasury. This burden can be brought under control by switching to privately funded pension schemes, lifting the retirement age, and raising worker participation by attracting women and immigrants to the employment pool.

EU governments sought to ease the pension crisis, largely the result of the demographic imbalance and generous retiree benefits, by initiating policy changes in the face of opposition from trade unions. The crisis called for a systematic overhaul of the existing arrangements. The numbers were ominous. First, the rising number of adults over the age of 65 in the European population from approximately 16 percent in 2000 to 25 percent in 2030 and 28 percent in 2050 was expected to tilt the ratio of workers (15 to 64 years) to nonworkers (65 years and above) from an average of over 4 to 2.4 in the U.K., 2.3 in France, 2 in Germany, and 1.5 in Italy in the next 50 years. In the absence of remedial measures, pension payments in Italy would jump from 13.3 percent of GDP in 1995 to 21.4 percent in 2040 and in Germany from 11.1 percent to 18.4 percent during the same period.

The remedies, demanding political will and votes from the center-left governments, were resisted by trade unions and left-wing political parties toward the end of the decade. In Italy, three rounds of reforms in successive governments managed to raise the retirement age and link pension benefits to worker contributions rather than to their earnings. Progress was slow on private pension schemes and generally inadequate to contain the fiscal pressures. In France, the pay-as-you-go system, sacrosanct to the ruling Socialist Party, was to be modified via the introduction in small and medium-sized companies of workers' savings schemes with ten-year tax-free maturity. A cutback in pension payments however was ruled out. In Germany, changes in the pension arrangements, worked up by the Social Democratic government involving the introduction of state-backed private pensions, faced a showdown with its coalition partners in the Green Party who demanded a speedier implementation of (state-subsidized) private pensions and effective trimming of state pension levels. In the midst of the halting, uneven pension payment changes in individual EU countries, the European Commission sought to create a pan-European pension market, valued at $2,028 billion. This would allow pension funds to be invested in diverse assets, including corporate bonds and equity, without being forced to concentrate in a given asset, such as government bonds. National regulators could however impose limits on pension fund investments in property and derivatives. The Commission was also busy drafting proposals aimed at improving taxation norms by persuading members to tax pension payouts rather than pension contributions.

The eurozone members needed to orient their inherited tax arrangements toward improved personal and business tax incentives.[1]

The Punitive Tax Arrangements

The eurozone's tax systems offered differing advantages to businesses when the euro created a unified currency area. The higher value-added tax at 20 percent in France was a disincentive for investors in contrast to the lower 16 percent tax in Germany, unless countered by other advantages. Luxembourg was an offshore banking haven because it welcomed savings without a withholding tax. EU value-added taxes, shown in figure 3.5, ranged from 16 to 25 percent. Corporate taxes, besides being generally high, also varied from country to country. Ireland, with low corporate tax, attracted massive foreign investments. Except for Finland and Ireland, with low rates of 29 and 24 percent, respectively, the top corporate tax rates in 1999 ranged from 34 percent in Austria to 40 percent in Portugal, 55 percent in Germany, and 60 percent in the Netherlands. Figure 3.6 shows that government revenues as a percentage of GDP were

Figure 3.5. Value-added tax (VAT). Standard VAT rate on purchased goods and some services. Rates are accurate as of May 1, 2001. *Source:* Directorate-General Taxation and Customs Union Tax Policy, European Commission.

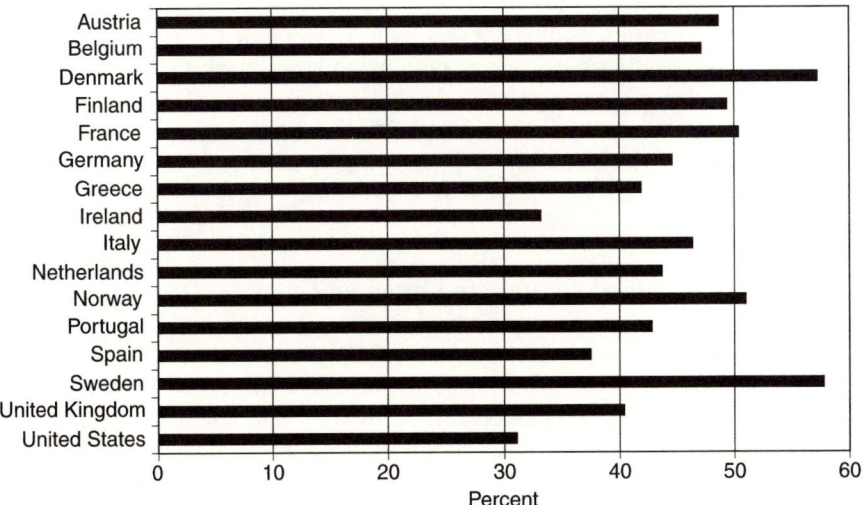

Figure 3.6. Taxes. Overall taxes as a percentage of gross domestic product, 1999. *Source:* Organisation for Economic Cooperation & Development.

over 40 percent in most economies in contrast to 40 percent in the U.K., 30 percent in the U.S., and 28 percent in Japan (*Financial Times*, September 29, 2000, p. 16). The high, across-the-board, export-led growth rates of 1999 and 2000, averaging 3 and 3.4 percent, the result of a growing world economy and a declining euro, needed to be sustained by a pickup in domestic demand requiring lower tax rates.

By mid-2000, taxation and budgetary reforms were beginning to spread in member countries. In Germany, the Social Democratic government of Chancellor Gerhard Schroeder reduced the basic income tax rate from 22.9 percent to 19.9 percent for 2001, 17 percent for 2003, and 15 percent for 2005. The highest rate was similarly targeted to decline from a high of 51 percent to 42 percent in 2005. Local business tax was slated to go down from 52 percent to 39 percent in 2001. In a strikingly radical move, the socialist government abolished the capital gains tax on inter-company stock sales with a view to promote restructuring of German companies linked via cross-company ownership. In the Netherlands, the combination of a rise in the value-added and environment taxes and reduced income tax rates was aimed, on balance, to provide an incentive to domestic growth. In Italy, the initial spurt of public finance cleanup, leading to the country's entry into the eurozone, had slackened in 2000: the overhaul of the regulated labor market and the bloating pension system faced a confrontation with the trade unions. But, in a bid to shore up the center-left coalition's prospects in the spring 2001 elections, the government announced a hefty tax reduction package aimed at reducing the tax burden of households and businesses by $19 billion in 2001.

On the whole, structural reforms involving labor market deregulation and pension benefits were halting. At the same time, the introduction of incentive-oriented tax systems, corporate management practices, and competitive business structures designed to take advantage of the unified capital market lagged behind U.S. arrangements.

The Americanization of European Corporate Traditions

Shareholder capitalism induces managers to concentrate on earnings for the company and dividends for the owners in contrast to stakeholder capitalism where they must worry about worker and employee welfare. Widespread share and corporate bond ownership, in contrast to investors' preference for safe, low-return government bonds, promotes such earnings-driven corporate culture. In 1996, the share of equities in the portfolio allocation of the French, German, Italian, and Dutch (as well the non-euro Japanese) private sector was much lower than in the U.S. and U.K. (*Financial Times*, April 30, 1998, p. 13). A variety of signals suggested however that European practices were beginning to change. Management remuneration was being tied to share prices; employees were being given stock options in companies; French and German companies were pressing their lawmakers for demands in legislation that would allow them share buybacks with cash on hand that would otherwise be used in low-return alternatives; and hostile takeovers had begun occasionally in defiance of incumbent management protected by interlocked share ownership among companies in France and Italy and by banks in Germany. The process called for the necessary legislative changes for it to gather speed (Details are in ibid.).

European business needed to rapidly adopt Internet technology in order for these new practices to contribute to economic efficiency and labor productivity. In this critical respect, Europe was miles behind the U.S. Cultural and economic factors constrained the growth of European business-to-consumer (B2C) Internet sites. These sites had to be translated into five languages in order for them to reach a large number of customers. Only about one in seven Germans and Italians owned a credit card that could facilitate B2C shopping. European e-commerce sales of $3.4 billion in 1999 were less than one-half of 1 percent of total sales (*New York Times*, September 28, 2000, p. C1). The switch to the technology of e-commerce also required abolition of restrictions allowing Internet sellers free listing of their items in regional directories. The U.S. was far less protectionist than the EU in this regard. As a letter to the editor in the Financial Times from a children's clothing seller of French origin claims, while her business was physically located in France, she was denied entry in some French directories because her Web site was in English. Subsequently she was also banned from English directories because her location was in France. However, her sales flourished in the U.S. market because she had no problem registering herself in American e-directories ("U.S. Understands Globalism Better than 'Protective' EU," *Letters to the Editor, Financial Times*, November 2, 2000, p. 16). As late as mid-2000, the EU had not worked up a legal framework to facilitate e-commerce.

At the same time, worried over the potential loss of high value-added tax revenue from the nontaxed Internet, the European Commission was considering controversial measures to ensure that digital items bought via the Internet did not escape taxation (details are in the *New York Times*, September 28, 2000, p. C1). Even if Internet customers surfing in cyberspace could be effectively caught in the tax net—a possibility that the U.S. Internet Tax Freedom Act of 1998 ruled out until 2001—the plan could constrain the growth of cross-national and cross-Atlantic B2C Internet commerce. Without rapid strides in the adoption of information technology, the eurozone could not be expected to overtake and surpass the slowing U.S. growth in 2000, arrest the cross-Atlantic flow of cash in Ameri-

Trans-Atlantic Deals

Figure 3.7. Trans-Atlantic deals. Acquisitions between U.S. and Western European firms, in billions of dollars. *Source: Wall Street Journal*, September 18, 2000, p. A25.

can business, and strengthen the euro. Aided by the availability of long-term euro financing in a unified capital market, European companies acquired an increasing stake in U.S. firms.

European Acquisitions of U.S. Business: A Double-Edged Sword

In 1999, European purchases of American companies, shown in figure 3.7, rose sharply in value and number of deals from their 1998 levels: by $47 billion to $193 billion and by 186 to 597, respectively. These deals represented a net inflow of European capital into U.S. business of $268 billion by mid-2000. European capital made inroads into a variety of U.S. activities including energy, chemicals, and financial and food services. This entry was eased by a number of factors, the principal among them being the unification of the European capital market under the euro umbrella. The unification provided companies with opportunities to convert their bonds denominated in weak, local currencies into long-term bonds denominated in euro that was expected to be stronger than its constituent local currency counterpart (except the D-mark). This redenomination of bonds implied a one-time spurt in bond instruments that was larger than their combined total in local currencies. In addition, European companies, taking advantage of the elimination of currency risk premiums, floated long-term bonds in larger amounts to finance their cash needs in euros at low interest rates, in the process reducing transaction costs for financing ambitious projects. New, euro-denominated bond issues by EU corporations by the end of September 2000 were ten times greater than issues before 1999 in their local currencies. According to an article by Ronald Mckinnon, "Two Sides of the Same Coin", "This improved availability of long term finance to European corporations has enabled them to launch numerous takeover bids for U.S. companies in the past year or so [noted above]" (*Financial Times*, September 28, 2000, p. 17). These companies were strategically positioning themselves for bigger market shares and higher earnings in U.S. industry and the financial sector marked by efficient management and advanced technologies.

The massive capital outflows (requiring the conversion of euros into dollars) weakened the euro by almost 30 percent against the dollar from its initial value on January 1, 1999 of $1.18 to a euro to below 85 cents in late September 2000. On September 22, the ECB, the Federal Reserve, the Bank of Japan, the Bank of England, the Bank of Canada, and the national central banks of the eurozone intervened in the foreign exchange market. They bought euros in exchange for dollars, yens, and British pounds and pushed the euro rate to 90 cents (it later settled at 87.87 cents). The decision makers intervened jointly in the currency market at the request of the ECB because they were concerned about the potential implications of a sharp decline in the euro for the world economy. At the same time, Treasury Secretary Lawrence Summers reiterated the U.S. policy stance in favor of a strong dollar that had kept U.S. inflation low in the midst of a sustained economic expansion.

The intervention raised several questions about the ECB's ability to successfully implement the triple policy arrangements of a floating euro, free capital mobility, and monetary policy autonomy, while maintaining economic growth with low unemployment. Would the support stabilize the euro? Would it be repeated if it failed in doing so? More to the point, should the ECB tilt its policy-making stance in favor of a strong or a weak euro?

Currency Intervention: Did It Stabilize the Euro?

The euro regained some of its loss because the concerted intervention in which the Federal Reserve joined in an unexpected policy move, conveyed a decisive interventionist signal. However, the capital outflows from Europe had been driven by European investors' search for higher returns in the growing and larger U.S. market rather than by speculative impulses of currency traders that could be arrested by a significant intervention. Ultimately, the downward pressure on the euro could abate if European productivity growth rate caught up with that of the U.S., reversing the long-term flow. The immediate fortunes of the currency were also linked with the short-term forecasts of the U.S. economy contributing to the currency's ups and downs. In view of the declared preference of U.S. policy makers for a market-determined value of the dollar, the Fed's participation in future efforts to arrest the decline of the euro could not be guaranteed.

Nor was it clear that the intervention had established an ideal floor for the currency's value in view of the conflicting choices facing the ECB between inflation control and continuing growth in the member countries. A weak euro combined with rising oil prices tended to push up inflation that could not be tamed via a higher interest rate without choking off the growth momentum in the zone. On the other hand, a slight orderly reversal of the decline could contain dollar- denominated prices of European imports, such as oil, minerals, metals, and fibers, and maintain the competitiveness of European exports, especially of construction and heavy engineering items to OPEC markets flushed with petrodollars.

The sharper-than-necessary slide of the euro, brought on by substantial long-term capital outflows in 1999 and continuing into 2000, confronted the ECB with the difficult choice between inflation control and continuing growth. At the same time, the bank's policy-making role was buffeted by pulls and pressures from various directions that went beyond the growth-versus-inflation control dilemma. Indeed, the euro's continuing decline brought out in the open clashes of opinions inside the zone and misgivings outside its borders posing a threat to its stability. The perceived lack of coherence in ECB policy pronouncements featured prominently in these debates pushing further in the future the emergence of an expanding Europe linked by a common currency and embraced by more member states.

The Pulls and Pressures Affecting the Euro's Stability

Despite the steely determination of European leaders stretching over four decades to transform Europe into a single monetary and economic union, the euro's progress was marked by doubts and differing views about its prospects. From the start, cohesive policies, in fulfillment of the requirements of the 2 percent inflation rate ceiling and budget deficit targets, had been difficult to hammer out among the eleven members, leading influential spokespersons to single out members by name for their foot dragging. Thus, Hans Reckers, a German Bundesbank member, said that Greece should not join the eurozone in January 2001 because it did not meet the criteria for inflation and budgetary discipline in a sustained fashion. In late April 2000, five leading German opinion makers declared that the U.S., in the view of the market, was poised to outperform the eurozone because the zone's policy makers were slow in overhauling their labor markets, tax arrangements, and welfare systems such as pension payments.[2] In the words of Hans-Olaf Henkel, head of the Confederation of German Industry, "Capital markets have little faith in the reform capability of the three most important Euroland countries, Germany, France and Italy. . . . Above all, these three countries are taking too long to reduce their debts" (*Financial Times*, April 27, 2000, p. 23).

Given the dissenting voices and the bottlenecks of forging a speedy policy framework among the members with vastly different economies and institutions, the task of managing the euro was tricky at best and nightmarish at worst. The ECB and its president, Wim Duisenberg, traveled in uncharted territories. The U.S. Treasury Secretary could firmly announce a preference in favor of a strong dollar except suggested to the contrary by the foreign exchange market. The situation facing the new ECB team was vastly complicated.

The Vacillating European Central Bank

The bank's operational routine was defined differently from that of the Fed. The ECB, unlike the Fed, provided a written policy statement raising speculations about its intentions. The Fed disclosed minutes of meetings or members' votes on decisions after the fact. Wim Duisenberg held press conferences and often gave conflicting signals; Alan Greenspan, the chairman of the Federal Reserve, made speeches on assorted subjects without revealing the Fed game plan except when he wanted to. Members of the Federal Open Market Committee sometimes differed with Greenspan on a given issue with nary a dent in his leadership acumen. While officials around Duisenberg made matters worse as they tried to salvage his inept pronouncements, Greenspan gave testimonies before congressional committees with the flair of a professor guiding his students through the intricacies of policy making. Duisenberg appeared before the European parliament and left the lawmakers mystified. On several occasions, the market perceived the ECB's exchange rate management as inconsistent and confusing.

Examples abounded. In April 1999, Duisenberg said the ECB policy stance did not neglect the euro exchange rate contradicting his earlier view that the ECB had a policy of "neglect" on the exchange rate. In September, Duisenberg switched from a tightening bias toward higher interest rates "gradually creeping into our considerations" of April to a bias "creeping at a snail's pace" (*Wall Street Journal*, April 27, 2000, pp. A1–A10). On September 22, 2000, Duisenberg, having described the ECB currency intervention in support of the euro as an attempt to "introduce an orderly reversal," confounded currency traders by saying that the ECB "has no strategy to continue and continue" intervening—a departure from his own promise to talk about intervention only after the fact, (*Wall Street Journal*, September 27, 2000, p. A21). In October, Duisenberg once again astonished analysts by declaring that the September timing of the joint intervention by several central banks in support of the euro was dictated by the significant time lag separating the decision from the U.S. presidential elections in November, signaling U.S. nonparticipation in additional rounds of intervention as the presidential election approached. He further explained his intervention strategy by suggesting that "it would be wrong to intervene to offset any impact on the euro from unrest in the Middle East" (*Financial Times*, October 17, 2000, p. 33).

The inconsistencies and indecisiveness reflected the ECB president's limited communication skills in signaling a credible scenario for the euro's stability to the markets. In all fairness, they also arose from the albatross imposed on his policy mandate by the Maastricht growth and stability pact for the eurozone members. The excessive emphasis on price stability in the context of inflation and budget deficit targets to be followed by the signatories turned out to be a steel-plated armor. The ECB chose to stay with interest rates that turned out to be high for a slow-growing economy because it feared that monetary easing would ignite inflation. The solution called for a counter-cyclical fiscal policy: deprived of an independent monetary policy, the slow-growing economies of Germany and Italy required budget deficits by mid-2001, while the fast-growing members had budget surpluses. But the pact prohibited such a fiscal adjustment for a weak economy by imposing automatic penalties including fines on countries that overshot the budget deficit target. Nor could the slow growers roll back their budget outlays and make room for tax cuts designed to revive their economies because progress on reforming the overburdened pension systems and unemployment compensations via promotion of flexible employment practices (noted previously) was slow. The ECB has therefore continued struggling with the growth versus price stability dilemma in the midst of a policy straightjacket that became severely constraining over time: the U.S. economic slowdown, followed by a recession after 9/11 in 2001, called for an active policy targeted to soften its impact on the eurozone growth and employment prospects even as the U.S. pursued resolute monetary and fiscal measures to overcome the recessionary drag at home.

In the midst of these problems and speculations about the ECB policy making and the euro's stability, the zone leadership faced Denmark's rejection of euroization and demands for EU entry by, among others, former members of the Soviet bloc to the south and east of Europe.

The Eurozone within an Enlarged EU: When and How?

On November 28, 2000, voters in Denmark rejected the euro by a vote of 53 percent to 47 percent in a referendum that conveyed their reservation about potential interference from a "European super state" in local affairs rather than about technical economic problems following entry in the zone. With Denmark representing just 2 percent of eurozone output, this decision was unlikely to unravel the zone or damage the currency significantly but it delayed the prospects of Britain and Sweden joining in, and revived debates about attempts from Brussels at undue political cohesion in the zone.

The enlargement also involved future entry of twelve countries, namely Bulgaria, the Czech Republic, Cyprus, Estonia, Hungary, Latvia, Lithuania, Malta, Poland, Romania, Slovakia, and Slovenia that desired EU membership. The Czech Republic, Cyprus, Estonia, Hungary, Poland, and Slovenia began membership negotiations in late 1997. Hungary and Poland (admitted to NATO membership along with the Czech Republic in 1999) desired membership in 2003.

The aspirants needed to fulfill strict criteria of a liberal market economy for gaining admission.[3] The candidates must not only be able to meet market pressures and compete economically with the current EU members but also must measure up to their rules and regulations. In early November, the European Commission released a schedule for the top contenders relating to their accession agenda to be negotiated in phases.[4] In its report card, the Commission ranked the tiny islands of Cyprus and Malta at the top in their ability to cope with the market pressures of the EU followed by Hungary, Poland, Estonia, and the Czech Republic in that order. However, EU membership would not qualify a new member to automatically adopt the euro by avoiding the fulfillment of the inflation and budget deficit norms laid down in the Maastricht Treaty for such euroization. Nor was the choice of exchange rate policies by potential members prior to their accession an issue that the European Commission would overlook.

The daunting task of the euro's enlargement designed to unify Europe was expected to extend over time requiring systematic negotiations in which the EU could expand to the south and east. The 2000 year-end Nice meeting of the EU leaders focused on two sets of issues in the existing EU and the enlarged EU with new members. The first related to the distribution of voting powers between large and small members (including prospective entrants) in the EU Council of Ministers where important decisions are made and the sharing of decision-making authority between the bureaucracy in Brussels and the current member government; the second pertained to developing clear and decisive signals about the entry of the new front runners in the Union.

From Horse Trading on the French Riviera to the Writing of an EU Constitution

In resolving the voting rights issue, the Nice summit ensured bigger clout in decision making in the Council of Ministers to Britain, France, Italy, and Germany by assigning twenty-nine votes to each, up from an earlier ten, and the retention of veto for members to block decisions. For example, Britain retained the veto on taxation, social security, and EU budgets; France on trade in cultural areas such as films and music; Germany on the free movement of professional workers within the EU. The summit hoped to abolish the veto in fifty new areas by introducing majority voting; it succeeded in doing so in twenty-nine policy areas. As for enlargement, the agreement did not set a target date or a queue for entry of all the aspirants but held out hopes for entry by 2004 for six countries. Each new entrant was assigned one commissioner in the European Commission, the core EU bureaucracy, until the commission reached twenty-seven members; at that point it was to be capped at a smaller, manageable size.

The negotiations marked by vigorous defense of national interests and active bargaining lifted the process from paralysis to incremental progress in institution building for a larger Europe. The task of writing a constitution for the expanding EU and formulating a cooperative model in which policy decisions could be shared by member governments and the EU institutions in Brussels was assigned in early 2002 to a constitutional convention of 105 members. Its recommendations would be debated and adopted in 2004. In the meantime, the decisions on streamlining financial, banking, and legal arrangements and implementing them within the smaller eurozone that could guarantee a strong, stable euro in a single currency zone were no less daunting. For example, the zone needed a pan-European corporate law, a banking code, and uniform accounting standards that could integrate national capital markets by ensuring cross-border movement of finances and their safe placements in high return activities in a competitive investment environment. The underpinning of this infrastructure was absolutely necessary for the speedy emergence of financial conglomerates, banks, and corporate businesses via mergers and acquisitions. The ongoing negotiations on these issues in the zone were time consuming and marked by backtracking and slow momentum. Unless these were speeded up, the eurozone could not hope to surpass and overtake the growth and productivity performance of the U.S. economy in the interest of a stable euro.

The Trans-Atlantic Scenario Affecting the Euro's Stability

The euro's strength depended on the prospects of robust, inflation free-growth in the zone. Rising oil prices, contributing to inflationary pressures and forcing the ECB to raise interest rates, could arrest eurozone growth rate. Another exogenous factor stalking the zone's performance was uncertainty over the growth prospects of the U.S. economy. A soft landing of the U.S. economy could enable the eurozone to maintain its growth rate without being clobbered by the dent in European exports and the earnings of European companies that a sharp decline in U.S. growth would imply. More critical to the realization of such a favorable outcome however was the relative productivity performance in the two areas.

Relative Productivity Growth Rates

The trans-Atlantic productivity race, with the U.S. outperforming the eurozone, was put in perspective by *Emu One Year On*, published by the Organisation for Economic Co-operation & Development (OECD) in early 2000. According to the report, eurozone output per hour of work at 70 percent of that in the U.S. in 1973 was 94 percent in 1998. This so-called closing of the gap however resulted from four factors: labor market participation of young and old workers in the zone was lower (than in the U.S.); their employment rates also were lower; female workers in prime working years had lower participation and employment rates; and everyone who was employed generally worked shorter hours (OECD, 2000). Enforcement of hiring and firing norms on employers, generous unemployment compensations, high minimum wages, and centralized collective bargaining practices, all attributes of the European welfare state (discussed previously), contributed to low workforce participation and employment in the zone. In such an exceedingly regulated labor market, the adoption of output-enhancing technical changes requiring superior skills evidently took place at the expense of the employment of the unskilled, and their subsequent withdrawal from the workforce because of the generous unemployment compensations. In order to reap the full benefits of the new technologies on output and employment growth, the members of the zone needed to rapidly liberalize their regulated labor markets.

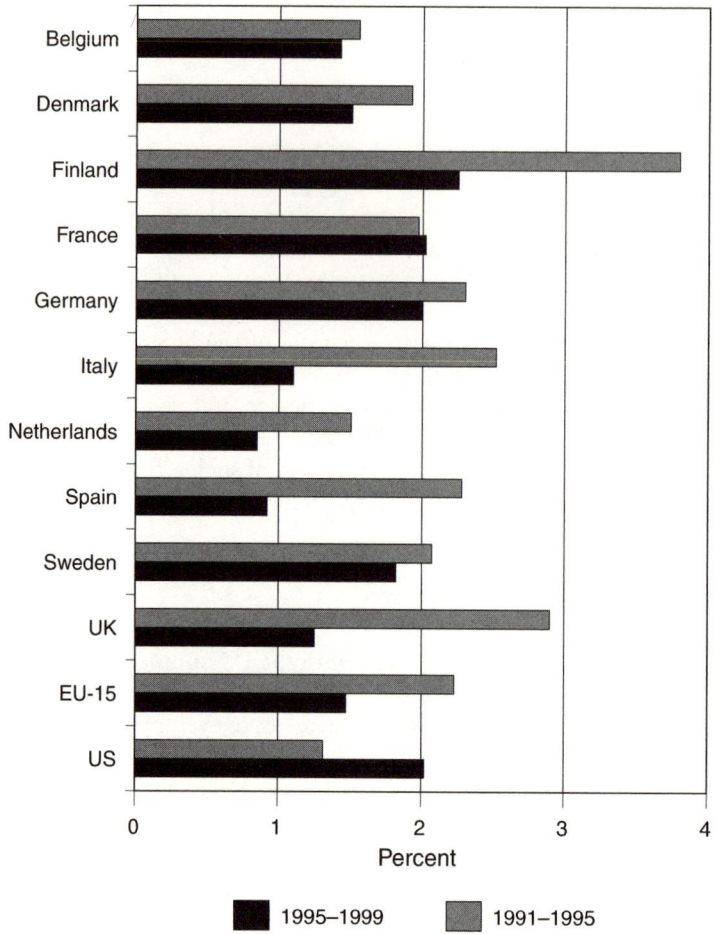

Figure 3.8. Hourly labor productivity growth in Europe and the U.S.
Average annual percentage change. *Source: Financial Times.*

The zone's long-term prospects of stabilizing the euro depended on the
speed with which it could raise labor productivity by adopting a competitive, deregulated employment regime bolstered by new technologies and a
streamlined capital market and corporate environment. From that perspective, hourly labor productivity growth *rates*, shown in figure 3.8, were
lower in all eurozone members in 1995–99 compared to those in 1991–95.

The higher productivity growth rates in the U.S. in the second half of
the nineties propelled the U.S. real GDP growth rates, outstripping the

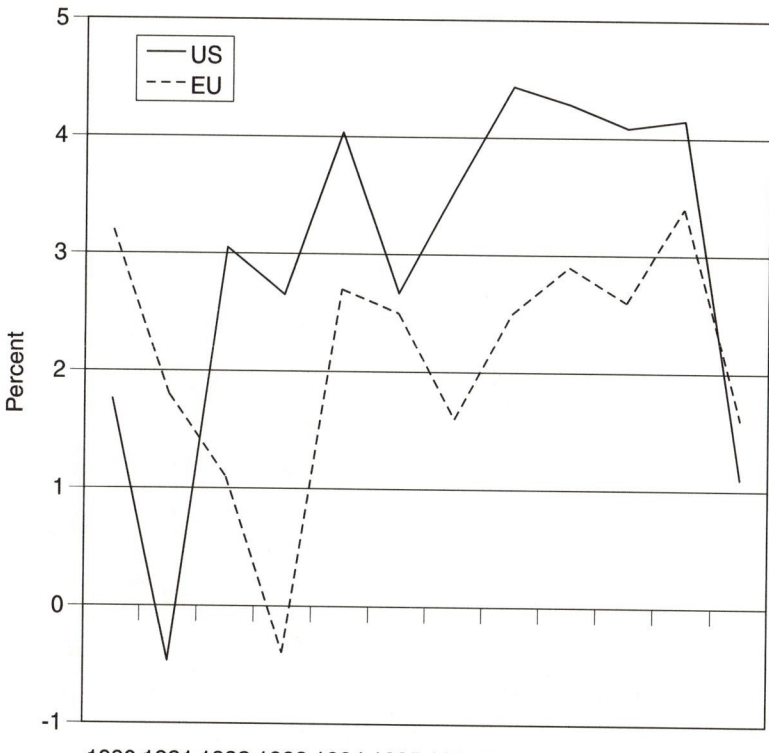

Figure 3.9. Real gross domestic product growth in the European Union and the U.S. Annual percentage change, 1990–2001. *Source:* Economist Intelligence Unit.

corresponding EU rates (figure 3.9). Higher economic growth also generated significant employment gains in the U.S. compared to the eurozone during this period (figure 3.10), leaving the zone struggling with a high structural unemployment rate exceeding 8 percent of the labor force.

Despite lagging productivity, could the eurozone outperform the U.S. economy as it struggled with an economic slowdown turning into a recession after 9/11? The answer depended on the resilience of the ECB in addressing the persistent conflict between growth and inflation and responding to the lowering of the U.S. short-term interest rate by the Federal Reserve by 4.75 percent between January 2001 and January 2002, supplemented by the fiscal stimulus (discussed in chapter 2), both of which were aimed at an early recovery in 2002 from the post-September recession.

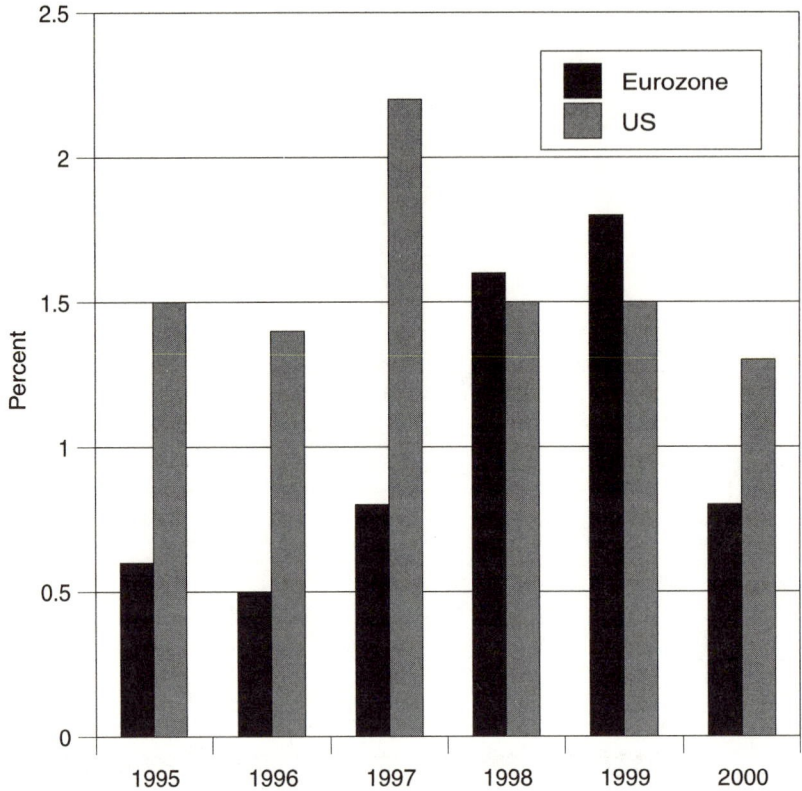

Figure 3.10. Percentage changes in annual employment in the eurozone and the U.S. *Source: Financial Times.*

Eurozone Prospects in 2002

Eurozone growth in 2001 had tumbled to 1.5 percent from a high 3.4 percent in 2000. The zone was marked in mid-2001 by slowing growth and creeping inflation rates as a result of high oil and food prices, a telecommunications sector battered by low earnings prospects, slowing exports to the U.S. and Asian markets, and sluggish consumption at home. After 9/11, the eurozone was headed toward a recession and low price expectations (contributing to a rise in real interest rates), requiring a monetary easing by the ECB on top of three benchmark interest rate cuts of August 30, September 17, and November 7. Germany, providing one-third of the zone output, had zero growth, plunging business confidence, and a surging unemployment rate at 9.4 percent which its policy makers could not counter with a fiscal stimulus without damaging the Maastricht pact's fiscal deficit norm. Overall economic decline in the zone, aggravated by a slump in travel, hotel, and airline business, had slipped into a recession by the end of 2001 marked by accelerating job layoffs, deteriorating business prospects, and declining consumer confidence. The U.S. economy, exhibiting a robust interplay between appropriate institutions, fine-tuned policies, and entrepreneurial risk-taking was better set to overcome the recession and move on to a higher growth than the eurozone caught in economic uncertainties emanating from policy indecisiveness and slow progress on structural, financial, and tax reforms.

The eurozone was thus not poised to fill the slack in the momentum to the world economic growth brought on by the events of 9/11. The continuing stagnation of the Japanese economy, to which I turn in the next chapter, also put the burden of global recovery on the performance of the U.S. economy in 2002.

Notes

1. Following Krugman and Baldwin (2001), I avoid the term harmonization implying a common EU tax rate on income from capital, for example. Krugman and Baldwin argue that the benefits of agglomeration, defined as the externalities arising from companies bunching together, are higher in the EU core consisting of France, Germany, Italy, Belgium, the Netherlands and Luxembourg. Despite higher taxes in 1965 on capital income, these historical centers did not fear capital flight because they offered advantages of strong infrastructure, common supply and service chains, and shared knowledge. By contrast, the periphery consisting of Greece, Ireland, Portugal, and Spain, lagging in the agglomeration advantages, had lower tax rates. Ultimately, the initial gap in the tax rates narrows as closer economic integration lowers the benefits of agglomeration for the core.

2. These were Theo Waigel, the former finance minister, Jurgen Donges and Horst Siebert, two government economic advisors, Michael Fuchs, president of the German Association for Wholesale and Foreign trade, and Hans-Olaf Henkel, head of the Confederation of German Industry.

3. The accession priorities in the economy related to liberalized prices, privatized industry, reduced subsidy burden in the budget, a robust banking system, agricultural reform, and environment upgrading. Government administration, the customs and tax services, and the judiciary must be toned up so that legislative measures could be implemented, crime and corruption could be brought under control, and minority rights (of the Roma in Hungary and Romania and of the Kurds in Turkey) were protected.

4. Free movement of goods, labor, and capital encouraged by legal guarantees and unencumbered by a protective environment followed by a well-placed taxation and legal system promoting competition would be negotiated in 2001. Negotiations on contentious issues, such as agricultural policy, were expected to be completed in the first half of 2002 allowing entry of the most advanced candidates by the end of the year.

4

Japan: The Lost Decade of the Nineties amidst Policy Paralysis

THE JAPANESE ECONOMY's prolonged decline in the nineties turned into a recession toward the end of 2000 marked by mounting price deflation. During this period, attempts to revive the economy via fiscal pump priming led to resource misuse into pork barrel projects. Monetary easing failed to stimulate consumer demand by households or capital spending by industry. A softening of the yen in late 2001 calculated to boost exports raised protests from Asian neighbors and the U.S. treasury. The prolonged policy paralysis, which I analyze in this chapter, arose from the leadership's failure to enforce a cleanup of banks that were burdened by massive nonperforming loans and free Japanese industry from widespread regulations and high taxes. The economy's decline also affected Japan's traditional role as an active investor and lender in the small Asian economies and affected their export sectors as the Japanese recession coincided with that of the U.S. after 9/11.

The Mounting Economic Malaise

In the late eighties, propelled by expansionary fiscal and easy monetary stimuli, Japan turned into a bubble economy of unparalleled asset price inflation especially in urban land values that rose sevenfold in less than a decade, in turn providing collateral against bank lending to companies that dizzily invested in real estate and urban property. The *keiretsu*, "happy-family" links between banks and industry groups marked by cross-shareholdings and low-margin corporate lending by banks, misallocated capital in dubious projects financed by bank loans to the tune of 12 percent of gross domestic product (GDP) when asset prices collapsed from their 1990 peak. Property prices continued tumbling for the ninth year in a row in 1999 forcing sales of some urban commercial properties at 80 percent or more below their peak values. The exposure of banks to declining prices of land, their principal asset, precluded chances of a sustainable recovery of the Japanese economy through monetary expansion via bank lending to industry. By February 1999, the Bank of Japan had pushed short-term interest rates to zero, essentially offering banks cost-free cash in the overnight lending markets without successfully inducing a spurt in the growth of money supply: bank lending shrank in the succeeding months as banks cut off weak borrowers, and strong borrowers paid off outstanding loans.

The government resorted to massive public spending to stimulate the economy via repeated fiscal packages, ten since August 1992, amounting to a staggering \$1,135 billion. Government outlays pushed the budget deficit to 10 percent of GDP by 2000, twice as devastating as what occurred in the U.S. in the worst days of the 1990–91 recession, and raised public debt from a manageable 60 percent of GDP in 1990 to an estimated, unsustainable 120 percent in 2001.

Monetary and fiscal stimuli failed to revive the economy as in the U.S. via a pickup in household consumption and business investment because Japanese banks, buried under a mountain of bad debts, were unable to serve as efficient lenders to consumers and companies. At the same time, households fearful of losing jobs in a declining economy held back their spending, and businesses battled the burden of debt repayment in the midst of bleak sales prospects. An American-style, wholesale cleanup of crumbling banks and bankruptcies of deadbeat companies was caught up in interminable policy differences between the Bank of Japan and the Ministry of Finance to which veteran party bosses and ministry bureaucrats contributed. An effective policy blueprint also required a streamlining of the tax system and deregulation of some sectors of the economy. The election of the charismatic and popular Junichiro Koizumi as prime minister in April 2001 raised hopes that he would embark on the necessary structural reform initiatives without which the best-designed policies could flounder. However, a 10 percent decline in the value of the yen against the dollar under his watch from November 2001 to February 2002, was viewed as a deliberate export-promoting strategy calculated to bypass a dysfunctional monetary policy and an overwrought government budget. It raised protests from near and far, from Chinese and South Korean leaders concerned about the loss of their export markets and from the U.S. treasury secretary who characterized the currency's decline as a deliberate "protectionist" move substituting for the long-delayed, more urgent banking-sector reforms. The year 2002 held little promise that Japan would emerge from its long drawn out slump (analyzed below) and embark on its traditional role of serving as a vigorous engine of growth for the Asian economies (as I argue later in the chapter).

The Protracted Slump which neither G (Government Outlays), nor C (Consumption), nor I (Investment), nor X (Exports) Could Revive

Japan's economic malaise was marked by up and down correlation in growth rates of GDP (figure 4.1), inflation (figure 4.2), and domestic investment (figure 4.3), all three exhibiting a declining trend amidst the volatility. The flip-flop in investment spending was again reflected in the

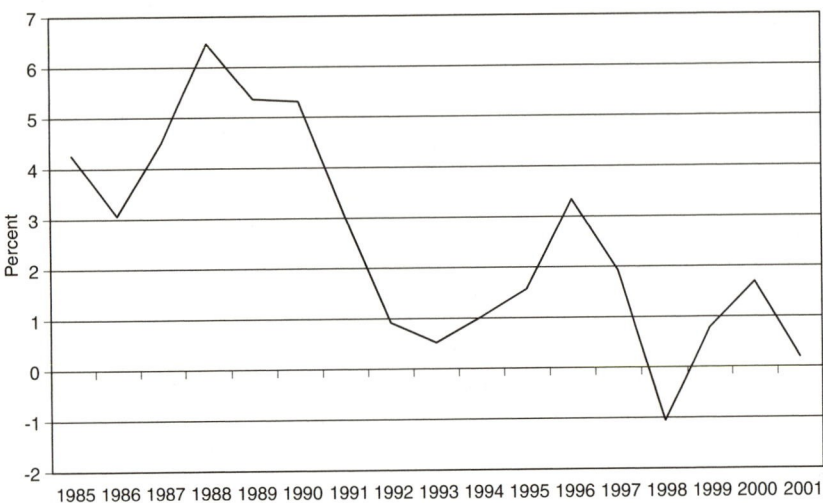

Figure 4.1. Japan: Change in real gross domestic product (GDP). Percentage change in real GDP over previous year. *Source:* Economist Intelligence Unit.

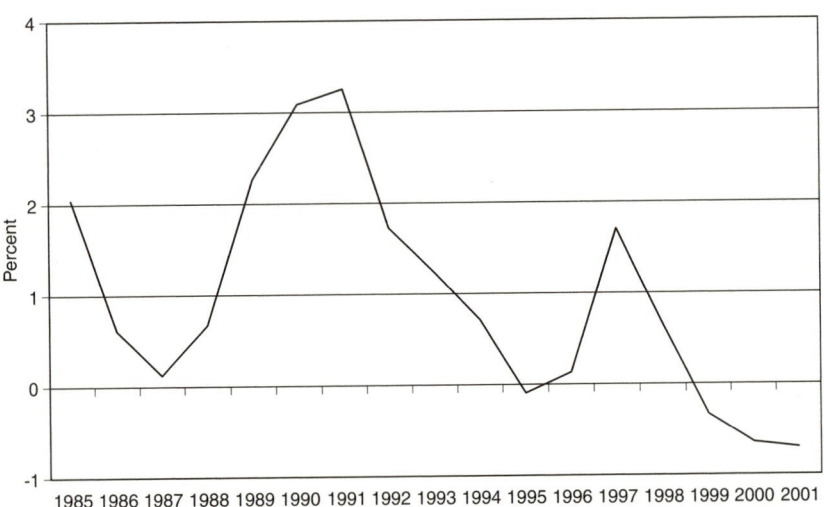

Figure 4.2. Japan: Inflation. Percentage change in consumer price index in local currency (period average), over previous year. *Source:* Economist Intelligence Unit.

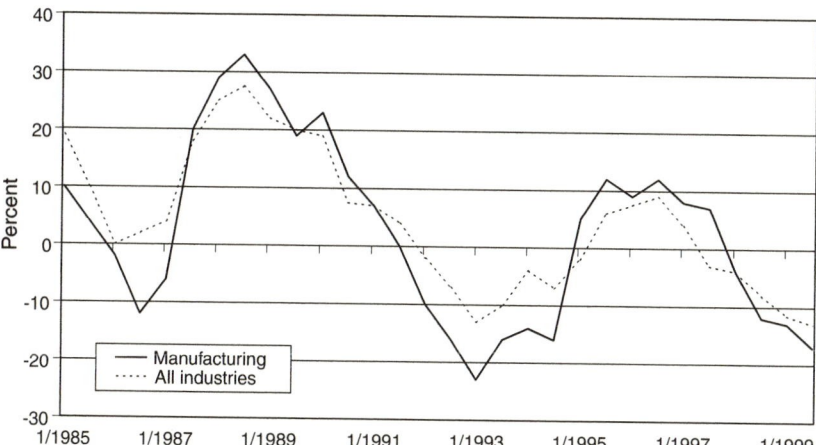

Figure 4.3. Japanese companies' capital spending plans. Business and investment survey of incorporated enterprises, annual percentage change. *Note:* Values for 1999 are estimates. *Source: Financial Times.*

index of industrial production until early 2002 (in figure 4.4). The high instability in these four indicators (GDP growth rate, inflation, investment, industrial production) pointed to the Japanese policy makers' loss of control over economic activity. Equally worrisome, unemployment had climbed from a low 2.3 percent of the workforce in 1965 to a high 5.6 percent in December 2001. The economy grew fitfully at an average annual 1.69 percent in the nineties marked by a continuing seesaw of growth followed by a pullback and declining prices. Real GDP, after adjustment for price deflation of 0.7 percent, barely grew by 0.2 percent in 2001, representing a nominal GDP growth rate of –0.5 percent.

The government's response for containing the economy's escalating downturn consisted in a massive fiscal stimulus.

The Failed Fiscal Stimulus

Budget allocations, financed via bond issuance, pushed the budget deficit to 8 percent of GDP in 2000 from a low of 2 percent in 1990 and doubled government debt to 120 percent of GDP in 2001 from 60 percent in 1990 (figure 4.5). However, public funding went into pork-barrel infrastructure projects, such as fishing ports and bridges, in the favored heartlands of the ruling Liberal Democratic Party (LDP). The new prime minister's political agenda pointed to the need, ironically procyclical, for trimming budget

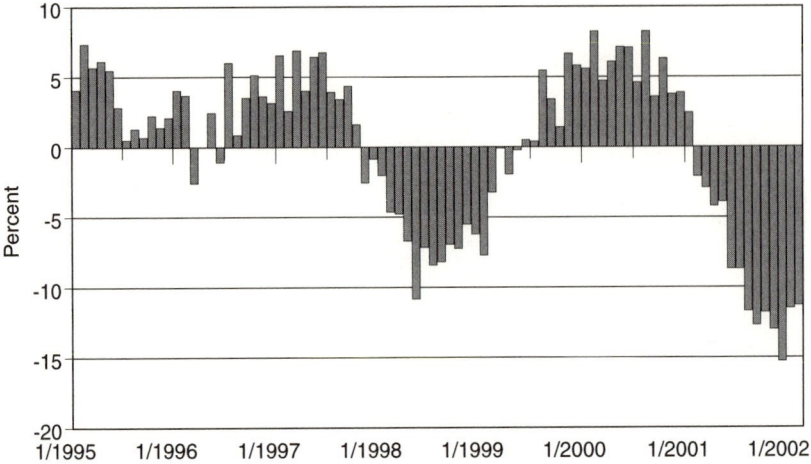

Figure 4.4. Industrial production. Percentage change in index of industrial production, over previous year. January 1995–February 2002. *Source:* Economist Intelligence Unit (1/95–1/01), Japan Ministry of Economy, Trade and Industry (2/01–2/02).

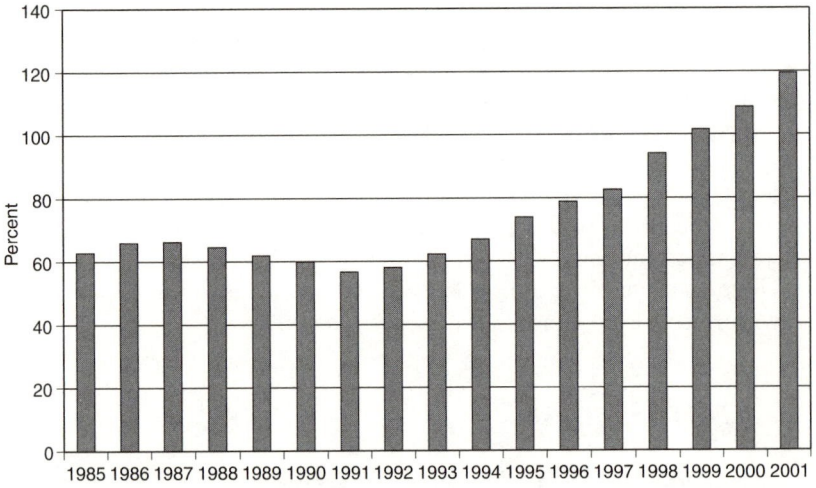

Figure 4.5. General government gross debt. Total debt (both local and foreign currency), owed by government to domestic residents, foreign nationals, and multilateral institutions, such as the International Monetary Fund, expressed as a percentage of gross domestic product. *Source:* Economist Intelligence Unit.

outlays that went into financing these schemes favored in their prefectures by the party's top echelons. These outlays were to be brought down gradually and diverted from roads, railroads, and bridges into efficient uses and into unemployment compensation. Again, party bosses used Japan's state-run postal savings system with $2,950 billion in saving deposits and life insurance premiums for financing boondoggles without concern for adequate returns. Koizumi put privatization of the postal system, vigorously opposed by the LDP senior members, on top of the reform blueprint. At the same time, the proposed fiscal restructuring initiated a scramble among ministry bureaucrats for pushing their efficiency-oriented schemes in the pool of ideas to be considered by the Ministry of Finance. At the start of the new leader's announcement to put the fiscal house in order, the battle lines were thus joined by political bosses and veteran bureaucrats bent on retaining a slice of the revenue pie for their use.

The chances of sustained recovery via growth of private consumption were not bright either.

The Overly Cautious Japanese Consumer

Japanese consumers, accounting for 61 percent of spending in national income and famous for their frugal spending habits, earned less because of job losses and spent less from their declining incomes because of fears of further layoffs as corporate restructuring moved apace. The low and uneven growth toward the end of nineties was also marked (as shown in figure 4.2) by a downward pressure on the price level as Japan imported lower-priced items from electronics to autos to motorcycles from its low-cost Asian operations. Cheap imports of consumer goods from China contributed to the pressure resulting in a substantial bilateral trade deficit with China, and an import flow from Asia into the Japanese market that exceeded the combined flow from North America and Western Europe. As relative prices in Japan approached those in low-cost Asian suppliers, the accumulation of excess capacity in Japanese industry added to the deflationary pressures. In early 2001, the benign impact of globalization and competition had turned into a worrisome deflation marked by falling demand. Consumers postponed spending in anticipation of lower prices and added to the downward pressure.

The increasingly unfavorable business climate could not promote capital spending in the economy that (with the exception of growth in 1993–95, as shown in figure 4.3) spiraled downward.

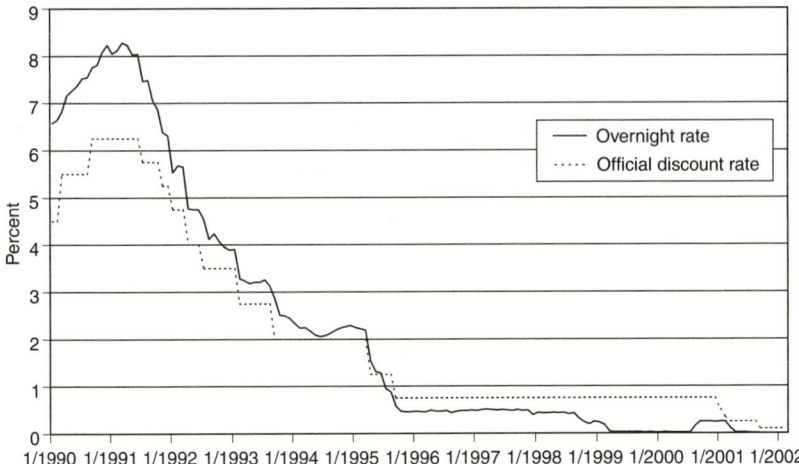

Figure 4.6. Short-term interest rate. Uncollateralized overnight call rate, monthly average data, and official discount rate. January 1990–February 2002. *Source:* Bank of Japan.

Volatile Growth Rates of Capital Spending

The price deflation escalated as bad debtors lowered prices to boost sales, adding to downward pressure on wages and household spending, thereby pulling marginally healthy companies into debt. The emergence of new debtors not only added to problem loans with banks but also aggravated deflation. Companies were under pressure to sell more in an increasingly competitive open economy in order to collect enough revenues to service their loans. Japanese banks, businesses, and consumers were locked in a vicious relationship, each contributing to the economy's downward spiral.

By early 2001, the consumer and investor outlook on the economy was so bleak that a flurry of monetary stimulus measures in quick succession failed to revive their confidence.

The Failed Monetary Stimulus

In February 2001, the Bank of Japan lowered its *discount* rate, the first time in six years (figure 4.6), from 0.5 percent to 0.35 percent, enabling banks to borrow from the central bank for their day-to-day funding needs. On the eve of his U.S. visit, Finance Minister Kiichi Miyazawa announced that the government's finances were close to "catastrophic," and that only more fundamental reform could help relieve the situation.

The finance minister evidently was passing the baton to the central banker, suggesting a switch from fiscal to monetary stimulus combined with banking sector reform. In a startling about-face, the governor of the Bank of Japan announced his decision to pump cash into the economy by buying government bonds from the market, and raising the reserves commercial banks held as deposits with the central bank. In effect, the central bank had abandoned its traditional policy of setting the *overnight interest rate* and moved to a radical policy stance of quantitative easing of money supply in order to push consumers and businesses to spend more and lift prices. The injections were to continue until the consumer price index gained stability or increased year-on-year. It would seem that the Bank of Japan was finally ready to adopt an expansionary monetary stance in line with a positive inflation target and an exchange rate ceiling[1] combined with commercial bank restructuring.

The measures had a slim chance of lifting consumption and investment spending. Investors were more likely to switch from yen to dollars in search of higher interest rates and weaken the yen, which was already under pressure from the deepening recession. In the words of Kenneth Courtis, vice chairman for Asia at Goldman Sachs: "No one buys a house or builds a factory with overnight money. The banks, the hedge funds, you name it are going to go to U.S. currency" (*New York Times*, March 20, 2001, p. C2).

Could a lower yen revive the economy by promoting Japanese exports?

The Lower Yen: A Controversial Option

A weaker yen could push Japanese exports in Asian markets and of autos and steel into the U.S. But the U.S. battled its own slowdown that began in mid-2000. At the Washington meeting in the spring of 2001 between the new American president and the visiting former Japanese prime minister, President George W. Bush reminded his visitor of the need to lift domestic growth via structural reforms. However, six months later, following the events of 9/11, a softening yen supported by monetary policy easing was motivated by domestic concerns. In less than a week, the key stock market index, the Nikkei 225, tumbled below the 10,000 level for the first time since the mid-eighties. This undermined the capital base of Japanese banks, which were required to mark their assets close to market values, and threatening progress on banking sector reform. Risk-averse Japanese investors were reluctant to invest abroad and even ready to bring home their overseas assets, estimated at 13 percent of Japanese GDP, as they habitually did during every major crisis. The Bank of Japan countered the resulting upward pressure on the yen-dollar exchange rate of

Y117 to a dollar by vigorously buying dollars on successive trading days and letting the yen holdings accumulate with commercial banks as reserves rather than "sterilize" them. By early 2002, the yen traded at Y135 to a dollar damaging the prospects of U.S. manufacturers seeking overseas markets for their products in the midst of an economic slowdown.

The opposition to such a deliberate lowering of the Japanese currency was categorical from the visiting U.S. treasury secretary Paul O'Neill and pronounced from Asian neighbors. The export-led recovery via a weakening yen thus faced limitations. Indeed, the prospects for such a recovery receded as the yen traded against the declining dollar at Y115 in early August.

Japan lost the decade of the nineties as a result of policy initiatives that failed to deliver and kick-start a recovery because of delayed structural cleanup in industry and in the banking sector.

Delayed Structural Reforms

Japanese companies made impressive gains in world markets in cars, cameras, computers, and video games but many sectors, such as chemicals, aircraft manufacturing, and financial services, remained noncompetitive and protected via a combination of regulated entry, government subsidization, and *keiretsu* collaboration. An urgent reform involving a simplified tax system and lower tax rates to stimulate the economy was not on the agenda. Starting in 1999, U.S. private-equity and venture-capital firms began investing in Japanese companies. But a variety of sectors, among them prescription drugs, medical equipment, and telecommunications, continued to be regulated barring competitive entry by foreigners. Reform of the banking sector, paralyzed by the burden of nonperforming loans, also called for an overhaul.

Why was bank restructuring delayed? Why did Japanese policy makers reject the idea of an American-type Resolution Trust Corporation which liquidated the bankrupt savings and loan institutions in the eighties and disposed of their assets?

Slow Bank Restructuring: The Unfinished Revolution

Banks had extended loans to companies during the Japanese boom which had peaked in 1989; when the bubble burst as in the East Asian crisis-swept economies, borrowers were unable to repay the loans. A rapid-fire write off of these nonperforming bank loans would force a closure of the affected banks and trigger a decline in the prices of assets in their balance

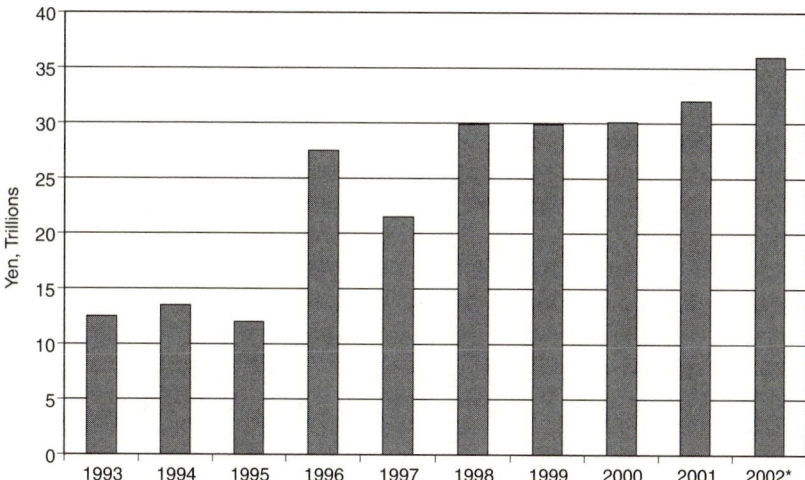

Figure 4.7. Nonperforming bank loans. In trillions of yen. Annual, by fiscal year. *Note:* Value for 2002 is for the first half of the fiscal period. *Source: Wall Street Journal.*

sheets, such as land and shares, which must be disposed of. It would also bankrupt businesses that were tied to the banks via *keiretsu* links, create substantial unemployment, and GDP loss. Rather than risk these consequences, Japanese policy makers sought to bail out selected banks with an on-again, off-again infusion of funds at their disposal, in effect, postponing the overhaul of the banking sector as a whole. More to the point, the bureaucrats in the Financial Services Agency in charge of providing a correct picture of bad loans and of persuading banks to write them off, failed in carrying out their mandate. In 1998, the government took over and sold the Long-Term Credit Bank and Nippon Credit Bank, two failed banks, and injected $224 billion into the banking system in the three years ending in 2000. The authorities also toughened bank regulation, compelled banks to price their assets at market values rather than at their acquisition costs from April 1, 2001, and allowed foreigners to buy Japanese banks. In an isolated bank restructuring milestone, a group of foreign investors bought the Long-Term Credit Bank "one of Japan's biggest lenders—a financial institution whose loan portfolio reads like a Who's Who of corporate Japan" (*Wall Street Journal*, March 23, 2000, A1).

The problem of nonperforming loans persisted rising from 12.5 trillion yen in 1993 to 32 trillion in 2001 (figure 4.7). In the week of March 12, 2001, turbulence hit Japan from outside. The stock market, already buffeted by declining earnings and continuing deflation, was jolted by a fallout from a dive in Nasdaq. The Nikkei Stock Average sank to its lowest level in 16 years. Japan's commercial banks, which held these shares as assets, faced another pell-mell cleanup. The government announced a plan, its twelfth emergency package of the past decade, requiring three banks to transfer their shares to a fund financed by bank loans, that would be guaranteed by the government to cover the losses arising from the gradual sale of this isolated pool of shares. Individual investors were offered tax incentives aimed at promoting stock purchases.

After more than a decade of marking time, Japan's worn-out policy makers had traveled full circle to square one by postponing a clearance of bad debts by banks. The economic conundrum pointed to the policy makers' inability to revive demand despite injections of cash into the economy by the Bank of Japan and frequent budgetary pump priming by the Ministry of Finance. These dogs had failed to bark. Neither the investors nor the consumers were reacting to the monetary and fiscal stimuli as I noted earlier. The failed, demand-push policies signaled the urgent need for structural reforms including the cleanup of the banking sector, lower taxes, deregulation, and privatization leading eventually to higher efficiency and supply-side response after an initial slowdown resulting from bank and business closures.

When Junichiro Koizumi became prime minister in April 2001, the Japanese economy was in the midst of a severe recession marked by a bear market in land, stock prices near 15-year lows, unemployment at a postwar peak of 4.9 percent, unused industrial capacity, a cutback in earnings projections by companies, low corporate orders for machines and equipment, a saving rate stubbornly high at 30 percent of income, and a slump in consumer demand. The election of the young and charismatic leader raised hopes that he would revive Japan's moribund economy by forging a consensus within the party and among the dissenting band of policy makers in the Bank of Japan and the government.

The Koizumi Magic: Will It Deliver?

The prime minister and his team faced conflicting economic signals, solid political resistance within the LDP, and bureaucratic pressures from a variety of vested interests. Putting up with pain today in exchange for gain tomorrow was the premise underlying Koizumi's early reform pronouncements. A proposed measure would allow the Resolution and Collection Corporation to buy and package bad bank loans of solvent banks with the use of public funds and at their book value, rather than the much lower market value, thus providing them a subsidy. The measure's implementation would require financial support from the government and speed up the process similar to what occurred in the U.S. savings and loan debacle, on a significantly smaller scale, but at a rapid-fire rate via the aggressive mandate of the Resolution Trust Corporation. The proposal raised hopes that the banking sector cleanup would proceed systematically and energetically in contrast to the earlier sporadic attempts.

However, the old questions kept resurfacing with renewed vigor as 2002 progressed. Were budget cuts aimed at clipping the clout of LDP brass advisable in the midst of a recession? Could the banking sector cleanup proceed despite mounting foreclosures of companies and rising unemployment? Would the Bank of Japan continue pumping cash into the economy as a stimulus to revive demand and lift prices? How far would the U.S. administration allow the yen to weaken, contributing to a surge of Japanese exports preferably in the U.S. markets as the U.S. economy itself recovered at a lower than expected rate? Would Koizumi's determination and popularity enable him to implement the triple policy mandate of systematic fiscal restructuring, continued monetary easing, and measured banking sector cleanup? Or would it face staunch resistance if not ultimate demise by ministry bureaucrats and LDP old guard in the legislature as they navigated it in a succession of committees and subcommittees?

An ideal textbook solution consisted of pegging the yen somewhat lower than Y130 to a dollar until an inflation target supported by the Bank of Japan with a matching pumping of yen was met. Exports would revive; consumer outlays too would pick up with the public choosing to spend now rather than later at higher prices. The fly in the ointment arose from the inability of Japanese decision makers, facing opposition from Washington, to push the value of the yen down to a level that would make Japanese exports competitive in declining world markets. The ultimate recipe was destined to consist of a little bit of fiscal restructuring, monetary easing, and banking sector cleanup.

Even this modest agenda came under threat as the Japanese policy makers struggled to formulate an appropriate response to the events of 9/11 and Koizumi's popularity dived in February 2002 when he fired the country's enormously popular foreign minister, Makiko Tanaka. After 9/11, the Japanese leadership came under greater pressure to implement measures for staving off the economic recession at home and worldwide, and also to contribute to the anti-terrorist alliance. It was hamstrung in these efforts by the worsening economic malaise and by the postwar constitutional ban on active military participation, limiting Japanese contribution to battling terrorism to intelligence and logistical assistance. Japan, the world's second largest economy, was thus economically, diplomatically, and militarily marginalized from being an effective alliance partner.

Of equal concern and consequence were the costs imposed on the small East Asian economies by Japan's prolonged economic decline and the

Source: "Unequal bedfellows in East Asia," Cartoonists and Writers Syndicate.

policy failures to overcome it. When it prospered, Japan, a formidable presence in East Asia, acted as a significant trading partner, a substantial long-term investor, and a major lender. These three channels of interaction worked to the mutual advantage of Japan and its neighbors as they grew and expanded their ties. The Japanese role from 1990 to 1997, when the East Asian crisis exploded and spread in the region, was affected however by Japan's protracted slump in the nineties marked by policy paralysis. Japanese policy makers extended financial help to the region after the crisis and sought to enhance Japanese trade and investment with a view to eventually pulling East Asia in a yen-dominated sphere, but they failed in pulling their economy out of its worsening on-off recession and transforming it into an engine of growth for the region via trade and investment interaction which I describe immediately below.

Japanese-East Asian Trade-Investment Links

The relative share of individual East Asian economies (excluding China) in Japanese trade in recent years continued to be small. For example, Japanese imports from Indonesia and Korea in the eighties and nineties were 3 to 4 percent of Japan's imports in the aggregate; Japan's exports to these countries accounted for even less in its total exports. However,

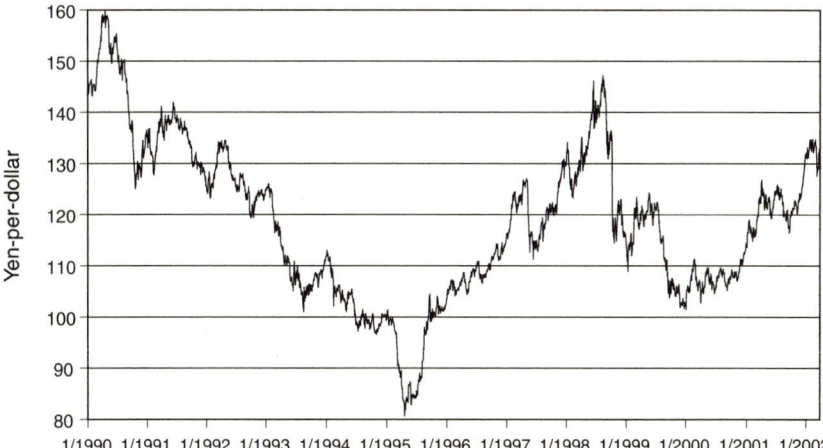

Figure 4.8. Yen exchange rate. Number of yen per one U.S. dollar, daily closing value. January 1990–March 2002. *Source:* Bloomberg.

trade with Japan constituted a significant fraction, ranging from 15 to 25 percent of each country's exports and imports. When all economies grew in the eighties, the trade interaction provided a growth impetus to Japan's East Asian partners.

The volume and pattern of trade were also affected by Japanese companies' investment activity in East Asia. They exported unfinished goods to be processed in jointly owned East Asian factories as finished products that were shipped to Japan. The movements in the yen/dollar exchange rate however complicated the interaction. The East Asian currencies pegged fully or largely against the dollar moved up or down as the dollar gained in strength or weakened against the yen. During 1985–95, when the yen appreciated against the dollar (figure 4.8), Japanese business, attracted by even greater relative wage advantage, invested long term in East Asia by locating industrial plants in the region. Japanese foreign direct investment in the Asian manufacturing sector rose from $441 million in 1985 to $7.8 billion in 1995 (Sazanami and Kawai, 1999).

During this same time (of appreciating yen against the dollar), as Japan grew in the first five years , the growing East Asian tigers posted substantial growth rates in their trade with Japan that subsequently declined in the second five years. It was at this point, the first half of the nineties, that Japanese growth faltered while East Asia barreled along. The massive 1998 Japanese recession depressed Japanese imports from East Asia, especially of transport and electrical machinery items that were part of the coordinated production networks in the region (Sazanami and Yoshimura, 1999, p. 8). The trade picked up in 2000 with signs of temporary revival in Japan and post-crisis growth restoration in East Asia; it again suffered an export-led downturn in late 2001 as the Japanese recession synchronized with that in the U.S.

Japan's foreign direct investment (FDI) flows worldwide, especially in East Asia, were affected by its prolonged slump. While world FDI flows remained generally stable in crisis-ridden East Asia in 1997 and 1998 (actually increasing in Thailand and Korea, declining only marginally in Malaysia and Philippines, and falling significantly in Indonesia in 1998), Japanese FDI, by contrast, fell in a year by 21.2 percent worldwide in 1998 and slumped by a substantial 44.3 percent in East Asia. Partly a reflection of the financial turmoil in the recipient countries, it resulted largely from the deep depression in electrical and transport machinery, and chemical industries that funneled investment flows in Japan as well as in East Asia (Sazanami and Yoshimura, 1999, p. 8).

Japanese Bank Lending in East Asia

Short-term bank lending by Japanese banks in the region followed a similar pattern, having collapsed from a peak of $123.8 billion at the end of June 1997 to a low of $74.8 billion by the end of June 1999. It fell by 50 percent in Thailand, 43 percent in Malaysia, 40 percent in Indonesia, and 37 percent in Korea. The interest rate differential in Japan and East Asia, that far exceeded comparable differential between U.S. and the region, had fueled East Asian short-term borrowing despite the pre-1996 appreciated yen to the dollar exchange rate. By the end of 1996, 61.5 percent of Asian bank borrowings had a maturity of one year or less (ibid., p. 4). However, Japanese banks, plagued by their nonperforming lending crisis, retreated from overseas lending activity in 1998 aggravating the payments crisis in the small Asian neighbors.

Japan contributed to the East-Asian bailout led by the International Monetary Fund (IMF) but failed to emerge as an assertive regional leader.

Japan, a Manager Rather than a Policy Leader

Japan committed $80 billion to the IMF bailout that was mounted in late 1997 to rescue the crisis-affected East Asian economies. It was followed in mid-July 1999 by a plan, announced by Finance Minister Miyazawa that was calculated to divert the cash of Japan's institutional investors into high-yielding, yen-denominated, government-guaranteed bonds floated by East Asian borrowers. The plan would further cement Japan's long-term trade-investment interests in the region, and promote the use of yen as a regional currency. Japan, however, could not snatch the policy initiatives for East Asia from the IMF. The Japanese-led idea in 1998 to float an Asian IMF, designed to garner the financial resources of the member countries of the region and give them a separate policy initiative forum suited to their needs and problems, was squashed by Washington. Instead, the multi-pronged approach, focusing on Japan's economic interests in the region, sought to compensate East Asian borrowers for Japanese policy makers' slowness in shoring up and restructuring its own economy in time. Even in the best of times, Japanese leadership failed to look beyond its economic interests and assume an active political and diplomatic role on the East Asian stage. Japan's economic role as a growth engine in the region was also impaired by a decade marked by three recessions (in 1991–93, 1997–98, and 2001; see figure 4.1), converting it from a regional partner to a victimizer. More significantly, it exemplified the failure of policy makers to devise and implement appropriate policies for overcoming a homegrown economic crisis by removing the economy's structural and institutional shortcomings. This lesson was to visit upon the East Asian economies via an externally-induced crisis when they were prematurely opened up to volatile capital inflows despite their lack of structural and institutional readiness to channel them in productive activities. The protracted consequences of the bursting of the Japanese boom of the eighties could have been avoided if Japan resembled and functioned like the U.S. A similar assumption with respect to the small economies of East Asia in their presumed ability to absorb massive short-term capital inflows to their advantage was not only farfetched, but disastrous, as I argue in the next chapter.

Notes

1. According to Martin Wolf (*Financial Times*, September 22, 1999, p. 112), "It would be possible by the Bank of Japan to conduct open market operations, by buying government bonds, as a counterpart to purchases of dollars by the Ministry of Finance. This would be unsterilized intervention—intervention whose effects are allowed to flow through to the domestic money supply. The Bank of Japan regards the distinction between sterilized and unsterilized intervention as academic. So this could be viewed, instead, as a policy of expanding reserve money dramatically whenever the yen appreciated above some ceiling (say, 110 to the dollar)."

5

The Asian Financial Crisis

THE ASIAN FINANCIAL crisis that originated in Thailand in the summer of 1997 caught everyone off guard by its unpredictability and scale as it spread in the neighborhood to Indonesia, Malaysia, and South Korea. It came as a shock because the affected economies had chalked up impressive private sector–led economic performance marked by high growth and low inflation rates, public sector balanced budgets, and economy-wide savings. Despite their evident strengths leading up to 1996, however, these economies displayed disturbing features, which I analyze in this chapter. I argue that the sudden and destabilizing reversals of short-term capital inflows, affecting their private banks that were weakly regulated and businesses that were tempted into risky investments, brought about the financial and currency turmoil that subsequently hit the Russian ruble in August 1998 and the Brazilian *real* in January 1999.

The attribution of crisis origin to short-term capital flows raises several conceptual and methodological issues. The crisis-swept Asian countries (figure 5.1) were inadequately prepared in terms of their institutional underpinning and structural features to absorb short-term capital inflows to their advantage. (I discuss these features in block 1.) As emerging market economies integrating into the world financial system with varying speed, they continue sharing this disadvantage of inadequate preparedness with others in the periphery which borrow from the developed market economies at the center of the global capital markets.[1] The uneven playing field between the lending center and the borrowing periphery raises important policy issues of the manner and the speed with which the emerging market peripheral economies can be integrated in the international financial system. I postpone to the final two chapters the analysis of the contentious issues of the pressured environment in which they liberalized their financial systems to volatile capital inflows, the unsatisfactory role of the International Monetary Fund (IMF) in mitigating the adverse impact of these flows, and the design of global financial arrangements which might ease the entry of the peripheral economies in the global capital markets.

In this chapter, I only demonstrate the vulnerability of the Asian economies to the potential reversals of short-term capital inflows. These are measured as fractions of total inflows and of available foreign exchange reserves (among several other criteria presented in table 5.1 for subse-

Source: The *Straits Times*, Singapore Cartoonists and Writers Syndicate

quent analysis). Next, in order to establish a cross-section, cause-and-effect link between volatile capital flows and financial crises, I compare the five crisis-prone Asian economies marked by large relative inflows with four other Asian economies (such as Hong Kong) with small or managed short-term flows that escaped the crisis impact.[2] However, I avoid a cross-section regression analysis by the two subsets of economies with and without substantial capital inflows (the sample in any case is small) in the hope that the loss of forced technical rigor is more than made up by the in-depth treatment of the sampled countries in this and the next chapter. Both groups in East Asia were similar in having robust macroeconomic performance in the immediate precrisis years.

Country Classification

I classify the East Asian economies into crisis-prone, crisis-immune, and crisis-safe for the cross-section analysis. (I use the phrase "crisis prone" ex ante, switching later to the ex post "crisis-swept" or "crisis-ridden" term for the same economy.) Indonesia, Malaysia, South Korea, and Thailand in the first category were overwhelmed by the seismic shifts in their financial health and currency values that hit their economies in 1997 and 1998. Philippines, which showed a steady improvement in its economic performance during the years leading up to the crisis in 1997, suffered less severely in terms of the collapse of its finances and currency. (I there-

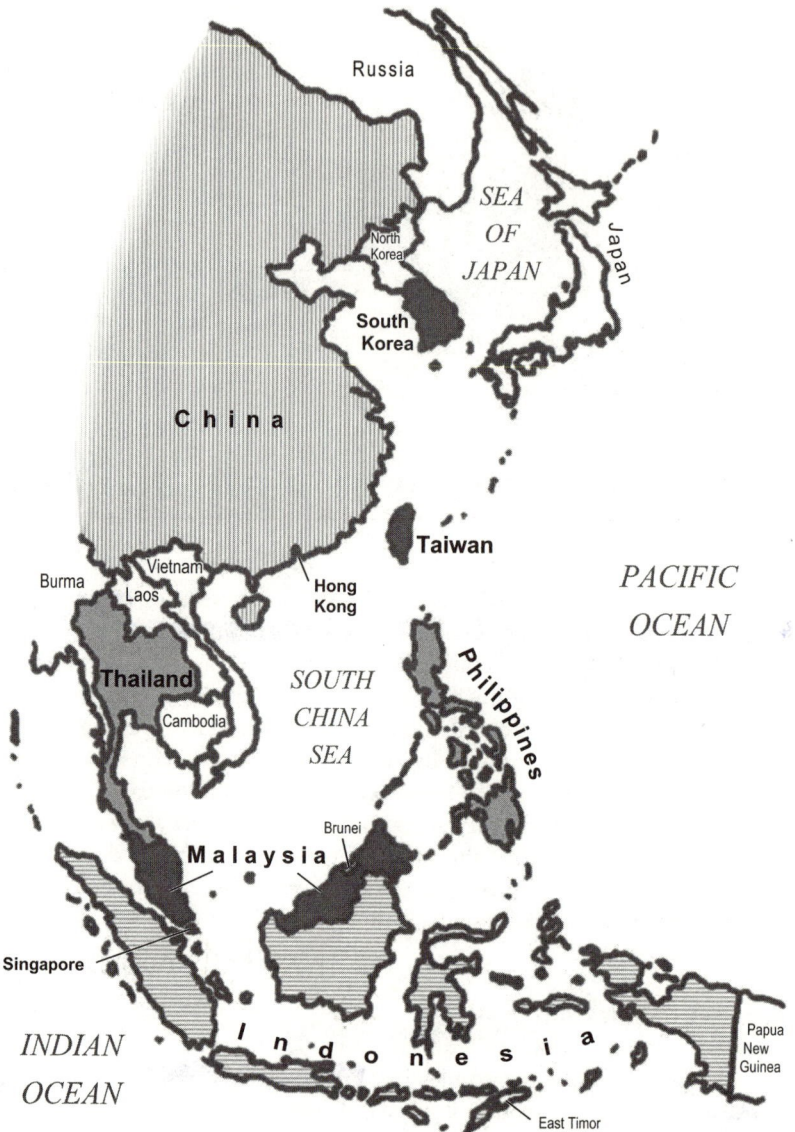

Figure 5.1. Map of East Asian economies. *Source:* Emil Czechowski.

fore do not narrate its crisis chronology at length in chapter 6.) However, the improvement in the Philippine economy thereafter was not sustained enough to prevent it from sliding into turmoil later. I therefore include it in the crisis-prone category here. By contrast the second group, consisting of China, Hong Kong, and Taiwan, managed to avoid the financial turmoil because of the immunity provided largely by their managed and limited exposure to short-term capital inflows. Finally, the minuscule exposure to such inflows allowed Singapore, the lone crisis-safe economy, to almost bypass the contagion.

These Asian economies exhibited solid economic performance in the nineties up to 1996 in terms of their growth and inflation rates, fiscal health, and current account balances. (These "fundamentals" are discussed in block 1.)

Robust Fundamentals

In table 5.1, the four crisis-prone economies (excluding Philippines) exhibit annual average growth rates ranging from 7 to 9 percent during 1991–96, low single-digit inflation rates, and high saving rates of 30 to 35 percent of gross domestic product (GDP) feeding into investment activity that was even higher at 32 to 41 percent. Each of these four economies had budget surpluses except South Korea with a minuscule negative number. Thailand, where the financial crisis exploded in mid-1997, had a budget surplus of 2.6 percent of GDP.

It is clear that with domestic investment exceeding domestic saving, the engine of growth was supported by foreign capital inflows that in turn were reflected in negative current account balances. (This relationship is explained in block 2). Indonesia and South Korea had manageable current account deficits of less than 5 percent of GDP, but Malaysia and Thailand were overboard, posting current account deficits of 8 and 7 percent, respectively, in 1996. Foreign short-term borrowing facilitated extravagant private sector overspending in dubious ventures and real estate expansion exposing all these economies to sharp declines in their currencies as speculators withdrew funds following bank and business failures (analyzed in chapter 6).

Philippines, the fifth economy in the group, recorded a modest 3 percent annual growth rate, a high 10 percent inflation rate, and a 4 percent current account deficit with improving performance in these indicators during 1991–96. The economy's performance during the period improved at various levels signaling a moderate impact of the crisis: its growth rate steadily increased from year to year (having gone up from –0.6 percent in 1991 to 10 percent in 1997); its annual inflation declined from 19

Table 5.1
Macroeconomic indicators for East Asian economies: 1991–96

	Growth rate (%)	Inflation rate (%)	Saving rate	Investment rate	Fiscal balance	Current account balance
			. . . . (% of GDP)			
I. Crisis-prone economies						
Indonesia	8.67	7.82	29.64	32.44	0.90	−2.80
Malaysia	8.65	4.20	31.21	38.99	0.22	−7.78
Korea	7.40	5.99	34.81	37.01	−0.07	−2.20
Philippines	2.80	10.13	18.34	22.64	−0.47	−4.30
Thailand	7.99	4.98	33.86	41.06	2.60	−7.20
II. Crisis-immune economies						
China	11.38	12.30	39.65	39.04	−0.71	0.61
Hong Kong	5.27	8.74	33.15	30.40	n.a.	2.76
Taiwan	6.48	3.64	27.91	23.68	−2.59	4.20
III. Crisis-safe economies						
Singapore	13.35	2.36	49.05	34.79	12.62	14.25

Source: The estimates, annual averages for 1991–96, are calculated from the IMF and from the sources mentioned in footnote 1 of chapter 6.

percent in 1991 to 5 percent in 1997; and its budget deficit of 3 percent in 1990 was transformed into a marginal surplus of 0.1 percent in 1997. More to the point (to be discussed subsequently), its current account deficit, hitting 5 percent in 1997, was supported by relatively low levels of short-term capital inflows at 15 percent of total foreign debt: its average short-term exposure during 1991–96 was the lowest among all the economies considered here except Singapore. Despite this steady improvement, however, the Philippine economy remained crisis-prone and could not avoid serious financial and currency problems in 1999.

Among the crisis-immune economies, China and Hong Kong present a number of contrasts: China had capital account controls that still persist and trade restrictions that are on the wane. Hong Kong, tied to the dollar via a currency board arrangement, has been an open economy of exemplary discipline. China, barreling along at an annual 11 percent growth rate, registered double-digit annual inflation and a 39 percent domestic investment rate almost entirely financed from domestic saving. Hong Kong, by contrast, grew at half the rate with a lower inflation and an excess of domestic saving over investment that materialized into a solid 3 percent (of GDP) current account surplus. Taiwan, a solid steady performer like Hong Kong, grew annually at 6 percent with a low inflation rate of 4 percent and a current account surplus of 4 percent despite a negative fiscal deficit of 3 percent. In other words, private net saving more than balanced the net deficit on public account. Therefore, China, Hong Kong, and Taiwan could minimize and even avert the impact of financial turbulence by drawing on their net savings to meet sudden claims of foreign creditors.

Singapore, combining the highest annual growth rate of 13 percent with the lowest inflation rate of 2 percent and posting a huge positive current account surplus of 14 percent, is a case apart not only in East Asia but around the globe. While it is included in the sample because of its location, its performance can hardly be replicated elsewhere underlining the futility of holding it as an example for others to follow.

What, however, was the secret of Singapore's success in bypassing the Asian financial crisis? Can it be uncovered in terms of its minimal exposure to short-term borrowing from abroad that did not spill over into bank lending to private business and into growth of money supply in the economy in turn damaging macroeconomic stability? By contrast, did the crisis-prone economies of the first group, displaying current account deficits of 2 to 8 percent, rely excessively on short-term borrowing from abroad to fill the gaps? Was their inordinate reliance on such funding also associated with large-scale bank lending to the private sector and growth in money supply in turn endangering the fundamentals? I address these questions immediately below.

Foreign Short-Term Borrowing: How Much Is Too Much?

In table 5.2, I present a number of indicators suggesting the exposure of the sampled economies to foreign borrowing during 1990–96. Among these are four descriptive measures, namely debt as a fraction of GDP, the share of short-term debt in total foreign indebtedness, short-term debt in relation to foreign exchange reserves, and the potential of these reserves to finance imports. Two estimates in the final columns of the table indicate the association of the foreign short-term borrowing to private sector bank lending and to money supply (M1) in the economy.

Turning first to the four descriptive measures. Singapore again was a strong, steady performer followed by China and Hong Kong: its debt as a fraction of GDP was a stable 10 percent during the period (China and Hong Kong each averaged 16 percent.). The share of short-term debt in Singapore's indebtedness was 17 percent (against China's 18 percent, and Hong Kong's 28 percent in 1996 from a high of 46 percent in 1990). Short-term debt as a fraction of foreign exchange reserves was a minuscule average of 2 percent in Singapore (China and Hong Kong, by contrast, registered high ratios of 24 and 22 percent, respectively, in 1996). Finally, China's foreign exchange reserves could on average buy six months of needed imports in contrast to three months' worth in Hong Kong.

Trailing far behind the impeccable norms of Singapore, the five crisis-prone economies in the sample lagged behind China and Hong Kong, the next best performers. Their record was poor in terms of all the four criteria. In 1996, the Thai and Philippine foreign debts were 50 percent of their GDP. Only Indonesia was worse with a ratio of 57 percent. Thailand's short-term debt, at 57 percent of total, was 107 percent of its foreign exchange reserves. Indonesian and South Korean short-term debts had deteriorated, respectively, to 177 and 203 percent of their reserves in 1996. Malaysia and Philippines, the least vulnerable among the five in terms of their short-term debt exposure, had nevertheless piled up short-term debt amounting to 41 and 79 percent of their foreign exchange reserves, respectively, in 1996.

In contrast to the five crisis-prone economies, Taiwan, with a low overall indebtedness of 10 percent of GDP, remained immune to the crisis. Its substantial short-term debt, 68 percent of the total in 1996, stood at a steady 22 percent of its foreign exchange reserves. Taiwan's foreign exchange reserves, evidently accumulated over the years, were so substantial that they could finance nine months of imports in 1996, which was higher than the 6 months' worth in China.

In sum, the crisis-prone economies had relied increasingly over time on short-term borrowing to fill their current account deficits. To what extent

Table 5.2
Foreign debt, foreign exchange reserves, money supply (M1) and bank lending to private sector in East Asian economies: 1990–96

Countries	Total foreign debt (% of GDP)	Foreign short-term debt (% of total debt)	Foreign short-term debt (% of foreign exchange reserves)	Average foreign exchange reserves in months of imports	Foreign short-term debt / bank lending to private sector (%)	Foreign short-term debt / M1 (%)
I. Crisis prone economies						
Indonesia	66—57 (falling)	16–25 (rising)	149–177 (rising)	3.40	21–26 (rising)	86–146 (rising)
Malaysia	36–40 (rising)	12–28 (rising)	10–41 (rising)	4.06	6–12 (rising)	10–35 (rising)
Korea	14–28 (rising)	31–50 (rising)	72–203 (rising)	2.34	8–23 (rising)	48–141 (rising)
Philippines	69–50 (falling)	15–19 (fluctuating)	152–79 (falling)	2.43	52–20 (falling)	116–89 (falling)
Thailand	33–50 (rising)	30–57* (rising)	63–107* (rising)	5.29	15–23* (rising)	110–246* (rising)
II. Crisis-immune economies						
China	16 (no trend)	18 (no trend)	67–24 (falling) (1992–96)	6.34	3 (no trend)	7 (no trend)
Hong Kong	16 (no trend)	46–28 (falling) (1990–95)	24–14 (falling) (1990-95)	3.20	4 (no trend)	48–64 (fluctuating)
Taiwan	10 (no trend)	88–68 (falling)	22 (no trend)	13–9 (falling)	10–5 (falling)	22–15 (falling)
III. Crisis-safe economies						
Singapore	10 (no trend)	17 (no trend)	2 (no trend)	n.a.	2 (no trend)	8 (no trend)

Source: The estimates are put together from IMF and from the sources mentioned in footnote 1 of chapter 6.
Notes: * The rising trends here show a sharp decline in the original figures for 1996. Therefore, the reported higher figure in the range is the average of 1995 and 1996.

did this imprudent reliance on short-term inflows in relation to their foreign exchange reserves spill into their bank lending to the private sector and to monetary expansion?

Short-Term Borrowing, Bank Lending to Private Sector, and Monetary Expansion

The ratios of short-term foreign debt relative to private sector loans by banks and alternatively, short-term foreign debt relative to money supply demonstrate the credit and monetary expansion associated with short-term borrowing.

Two caveats are in order before I interpret these ratios. First, cash inflows from abroad that found their way in the coffers of central and commercial banks added to money supply and bank lending. However, financial companies, that did not operate as banks in the sampled economies, also borrowed from outside and loaned to private sectors. While the numerators in the ratios include all short-term borrowing, the denominators refer to bank lending only. Second, long-term capital inflows that also added to the liquidity of the banking sector, raising its potential for credit and money creation, are excluded from the estimates. From both perspectives, the ratios reflect only part of such expansionary transactions. They are however a critical slice because a reverse flow of short-term funds compelled commercial banks to recall loans and the central bank to cut back monetary expansion setting in motion collapsing banks and businesses. The ratios are therefore relevant in signaling the likelihood and onset of financial crises.

In the five crisis-prone economies, short-term borrowing amounted to almost a quarter of bank loans to the private sector in 1996, except in Malaysia where it was 12 percent. The comparable ratios were a firm 2 percent in Singapore, 3 percent in China, and 4 percent in Hong Kong. It had fallen to 5 percent in Taiwan. More damaging to the financial stability of the crisis-prone economies were the excessively high ratios of foreign short-term debt to money supply. Except in Malaysia, where it was 35 percent in 1996, the ratio was 89 percent in Philippines, 141 percent in South Korea, 146 percent in Indonesia, and 246 percent in Thailand. In a staggering contrast, it was a steady 7 percent in China and 8 percent in Singapore. By 1996, it had declined to 15 percent in Taiwan. Hong Kong's ratio, fluctuating between 48 and 64 percent, reflected the currency board arrangement requiring an expansion of money supply in response to net accruals of foreign exchange.

Three major observations emerge from this analysis of the economic and financial record of these East Asian economies in the years before the onset of the financial turbulence that swept the region. First, all of them showed impressive fundamentals in terms of high growth and low inflation rates and formidable domestic saving and investment rates, but the severely crisis-prone economies of Indonesia, Malaysia, South Korea, and Thailand had built their prosperity by foreign borrowing. In the worst case scenarios this was reflected in Thailand's current account deficit of 7 percent and Malaysia's current account deficit of 8 percent. Second, low current account deficits of 2 to 3 percent of GDP for Indonesia and South Korea did not spare these economies from financial upheaval: these deficits were covered by short-term debts reaching 177 and 203 percent of foreign exchange reserves, respectively, in Indonesia and South Korea, covering up to a quarter of bank loans to their private sectors, and hitting 146 and 141 percent of their respective money supplies.[3] By contrast, Philippines had managed to tame the potential onset of crisis by a steady improvement in short-term debt exposure for financing its current account deficit. Finally, crisis- immune China, Hong Kong, and Taiwan, with positive current accounts, were firmly anchored in low debt exposure and limited commercial bank lending and monetary expansion in relation to short-term cash inflows.

Why were some of these Asian economies inundated with short-term capital inflows rendering them vulnerable to financial turmoil?

Why the Deluge of Short-Term Capital Inflows?

These inflows in East Asia resulted from liberalization of domestic credit and financial markets by their policy makers followed by swift removal of capital account controls. (I give details of these liberalization measures in block 3.) At the same time, their banks and financial institutions were poorly supervised and their capital/asset ratios were inadequate. Lenders and borrowers were linked via special ties and traditional norms of financial practices. Risk management of portfolios was rudimentary. Banks and financial institutions borrowed short term and lent long term to domestic borrowers who invested the funds in real estate and businesses of questionable worth.

Neither over-investment nor the presumed diminishing returns to too much capital can however explain the *sudden* financial collapse that shook the East Asian economies. The premature opening of their economies to foreign capital, that was massively short term (as I noted previously) and speculative, accounts for the swiftness, depth, and spread of the crisis in the region. (I discuss these opposing views of the crisis resulting from over-investment and alternatively, to the unsustainable inflows of speculative capital following premature liberalization of capital account controls in block 4.) Investors, among them hedge funds and speculators, rushed in hoping to earn hefty financial rewards by bearing risks in short-term exposure in emerging markets rather than undertaking buy-and-hold, long-term investments. In the words of Martin Wolf: "If the U.S. banking system, for example, had short-term D-Mark liabilities of $1,500bn (DM920bn), the Federal Reserve would be very anxious indeed. Yet, proportionately, that was the size of the short-term foreign currency liabilities of a Thailand or a Korea" (*Financial Times*, March 1999, p. 13).

The hasty opening up to short-term capital inflows conformed to the prevailing view of globalized capital markets repeatedly articulated from across the Atlantic by the U.S. Treasury, the IMF, and Wall Street financiers. Robert Wade (1998b, p. 1546) provides details of the decision-making environment in which emerging market policy makers operated.[4] James Tobin's description was graphic and his judgment unequivocal: "South Koreans and other Asian countries—like Mexico in 1994–95— are . . .victims of a flawed international exchange rate system that, under U.S. leadership, *gives the mobility of capital priority over all other considerations*" (ibid.).

In practice, the doctrinaire official positions in total agreement with Wall Street's natural preference for unrestricted capital flow ruled out departures from the free mobility mantra. The downside of short-term flows, which, according to Kindelberger, create panics and crashes, was overlooked even as academic economists and influential policy makers raised critical questions. In the words of Paul Volker (Wade and Veneroso, 1998, p. 14): "The visual image of a vast sea of liquid capital strikes me as apt. The storms through which a great liner like the U.S.S. United States America can safely sail will surely swamp even the sturdiest South Pacific canoe."

Full capital mobility resulting in massive flows of hot money also prompted a debate on sequencing issues. For example, emerging market economies should first remove the regulatory handicaps in their banking and financial institutions before plunging headlong into free capital mobility in order to minimize the negative impact of speculative movements. They should free up trade before allowing unrestricted entry of short-term capital. They should encourage foreign direct investment that brings capital *and* technology to the exclusion of destabilizing short-term lending and borrowing transactions by nationals and non-nationals.[5] Foreign direct investment flows may be smaller as a result but such losses cannot be large as the massive foreign investment flows into China under a regime of restricted capital account convertibility demonstrate. In any case, the free capital mobility enthusiasts have not come up with measures of gains from free, across-the-border access to short-term capital (Rodrik, 1998).[6]

Lobby-laden images of the Wall Street-Treasury complex (Bhagwati, 2000a)[7] and the Wall Street-Treasury-IMF complex (Wade, 1998a) colored these debates on the advisability of the blanket, unconstrained opening up of emerging markets to foreign capital inflows.

Ultimately, haste not only made waste but it also brought into disrepute the allocatable efficiency of global markets in moving loanable funds aimed at raising collective gains. In the next chapter, I trace the sequence of events that brought about the financial and currency maelstrom in the four East Asian economies that chose to prematurely allow unsustainable, short-term capital inflows in their economies.

Notes

1. Fischer (2001) provides a list of twenty-two developed market economies, which include Hong Kong and Singapore, and thirty-three emerging market economies as of December 31, 1999. The first list of the developed market economies with almost complete integration in the global financial system includes the Organisation for Economic Co-operation & Development (OECD) members. The second list includes former developing countries, such as India, Argentina, and Brazil, as well as former centrally planned economies currently in transition to liberal market systems such, as Hungary, Poland, and Russia. Defined in terms of the speed of its integration in global capital markets, a developing country or a transition economy can thus qualify for inclusion in the emerging market category. It is not clear why Estonia, Latvia, and Lithuania are excluded by Fischer from the group of emerging market economies.

2. I employ a similar cross-section analysis in chapter 10 for contrasting the global financial contagion of 1997–98 triggered by excessive short-term capital flows by large common lenders in emerging market economies and the lack of such cross-border global flows as transmission mechanisms in the subsequent 2001–02 Turkish and Argentine crises.

3. According to Frankel (1999d, p. 6), "The composition of capital inflows is often a better warning indicator than the total inflow. By this I mean that the amount of debt that is short-term, dollar-denominated, and intermediated through the banking system—particularly relative to the level of foreign exchange reserves—is a useful indicator of future trouble."

4. The extended Wall Street-U.S. Treasury-City of London-U.K. Treasury complex "has over the past year led the process of amending the IMF's articles of agreement to *require* member governments to remove capital controls and adopt full capital account convertibility. The extended complex has likewise worked to promote the World Trade Organization's agreement on liberalizing financial services being hammered out in 1996–97. Many developing country governments, including prominently several Asian ones, opposed the WTO's efforts to liberalize financial services. In response, Executives of groups including Barclays, Germany's Dresdner Bank, Societe Generale of France and Chubb Insurance, Citicorp,

and Ford Financial Services of the U.S., agreed discreetly to impress on finance ministers around the world the benefits of a WTO deal."

Opposing my argument in favor of a slow pre-accession liberalization of financial services for Russia, leaders of the U.S. and European lobbies recently declared their preference for the rapid opening up of these services in Russia prior to its WTO entry by misleadingly comparing their speedy pre-entry liberalization in China. Details are in Padma Desai, "Help Russia to graduate," Personal Opinion, *Financial Times*, July 11, 2002, p. 13; Christopher Roberts and Robert Vastine, "Russia should liberalise before WTO accession," Letters to the Editor, *Financial Times*, July 17, 2002, p. 14; Padma Desai, "Russia compared unfairly with China," Letters to the Editor, *Financial Times*, July 22, 2002, p. 14.

5. According to Frankel (1998a, p. 2; 1999c, p. 4; and Frankel and Rose, 1996, p. 17), "Higher debt, lower reserve, and a more over-valued real exchange rate [its implications are analyzed in block 2] all seem to raise the odds of crash incidence." According to Rodrik and Velasco (1999, p. 16), crisis probabilities "increase with the overall debt burden (measured by the debt-GDP ratio), the current account deficit (as a percentage of GDP), and the appreciation of the real exchange rate (measured over the previous three years)." Again, ". . . potential illiquidity—in particular, the ratio of short-term foreign debt to reserves—is an important precursor of financial crises triggered by reversals in capital flows. Our evidence is consistent with the idea that illiquidity makes emerging market economies vulnerable to panic. At the same time, it bears repeating that such crises remain highly unpredictable."

6. Rodrik (1998) found no evidence that countries without capital controls grew faster, invested more, or experienced lower inflation. He used the proportion of years for which the capital account was free of restrictions (according to IMF classifications) as the indicator of capital account liberalization. The exercise covered a post-1975 sample of around 100 countries. According to Bhagwati cited in Wade (1998b, p. 1546), "Many countries have grown well without capital account convertibility, including China today and Japan and western Europe earlier. 'In my judgment, it is a lot of ideological humbug to say that without free portfolio capital mobility, somehow the world cannot function and growth rates will collapse.' "

7. "Just like in the old days there was this 'military-industrial complex', nowadays there is a 'Wall St.-Treasury complex' because Secretaries of Treasury like Rubin come from Wall Street . . . . So today, Wall Street views are very dominant in terms of the kind of world you want to see. *They want the ability to take capital in and out freely. It also ties in to the IMF's own desires, which is to act as a lender of last resort.* They see themselves as the apex body which will manage this whole system. So the IMF finally gets a role for itself, which is underpinned by maintaining complete freedom in the capital account" (Wade, 1998b, p. 18.)

Block 1

What Are Fundamentals?
What Are Structural Issues?

FUNDAMENTALS REFER to macroeconomic indicators, the choice depending on the analyst's concern. Gross domestic product (GDP) growth and unemployment rates, government budget deficit, and the economy's current account deficit, both in relation to GDP, top the list. The choice also includes a second tier of macroeconomic measures affecting the health of the economy's current account balance. Among these are the ratios of external debt to GDP, of the short-term debt to total debt, and of export earnings to total debt liability. These reflect the economy's potential to continue growing while meeting its external debt obligations. However, trade-related problems in the structural category, such as quantitative restrictions and high import duties and export taxes that distort trade patterns, were absent in the countries included in this book.

Structural problems, on the other hand, focus on mismanaged banks, businesses, and finance companies. Thus, banks may have massive nonperforming loans and inadequate capital/asset ratios because they are poorly regulated and supervised. Businesses may be dangerously leveraged, displaying high debt-to-equity ratios.

Most critically, banks and finance companies (and businesses directly) may borrow heavily from abroad, accumulating short-term, unhedged liabilities, and lending long term to finance risky and dubious investments. Close ties between banks and borrowers promote such mutual deals. As a result of these structural abnormalities, the ratios of corporate debt to equity averaged 395 percent in South Korea and 450 percent in Thailand as the borrowing boom accelerated compared to 144 percent in Germany, 154 percent in Sweden, and 106 percent in the U.S. Real estate loans in total ranged from 30 to 40 percent in Thailand, 20 to 30 percent in Indonesia, and 15 to 25 percent in South Korea by the end of 1997 (IMF, 1999, p. 10).

The borrowing boom paved the way for the onset of the currency crisis in the East Asian economies. The crisis in turn prompted a fresh search for models aimed at explaining its occurrence despite strong fundamentals in these economies. Conventional stories of

· Structural issues not necessarily reflected in fundamentals

currency crisis that include Krugman's illuminating distinction (1998) between "first generation" and "second generation" models focus, in his view, on weak fundamentals and therefore could not explain the Asian crisis.

Fundamentals and Models of Currency Crisis

In the simple "first generation" models (Krugman 1979; Flood and Garber 1984), a government that routinely runs budget deficits year after year and fills them via borrowing from the central bank and creating cash in the domestic economy, shakes the confidence of creditors, both insiders and outsiders, who have invested in deposits, bonds, and stocks denominated in the economy's currency. A speculative attack on the currency begins when these investors believe that the currency peg cannot be maintained with the foreign exchange reserves at the command of the central bank.

In the smarter, "second generation" models (Obstfeld 1994, 1995), the policy makers deliberately choose to run budget deficits for a time, knowing well that they risk their ability to maintain the exchange rate parity if the recourse to budgetary overspending ceases to be temporary. They may then defend the parity by raising the interest rate, once more rattling the confidence of investors who anticipate that interest rates may have to be pushed higher, damaging the fundamentals: the growth rate may deteriorate creating high unemployment. And investors walk out as the fundamentals begin to weaken in a self-fulfilling manner.

The Asian crisis, by contrast, "is best seen not as a problem brought on by fiscal deficits, as in 'first-generation' models, or as one brought on by macroeconomic temptation, as in 'second-generation' models, but, rather, as one brought on by financial excess and then financial collapse" (Krugman, 1998).

Causes and Consequences of Financial Excess

In these economies, "financial excess" resulting, in my view, from premature opening up of capital accounts consisted of short-term external borrowing in dollars or yen by financial intermediaries (among them banks in Thailand and South Korea and directly by corporations in Indonesia), which then lent them long term into assets that gave returns in local currencies. The two unwise transformations, namely borrowing short term and lending long term, and borrowing in dollars and yen, and investing in assets that gave returns in domestic currencies created an inherently vulnerable situation (Cooper, 1999).

Such regimes, stable in terms of fundamentals but vulnerable in terms of the financial activity of intermediaries, get destabilized as a result of an external shock. For example, the appreciation of the dollar against the yen in 1995 strengthened the East Asian currencies pegged against the dollar, in turn weakening their export competitiveness and enlarging their current account deficits beyond sustainable levels. The Thai current account deficit, reaching 8 percent of GDP toward the end of 1996, was perceived by foreign creditors as threatening the stability of the Thai baht (that was essentially pegged against the dollar). As they began getting rid of their Thai stockholdings posting net equity liquidations, Thai banks rolled over old loans and stopped making new loans, straining the finances of their business clients. The Thai central bank, faced with declining net inflows of foreign exchange, initially supported the currency by drawing down its reserves, but ultimately withdrew from the foreign exchange market. The pressure on the exchange rate accelerated as domestic residents began converting local currency into foreign exchange; the process developing into a full-blown currency crisis as foreigners joined the exodus.

Clearly, the distinction between fundamental and structural problems was energized as a result of the Asian economic crisis, "fundamentalists" and "structuralists" offering their postmortems and remedies on the basis of their preferred perspective. In particular, the IMF judgment and rescue packages were seriously called into question: Why did the IMF choose to apply the standard painful remedies, designed for correcting fundamental imbalances, to East Asian economies that displayed good, even robust, macroeconomic health in terms of high growth and low inflation rates, minimal government budget deficits, and manageable current account deficits? The IMF imposed strict austerity measures as part of the rapid-fire rescue in East Asia, linked them with the need for the necessary legislative backup in support of profit-oriented corporate governance in the affected region, and insisted on the enactment of bankruptcy laws in Russia. However, the structural cleanup of the crisis-ridden economies under its watch (which I describe subsequently) continued to be halting at best in South Korea, and lawless at worst in Russia. More critically, everywhere, including Japan (which I discussed in chapter 4), the sheer size of the overhaul in the recovery phase raised a specter of factory closures, worker layoffs, declining outputs, and political instability, and slowed its speed. Foreign direct investment flows could hasten the process by providing cash, technology, and management. However, these prospects were dampened in Russia, for example, not only by the risk-prone environment but also by an implicit collusion between Russia's big business and left-wing legislators. Having captured the "commanding heights" of the economy via ruthless internal mergers and acquisitions, the former desired that foreign investors step into Russian industry on its terms, whereas the latter insisted, on ideological grounds, that the presence of foreign investors in the Russian economy be minimized. Finally, the overhaul required that the emerging market economies in East Asia and elsewhere discard their traditional, long-term practices of the financially strong player bailing out the weak in a locked relationship, and adopt new rules of market economies. Everyone must sink or swim in the globalized world of profit orientation.

Structural Cleanup: Slow in South Korea and Lawless in Russia

Restructuring of the industrial and banking sectors required proper laws and their speedy implementation. In South Korea, policy makers successfully enacted new laws but let *chaebol* tycoons restructure their conglomerates in slow steps. In Russia, a lawless corporate jungle, industry bosses and bankers manipulated balance sheets, stripped assets, and violated shareholder rights.

South Korea: New Laws and Old Structures

The legislative coverage was comprehensive in South Korea. The Financial Supervisory Commission was empowered to enforce international accounting norms in banks and businesses. They had to absorb rather than defer losses or gains from exchange rate movements in their balance sheets; they were required to value shares at market prices and produce financial statements audited by independent accountants; family-owned *chaebols* were obliged to produce three sets of accounts—their individual accounts had to be consolidated to include the financial health of their subsidiaries, and further combined to cover their financial dealings with outside companies. Penalties for fraud were raised. Auditors faced jail terms of up to three years and fines of 30 million wons if they failed to detect accounting fraud. In mid-1999, South Korean business conglomerates were prohibited from acquiring more than 25 percent of their assets in affiliated companies. *Chaebol* executives were held personally responsible for losses they incurred from shaky investments. Lee Kun Hee, the chairman of Samsung Group, covered losses of the group's bankrupt auto maker, Samsung Motors, Inc., by handing over $2.3 billion of his personal wealth.

The new laws produced few restructuring successes simply because the task was enormous. South Korea's banking sector was overwhelmed by massive loans to 70 *chaebols* whose bankruptcies would have forced the banks to write off more loans. Banks could not replenish their capital from the government bailout fund because it had run out of cash or from the market by floating new shares because they had low credit ranking.

The government ended up owning most banks. In late July 1999, South Korean creditor banks salvaged Daewoo from an imminent insolvency by rolling over some of its short-term debt and providing it with new loans. At the same time, the *chaebol* chiefs continued their practice of throwing lifelines to sinking subsidiaries via cash injections from one affiliate to another. According to a study released by the South Korean stock exchange, the average internal shareholding in ninety-one listed companies, that constituted subsidiaries of South Korea's ten biggest *chaebols*, rose from 27.2 percent before the financial crisis to 34.6 percent at the end of August 1999. For example, the Hyundai Electronics Company, the chipmaker affiliate of the Hyundai Group, required cash infusion to reduce its debt/equity ratio. Rather than sell its assets and raise capital, the Hyundai Group transferred cash from its Hyundai Engineering and Construction Company into the chipmaker affiliate, making the Hyundai Group chairman the largest shareholder of the chipmaker. The new laws could not overcome the old practices of bailout by banks and companies of heavily indebted businesses. But practical problems arose also from the presence of powerful trade unions and government concern to protect worker jobs that could be threatened by rapid restructuring.

Daewoo and Hyundai: A Tale of Two Chaebols

The traumas of two of South Korea's leading *chaebols*, Hyundai and Daewoo, disintegrating under mountains of debt, dominated the South Korean post-crisis restructuring. Daewoo, a small textile trading company, had expanded in thirty years into shipbuilding, electronics, and construction at home, and automobile factories in Poland, India, and Uzbekistan. During that period, Hyundai emerged as South Korea's market leader in semiconductors, ship-building, construction, autos, steel, oil refining, and brokerage services. Hyundai was less exposed to short-term debt than Daewoo and more successful in floating shares on the South Korean stock exchange but overall, both were massively indebted. With proper asset revaluation, Hyundai's debt/equity ratio was 1,328 percent against Daewoo's 720 percent! In January 2000, foreign creditors of Daewoo paved the way for its overhaul by proposing to sell their loans owed by the conglomerate to South Korean banks at 35 percent of their face value. Hyundai also floated plans to reduce its subsidiaries from seventy-nine to twenty-six and break itself into five business groups by 2003, each headed by a son of the founder, Chung Ju-Yung.

The restructuring challenges were more daunting in Russia.

Restructuring: Russian Style

The systematic recapitalization of Russian banks in the period since the collapse of the Russian ruble in August 1998 was deadlocked by conflicting authority between the Agency for the Reconstruction of Commercial Organizations (ARCO) and the Central Bank of Russia, ARCO's meager finances, and its search for objective criteria for salvaging banks. Most banks lacked reliable balance sheet information; unscrupulous managers stripped their assets and formed new banks. Russia's banking reform, critical for the continuation of the economy's revival beyond 2000, was dead on arrival.

At the same time, Russia's big business was marked by shoddy corporate governance, nontransparent balance sheets based on questionable accounting practices, disregard for creditor interests, and abuse of minority shareholders. The pervasive lack of concern for fulfilling contractual obligations and observing correct business practices extended from state-owned concerns to privatized industry. Sberbank, the savings bank with state ownership of 70 percent, floated a plan to issue a large chunk of new shares at 75 percent book value, setting aside concerns for a steep decline in share valuation for existing shareholders. Lukoil, Russia's largest oil company, missed several deadlines for issuing its accounts for 2000. The management of Norilsk Nickel, the world's largest nickel producer, diluted investors' holdings by swapping some of them with shares in a London-based trading company. The executives of Gazprom, the world's largest natural gas concern, set up extensive business connections with Itera, a U.S.- based hydrocarbon company, ostensibly transferring the parent company's assets to the overseas affiliate.

The restructuring of Russia's natural monopolies in the power and natural gas sectors was caught up in decisions relating to the breakup of power-generating and transmission units in the former, and the separation of natural gas production and pipeline distribution rights in the latter. Minority foreign partners, who owned 25 percent of United Energy Systems (UES) stock, wanted the valuations of the generating units lifted via a raise in electricity rates before they were put up for sale, a suggestion that the UES chairman Anatoly Chubais found politically unenforceable. A rapid rise in energy prices could facilitate the company's overhaul but it could impose unsustainable costs on households and industry and threaten the government's inflation control targets for 2002. As a result, plans to restructure UES and Gazprom, the natural gas monopoly, made little progress as late as 2002.

Why the Delayed Restructuring?

As the economies revived in East Asia and Russia in 1999 and growth rates picked up in 2000, the urgency to restructure slackened. Policy makers feared that speedy overhauls of banks and companies might even slow the growth performance.

From South Korea to Russia, the overhaul of industrial, financial, and banking units could acquire speed with foreign participation and acquisition. It was indispensable in Russia, which needed vast inflows of foreign capital and technology. These were held back by lack of ownership guarantees, shifting laws, nontransparent accounting standards, and outdated management practices. But even if these handicaps could be steadily repaired, the speed of entry by foreign capital in Russia's natural resource sector and manufacturing faced a political bottleneck. Russia's big business, actively engaged in mergers and acquisitions in Russian oil, aluminum, pulp and paper, and chemical industries, desired the entry of foreign investors on its terms. At the same time, Russia's left-wing legislators, committed to their ideological viewing of foreign investment as exploitative, defined a marginal role for it. Foreign investors faced unusual risks as well as bureaucratic hurdles and equity participation ratios that were confined to a low 5 percent in Gazprom and 25 percent in UES. In South Korea, Western businesses succeeded in completing deals in small and medium-sized companies but found it difficult to overcome negotiating barriers arising from the incomplete disclosures in company balance sheets and local owners' insistence on recovering their initial investments rather than the depreciated market valuations.

Finally, an unwillingness to switch from the traditional interlocked ties between banks and businesses to new arrangements of Anglo-American style shareholder capitalism, in which banks and corporations deliver profits to equity holders and dividends to bond holders, has slowed the overhaul. The failure arises as much from practical realities as from the rejection of an alien corporate model.

The New Arrangements of Shareholder Capitalism

The traditional, living-together arrangements evidently geared toward long-term returns and investments needed to be replaced by profit-conscious businesses that practiced corporate governance with a shorter horizon. Again, stock and bond markets, rather than banks, must increasingly provide finances to companies. The change would contribute to shareholder interest in company performance, induce bank managers to carefully assess loan risks, weaken interlocked stock holdings, and rule out routine support of a weak component via preferential treatment in giant conglomerates such as the French and German industrial-banking groups, South Korean *chaebols,* and Japanese *keiretsu.* The profit orientation implied that company balance sheets be transparent and their accounting systems follow international standards. Emerging market leaders and policy makers viewed such changes as invasion of Anglo-American norms in tradition-bound cultures rather than new economic rules aimed at bringing in the benefits of capital inflows in an open world economy. The resistance slowed the pace of structural reforms.

Block 2

The Current Account and the Exchange Rate

MULLING OVER the lessons of the Mexican financial crisis of 1994, U.S. Treasury Secretary Lawrence Summers, then a major player in handling the crisis as the country's deputy treasury secretary, noted that a current account deficit of over 5 percent of gross domestic product (GDP) was a cause for concern. What is a current account?

The elementary distinction, often overlooked in journalistic accounts, is that the current account differs from the trade account: the latter includes only exports and imports of goods. If a country imports more goods than it exports, it runs a trade deficit. The current account additionally includes services, among them tourism, shipping and insurance, and earnings on foreign investments. The U.S. economy earns substantially from interest and dividend receipts on foreign bonds and stocks owned by Americans, and profits from manufacturing facilities owned abroad by American companies. These "factor incomes" are included as credit entries in the U.S. current account. Payments made to foreign holders of U.S. assets, for example, U.S. treasury bills, are entered as debit items in the U.S. current account. The net flow of payments on service items and on past investments are added to the trade balance giving us the current account balance.

If a country runs a current account deficit, it must finance the deficit by borrowing from abroad or running down its foreign assets. This is no different from the case of an individual who spends beyond his or her income except that for an overspending economy, help must come from outside. When the Thai economy runs a current account deficit, it brings in less foreign exchange than it sends abroad. It must acquire foreign exchange from abroad to close the gap. It manages to do that when foreigners offer foreign exchange to Thai banks for acquiring high-interest-yielding Thai government bonds, or stocks of profitable Thai companies or buying a Thai factory. When foreigners (including their governments) undertake these activities in Thailand in larger amounts than Thai residents (and the Thai government) carry out abroad, investment flows into Thailand exceed outflows of savings from Thailand. In other words, the deficit on current account is filled by a net flow of investment in Thailand. The excess of imports over exports in the current account representing overspending by the Thai economy is filled by the excess of investment over savings in Thailand's capital account. In other words, Thailand depends on foreigners' thriftiness for supporting its excessive spending.

But is this necessarily bad? How high should a current account deficit be before it turns into a serious problem? In an early stage of development, a country may have substantial productive investment opportunities that cannot be financed with domestic saving because developing countries tend to save less. Capital inflows from abroad, representing a capital account surplus, to finance the investment would be profitable for borrowers and creditors alike. East Asian countries had high levels of saving, and even higher levels of investment. Their open economies attracted funds from abroad fueling years of growth. However, their rapid, premature opening up led to massive short-term capital inflows that were channeled by financial intermediaries into long-term risky investments, such as real estate, which ultimately contributed to the financial crisis.

These economies also operated under fixed exchange rates pegged largely against the dollar. A rise in the dollar against the yen would lift their currencies and damage their export competitiveness. I discussed the consequences of such an external shock for the Thai baht, associated with the 1995 appreciation of the dollar against the yen, earlier in block 1.

Such an appreciation need not invade a currency from outside.

The Hazards of Real Currency Appreciation

Currency appreciation under a fixed exchange rate regime can occur because, while the emerging economy stabilizes under the discipline of the fixed exchange rate, prices and wages may continue rising out of inertia. If the inertial inflation rate continues to be higher than those of trading partners, the real exchange rate of the domestic economy (with the fixed nominal exchange rate) will appreciate. This will damage export competitiveness because domestic costs of producing the exportable item will be higher than the domestic earnings (converted at the fixed nominal exchange rate) from exporting it. A strong currency may attract capital flows from outside, strengthening it even further but making the economy's exports less competitive. At some stage, overvalued real exchange rates create a conflict between the management of the capital and current accounts in the balance of payments and thus become incompatible with sustainable current accounts.

Selling goods in foreign markets and earning hard currencies is crucial for countries that must repay foreign debts that are denominated in foreign currencies. Export earnings must add to foreign exchange reserves signaling to creditors that debt obligations will be paid on time. The ratios of short-term foreign debts to foreign exchange reserves in 1996 ranged from 41 percent in Malaysia to 203 percent in South Korea (in chapter 5). At the same time, their real exchange rates were generally believed to be overvalued in the run-up to the currency crisis thus damaging their export competitiveness and foreign exchange buildup. According to Goldman Sachs, while the degree of real exchange rate overvaluation in June 1997 was modest in Indonesia, South Korea, Malaysia, Philippines, and Thailand, "it had persisted for a number of years: in Indonesia, the real exchange rate had been overvalued since 1993, in Korea since 1988, in Malaysia since 1993, in the Philippines since 1992, and in Thailand since 1990." (Edwards, 1999, p. 7).

In contrast to the East Asian economies with a virtual fixed exchange rate regime, the Russian ruble operated under a managed float until July 1, 1995, and under a managed band until its collapse in August 1998. The Central Bank of Russia, pursuing active macroeconomic stabilization, allowed the ruble to appreciate in real terms from 1993 until the end of 1995, after which it remained appreciated until August 1998. Its subsequent depreciation offered price advantage to Russian goods in comparison to imports and contributed to an across-the-board revival of Russian industry.

The Argentine peso, fixed against the dollar under a currency board type arrangement in 1991, moved with the strengthening dollar and damaged the competitiveness of Argentine exports since early 1999 when the Brazilian *real* was devalued. The competitive advantage of Argentine goods under the fixed exchange rate regime could be maintained only by lowering domestic prices and wages, and by slashing the budget deficits that contributed to inflationary pressures. These requirements imposed unmanageable political choices on Argentine policy makers in the middle of the financial crisis which I analyze in chapter 9.

Block 3

Financial Liberalization, Capital Account Decontrol, and the Regulatory Framework

UNTIL THE MID-EIGHTIES, the Asian tigers were reined in by financial and capital account controls marked by regulated banks and financial institutions.

Thus, domestic credit flows were regulated via ceilings on interest rates and state-directed credits in prescribed areas. Foreign direct and portfolio investments faced limits on repatriation of principal, interest, and dividends. Indeed, foreign investors were denied opportunities to acquire a stake in certain types of companies and in real estate. Domestic banks and residents could not borrow abroad without a permit from the central bank. At the same time, the rules governing the activities of banks and financial institutions were inadequate or ignored.

The liberalizing sequence proceeded from the lifting of controls on domestic activity in borrowing, lending, and investing followed by current account convertibility of the currency ending with its full convertibility.

Current account convertibility implies that only recurring expenses involving foreign exchange are exempt from official approval or permission. Resident companies can freely buy foreign exchange from local banks for importing goods from abroad but exporters must bring it back and sell it to banks or to branches of the central bank or in the foreign exchange market. They cannot keep foreign exchange abroad except with the permission of the central bank. Again, foreign companies can repatriate profits after paying taxes, pay interest on foreign debts, and remit salaries of foreign employees.

By contrast, full capital account convertibility implies that resident individuals and corporate entities can convert local currency into foreign exchange in the desired amount and use it for the intended purpose. If they earn foreign exchange, they should be able to use it freely while abiding by local laws that prohibit its use for illegal arms purchase or drug trafficking. Nonresident individuals and corporate entities should similarly be free to convert a currency into their own. The dollar, the euro, and the yen are fully convertible major currencies.

The goal of capital account controls is to retain foreign exchange at home. If citizens were allowed to buy equity in foreign companies or deposit local cash into foreign banks (both requiring conversion of domestic money into foreign exchange), the demand for foreign exchange may outstrip supply. An ideal liberalizing progression may start with current account convertibility followed next by gradual freeing of foreign direct investment, which locks in capital and brings management and technology. Resident companies may then be allowed to invest long term in foreign businesses. Next, foreigners can acquire equity in domestic companies at a pace marked again by rules and exceptions. This may be followed by foreign entry into government and corporate bonds. In the final step, residents are allowed to acquire foreign stocks and bonds.

In practice, the whole process, moving back and forth, is influenced by the pulls and pressures of local political considerations and bureaucratic judgments, domestic business lobbying, and foreign investors' calculations or miscalculations of risks and rewards of alternative opportunities. In the four economies analyzed here, in which the liberalization began in the late eighties and proceeded in zigzag steps, private portfolio acquisitions and short-term borrowing exceeded long-term direct investment flows by 1996. In Russia and Argentina, government borrowing from abroad dominated portfolio and long-term investment flows into the private sector. Brazilian policy makers promoted foreign investment after 1994, but the flows (unlike in China) did not generate sufficient foreign exchange earnings to adequately cover its accumulating debt repayment obligations by 2002. Turkey lagged farthest behind among the sampled countries in cleaning the web of rules on foreign direct investment until 2001 when measures to straighten up the procedures under the initiatives of Kemal Dervis, the economy minister, were thrown aside in the political turmoil of mid-2002. China marked a striking exception to this pattern: foreign direct investment initiated at the start of the liberalization far exceeded borrowing by the government and businesses and equity flows by foreign investors.

The decade of the nineties witnessed liberalizing measures relating to domestic and foreign financial markets in the four Asian economies.

Thailand

Progress was most rapid in Thailand beginning with the removal of controls on interest rates from 1989 to 1992 for domestic commercial banks by the central bank, the Bank of Thailand. At the same time, foreign investors in mutual funds and equities were taxed less and allowed free repatriation of principal, interest, and dividends. Three mutual funds were set up in 1990 to attract foreign investors. Reform of foreign direct investment gathered speed: beginning in 1991, companies that promised to export all outputs were allowed 100 percent foreign investment. Thai residents were gradually permitted to invest abroad.

In a radical innovation, the government set up the Bangkok International Banking Facility (BIBF) in March 1993 with the goal of advancing Bangkok as a regional financial center. The member bank licensees, forty-nine by 1996, could borrow in foreign currency abroad and lend to Thai residents and companies (an out-in transaction) or nonresidents (an out-out transaction). These loan activities enjoyed a series of tax breaks (Alba, Hernandez, and Klingebiel, 1999).

As the economy, flushed with funds, started heating up, some old practices resurfaced in 1995. The Bank of Thailand sought to curb bank loan activity and channel it in desirable directions. In 1996, it raised the minimum loan amounts extended by a BIBF member bank thereby diverting them to large customers; pushed up the reserve requirements for nonresident baht accounts to 7 percent, the same as for other short-term accounts in banking and finance companies; and lowered the tax credit concession for BIBF business (ibid.). These measures however were not effective in curtailing the credit operations of BIBF banks in view of the substantial difference between domestic and foreign interest rates.

More precarious for the health of the financial system was the lax regulatory framework that followed these fast-paced liberalization measures.

Inadequate Regulations and Poor Performance Standards

Around the mid-eighties, the financial sector, consisting of commercial banks, government savings banks, private and public insurance companies, and financial institutions with special functions, was dominated by commercial banks, fifteen domestic and fourteen foreign. The banking industry in turn was highly concentrated with four banks accounting for 63 percent of total bank assets (ibid.). Foreign commercial banks accounted for only 5 percent of bank assets because of government restrictions. At the same time, external borrowing made up only 3.9 percent of total bank liabilities. All this was to change dramatically as a result of the decontrol measures described previously.

Thai banks lacked a regulatory framework aimed at promoting prudential banking activity on their part. Banks, the main providers of funds to industry, depended on collateral values rather than on borrowers' creditworthiness in terms of cash flows or project viability. The capital-to-asset adequacy ratio of 8 percent, prescribed by the Bank of International Settlement, was in fact ignored—40 percent of total assets in 1989 were exempted by the Bank of Thailand from the adequacy guidelines. In any case, asset values were overstated. They could not be monitored for banks as well as for businesses because of poor accounting standards and inadequate disclosure of financial statements that were in turn based on doubtful norms of classifying assets and financial losses. Linked ownership among banks and businesses, the latter again dominated by family insiders, further complicated the critical issue of raising accounting norms and standards to global levels in a transparent environment. These features prevailed in banks and businesses in South Korea, Indonesia, and Malaysia as well. Beginning 1993, the Bank of Thailand sought to raise capital/asset ratios across the board for banks and financial institutions for curbing excessive risk taking in their loan activities, and assert its supervisory role. But by the end of 1996, the Thai financial sector had already become, in substance and size, a bubble ready to burst.

The liberalizing and opening up of financial activities proceeded along a similar track in Indonesia, South Korea, and Malaysia, although the speed and sequencing of the measures differed from country to country.

Indonesia

In Indonesia, interest rates were freed and direct credit controls on banks were removed in 1983. By 1989, banks could borrow freely from nonresidents. New foreign banks were licensed leading to their active participation in the financial sector. Foreign investors could invest into the stock market up to 49 percent of the ownership of listed stocks. In July 1996, the central bank, Bank Indonesia, issued Indonesian-government Yankee bonds on the New York Stock Exchange, in the process raising resources for the treasury. Increasingly, foreign direct investment was allowed in more sectors and for longer times in targeted activities before these were required to be converted to domestic ownership. By 1989, foreign direct investors could sell foreign exchange directly to commercial banks instead of routing it through the central bank. In mid-1996, the government launched infrastructure investment by foreign companies offering them a ten-year tax holiday.

Not surprisingly, as in Thailand, the measures attracted funds from abroad, resulting in booming investment, a surging economy, rising inflation and interest rates, and a widening current account deficit. In response, foreign borrowing by banks and state enterprises was reined in via direct controls; banks faced limits on their foreign exchange transactions and ceilings on their swap positions in relation to their capital base. In September 1996, Bank Indonesia operated between a rock and a hard place: it widened the foreign exchange band of the Indonesian rupiah to maintain the country's export competitiveness while increasing the minimum reserve requirement for commercial banks in a tightening policy stance. Interest rate differential at home and abroad attracted capital inflows contributing to the appreciation of the currency.

Deregulation of the financial sector started somewhat late in Malaysia.

Malaysia

In 1991, the central bank, Bank Negara Malaysia, lifted all controls on interest rates and raised its supervisory oversight over the country's twenty-two domestic banks and their proliferating branches, requiring a higher than 8 percent capital/asset ratio and promoting a high liquidity in banks. The bank liquidity got a further boost with the liberalization of the capital markets in mid-1995, permitting banks to secure loans with shares as collateral. At the same time, Kuala Lumpur, the capital, was launched to compete with Bangkok as Asia's leading financial center.

Among the East Asian economies in our sample (South Korea is discussed immediately below), Malaysia ranked at the top in attracting foreign direct investment via its commercial banks that transformed its industrial sector. As a result, in their run-up to the financial crisis, Malaysian banks were flushed with enormous liquidity that they lent aggressively to the country's burgeoning real estate market.

South Korea

In South Korea, as in Thailand, Indonesia, and Malaysia, financial liberalization and opening up resulted in escalating inflows of capital from abroad leading to an investment boom. As with these neighboring economies, the authorities brought back controls for cooling economic activity, when necessary, as in the eighties.

Chaebols, the industrial conglomerates, dominated the South Korean economy through their significant ownership of banks and financial institutions. However, in the run-up to the crisis, the vulnerability of several *chaebols*, rather than the insolvency of banks and finance companies, "triggered concern." (Haggard and MacIntyre, 2001, p. 8). Next, the bait of entry into the Organisation for Economic Co-operation & Development (OECD) hastened the abandon with which the authorities eliminated barriers to short-term external borrowing by South Korean banks and finance companies in early nineties. "Interestingly enough, and in spite of the reluctance to open the stock market to foreign funds, Korea allowed its banks to borrow very heavily and at very short maturities, from international banks. By the end of 1996, for example, Korean banks had borrowed US$67 billion from OECD banks, of which US$50 billion is estimated to have had a maturity of less than one year" (Edwards, 1999, p. 13).

As elsewhere, the process began with decontrol of interest rates in 1991. It was followed by removal of administrative controls on foreign borrowing by banks and financial institutions and on foreigners investing in commercial and financial securities in South Korea. "In a heavily politicized process, the government converted 24 relatively weak finance companies into merchant banks in 1994–96 in order to provide them new business opportunities. Merchant banks lent aggressively, engaged in a variety of speculative activities such as investment in Russian bonds, and subsequently proved themselves the Achilles heel of the financial sector" (Haggard and MacIntyre, 2001, p. 8).

In these countries, the allocation of credit via administrative controls gave way to interest-rate determined flows that were followed by the removal of controls on capital flows. However, the sequence of internal financial liberalization followed by international financial liberalization occurred without a successful implanting of prudential regulation and supervision of their banking sectors. The final step in the incomplete agenda consisted in confronting the traditional practices of financial activities governed by family ties and informal networking relations, dominated by long-standing arrangements in Turkish Islamic banks, South Korean *chaebols*, and Japanese *keiretsus*. A forced transformation of these institutions so that they conformed to the demands of global financial standards, accounting practices, and balance sheet disclosures aroused political pressures and cultural resistance, raising serious issues about an optimal sequencing of financial liberalization. The theory of the second best, that provided an ideal textbook sequencing of which distortion should be removed first, was of limited relevance in dealing with the reality on ground.

Even in the model U.S. economy, a serious infringement of accounting and financial disclosure rules came to light when Enron, the energy conglomerate with a $70 billion market capitalization, collapsed in December 2001. Arthur Anderson, the company's auditors, understated its risk exposure by finagling the accounts of its off-balance sheet partners. Evidently, the U.S. regulatory requirements lagged behind the giant strides in the complex financial instruments that facilitated accounting manipulation by auditors for their corporate clients for whom the auditors occasionally served as consultants, raising serious conflict-of- interest issues. The measures to bridge the gap, however, were swift and multi-pronged as the bankrupt company fired Arthur Anderson, the Justice Department launched an investigation of Enron's financial practices, Congress began an enquiry in its employees' retirement plans that had wiped out their savings locked in Enron stocks, and the Securities and Exchange Commission announced its readiness to tighten its supervision of corporate auditing procedures and business practices. Congress enacted laws that put the accounting industry under the surveillance of an independent oversight board and forbade auditors from providing lucrative consulting services to their corporate clients whose accounts they audited on behalf of the public. They made corporate executives liable for misleading information provided by their companies. Corporate malfeasance and accounting mismanagement pervade all cultures, but the U.S. response in dealing with the consequences of "infectious greed" was remarkably swift and focused.

Block 4

The East Asian Crisis: A Crisis of Over-Investment or Unregulated, Premature Capital Flows?

WHY DID THE East Asian miracle of unprecedented growth over three decades suddenly turn into an unexpected debacle?

Diminishing Returns to Over-Investment and Declining Factor Productivity →Desai claims not cost

According to Krugman (1998), the miracle, the result of escalating investments, was bound to lead to diminishing returns and growth rates: as more capital is combined with a slower growing labor force, the marginal product of capital declines. This argument was further buttressed by the lack of measured factor productivity as a source of growth in East Asia (Young, 1995).

These exercises drew a parallel from painstaking analysis by economists, among them Desai (1976, 1987) and Weitzman (1970) who sought to explain postwar Soviet growth retardation by capturing production activity spanning different years in the economy and industrial branches with alternative data. But the latecomers on the scene, keen to contrast Soviet growth exhaustion with East Asian economic expansion, were not aware that the results of the earlier attempts to explain Soviet growth slowdown had been inconclusive. Depending on the choice of data and the years, the "best" production function suggested either diminishing returns to excessive capital formation or declining factor productivity as the source of slowing Soviet growth rates. The econometric search for explaining East Asian growth could be equally elusive.

On the other hand, East Asia's miraculous growth rates may have resulted from smart policies (Bhagwati, 2000b).

The Role of Correct Policies

Capital accumulation in East Asia was driven by the decisive goal of export orientation and steady absorption of better technologies for the purpose (Bhagwati, 2000b). The superior technologies that were brought in via imported capital goods could be expected to boost output gains over time because of the policy emphasis on education. With better absorption of technologies, factor productivity must have improved in later years, a point evidently missed by Young whose econometric exercise did not include periodization (ibid.).

But if the Asian growth miracle was bound to end because of diminishing returns to capital accumulation à la Krugman, or weak factor productivity push à la Young, why did it collapse suddenly instead of tapering off smoothly?

Why the Sudden Collapse?

In the Krugman version endorsed by Phelps (1999), excessive investment became a crisis of over-investment because it was financed by massive short-term borrowing from abroad by financial intermediaries (finance companies in Thailand, and banks and businesses in South Korea), who loaned the cash long-term to speculators-investors in the stock market and real estate. The intermediaries lent recklessly because, in Krugman's initial analysis, they had implicit guarantees of bailout by policy makers in high places. The soaring prices of some assets, among them stocks, land, and property, took on the marks of an investment-boom marked by "unsustainably optimistic expectations about the future returns on the investment they [the heads of enterprises] were undertaking and/or about the future interest rates on the loans they were getting from domestic banks" (ibid.).

The inevitable financial bust resembled the let down that follows a drinking binge. "When these expected returns began to look unrealizable and furthermore when the banks saw they had to call in loans or raise interest rates, as the government could not guarantee on the expected scale, the real prices of these assets had to fall back" (ibid.). The meltdown was marked by the puncturing of the asset bubble that had resulted from misdirected over-investment.

Countering over-investment as the source of Asian collapse, several oppositionists (Bhagwati, 1998; Wade, 1998a, 1998b; Eichengreen, 1999a & b) attributed the cause to the "hasty opening to freer capital flows," the result, moreover, of outside pressure. The agents exercising pressure included Wall Street in Eichengreen, the Wall Street-Treasury complex in Bhagwati, and the Wall Street-Treasury-International Monetary Fund complex in Wade.

6

The Asian Crisis Chronology

THE ASIAN CRISIS was set in motion in Thailand, Indonesia, Malaysia, and South Korea by highly leveraged local banks, financial institutions, and companies that had borrowed short term abroad and lent long term at home to questionable investors in real estate and other dubious ventures. As these borrowers missed debt payments and declared bankruptcies, foreign creditors withdrew funds aggravating the finances of these borrowers and dragging with them the values of currencies they dumped. The financial crisis became a currency crisis. In response, East Asian central banks raised interest rates with a view to stemming the outflows by nervous currency speculators and equity holders, and declared that the currency pegs would not be abandoned. Despite the hikes, the currency and stock values continued their rapid slide, denting central bank reserves of foreign exchange and forcing authorities to abandon the pegs and seek financial rescue from the International Monetary Fund (IMF).

These salient features, which I analyze in this chapter, were similar across countries, but their severity and duration varied. The financial turmoil interacted with political uncertainty affecting the ability of policy makers to implement the necessary rescue measures under IMF monitoring. Elections and their outcomes complicated the process further. South Korea and Thailand experienced upheavals during the economic crisis, but the political changes in both were constitutional, serving to reassure the citizens. The new governments started riding out the ill effects of the crisis sooner than in Indonesia under B. J. Habibie who was handpicked by President Suharto as his deputy, and approved by a compliant parliament in the summer of 1998. Indonesia's freewheeling Suharto-Habibie brand of politics in the midst of the turmoil also contrasted with Malaysia's autocratic regime under Prime Minister Mahathir Mohamad who launched his own economic blueprint bypassing IMF support.

The IMF could have intervened earlier with a larger-rescue effort, less severe policy strictures, and innovative initiatives of timely and orderly debt restructuring which could have moderated the need for large IMF funding for the crisis-swept economies. The option of imposing Malaysian-style temporary controls on capital outflows also ran contrary to its "one-rule-fits-all-situations" bureaucratic approach and its ideological

Source: "The collapse of the Thai baht," Nop's World, *Bangkok Post*, July 3, 1997.

predisposition against such controls for member countries seeking its financial support. It not only misjudged the seriousness of the Asian crisis but also failed to learn new lessons, which could have prepared it for managing future crises in Argentina and Turkey. (I discuss these issues in chapter 11.)

Crisis watchers mark July 2, 1997 as the historic date in the chronology. On that day, the Thai authorities ended their defense of the Thai baht, allowing it to float. In the following months, this decision engulfed other countries of the region in financial and currency turmoil that hit the Russian ruble on August 17, 1998 and the Brazilian *real* in January 1999.[1]

Crisis Origins

Financial hardships of highly leveraged banks and companies that had invested heavily in the real estate boom in East Asia predated the July 1997 collapse of the baht. In early January 1997, Hanbo, a South Korean *chaebol*, declared bankruptcy, crumbling under the weight of $6 billion in debt. Samrasong Land, a Thai company, missed payment on its foreign debts a month later. In South Korea, Sammi Steel and Kia Motors of Korea folded a little later prompting fears about impending corporate failures.

Regional authorities announced policy measures to contain the damage to their economies from the unfolding bankruptcies. The central bank of

Malaysia issued a directive in late March 1997 limiting real estate credits and capping the fraction of loans that could be secured by stocks and bonds. The Bank of Thailand also followed a similar strategy, limiting loans by banks and finance companies for real estate deals.

These measures did not hold the crisis at bay. In mid-May 1997, the Thai baht was hit with a massive speculative attack, prompting the central bank to spend nearly $10 billion in defense of the currency. The bank had committed almost all its liquid foreign exchange reserves in forward contracts, most of them to speculators betting on devaluation (Radelet and Sachs, 1998). In the midst of the depletion of its usable reserves, it defended the currency and insisted that the peg would be held. The simmering crisis saw the departure of Finance Minister Amnuay Viravan, as Prime Minister Chavalit Yonchaiyudh continued defending his decision to stick to the currency peg. The central bank banned repatriation of baht funds by foreign investors, when they sold Thai shares, to stem the outflow while committing itself to stay with the currency peg. It suspended operations of sixteen finance companies, pushed up the interest rate, and tightened currency controls. On June 30, Yonchaiyudh assured the nation on TV that the currency would not be devalued. The measures failed. On July 2, 1997, the Bank of Thailand announced its decision to float the baht and called on the IMF for technical assistance as the currency tumbled by 18 percent, reaching a record low.

Après Baht, le Déluge

The fall of the baht set off a process that reverberated throughout the region in a full-blown panic attack by speculators on the Malaysian, Indonesian, and Philippine currencies. By October 1997, most of the currencies in the region had been battered, the South Korean won being an exception. The Thai and the Indonesian currencies had lost more than 50 percent of their values and the Malaysian and Philippine currencies about 30 percent from before the start of the crisis. The Singapore dollar registered depreciation. The Hong Kong dollar remained stable because the authorities intervened without public fanfare, spending $1 billion and increasing overnight interest rates to defend it. The crisis spread internationally. On October 27, the decline of the Hong Kong Hang Seng index hit Wall Street—the Dow Jones dropped 554.26 points to 7161.15, one of the biggest point losses in one day, leading to suspended trading. The tremors were felt in Latin America as well, with the Mexican, Argentine, and Brazilian stock markets experiencing losses in stock prices.

Source: "Thai prime minister serenading the IMF," Nop's World, *Bangkok Post*, December 16, 1997.

Malaysia, the Maverick

Malaysia stood out as a policy maverick despite similarities in the essential symptoms of the crisis marked by withdrawal of short-term capital by foreign speculative investors and a declining currency despite administrative measures to stem its fall. The central bank finally abandoned the peg.

The pluses contributing to an independent policy stance arose from Prime Minister Mahathir Mohamad's strong political standing,[2] the relatively higher presence of foreign direct investment in the economy, and a slightly better capital/asset ratio in the industrial sector than in the neighboring economies. The negative elements arose from rising labor costs, excessive reliance on imported inputs, and leveraged banks and financial institutions.[3] A steady annual growth rate of 8 percent masked the growing economic stresses.

Through the crisis months, Mohamad insisted on lower interest rates, optimistic growth forecasts, and budgetary support of infrastructure projects to stem the recessionary impact of the financial crisis. In the process he isolated his deputy and finance minister, Anwar Ibrahim, challenged U.S. Treasury Secretary Robert Rubin and the managing director of the

IMF, Michel Camdessus, and accused financier George Soros of being "a racist speculator" seeking to destabilize the Malaysian economy. The central bank imposed direct measures to curtail outflows of foreign capital (details follow subsequently). The growth forecasts were scaled down following an earlier optimistic announcement; mergers of banks and financial companies were postponed after an initial declaration of plans to overhaul the financial sector; and infrastructure projects were halted or trimmed after a go-ahead signal. Throughout the zigzag, the Malaysian leader, outspoken and autocratic, kept the upper hand, ultimately sending his deputy to jail and keeping the IMF at an arm's length.

Malaysian Exchange Controls

The selective exchange controls, imposed by the central bank on September 1, 1998, were targeted at preventing the speculation of the ringgit and controlling short-term capital flows. The following day, the bank also fixed the exchange rate of the ringgit at 3.80 to the dollar. The measures distinguished between residents and nonresidents and between current account transactions and investment flows.

Detailed rules, some of which were gradually removed or relaxed, were imposed on resident and nonresident travelers with a view to regulating the outflow and encouraging the inflow of foreign exchange. All travelers entering Malaysia are required to declare the foreign currency they carry irrespective of the amount. Nonresident travelers may bring in an unlimited amount of foreign currency, provided they do not take out more than they bring in. Resident travelers are required to get prior permission from the controller of foreign exchange for exporting or importing ringgits or for exporting foreign exchange in excess of the permitted amounts.

Current and capital account transactions were regulated as well. Imports must be paid for in foreign exchange (but nonresidents can import goods and services without restrictions). Export earnings must be brought back within six months and converted into ringgits. They may be retained by residents within specified limits in approved foreign currency accounts with onshore banks. The currency controls also limited the movement of foreign direct investment; these, however, were gradually terminated. On February 15, 1999, the rule requiring nonresidents to hold their principal sum for at least twelve months was relaxed. They could repatriate the capital and profits any time after paying a tax ranging from 10 to 30 percent. The tax on profits was standardized to 10 percent on September 21, 1999. Currently, "foreign direct investors are freely allowed to repatriate their investment, including capital, profit and dividends, without being subject to any levy" (Wang, 2000, p. 2). Foreign exchange controls limit resident investment in foreign currency accounts and their transactions in offshore financial centers.

South Korea Abandons the Currency Peg

A foreign debt crisis was emerging in South Korea, which had been immune from speculative attacks until the late summer of 1997. The market was saddled with bankruptcies of several mid-sized corporations. In August 1997, Standard & Poor's demoted its credit rating to "negative." By October, stock prices began plummeting as foreigners dumped stocks prompting the central bank to raise the interest rate and run down its reserves. The stock market nevertheless crashed to a five-year low in November.

The ruling party announced a plan to clean up debt-ridden banks as an inducement to foreign investors to return. The policy announcement (that in the end failed to pass the National Assembly) could not stop the attack on the currency. A new economics minister tried shoring it up by halting currency trading for four consecutive days during which it declined daily to its maximum permissible low, while interest rates rose and currencies in the region continued sliding. On November 17, 1997, South Korea joined the ranks of East Asian countries that had abandoned the defense of the currency, sending the won plummeting past the 1,000 won per dollar barrier. Stocks plunged, money market interest rates were pressured upward, and the Thai, Malaysian, Indonesian, and Philippine currencies declined further. On November 21, the government announced that it would seek assistance from the IMF.

Indonesia, a Tale Apart

Indonesia had all the features of the escalating financial crisis in the region: foreign speculators dumped local stocks, fled from the currency, and forced the central bank to raise the interest rate, which in turn devastated the financial viability of banks and companies. Debtors turned to the foreign exchange market to replace the lost foreign exchange, pushing the rupiah down and the local-currency interest charges up, putting further pressure on the banking system. Bank closures, bank runs, thinness of the financial markets, and maturing short-term external debts battered the currency. In late September 1997, the rupiah reached a new low against the dollar, and the Jakarta stock market also sank to 550 from around 700 in August. The flip-flops in government decisions—that at one stage canceled 150 investment projects, but was later limited to the cancellation of the fifteen largest of these projects (Radelet and Sachs, 1998)—undermined its credibility and added to the confusion of foreign investors reeling from panic.

Indonesia contemplated seeking IMF assistance in early October. The stock market temporarily revived, buoyed by Japanese readiness to offer technical assistance to the economy. The government, motivated by concerns to soften the liquidity crunch blundered again by cutting back interest rates and aggravating the currency slide. The approval of an IMF loan in early November, linked with support from the World Bank and the Asian Development Bank, did not halt the crisis. From being a country with one of the strongest fundamentals at the start of the crisis, Indonesia became a pariah in the eyes of foreign investors in the course of a few months. Deposits continued fleeing the country for lack of investor confidence.

The 1998 Blues: South Korea

The South Korean and Indonesian economies deteriorated further in 1998 despite IMF financial support. In both countries, bank cleanup and closures failed to restore confidence in the banking sector. Non-economic factors, among them the upcoming presidential elections in South Korea, added to the confusion. In Indonesia, rumors of President Suharto's ill health and the unclear succession scenario added to investor panic. The chaotic signals ricocheted to the countries that were the original targets of speculative attacks: the sinking fortunes of the won and the rupiah sent the neighboring baht and ringgit to record lows.

Three factors plagued the South Korean economy and currency in 1998: the inadequate size of the IMF rescue package and its delayed implementation, the conflicting signals from the authorities about the economy's precarious finances, and the massive debt owed by the private sector to foreign banks.

The $57 billion rescue package arranged by the IMF failed to restore investor confidence because the corporate sector was too highly leveraged to crawl out of the financial burden. Another *chaebol*—the Halla group—failed to make payments on its debt underscoring the tenuous financial health of the country's corporate companies. Over half of Halla's debts were owed to merchant banks that were in a precarious situation of their own. Yet another bankruptcy of Coryo Investment and Securities—the first such bankruptcy in more than three decades—demonstrated continuing financial woes. As *chaebols* collapsed and corporate debt burden accumulated, the IMF package turned out to be severely inadequate, requiring speedy action to halt impending defaults of international loans. Pressures appeared for changing the terms of the agreement between the IMF and the government, even as the international institutions and the U.S. government continued emphasizing the need to fulfill the original plan, and Standard & Poor's downgraded South Korea's long-term foreign currency rating to just above junk bond status.

Next, lack of transparency relating to the seriousness of the South Korean financial situation worsened market confidence. Official foreign exchange reserves at $23.9 billion in December 1998, most of them illiquid, were dangerously low. At the same time, the country's short-term external liabilities, reaching $100 billion at the end of September, turned out to be vastly higher than the original estimate of the finance ministry at $65.6 billion. The disparities in these numbers contributed to the overly negative assessment by the market of the South Korean situation.

Finally, the delayed restructuring pulled more businesses into bankruptcies. In mid-December, the IMF announced that it was considering a renewed fund disbursement schedule for the country involving a plan for debt rescheduling. By December 24, several foreign financial institutions considered rescheduling South Korean corporate debts in view of the dim prospects of recovering their on-time repayment. On the same day, the IMF announced a refurbished package for the country that encouraged negotiations between foreign creditor banks and the authorities on rescheduling commercial bank short-term credits. Debt restructuring moved forward as several U.S. banks—including Goldman Sachs, Lehman Brothers, Merrill Lynch, and Salomon Smith Barney—completed the necessary details followed by similar arrangements with European and Australian banks. The plan involved conversion of bank debts into government bonds of varying maturities. By mid-January 1999, about $24 billion of short-term debt through March 31, was exchanged for government-guaranteed bonds. These measures, actively supported by the newly elected president, Kim Dae Jung, helped revive market confidence. The official foreign exchange reserves began moving up. Policy makers turned, albeit haltingly, to the formidable legislative issue of adopting laws enabling company executives to shed labor, downsize factories, and convert *chaebols* into competitive players. (These details are in block 1.)

The South Korean economy moved into 1999 with hopes for financial stability and economic turnaround. Market confidence began reviving in Thailand and Philippines somewhat later, after an initial plunge of their currencies to record levels. Reassuring statements from U.S. authorities and the IMF helped assuage investor nervousness. The negative trends of late 1997 and early 1998 in the critical indicators of exchange and interest rates and stock market indexes gradually turned positive. Toward the end of 1998, bargain hunters appeared with offers to pick up cheap stocks and negotiate deals for joint ventures.

Indonesia, however, continued to be an exception to these recovery signals in the rest of the region.

Indonesia, the Exception

While the rest of the region had resolved political uncertainties via elections (in Thailand and Korea) or suppression of a political rival via authoritarian means (in Malaysia), Indonesia remained politically turbulent to the end of 1999. Major reform decisions involving a budget, IMF fund disbursement, cleaning up banks and businesses under IMF monitoring, and debt rescheduling continued to be embroiled in delays, policy muddles, and battles of leadership succession involving corruption scandals and street riots. In 1998, the market seesawed in reaction to a string of uppers and downers experiencing a full-scale meltdown in January: stocks declined sharply, and the rupiah reached the 10,500 to the dollar barrier, losing 70 percent in value since the start of the Asian crisis. The disbursement of IMF credits did not contain the negative impact of market reaction to the budget as being inadequately austere.[4] Political uncertainty and escalating social unrest, policy confusion and lack of commitment to IMF measures, the IMF occasionally stepping out and back in, interacted with one another through the year.

In the midst of the escalating financial deterioration, rumors of the Indonesian currency being fixed against the dollar circulated in Jakarta in February. This pie-in-the-sky idea fed the uncertainties from two directions: the public demanded local money in anticipation of selling it later at a more favorable government-determined rate. The specific currency board plan, evidently favored by the government, faced vehement opposition from the IMF and the U.S. Treasury, the former threatening to withhold cash from the rescue package if it went ahead, and the latter sending a prominent envoy, Walter Mondale, to underscore the importance of its opposition. The plan was shelved, but not before the governor of the central bank had lost his job over his reported opposition to the government plan favoring a currency board.

The IMF and the government policy makers continued being at loggerheads in the spring months. The government worked up a plan to subsidize imports of food and other essentials for capping prices in technical violation of the bailout package. The IMF postponed disbursal of the next $3 billion tranche, originally scheduled for March, into April. In May, students frustrated by lack of economic turnaround and hurt by unemployment and rising prices, protested and demanded Suharto's resignation. Although he initially tried to ride out the protests, Suharto resigned on May 21, declaring that he would not defy the will of the people. The Indonesian leader, who had transformed the country from a dirt-poor economy into a credible powerhouse of the region, was unable to contain the crisis that had shriveled the economy by 8 percent in a few months, and had knocked the value of the currency by over 80 percent in less than a year. It was not clear how long his successor, B. J. Habibie, could last in office, even though he seemed to have the support of the military. At issue was his credibility: as a handpicked successor of Suharto, he failed to inspire confidence and provide leadership for mounting new policy initiatives. Some of his favorite projects had been targeted for cancellation by the IMF as preconditions for Indonesian rescue.

The survival of the Indonesian economy however depended on the infusion of IMF emergency funds. On May 25, four days after taking office, Habibie announced that he would press ahead with economic reforms and follow IMF prescriptions to qualify for the next installment of the Fund's $10 billion balance-of-payments loan. A strategic decision, granting policy-making independence to Bank Indonesia, the country's central bank, contributed to inflation control and currency stability. In October 1998, a year after the initial request for IMF support, market sentiment began changing, and the rupiah appreciated from an all-time low of 16,650 against the dollar. The economy began recovering although critical political problems and restructuring issues remained unresolved.

As noted earlier, the crisis manifested similar features from country to country in East Asia. Each suffered from speculative short-term capital outflows linked with bank and company failures: policy makers in each country, having tried interest rate hikes and other measures ultimately discarded the currency pegs, and (except Malaysia) sought IMF rescue packages. Unlike in the other three economies of Thailand, Malaysia, and South Korea, political turbulence in Indonesia, brought on by the continuing economic uncertainties, delayed their timely resolution. In the years following the onset of the crisis in mid-1997, these Asian economies (including Philippines) battled the problems of reviving growth, repayment of debts incurred during the previous phase of premature capital account liberalization, and loss of foreign investor confidence that intensified with the emerging financial problems in Argentina and Turkey.

Free Capital Mobility and the Lost Years of the Nineties

The fast-paced opening of these economies to capital inflows in the early nineties was expected to integrate them into the world financial system. At the end of the decade, emerging market economies in general, with the exception of China and Mexico, had disappeared from the activity of global investors. The Crisis Five in East Asia shifted their gear in the reverse by retiring their external debt collectively to the tune of $100 billion since 1997. At the same time, foreign investors lost faith in new stocks and bonds in emerging markets as they watched their gains in old holdings disappear with repeated assaults from the collapse of East Asian currencies followed by the meltdown of the Russian ruble in August 1998, the subsequent plunge of the Brazilian *real* in January 1999, and the devaluation of the Turkish lira in 2000. Anticipating a devaluation of the Argentine peso or a default of its $130 billion debt of 2000, or both, they slashed their Argentine bond trading to about one-tenth of its volume of 1997.

The Asian economies revived at varying paces in the post-recovery years until the prospects for sustained growth were again stymied in 2001 by the U.S. economic recession, which contributed to and synchronized with the recessions in the eurozone and Japan. Their performance was affected not only by reduced export demand from their major overseas buyers but also by their pell-mell structural reforms and weak stock markets that contributed to slowing capital flows from risk-averse foreign investors. Despite the post-1998 economic revival continuing into 2000, these economies were not geared to battle the fallout from the U.S. economic slowdown and the financial turmoil in Turkey and Argentina that began in mid-2000. Japan's continuing economic slump and the anemic growth in the eurozone, which the European Central Bank failed to counter with a decisive monetary policy, added to the negative pressures in emerging markets as a group. The low presence of risk-averse global investors in these economies minimized the financial contagion, but the synchronized economic slowdown in the world's three largest areas affected their exports, especially in critical sectors such as semiconductors and electronic components in South Korea and Malaysia. As a result, the weak and uneven progress in structural and institutional cleanup suffered a further setback from the economic hardships imposed by the global downturn that led to "reform fatigue." These hardships intensified as the U.S. economic slowdown turned into a recession following the 9/11 terrorist attacks and the subsequent military action in Afghanistan.

The first decade of financial globalization that began in the early nineties had therefore failed to integrate the Asian Crisis Five in the world financial system. Toward the end of 2001, they were a fragmented and isolated group. Investors that had hoped to spread out in these economies with a view to diversifying their portfolios in profitable holdings not only focused on another emerging market, Mexico, for example, but also on individual companies in specific countries. The Crisis Five economies posted growth rates ranging from 2 to 3 percent, positive current account balances, and manageable debt-servicing ratios of export earnings to debt-servicing obligations in 2000. But the structural reforms were lagging.

Post-Crisis East Asian Recovery

Three features relating to the slow speed of structural reforms, its consequential impact on economic performance, and efforts at devising regional trade and financial arrangements marked the post-1998 upturn in the East Asian region analyzed here.

First, the overhaul of the traditional tightly knit banking and business structures was inadequate. (Details for South Korea are in block 1.) The swiftness, depth, and spread of the crisis had raised hopes that the necessary reforms for averting future occurrences would gather momentum in these economies. More than four years to the origin of the crisis that knocked the Thai baht in July 1997, progress in the East Asian Crisis Five in financial market regulation, banking sector cleanup, and corporate restructuring was limited. In the recovery phase of 1999, it lacked urgency, and in the downturn of 2000, it was deemed difficult. As the growth in the affected economies reached a precrisis average 4 to 6 percent in 1999, the adjustment pressures slackened despite pervasive problems in the financial and business sectors. In both phases, the process encountered problems of political uncertainties ranging from new elections, government changes, and ministerial resignations to upheavals marked by presidential impeachment and ethnic-religious turmoil. The region, buffeted at best by political uncertainty in Thailand, and at worst by physical fragmentation in Indonesia, failed to forge independent financial, judicial, and political institutions that could provide the institutional underpinning for orderly, transparent, and rule-based economic activities in a highly competitive global environment.

Second, slow structural reforms and the synchronized economic slowdown in the global economy affected growth performance and the slowing growth (except in 2000) affected financial market health, currency values, and investment flows in the struggling economies of the region. Figure 6.1 illustrates real GDP growth rates in these Asian economies from 1996–2001. All economies showed a lower growth rate in 2001 than in 1996. Figure 6.2 shows that the per capita real GDP indexes in the region, with 1995 equaling 100, ranged between 63 to 89 in 2001. Finally, country stock market indexes (figure 6.3) steadily declined between mid-1999 and mid-2001. The weakening currencies and declining stock markets in the region during the period highlighted its incomplete structural adjustment signaling to investors that its growth rebound was uncertain. Figure 6.4 shows that the small positive capital flows in 1999 declined to $20 billion in outflows in 2000. Given the discouraging growth prospects of the region, foreign investors focused on quality investments in the U.S., the European Union, and Japanese markets. The

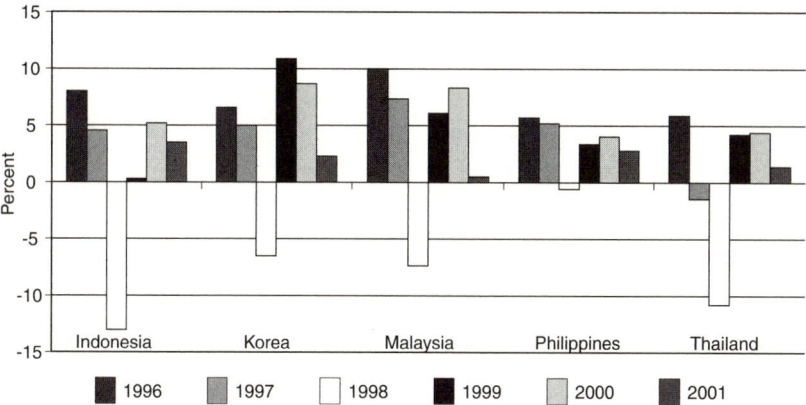

Figure 6.1. Change in real gross domestic product. Percentage of annual change. *Source:* Economist Intelligence Unit.

U.S. was the largest recipient of the flows that fed into cross-border mergers and acquisitions. The spike in oil prices also took a toll on the investment prospects in East Asian markets. On the positive side, low inflation and interest rates contributed to higher domestic demand and intraregional trade. The post-crisis performance however brought out the region's dependence on the U.S. economy. Economic expansion in the U.S. helped the East Asian economies recover from the crisis in 1999. But U.S. economic slowdown, continuing high oil prices, and Japan's persisting doldrums affected their performance in 2001.

Finally, the post-crisis years witnessed an active search for financial and economic cooperation among the ten members of the Association of Southeast Asian Nations and the three northeastern, large economies of Japan, China, and South Korea (the so-called "ASEAN + 3" collective).[5] These suggestions for regional trade and currency arrangements gathered momentum in recovering East Asia as it struggled with the impact of the U.S. economic slowdown and the continuing Japanese recession. Even if these schemes succeeded, they were a backward step from the region's full integration in the world economy that the free flow of global capital was supposed to promote.

Three lessons of contrasting recovery scenarios relating to the U.S. and Japanese economies of the center (analyzed in the earlier chapters) and the East Asian economies of the periphery (discussed in this chapter) emerge from the chronology spanning the crisis origins in the latter, and their brief upswing followed by poor growth performance in 2001. First, the boom in the East Asian periphery was fed by speculative investors from outside who simultaneously withdrew their cash thus aggravating

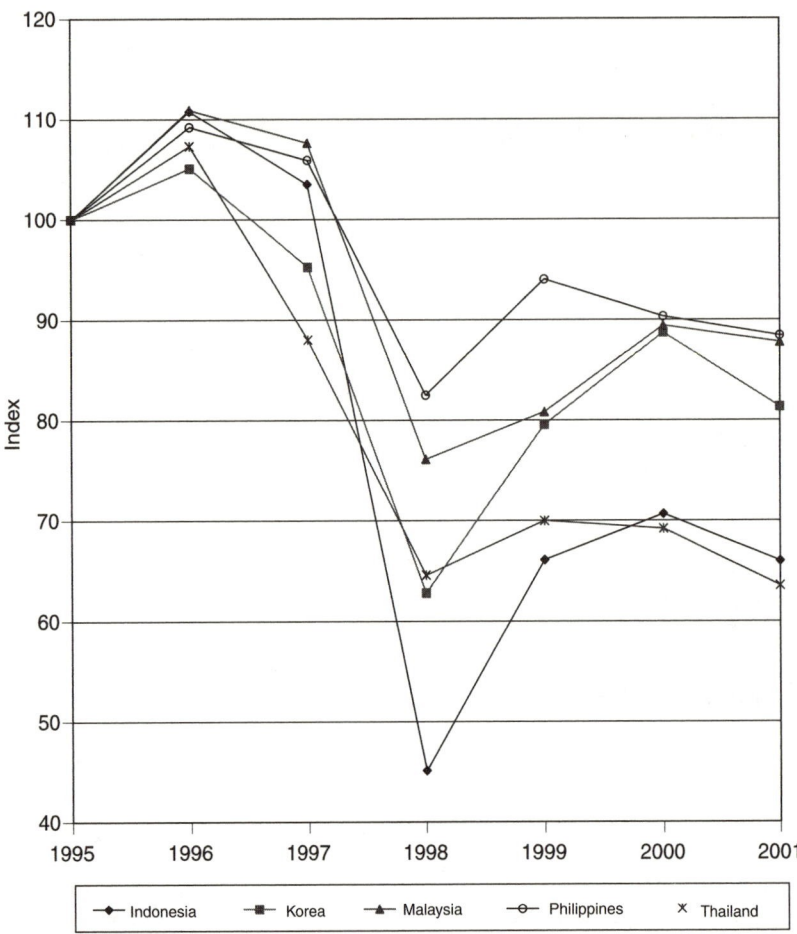

Figure 6.2. Gross domestic product per head. Index, 1995 = 100. *Source:* Economist Intelligence Unit.

the currency collapses and economic declines. Second, their policy makers (except in Malaysia) turned to the IMF, an external rescuer, for financial support inviting extreme recessionary consequences in its trail: the size of the bailout package was inadequate and the policy mandate was severely procyclical. (I assess IMF bailout activity at length in chapter 11.) By contrast, the U.S. and Japanese economic expansions and contractions were internally driven as were the homegrown stimulus policies during the latter phase that succeeded in the U.S. as a result of its special autonomous features, and failed in Japan because of self-imposed vacillations. Finally, the downturn of the East Asian economies in 2000, continuing

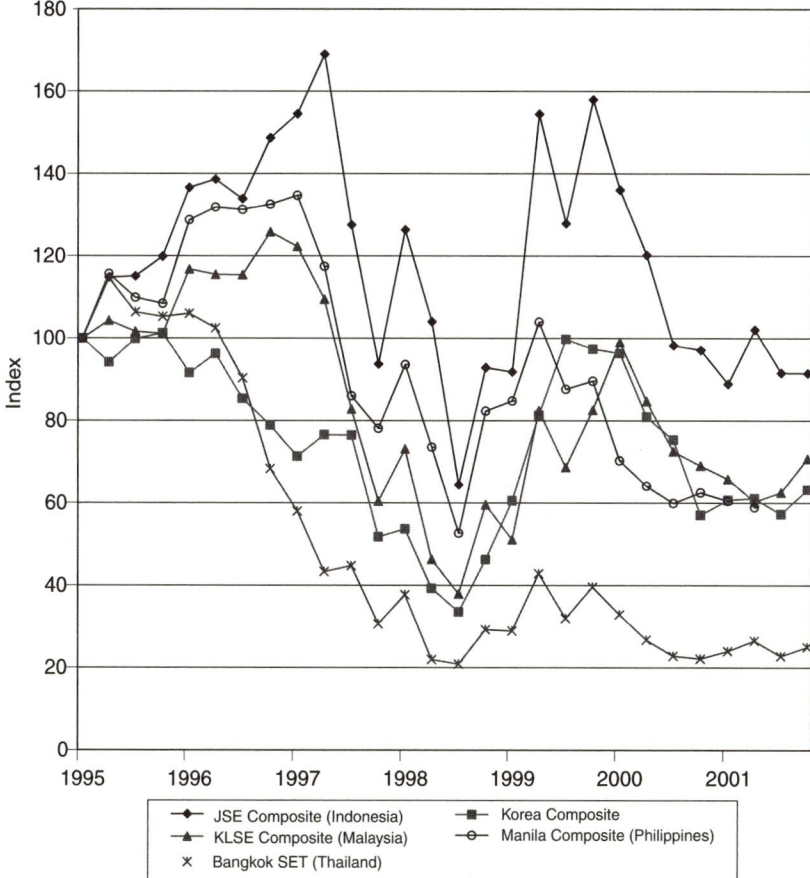

Figure 6.3. Stock market indexes. Rebased, 1995 = 100. *Source:* Economist Intelligence Unit.

into early 2002, was again externally driven by a drop in their exports to the synchronized slowdown in the U.S., the European Union, and Japan. It raises an important analytical issue however of the difference between this trade-induced transmission and the 1998 financial contagion that spread from Bangkok to Brasilia via Moscow, although both were similar in being imposed from outside. The virus that caused the Asian crisis and transmitted it to Russia and Brazil could be traced to a common external trigger and explained in terms of an exogenous transmission mechanism. Before turning to an in-depth contagion analysis in chapter 10, I address the impact of the Asian financial and currency turmoil on the Russian ruble (in chapter 7) and on the Brazilian *real* (in chapter 8). As I explain in

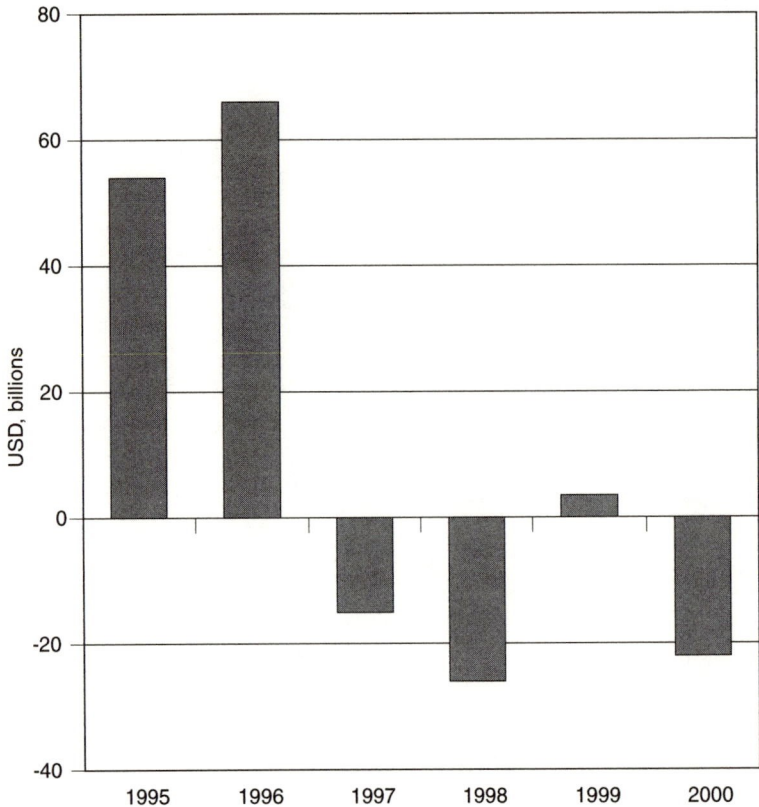

Figure 6.4. Capital flows into the East Asian economies. Flows into Indonesia, Korea, Malaysia, Philippines, and Thailand, in billion U.S. dollars. *Source: Financial Times.*

the next chapter, massive short-term foreign debts of commercial banks, treasury inability to raise resources to pay mounting interest charges, declining oil prices, and continuing political wrangling in the midst of an escalating financial crisis interacted with one another and contributed to the ruble meltdown of August 1998.

Notes

1. See Corsetti et al. (1998), Radelet and Sachs (1998), Wade (1998b), and Wong (1998) for details of the crisis onset and its spread. Crisis chronologies are also available on the Internet, at two Web sites in particular, compiled by Nouriel Roubini of New York University (http://pages.stern/nyu.edu/~nroubini) and Kar-

yiu Wong of the University of Washington (*http://faculty.washington.edu/karyiu/*). These are put together from crisis monitoring in sources such as the *Far Eastern Economic Review*, the *Economist*, *Business Week*, Reuters, the *Wall Street Journal*, the *New York Times*, CNNfn, the *Financial Times*, and Bloomberg. This chapter draws from Roubini and Wong.

2. Kaplan and Ke (1999) attribute the prime minister's exceptional political strength to his creation, via deliberate preferential treatment over three decades, of a corporate class of native Malays that, he feared, an IMF-led program would seek to dismantle.

3. According to Kaplan and Ke (1999), directed lending by banks in Malaysia was less than in South Korea and the capital/asset ratios of banks were less unfavorable than in Thai, Indonesian, and South Korean banks.

4. Radelet and Sachs (1998) argue that unfavorable exchange rate movements rather than insufficient reform commitment by the government, as suggested by the IMF and the U.S. Treasury, contributed to budgetary problems. Declining currencies raised repayment costs of dollar debts.

5. Arrangements for bilateral currency swaps, in which the signatories agreed to lend each other part of their hard currency reserves if their currencies came under attack, proliferated. Actual swaps might not be necessary because the currencies operated under floating regimes. However, ASEAN + 3 needed to overcome their long-standing animosities and significant economic disparities before they could form a free trade area or plan a monetary union. The first step required a freeing of their trade along multilateral lines. Actual economic cooperation among ASEAN +3 was expected to remain anemic and proceed in a pell-mell fashion despite occasional euphoria in the region and enthusiastic pronouncements by some of its leaders.

7

The Ruble Collapses in August 1998

Russia, marked by a fragile economy in the midst of continuing political instability, was an exception among emerging market economies. Its fundamentals were weak, its institutional underpinning was inadequate for the challenges of a market economy, and its politics were volatile. These three features coalesced into a financial meltdown when the government of Prime Minister Sergei Kiriyenko devalued the ruble on August 17, 1998, defaulted on the government's domestic debt, and declared a moratorium on payments by Russian commercial banks to foreign creditors. As a result, inflation control, a stable ruble, and a fragile turnaround of gross domestic product (GDP) growth, visible toward the end of 1997, came to a sudden halt.

The dismissal of the Kiriyenko government on August 23 was followed by dizzying nominations by President Yeltsin and confirmations by the Duma (lower house of the parliament) of three prime ministers in the span of less than a year. The government of Prime Minister Vladimir Putin, a caretaker body appointed on the eve of the forthcoming December 19, 1999 parliamentary elections to be followed by the March 26, 2000 presidential elections, could not be expected to launch major policy changes.

However, after Putin's election to the presidency, a series of legislative initiatives involving the tightening of federal authority, adoption of simplified personal tax rates and customs duties, and market transactions in land unfolded in measured steps. The economy grew at a brisk 8 percent in 2000 in response to the relative price changes in favor of domestic items following the sharp depreciation of the ruble. The budget posted a surplus as higher oil prices in world markets augmented budgetary revenues from oil companies enabling the treasury to pay off debt obligations that stood at one ruble out of four in the 2001 budget. Putin's active foreign policy moves, calculated to boost sales of defense industry hardware in Russia's traditional markets of China, Cuba, India, Iran, and Vietnam, were also expected to complement industrial revival. These gains in turn served to provide relief to the economy that had registered policy and performance pluses since 1992 (that I analyze subsequently), but was still constrained in 2002 by an appreciating real exchange rate, significant debt burden, and slow reform momentum. In particular, despite the leadership's antiterrorist alliance with the West, an implicit coalition of political, bureaucratic, left-wing legislative, and corporate forces constrained substantial flows of foreign direct investment that could help transform the Russian banking and energy sectors and manufacturing activity.

The Push to a Liberal Market Transition in 1992

At the very outset, the balance sheet of reform from its onset in January 1992 to the financial setback of August 1998 showed an array of policy pluses. Despite the fractured politics and institutional vacuum, several policies were pushed through. Most prices, except those of monopoly suppliers, among them the energy sector and the railroads, were freed from their administered levels. Inflation was brought down to annual single digit toward the end of 1997 and foreign trade was liberalized. By early 1998, import duties averaged 14 percent, export quotas had been largely removed, and export taxes lowered. Finally, most assets, including farms, were converted into joint stock companies with diversified stock ownership. Small businesses, shops, and trading outlets were sold off or auctioned. The market orientation of the Russian policy agenda however aroused controversies because of its enormous costs in imposing a prolonged recession on the economy and in immiserizing the masses. The process was seen as neglecting its economic and human costs altogether. It also witnessed the emergence of widespread corruption. Ultimately, the policy measures failed in staving off the collapse of the ruble and the debt default of August 1998.

The key policy decisions and specific measures that shaped economic outcomes in Russia were constrained and shaped by the political context that, in turn, evolved (unlike in the East Asian emerging market economies, with the exception of Indonesia) into a destructive mode as a result of the economic decisions that began in early 1992. The confrontational politics between the technocratic team of reformers and the left-wing lawmakers escalated from ideological differences in 1992 to unbending opposition by mid-1998, as the Duma's Communist-dominated left majority moved from "we disagree with your program" to "we will wreck your policy agenda." The initial opposition to acting Prime Minister Yegor Gaidar's shock therapy measures of January 1992 by the old Supreme Soviet (the parliament), elected in 1990 during the Communist days, had hardened into stonewalling by the left majority of the Duma that came to power in the December 1995 parliamentary elections.[1] (Four years later, the December 1999 elections brought down the Communist presence in the Duma to almost a quarter of its members.)

The Fractured Politics

The mounting political turmoil that followed the launching of shock therapy operated at three levels. The fast-paced program led to increasing polarization over time between the executive and legislative branches at the center, and between Moscow and the eighty-nine territorial units of the Russian Federation. The process also witnessed the exit and entry of cabinet ministers with President Yeltsin orchestrating an apparent centrist balance between reformers and conservatives in the government and staving off the prospects of anyone else hijacking his liberal agenda by staking a claim on the presidency. These three polarizing features fed one another in contentious interaction up to the collapse of the ruble.

The Executive Branch versus the Legislative Branch

The legislators elected to the old Russian parliament in 1990 were a mixed bag of reforming democrats, ardent Communists, and a fringe of diehard nationalists and extreme (Soviet) unionists ready to go beyond the war of words to resurrect old times. The membership was one-third reformist, one-third antireform extremists (including the Communists), and the remaining uncommitted element, known as *boloto* or marsh, that moved in either direction.

The January 1992 shock planned a sharp cutback in budget deficit to zero in the first quarter of 1992 from the 17 to 21 percent of GDP in 1991 estimated by the International Monetary Fund (IMF) via a slashing of subsidies to industries and consumers and of military procurement. The program brought out a variety of voices. Increasingly, pro-reform centrists, who were against the program's swift pace, joined ranks with the old faithful who saw it as designed to accomplish the political goal of destroying the Communist-planned system. By August 1992, the Supreme Soviet had forced the government to bail out bankrupt factories. By September 1993, it was ready to push the 1993 budget deficit to 25 percent of GDP. The escalation culminated with the dissolution of parliament, the attack on the parliament building in Moscow, and the December elections.

The Center versus the Periphery

Friction between the central government and Russia's regions and municipalities was brought out into the open over time by the hasty fiscal measures of early 1992. In the grand swoop designed to roll back the federal deficit, a number of items were summarily taken out of the budget and passed on to lower levels without a proper agreement on the principles of financial arrangements between the center and the regions. In the Soviet era, the regions had been responsible for education, health care, culture, housing, local road building, and the like, but they received the necessary funds from the center. In 1992, federal programs such as capital investments in rural areas, subsidies for livestock products, and development of local passenger transport were shifted to the regions without matching finances. The ad hoc nature of the rearrangements continued into the future. The regions were allowed to keep varying fractions of value-added and corporate taxes that they collected as the center selectively capitulated to the more vociferous claimants, further weakening the tenuous fiscal arrangements. On average, more than half of the eighty-nine Federation members unilaterally cut back their tax contributions to Moscow between 1992–97.

From local → central control

The Polarization in the Cabinet

With the 1992 initiation of reforms, Boris Yeltsin maneuvered a centrist cabinet composition just enough to keep the reform momentum going but more than adequate to forestall the emergence of a political rival. This balancing act went out of control in March 1998 with the firing of Prime Minister Viktor Chernomyrdin, who, while remaining loyal, had grown in stature, and his replacement with the young, balding, bespectacled, Bambi-like Sergei Kiriyenko. Frequent cabinet changes, actual and impending, contributed to political instability.

In sum, Russian politics had failed to settle down into a resolute give-and-take mode within and between the various branches and levels of government, the pattern continuing after the parliamentary elections of December 1993 and December 1995 and the presidential election of June 1996. In a settled democracy, the combination of a reformist president and a left-of-center parliament would perhaps herald the politics of consensus building. In Russia, the executive and legislative branches were at loggerheads. The refurbished reformist cabinet appointed in March 1997 raised hopes for a policy momentum by presenting a string of legislation for consideration of the Duma, but Russia's left-wing lawmakers scuttled it with a sustained ferocity which went beyond ideological opposition to market reforms in the initial phase.

The Duma on a War Path, March 1997–July 1998

Among the new items on the government's legislative agenda were housing reform aimed at abolishing the massive across-the-board subsidies on rents and utilities (except for the poorest) by 2003—housing subsidies annually amounted to more than the payments to the army or the police; a systematic overhaul of the pension system involving voluntary contributions by prospective pensioners in place of the existing system based on employer contributions that was busting the Pension Fund as employers put in less and less; a bold production sharing agreement (PSA) plan calculated to attract foreign investors into Russia's natural resource sector; a tax code aimed at reducing the number of taxes and their rates and numerous tax exemptions; the restructuring of Russian monopolies (among them the energy sector and the railways) combined with rational energy and railway charges. The Duma threw out most of the proposed legislation, passed an anemic PSA law granting foreign investors concessions in eight least attractive sectors with a number of strings, and attached scores of amendments to the tax code on its first reading. The pension reform plan was shelved. The government's legislative agenda was dead on arrival.

In the absence of the legislative mandate, Government expenditures remained high, the tax system lacked simple, transparent rules and reasonable rates, auction-based sale of assets was hampered, and the pricing policies of Russia's monopolies continued to be "exploitative." Legislative intransigence thus deprived inflation control and price liberalization policies of a firm, credible foundation. In particular, as I argue below, macroeconomic stabilization was marked by poor fiscal management, and inflation was brought down largely by a stringent monetary policy combined with external borrowing that was sufficiently large to raise the prospect of panic-driven outflows.

Macroeconomic Stabilization amidst Fragile Budgetary Management

Macroeconomic stabilization policies were aimed at eventually reviving economic activity under a stable inflation regime. Inflation, measured in terms of change in the consumer price index in figure 7.1, was brought down to less than 1 percent a month by September 1997 via a slowing down of money supply growth rates from quarter to quarter, as shown in figure 7.2. But budgetary management continued to be shaky. Federal budget deficit (figure 7.3) remained high, in the range of 7 to 8 percent of GDP during most of 1996–97. Two ominous structural features marked this performance. The revenues of the federal government (figure 7.4) declined from 12 percent of GDP at their highest in December 1997 to a little over 10 percent in the months prior to the meltdown. More to the point, monthly interest payments from the budget (figure 7.5), 23 percent of the revenues in January 1998, had jumped to a whopping 51 percent in July 1998. The fiscal health of the federal government was more critical

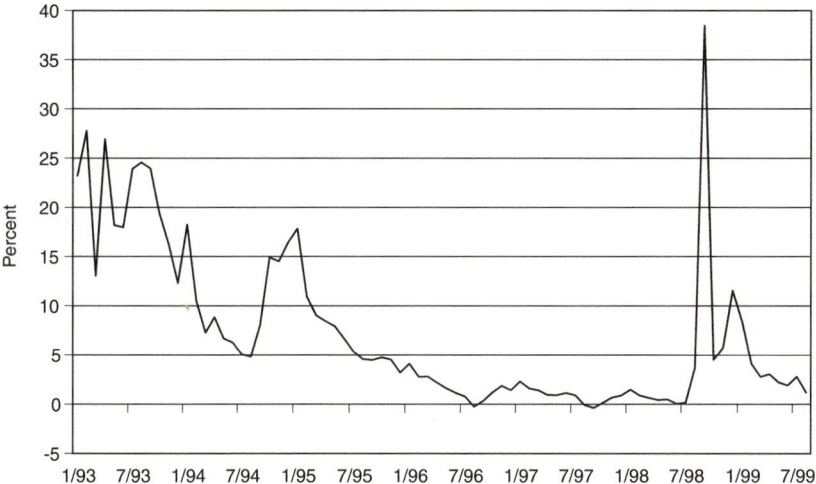

Figure 7.1. Inflation rate. Monthly percent change in consumer prices, January 1993–November 1999. *Source: Russian Economic Trends.*

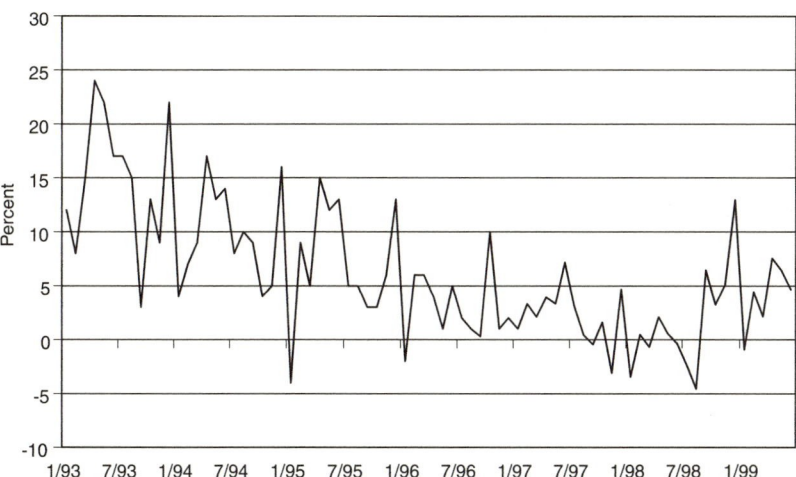

Figure 7.2. Growth rate of money supply. Monthly percentage change in M2 money supply, January 1993–June 1999. *Source: Russian Economic Trends.*

Figure 7.3. Federal budget as a percentage of gross domestic product. December 1993–June 1999. Annual data 12/93–12/95, monthly data 1/96–9/98, quarterly data 12/98–6/99. *Source: Russian Economic Trends.*

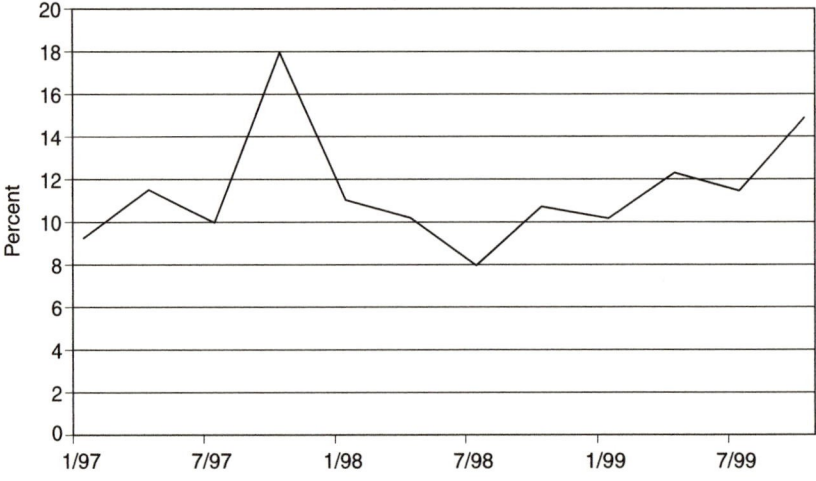

Figure 7.4. Federal revenues as a percentage of gross domestic product. January 1997–June 1999. *Source:* Economist Intelligence Unit.

than was suggested by these numbers. The government struggled to contain the deficit by diverting cash from the off-budget funds, among them the Pension Fund. It also failed to enforce timely wage payment to budget sector employees from federal funds assigned for the purpose in local budgets to be disbursed by local administrations.

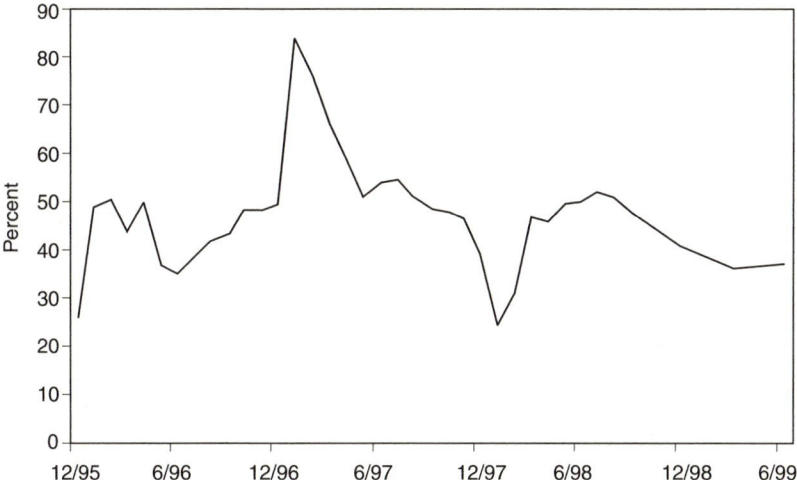

Figure 7.5. Debt burden. Federal budget interest outlays as a percentage of federal revenues. International Monetary Fund definition of revenues. *Source: Russian Economic Trends.*

Unable to raise adequate taxes and prohibited by the IMF to borrow from the Central Bank of Russia in 1995, the government turned to borrowing from the market, increasingly relying on foreigners to pick up government short-term bills (GKOs) and long-term bonds (OFZs). In the process this attracted short-term foreign funds in excess of foreign exchange resources available to finance their sudden withdrawal. At their lowest levels in the final quarter of 1997, the annualized yields on government securities averaged 25 to 30 percent, far higher than comparable rates abroad. The restrictions on foreign capital flows targeted at taking advantage of these differentials were removed: this was a colossal mistake. Thus, in 1997, the earlier requirement limiting purchases of government securities by *domestic* investors was lifted, allowing foreign speculators easy access. In November 1997, nonresident holders of GKOs signed forward contracts with the Central Bank of Russia in anticipation of a decline in the ruble following the collapse of Asian currencies. Not to be left out from gainful speculative transactions in government securities, Russian banks borrowed heavily in foreign markets, registering a rise in their foreign liabilities as a proportion of assets (mostly in domestic government securities that were to become worthless) from 7 percent in 1994 to 17 percent in 1997.

Russia was thus poised for a financial disaster at the slightest indication of a weakening ruble. The IMF-led policy agenda of unsustainable inflation control to low, single-digit annual rates by the end of 1997 lacked fiscal consolidation. This required a consensus between the reformist government and the intransigent Communist-led lawmakers in the Duma on issues ranging from the adoption of a tax code and tax rates to their effective implementation. The lessons of Russia's macroeconomic management in the years leading to the collapse of the ruble in August 1998 were writ large: Russia resembled an obese patient whose weight loss could be guaranteed only with a gradual but firm and feasible diet program under meticulous monitoring. The Russian economy was hastily being brought to macroeconomic stability via monetary control but the significant weaknesses in fundamentals of fiscal policy requiring budgetary support from short-term, foreign funds made the ruble vulnerable to a large external shock related to the unanticipated East Asian financial crisis. Moreover, the hard currency transactions were not confined to short-term external borrowing by the Russian government and banks but also allowed households to convert domestically held rubles into dollars. (I describe the hasty evolution of these policies in block 5.) The stage was thus set for an impending financial crisis spilling into a currency crisis in the event of external shocks to Russia's balance of payments.[2] In the formal analysis of Paul Krugman (1979, 1998), the Russian malaise combined elements of the first- and third-generation currency crisis models: Russian policy makers' attempts to maintain a stable ruble in the midst of a government-borrowing-financed budget deficit were overwhelmed by plummeting values of government GKOs as external shocks hit Russia's balance of payments. I also argue that, instead of the policy mistake of August 1998 requiring an unplanned, disorderly default of domestic debt and moratorium on payment of foreign commercial debt, a timely, IMF-led decision toward the end of 1997 in favor of temporary exchange controls as an emergency measure, combined with an exchange of short-term foreign debt into long-term instruments, would have been a better alternative, obviating the de facto partial and unilateral resort to controls that the moratorium and default implied.

Exogenous Shocks to Ruble Stability

These shocks appeared from two exogenous factors: the collapse of the East Asian currencies starting in mid-1997 and the decline in oil and non-ferrous metal prices that began in December of that year.

The decline in oil prices from $23 a barrel in mid-1997 to $11 a barrel a year later, accompanied by falling prices of nonferrous metals hit Russian foreign exchange earnings from these two major exports and affected its trade balance. Figure 7.6 shows the trade balance as it shrank to $2.4 billion in the first half of 1998 compared to its average range of $10 to $11 billion in the first half of the preceding three years. Combined with

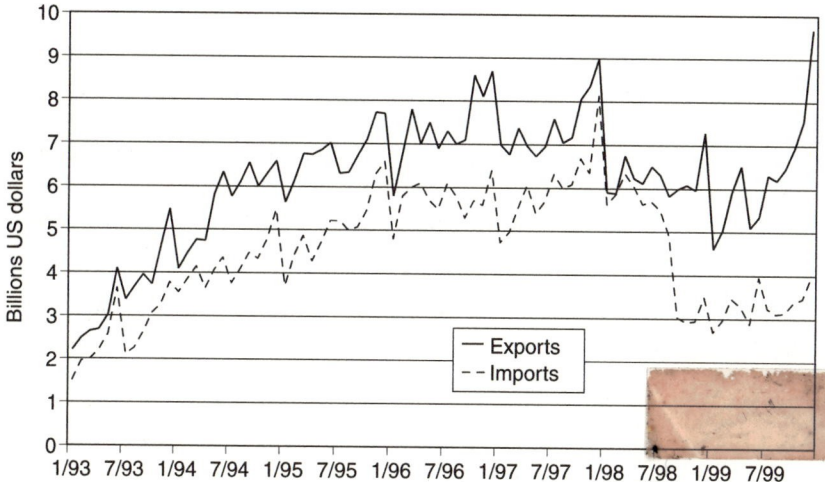

Figure 7.6. Exports and imports. January 1993–December 1999. Monthly data.
Source: Economist Intelligence Unit.

soaring interest costs of foreign borrowing, the current account balance
turned negative in the amount of $5 billion for the first half of 1998 in
contrast to positive amounts of $4 to $6 billion in the first half of the
preceding three years (Alexashenko, 1999, p. 3). The flight of nonresidents from government GKOs and the ruble could not be stopped despite
a hike of the central bank interest rate to 150 percent in June 1998. The
first installment of $4.8 billion of the IMF assistance package of $22 billion announced in July in support of the currency disappeared in two
weeks. The substantial purchases of foreign exchange by households
across Russia's major cities depressed the ruble by 10 to 15 percent in
mid-August (ibid., p. 5).

The crisis marked by the inability of the government to redeem the
GKOs held by foreigners and of the Russian banks to pay their foreign
creditors called for drastic measures.

Government Debt Default and Commercial Bank Debt Moratorium

In early August, the foreign exchange resources available to the government (after the disappearance of the IMF funding of $4.8 billion) fell
short of its ability to redeem the foreign share of the GKO-OFZ securities
that fell due by December 1998 and the foreign debt of Russian commercial banks. The former was approximately $6 billion, and the latter $16

billion, of which the critical part of $6 billion was forward currency contracts with nonresident investors in GKOs.

The foreign exchange liabilities of Russian banks threatened to destroy their balance sheets. As with banks and financial institutions in East Asia, their debts, mostly short-term of 6- to 9-month duration, were backed by fast depreciating government securities and had cross-default clauses holding a bank responsible for the debt default of another bank. Facing substantial margin calls and refusal of creditors to roll over their liabilities, they bought foreign exchange to repay debts, in the process drying up their liquidity and creating interbank loan defaults.

The gross foreign exchange reserves (excluding gold) with the central bank for clearing the foreign short-term obligations of $22 billion noted above (not counting public demand for dollars) averaged $10 billion. At the same time, all available sources of external financing had dried up. With eurobond spreads exceeding 700 points, the Ministry of Finance could not borrow abroad; the government could not find investors to buy its stake in privatized companies (Alexashenko, 1999, p. 6). The government could either borrow directly from the Central Bank of Russia after getting the legal authorization from the Duma, start a deluge of currency emission, and wreck macroeconomic stability; or it could mandate a nonvoluntary restructuring of the short-term debt. It chose the latter course.

The measures implied a default by the government on its GKO debt (domestic and foreign) and a ninety-day moratorium, agreed by the IMF, on foreign debt payment by Russian banks. The original GKO-debt restructuring plan had a dual approach allowing conversion of foreign-held GKOs into dollar-denominated securities with no immediate cash payment, and allowing 20 to 25 percent cash payment to resident holders, mostly banks, to bolster their liquidity. Having initially agreed with this unequal treatment approach, the IMF changed its position, evidently under pressure from the U.S. Treasury. The final plan, allowing 20 percent cash payment to all investors, imposed a higher burden on the Russian budget forcing it to generate the cash via inflationary means (ibid., 1999, p. 7).

Was Ruble Devaluation a Desirable Option?

Could Russia's policy makers have avoided these drastic measures if they had abandoned defending the currency and devalued it in time? The protagonists of devaluation summarized in Popov (1999) argued that the ruble was overvalued in real terms, and that the Central Bank of Russia mistakenly stuck to its policy of defending the ruble band despite losing massive foreign exchange reserves. The substantial 1993–94 real appreci-

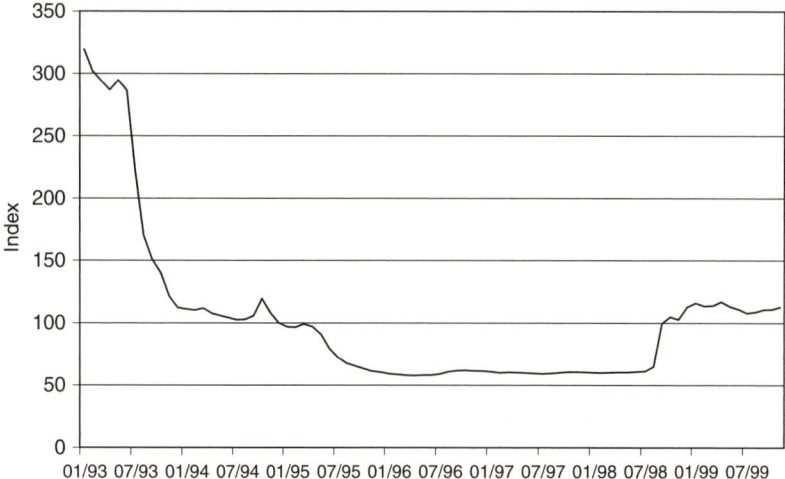

Figure 7.7. Real exchange rate. Index, 1994 = 100. A declining trend represents real appreciation of the ruble. *Source: Russian Economic Trends.*

ation of the ruble (figure 7.7) under a managed-float regime was designed to rein in inflation from 2000-plus percent of 1992 to a double-digit 95 percent in 1995. The nominal exchange rate of the ruble was allowed to depreciate at a lower rate than the inflation rate differential between the Russian and U.S. economies. This exchange rate regime, tilted in the direction of inflation control at the expense of maintaining the competitiveness of Russian tradables, also bridged the gap between the highly depreciated ruble following the massive currency emission of 1992 and its purchasing power parity rate (Desai, 1998). The policy stance was moderated subsequently: the real exchange rate, shown in figure 7.7, remained constant under a shifting nominal ruble band regime (Desai, 1997). When the ruble came under attack in November 1997 and June 1998, the government considered letting the ruble float but chose instead to defend the band, losing $6 billion and $5 billion, respectively, in the process (Alexashenko, 1999, p. 12).

Could it have avoided the catastrophe if it had settled for a 15 to 20 percent devaluation in, say, mid-November, 1997? I agree with Alexashenko that, while marginally improving the competitiveness of Russian goods, it would have pushed up the ruble cost in the budget of servicing Russia's foreign debt and compelled nonresidents to sell their GKOs right away, adding to loss of confidence in the currency destabilizing it further. In other words, a devaluation of the ruble in late 1997 could have been a feasible option if it were linked with an IMF-led timely and orderly restructuring of Russia's sovereign and commercial bank debt. Russia's policy makers did not manage to get financial support from the IMF despite repeated requests in November 1997 and February and March 1998. The support that did come in July 1998— in the amount of only $4.8 billion—was too little and too late. Through the crisis months, Russia's treasury, short of cash, sought and failed to raise cash at home and abroad. At the same time, Russian politics continued to be volatile. President Yeltsin sacked Prime Minister Chernomyrdin in March in the midst of financial turmoil. The Duma merrily debated the confirmation of the new appointee, Sergei Kiriyenko, for the full month of April. Having confirmed his appointment under the threat of a parliamentary dissolution by Yeltsin, it turned down his austerity budget in July.

Restoring Exchange Controls, Russian Style

Ultimately, therefore, the policy makers turned to debt default and moratorium, in fact overturning the de facto convertibility of the earlier period. With a devaluation inappropriate, and with inadequate external support from the IMF and with no assistance from other sources, Russian authorities were left without an option. The 90-day moratorium legally exempted Russian banks from clearing their margin calls and forward contracts. The Central Bank of Russia was allowed by law to ban these transactions (Alexashenko, 1999, p.12). In the process, it damaged the economy's credit rating and future borrowing potential. The question must then be raised: Was a better option not available, even if the IMF could not bring itself to increase its assistance above $ 4.8 billion? I would argue that Russia did have the choice of adopting temporary exchange controls toward the end of 1997 as an emergency measure supplemented by conversion of short-term foreign debt into long-term obligations with IMF and U.S. Treasury sanction and linked with an orderly devaluation of the ruble. This would have been less damaging than the de facto and partial exchange control, and the disorderly and unilateral moratorium and default of August 1998.

Which Way Next?

The default put the economy back to the start of 1995, with limited maneuverability for a sustained economic recovery in the face of uncertain macroeconomic stabilization, a heavier debt burden, a banking system in disarray, and shattered investor confidence. Inflation in 1998 jumped to 100 percent.

Two events held out hopes for measured macroeconomic stabilization and economic recovery as the millennium ended. The December 1999 parliamentary elections resulted in a centrist Duma with substantially diminished representation of the Communist Party of the Russian Federation and the emergence of President Putin's Unity block combined with the reformist Union of Right Forces as major contenders in legislative decision making. The centrist composition of the Duma offered prospects for the new lawmakers' acceptance of the reformist legislation noted above that the old Duma had scuttled in 1997. Yeltsin's resignation on December 31, 1999, and the election of Vladimir Putin in March 2000 as the Russian president, reflecting the electorate's support for the Chechen war as well as its desire for a strong, stable, and predictable leader, added to the chances of a pro-reform alliance between the executive and legislative branches.

As a result, the old model of Russian reform, according to which the international financial institutions negotiated the policy details with successive reformist governments that in turn sought to implement them via presidential decrees and government resolutions to the neglect of the legislative watchdogs in the Duma, had in all probability disappeared from the scene. Crafting a consensus with the Duma that managed nonetheless to keep reforms on track required realistic policy proposals. Thus, for example, the Russian economy could not be expected to reach the nirvana of a single-digit inflation rate despite the surplus primary budgets of 2000 and 2001 resulting from sumptuous revenue flows from high oil prices— the monumental evidence of the 1995–98 years provided a stark lesson in that regard. A credible policy agenda marking low double-digit inflation rates with corresponding targets of monetary growth rates and budget deficits over a period of three to five years would create greater confidence about its implementation and hence produce stable outcomes than the unrealistically ambitious macroeconomic targets of the past favored by the IMF.

Second, the prolonged real appreciation of the ruble in the interest of inflation control that put Russian tradables at a competitive disadvantage turned into a real depreciation in 1999 (see figure 7.7) as the ruble tumbled from six rubles to a dollar in the first half of 1998 to twenty-six to twenty-eight rubles in the subsequent months, generating sizeable price advantages for domestic import substitutes.[3] The domestic price structure, shown in figure 7.8 shifted radically in response, displaying a changed pattern of competitive advantage to domestic producers. Thus, the producer price indexes of electrical power, construction materials, and fuel industries ranking in that order at the top in the pre-August 1998 phase had moved in the middle with the fuel price index subsequently close to the bottom. By contrast, nonferrous metallurgy index, earlier at

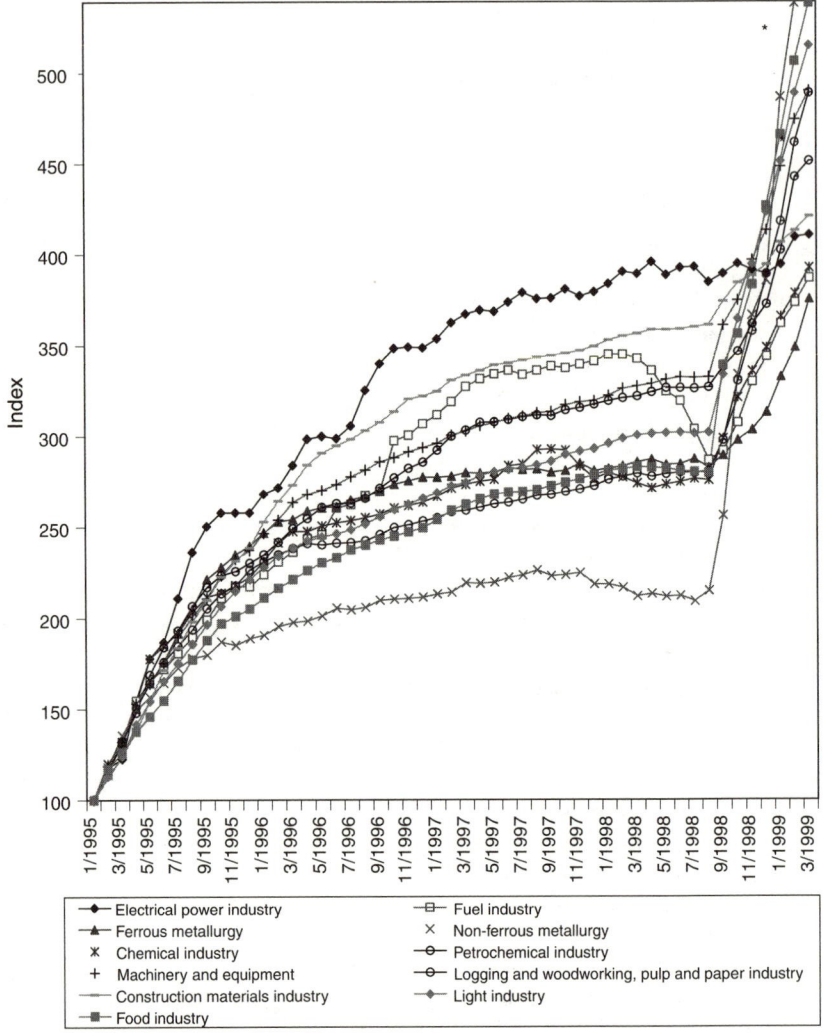

Figure 7.8. Producer price index, January 1995 = 100. Asterisk indicates that the value for nonferrous metallurgy for March 1999 is 566. *Source:* Goskomstat.

the bottom, was later at the top. Food and light industry indexes of concern to consumers had moved to the second and third highest positions in the second period from their close-to-bottom rankings in the first phase. Ferrous metallurgy index, earlier in the middle, later slumped to the bottom. Rendered noncompetitive by substantial price disadvantages vis-á-vis imported items in the old days, several "virtual" producers turned into "real" performers, laying to rest the blanket notion of a virtual economy. The economy registered a growth rate of 8 percent in 2000, one of the highest since the Second World War. The conversion of the pulse of recovery into sustained growth however was impeded in 2001 by the emergence of potentially discouraging economic signals, lack of reform momentum especially in the banking sector, weak implementation of enacted laws, and an implicit coalition of domestic lobbies bent on slowing substantial entry of foreign investment in the economy.

The Slowing Economy in 2001

The economy was expected to grow at lower rates, (actual) 5 percent in 2001 and 4 percent in 2002, post high inflation rates of up to 18 percent, and allocate increasing shares from the primary budget surplus for debt repayment at one ruble out of every three by 2003. The continuing inflow of foreign exchange in the Central Bank of Russia from higher oil earnings, reminiscent of the "Dutch Disease,"[4] resulted in money supply growth, and heightened inflationary pressures that the central bank was unable to control via sterilization by issuing bonds for which there were few takers. With inflation marching ahead of the nominal exchange rate of the ruble, the real appreciation of the currency put the Russian manufacturing sector at a competitive disadvantage vis-à-vis imports. At the same time, any softening of oil prices threatened Russia's budgetary revenues and debt repayment potential: the oil sector contributed up to 30 percent of revenue inflows in the budget.

Economic reforms, that could push growth into a sustained, higher trajectory, unfolded at a measured pace in 2000 and continued without a sense of urgency in 2001 and 2002.

Slow-Track Economic Reform

Among the major reforms were the introduction of the low, uniform personal income tax rate at 13 percent; the lowering of the corporate tax rate (effective January 1, 2002) from 34 percent to 25 percent; the significant trimming of off-budget contributions by industry; and the streamlining of customs duties. Important legislation of 2001 related to sales-purchases of urban land and reform of the judiciary and the labor market. The Federal Commission for the Securities Market prepared a draft code for the Duma's consideration in 2002 designed to protect shareholder rights and promote corporate governance practices by Russian companies with a view to promoting investment in the economy. The Duma also passed a law allowing transactions in agricultural land. It assigned a decision-making role to regional authorities and limited foreign participation in land purchases.

There was little progress however in scaling back Soviet-era budget subsidization of apartment rents and utility charges for households, and in reforming and stabilizing the moribund banking system. Gazprom, the natural gas supplier, and United Energy Systems (UES), the electricity company, both monopolies which could undertake efficient restructuring by charging higher prices to private consumers and industry, were held back by the government which worried about the impact of the price increases on inflation and the appreciating ruble.[5] The continuation of the subsidies in the budget affected fiscal management, and the absence of banking services deprived small businesses of loan financing. The Agency for Reconstructing Commercial Organizations (ARCO) had scant resources for recapitalizing banks, lacked systematic norms for the purpose, and had conflicting authority with the Central Bank of Russia which was under the tight grip of Victor Gerashchenko, once described as "the world's worst central banker." His enforced resignation in March 2002 raised hopes for starting the much-needed and long-delayed commercial bank reforms. Russia's small businesses were also reined in by a nightmare of licensing procedures whose continuation was favored by the vast network of bureaucrats in the ministries inherited from the Communist days. An entrepreneur needed up to fifty signatures before he or she could launch a small to medium-sized business! In mid-2001, the efforts to reconstruct UES by expediting licenses to new entrants in power generation encountered bureaucratic intransigence. The licensing requirements were mostly retained.

A bigger problem arose from the gargantuan gap between laws and their implementation.

The Gap between Laws on Books and Laws in Practice

New laws designed to introduce market economy norms could not obliterate the attitudes and practices of old times. Few managers were inclined to fire workers under the authority granted them by the new labor laws. Fewer judges, committed to the welfare orientation of socialist days, were ready to uphold such job losses. Nor could the workers relocate to new jobs in the absence of a functioning labor market and available housing. The institutional vacuum, the pervasiveness of old attitudes, and the daunting practical problems of enforcing existing laws interacted to create a legendary environment of lawlessness and corruption that the well placed in the world of Russian business, bureaucracy, and politics fully exploited and enlarged. They also facilitated the emergence of a handful of oligarchs who established a firm hold over specific sectors of the economy via means that were illegal at best and criminal at worst.

The Antiforeign Investment Coalition

Nowhere was this practice more prevalent than in Russian oil and metals, which underwent a ruthless process of mergers and acquisitions marked by asset grabbing and violation of shareholders' rights, a consolidation which proceeded apace while President Putin talked about a "law-based state" and a "dictatorship of laws." It endowed the new owners with the competitive clout and the negotiating potential to invite foreign investors on their terms. There was not a whimper from the Kremlin when the oligarch Oleg Deripaska captured 70 percent of Russia's aluminum industry. The president also turned down German Chancellor Gerhard Shroeder's suggestion that a fraction of Russia's Soviet-era debt owed to Germany be converted into equity in Russian companies. (At the same time, Russian negotiators were keen to convert the debt owed by buyers of Russian natural gas in Georgia and Moldavia into equity ownership in their debtors' companies.) The ministry bureaucrats also favored retaining the licensing procedures that hampered the growth of small and medium businesses desiring participation of foreign investors. This authoritarian-corporatist-bureaucratized nexus had a positive nod from Russian legislators on the left who opposed unrestricted flows of foreign direct investment on ideological grounds. The proposal by the U.S.-Russia Business Council to work up a legislative framework to promote long-term investment flows in Russia's energy sector via PSAs did not make significant headway in 1997 (as I have noted earlier) because it was viewed by the Communist legislators, in particular, as an American takeover bid to capture Russia's energy sector. U.S. Treasury Secretary Paul O'Neill's suggestion in July 2001 that special investment zones, in which foreign investors could be provided exclusive investment guarantees, did not gain acceptance either. As a result, foreign investment flows remained a political issue on which the Russian president, the legislators and bureaucrats, and Russian big business continued presenting a united front of extreme caution. Western business could only hope to get limited entry on a factory-by-factory basis via long-term, time-consuming negotiations in which the foreign partner was generally constrained to utilize existing capacities and skilled workforce.

This calculated approach prevailed in the post–antiterrorist-campaign phase of increased Russian-Western togetherness. Politically Russia was stable. President Putin's popularity rating remained high at 70 percent.

But Resisted foreign inflows

However, he held back from launching dramatic economic initiatives despite centralized federal authority and a pliant legislature in Moscow. The prospects for a decisive cleanup of across-the-board entitlements to households from the budget, a speedy restoration of functioning banks, and a fast-paced restructuring of Russian companies (among them the energy and natural gas monopolies) with active foreign participation, continued to be limited. Even if foreign investors' rights could be legally guaranteed, the implicit collusion among Russia's big business (who would welcome foreign investors only on their terms), its left-wing legislators (who would oppose them on ideological grounds), and its widely scattered bureaucrats (who would only grudgingly part with their restrictive licensing privileges) was poised to limit foreign inflows of management expertise and technology. The Russian president, a pragmatic politician and strategic gradualist, with no challenger in sight, would perhaps embark on these urgent initiatives after the presidential elections of March 2004.

By contrast, Brazil's outward orientation to foreign direct investment flows placed its policy makers at an advantage in sorting out problems of the government's fiscal deficit spilling into a current account imbalance (which I analyze in the next chapter) when the *real* was threatened with a ruble-infected collapse in 1998.

Notes

1. For more details, see Desai (1994, 1995a).

2. By contrast, privatization of Russian assets, which began on October 1, 1992 with the distribution of vouchers in the amount of 10,000 rubles each that the recipients could use for acquiring company stocks, was not responsible for the ruble's meltdown on August 17, 1998. The program, fully indigenous in design and implementation, was spearheaded by the ideological motivation to banish the state from asset ownership and by the tactical necessity to keep the reform momentum alive. As macroeconomic stabilization faltered by mid-1992, a new reform front was opened up. The scheme to sell vouchers to every Russian man, woman, and child, originally planned for 1993, was brought forward in October 1992, enticing one and all to asset ownership and instant wealth. In effect a boondoggle, the voucher program gave a resounding "yes" to Boris Yeltsin and his reforms in the subsequent April 1993 referendum. In the next phase, the program reached its climax in the spring of 1996 when the "semibankiri" (the seven bankers) floated the "loans for shares" scheme with a promise to manage (and subsequently own) part of government stock in some of Russia's lucrative companies in exchange for credits to the cash-strapped treasury. The impact of this second phase of privatization, which was thus undertaken to support the unsustainable budget deficit targets imposed by the IMF, was however socially devastating. It was seen as a corrupt scheme to enrich a few at the expense of the many, while

depriving the masses of their legitimate share in assets created collectively in Soviet days. In the end, the people got potato patches to subsist on. Details are in Desai (1995b and 1999).

3. Rodrik (2000, pp. 8–9) emphasizes the contribution of real exchange rate depreciation in setting off growth spurts in a number of countries in the last two decades.

4. According to Corden (1984, p. 359), "The term Dutch Disease refers to the adverse effects on Dutch manufacturing of the natural gas discoveries of the nineteen sixties, especially through the subsequent appreciation of the Dutch real exchange rate." The booming oil exports resulting in the real appreciation of the ruble similarly contributed to the cost disadvantage of Russian manufacturing from 2001.

5. The World Trade Organization's working party on Russia's entry into the organization suggested that Russian energy charges at 25 to 30 percent of world prices afforded a cost advantage to the country's manufactured exports in world exports.

Q: how did ruble collapse because of Asian crisis?

Block 5

The Ruble: Premature Capital Account Convertibility

— Russia had different ex∆ rates?

THE RUBLE THAT traded at 6 rubles for a dollar in the first half of 1998 exchanged for 26 to 28 rubles toward the end of 1999. What went wrong?

August 17 '98: Ruble collapse

The Background

The ruble's course spanned two phases: the first one from 1992 to August 17, 1998, when it was sharply devalued, witnessed its liberalization from a variety of exchange controls operated by the Central Bank of Russia. Some exchange controls were restored subsequently. The rules governing current account transactions for exporters and importers were simplified and relaxed gradually in the first phase.

Current Account Transactions

Foreign exchange auctions, which appeared in Moscow in early 1991, provided dollar sources for importers and sales outlets for exporters. The Moscow Interbank Currency Exchange (MICEX) began trading the dollar once a week on January 8, 1991. Initially, a few banks participated with small offerings and the central bank operated with substantial intervention. The resulting interbank exchange rate, hardly a market rate of exchange, was influenced by enterprises' limited access to the auctions, central bank restrictions, and its intervention in the auctions. Despite these limitations, the proliferating currency exchanges opened alternatives for exporters and importers. Having carried out the mandatory surrender of 50 percent of foreign exchange earnings to the central bank at a less than favorable rate, exporters could sell their remaining holdings on the MICEX, or spend them on imports, or deposit them, as required by law, in their resident bank accounts. Importers could buy foreign exchange at the market rate from the MICEX, or at a subsidized rate from the central bank for importing essential items.

A major change in these arrangements was introduced by the government of acting Prime Minister Yegor Gaidar when, on July 1, 1992, it enacted measures to unify the exchange rate for current account transactions. Furthermore, the exchange rate of the ruble in terms of the dollar was allowed to vary and followed the quotations, twice a week, of the MICEX.

Changes occurred on all fronts in 1993 and continued in 1994. From July 1, exporters were required to surrender half their export earnings directly to the market through their banks instead of to the central bank. Despite this compulsory surrender requirement, the repatriation of foreign exchange earnings continued to be a major concern of policy makers. As for imports, the exchange rate coefficients (favoring imports of essential commodities such as baby food) were abolished in 1993.

Thus, a flexible, current-account-convertible and unified exchange rate was in place in Russia at the start of 1994. The managed float (until July 1, 1995) and the crawling corridor regimes thereafter operated under selective convertibility of the ruble: exporters could keep foreign exchange abroad in specified amounts with the permission of the central bank bringing home the rest and converting it into rubles.

Capital account transactions for residents and nonresidents, individuals and corporate entities, were relaxed gradually and selectively.

Arrangements with Regard to Capital Account Transactions

Russian *citizens* were allowed to open foreign exchange accounts and deposit foreign exchange (which they could buy from authorized foreign exchange bureaus operating in large cities) in resident banks. Residents traveling abroad could take foreign exchange with them permitted by the central bank, which raised the amounts from time to time. *Resident corporate entities,* enterprises, for example, needed to acquire a license and approval from the central bank in order to borrow abroad. Enterprises were not allowed to keep accounts in foreign banks, including branches of Russian banks, without central bank authorization. Finally, Russian commercial banks that had a general foreign exchange license did not require a license to borrow abroad, maintain a foreign account, or import and export foreign currency, banknotes, bonds, and securities. These banks also could carry out these transactions for other authorized banks. This was a major legal conduit through which enterprises could transfer ruble earnings into dollars by depositing the former into Russian banks licensed to carry out transactions with foreign banks and companies.

Detailed rules also existed for foreign exchange transactions by *nonresident individuals* and *corporate entities*. (Details are in Desai, 1997.) These arrangements relating to current account convertibility for exporters and importers and capital account transactions for Russian corporate entities opened up massive opportunities for *legal* holdings of foreign exchange earnings abroad and of permissible outflows from Russia of rubles (converted into dollars) by Russian companies.

Policy Rules and Permissible Capital Outflows

First, Russian citizens could freely convert rubles into dollars which they were required to keep at home or in a Russian bank. The deliberate "dollarization" of the economy was perhaps encouraged with a view to fill treasury coffers with greenbacks when people eventually exchanged them for rubles as market reforms took hold. Illegal outflows by citizens in suitcases or with departing friends who traveled abroad were minuscule compared to transfers by companies via banks as described below.

Second, Russian companies could convert their ruble earnings into dollars in MICEX and deposit them into a bank that had the license to hold dollars abroad. If they transferred the cash before paying a corporate tax, they violated Russia's tax law but not the foreign exchange regulation.

Third, exporters were required to bring most of their foreign exchange earnings back home, keeping the rest abroad with central bank permission. The repatriation requirement encouraged exporters to understate their foreign exchange earnings by procuring a false invoice for Russian customs authorities from a foreign partner while depositing the extra earnings in a foreign bank. The concealment arising from under-invoiced exports implied an infringement of Russian tax laws and exchange control regulations.

Fourth, Russian importers were tempted as well to under-invoice imports thereby paying lower import duties (averaging 14 percent in early 1998) and breaking Russian customs regulations. They managed to pay their foreign suppliers the additional amounts via accounts held in offshore companies.

These arrangements resulted in legal capital outflows (in the second feature noted above) that could not be distinguished from illegal transactions (as described in the last two activities). The illegal drain of foreign exchange took additional forms. Russian traders who bought arms and weaponry at favorable prices from generals departing from the former German Democratic Republic sold them to arms merchants dealing with Iraq or Libya and deposited the dollar cash in an offshore bank. Russian middlemen, who extorted payments from Russian exporters based in Italy (who bought consumer goods in Italy for shipment to Russia), deposited the cash in offshore banks. Russian mafia collected levies from Russian prostitutes operating from Bulgaria to Bangkok. These bounties, defined as criminal money mingled with legal and illegal flows as the cash, traveled from several accounts and landed in a U.S. bank. In practice, they could only be distinguished on the basis of a voluminous paper trail involving various operators, agencies, and banks located in various countries requiring cooperation of several governments including, above all, the Russian state.

Fifth, Russia's authorized banks borrowed short-term abroad and invested in government treasury bills (GKOs) and long-term bonds that offered a substantially higher return. Their foreign currency liabilities were backed by ruble-denominated government paper of varying duration that started losing its value as the ruble began its decline in early 1998. In this respect, the loan transactions of Russian banks were similar to East Asian banks and financial companies which borrowed short-term abroad accumulating hard currency debts, and loaned long term to domestic borrowers thereby acquiring local assets of questionable worth.

Sixth, the rule prohibiting foreign entities from holding Russian government paper was abolished in 1997. In practice, therefore, a foreigner who bought Russian government bonds could dump them, convert the rubles into dollars, and walk out if he or she desired. The overly hasty inflation control policy, that was unsustainable in view of the fragile budgetary management (as I argued in chapter 7), imposed unmanageable budget deficit norms on the government that sought to fulfill them by letting foreign speculators invest in short-term treasury bills.

These arrangements contributed to massive capital outflows by Russian banks and businesses *before* Russia was hit by the exodus of foreign investors that began in November 1997 as a result of the East Asian crisis. A significant fraction of the pre-crisis outflow by Russian companies (which has continued) was induced by the decision allowing some banks to deal in foreign exchange transactions and was therefore legal. This hasty policy move, devoid of an orderly liberalizing sequence which I described in block 3, sets Russia apart from a number of emerging market economies. Again, the East Asian economies undertook their capital account liberalization during years marked by strong fundamentals of high growth and

low inflation rates, healthy government budgets, and stable governments. There was some backtracking in the process (which I described in block 3), but none of the countries experienced Russian-
style capital outflows engineered by local businesses during their
pre-crisis liberalization phase: domestic capital stayed in although
it could step out. From that perspective, Russia was not ready for
capital mobility legally sanctioned through banks. On the other
hand, emerging market economies, such as China and India, gradually lifted controls on foreign exchange transactions by commercial
banks for their business clients and on retention of foreign exchange
earnings by exporters in foreign banks. These arrangements were
not foolproof, but they did prevent the deluge of capital outflow
undertaken by Russian private business.

The Post–August 1998 Situation

The policy rules related to export and import transactions and banking sector activities.

Exporters must bring back 75 percent of foreign exchange earnings (cut back to 50 percent in 2001) and sell it in MICEX. Importers must deposit the full ruble value of their imports with the central
bank until the goods arrived in Russia. Licensing fees prevailed for
importing alcohol, audio-visual equipment, large color televisions,
and so forth, that were again subject to steep excise taxes. Importers
must pay U.S. $210,000 for each one-year license on four different
categories of alcohol products.

Banks could borrow abroad but in practice most of them found
it difficult to catch willing creditors. Nor could the Ministry of Finance float new GKOs in the market in 2000, although new government paper was available to foreigners who could use the funds
they received from the recycling, at heavy discount, of old GKOs.
Exporters continued to face the requirement of repatriating half
their export earnings in their resident banks. Banks breaking the
rule, which was intended to increase the supply of dollars, risked
losing their licenses. The Central Bank of Russia replaced the Ministry of Finance as the regulatory agency in charge of enforcing currency trading rules. It could suspend for a month the currency trading licenses of banks that violated rules.

In sum, as a result of hasty and unplanned deregulation of capital
account transactions that led to the collapse of the ruble in August
1998, Russia's subsequent arrangements with respect to foreign
trade and currency regulations regressed, lagging far behind those

of the East Asian economies. Viktor Gerashchenko, the chairman of the Central Bank of Russia, attributed the increased capital flight of $4 billion in 2001 to the lowering of the repatriation requirement that was legislated to 50 percent of export earnings (from the earlier 75 percent) by the Russian Duma with the support of the reformist and pro-Putin groups. At the start of 2002, the Russian central bank and the government continued to be at loggerheads, the former favoring the retention of exchange controls and the latter arguing for their removal in view of the increased foreign exchange earnings brought on by higher oil prices. The International Monetary Fund watched this internal policy debate long distance, especially because the Russian central bank had paid $4.3 billion owed to the Fund by early 2002.

8

Contagion from the Ruble to the *Real*

TOWARD THE END of 1997, the Brazilian government of President Fernando Henrique Cardoso sought to ward off pressure on the *real* as nervous investors reacted to the Asian crisis by pulling out of the Brazilian currency: the central bank raised the basic lending rate to 43 1/2 percent and the government cut back budget outlays by 2.5 percent of gross domestic product (GDP). After a temporary respite, the old pressures on the *real* resurfaced following the meltdown of the Russian ruble in August 1998 and the declaration of debt moratorium by Minas Gerais, one of Brazil's largest constituent states. Further fiscal tightening and interest rate hikes failed to halt the outflow of capital at the rate of $1 billion a day. Foreign exchange reserves, $70.2 billion toward the end of July 1998, had dwindled to $39 billion by the end of December 1998 as the government desperately sought to support the currency. It turned to the International Monetary Fund (IMF) for immediate financial support for halting a payments crisis, and buckled down to launch short-term measures for trimming fiscal deficits and long-term plans for overhauling budgetary imbalances. Despite IMF support, the exchange rate regime of managed devaluation of the *real,* in place since mid-January 1998, did not last. The *real,* which was allowed to float on January 18, 1999, declined from R$1.32 per dollar on January 14 to R$2.14 on January 29. At the same time, the IMF package was revised involving stricter fiscal targets in the midst of a declining economy. (Details are in chapter 10.)

The chronology of circumstances leading to the fall of the *real* resembled events in the crisis-prone East-Asian economies with one major difference: subsequent to the adoption of the *Real* Plan in July 1994, Brazilian inflation had declined and the real growth of the GDP had picked up to 3.2 percent in 1997; however, the consolidated budget and current account deficits had remained at unsustainable high levels. (Details follow in the next section.) The fiscal deficit spilling into current account deficit resulted from the lax control of the central government over the continuing profligacy of the constituent states amidst destabilizing political tensions.

The fiscal discipline imposed by the IMF-monitored bailout brought the earlier unsustainable budget deficits under control in 2000, but lagging exports and mounting current account deficits, supported by foreign investment flows, brought the *real* under pressure in 2001. The currency plunged to a historic low of R$3.47 to a dollar in early August 2002 as foreign creditors concerned about the emergence of a left-wing president in the October elections began pulling out of Brazil. On August 7, the IMF agreed to provide a $30 billion funding to the government, one of the largest ever by the IMF, in order to restore investor confidence, preempt a debt default, and above all, preserve the gains of price stability painstakingly hammered out over a decade-and-a-half, beginning with the *Real* Plan of July 1994 (which I discuss immediately below).

The *Real* Plan of July 1994: Pluses and Minuses

Brazil in the early nineties was plagued by "the stultifying influences of the old regime elites and the military; and the weaknesses of the political parties—i.e., their dependencies on personalities rather than platforms and their failure to address the basic social and economic problems confronting the nation" (Petras and Viewux, 1992, p. 3). The shift from the military to the civilian authority in March 1985, when the military appointed Tancredo Neves as the Brazilian president, was followed by almost a decade of fragmented politics marked by skirmishes between legislators and the government, corruption scandals, and currency reforms mixed either with wage price controls in the early years to widespread indexation arrangements as inflation soared to almost 2,000 percent toward the end of 1993. During that period, Brazil fit General de Gaulle's description of lacking the features of a "serious country." The *Real* Plan, an anti-inflation package, drafted by then Finance Minister Cardoso in the government of President Fernando Collor de Mello and successfully negotiated with the warring political factions, was calculated to turn the situation around. And it did. Inflation dropped to 1000 percent contributing to the landslide election of Cardoso as the Brazilian president in November 1994, followed by his reelection in October 1998.

The plan, a multiphased program based on minimizing state intervention, was aimed at tightening the fiscal arrangements in the federal state while privatizing large banks and businesses and opening up the economy to foreign trade and capital inflows. Brazilian states and municipalities would repay old debts to the federal treasury. State banks were to be brought under stricter supervision with a view to controlling their habitual reliance on widespread borrowing from the center calculated to closing state budget deficits. Asset privatization was aimed at trimming costs, raising productivity, and enhancing the revenue base while bringing in one-time cash inflow to the treasury. The new currency *real,* to replace the old Cruziero, would reflect correct wages and prices unencumbered either by wage and price controls, or by the indexation of wages to prices. The old currency bills, crumpled, torn and defaced, occasionally littering the streets, were replaced by crisp new bills. The exchange rate, linked to the dollar under a crawling peg, initially fluctuated without intervention from the central bank. The bank however began intervening in the market toward the end of 1994 when the rate, having traded on par with the dollar, closed at R$0.82 to the dollar in October 1994, thus damaging the competitiveness of Brazilian exports.

During 1995–97, before the East Asian crisis followed by the ruble collapse hit Brazil, the *Real* Plan had scored a few pluses in the economy's fundamentals: it had reined in inflation while maintaining the economy's growth with a low unemployment rate. Thus, annual inflation (shown in table 8.1) was brought down from 2078 percent in 1994 to 7 percent in 1997; GDP growth rate, which was 4 percent in 1995, however, had moved down to 3 percent in 1997; and unemployment, which was 5 percent in 1994, rose to 5.7 percent in 1997. The performance in the real economy was also marred by high fiscal deficits spilling into current account deficits. In contrast to the crisis-prone economies of East Asia, for which current account deficits reflected net dissaving by their respective private sectors, the Brazilian current account deficit, rising from 2.6 percent of the GDP in 1995 to 3.8 percent in 1997, reflected the net dissaving of the economy arising from the negative balance in the consolidated government accounts that has continued posing problems to the present.

Why Does the Brazilian Budget Continue To Be in the Red?

Brazil's budgetary problems persist from definitional, habitual, and structural factors.

How Is the Budget Defined?

According to the Memorandum of Economic Policies sent to the IMF on November 13, 1998 by Finance Minister Pedro Malan and (former) chairman of the central bank, Gustavo Franco, the Brazilian budget carried the finances of the entire nonfinancial public sector (NFPS) that included the federal, state, and municipal administrations, the social security fund, the central bank, and public enterprises under federal, state, and local jurisdiction. Fiscal inclusiveness however failed to result in consolidation via fiscal discipline. The center represented by the Ministry of Finance and Central Bank of Brazil lacked effective control over the constituent NFPS members. In fact, the center itself was lax in balancing its budget with tax revenues because of the inflation tax generated by high inflation.

Table 8.1
Macroeconomic indicators for Brazil: 1990–2001

	1900	1991	1992	1993	1994	1995	1996	1997	1998	1999	2000	2001
1. Growth rate of GDP (annual percent)	−4.39	1.24	−0.47	4.80	5.85	4.01	2.82	3.21	−2.43	2.72	4.20	1.50
2. Inflation rate (annual percentage change in consumer price index)	2947.73	432.79	951.96	1927.38	2078.01	65.94	15.77	6.94	3.18	4.86	7.06	6.83
3. Unemployment (percent of labor force)	4.28	4.83	5.66	5.32	5.06	4.65	5.43	5.67	7.60	7.56	7.14	6.20
4. Saving rate (percent of GDP)	20.51	19.21	20.34	18.34	21.94	19.71	17.92	17.72	16.82	15.50	17.60	15.90
5. Investment rate (percent of GDP)	20.78	19.57	18.78	18.34	22.15	22.29	20.92	21.50	21.12	20.29	21.76	20.62
6. Fiscal balance (percent of GDP)												
a. Total operation balance			−2.20	0.30	0.50	−4.80	−3.80	−4.30	−7.40	−3.40		
Operational balance of central government				0.00	1.60	−1.60	−1.60	−1.80	−5.10	−3.20		
States and municipalities			−0.80	0.30	−1.00	−2.30	−1.80	−2.30	−1.80	−0.50		
Public enterprises			−0.60	0.00	−0.10	−0.80	−0.30	−0.30	−0.50	0.30		
b. Interest payment (net)			4.40	2.30	3.80	5.10	3.70	3.30	7.40	6.70		
c. Primary balance			2.30	2.60	4.30	0.30	−0.10	−1.00	0.00	3.20		

Source: Economist Intelligence Unit, International Monetary Fund; Nyambi, 1999.

Table 8.1 *cont.*
Macroeconomic indicators for Brazil: 1990–2001

	1900	1991	1992	1993	1994	1995	1996	1997	1998	1999	2000	2001
7. Current account deficit (percent GDP)	−0.28	−0.36	1.56	0.00	−0.21	−2.58	−3.00	−3.78	−4.29	−4.78	−4.15	−4.70
8. Foreign direct investment (percent of GDP)	0.20	0.25	0.60	0.25	0.50	0.80	1.30	2.10	3.30	5.70	4.75	
9. Total foreign debt (percent of GDP)	8.69	30.08	32.97	11.93	27.68	22.59	23.37	24.58	31.08	46.07	39.80	47.00
10. Foreign short-term debt (percent of total debt)	19.78	21.76	18.71	21.29	20.77	19.17	19.57	17.34	12.30	12.07	13.61	12.40
11. Foreign short-term debt (percent of gross international reserves)					81.58	59.25	59.38	66.59	68.61	84.88		
12. Debt service ration (percent)	0.59	2.07	2.22	0.93	2.97	3.08	3.14	5.08	5.76	12.71	10.19	8.20
13. Import cover (in months)					8.40	7.90	8.60	6.40	5.30	4.80		

Source: Economist Intelligence Unit, International Monetary Fund; Nyambi, 1999.

The Old Practices

In the years before the *Real* Plan curbed inflation, the center and the periphery in the NFPS converted ex ante disequilibrium in their budgets into ex post equilibrium by indexing nominal revenues fully and expenditures partially to rising inflation. This gimmick obviated the need for real efforts to raise tax revenues and slash expenditures. With falling prices, the automatic inflation tax (contributing to revenues) and the slashing of real expenditures (easing budgetary outlays) vanished. Another carryover from the old days related to the hasty parceling of revenues and spending between the center and the states in the 1988 constitution that delegated spending obligations to the states and municipalities without matching resources creating structural imbalances in overall budgetary management.[1]

The Structural Issues

Fiscal freedoms not only turned into spendthrift practices as a result of unplanned sharing of revenues and outlays between the center and the periphery of the NFPS but also from the presence of multiple political parties that freely indulged in populist spending. Twenty-six political parties, as many as eleven of them represented in the federal cabinet, contributed to the volatility of Brazilian politics under President Cardoso. In the October 1998 gubernatorial elections, Cardoso's Party of Brazilian Social Democracy lost control of key states, among them Rio de Janeiro, Minas Gerais, and Rio Grande do Sul. Abandoning fiscal restraint, the states bankrupted their treasuries, allocating anywhere from 50 percent to slightly over 80 percent of revenues in their budgets to employee payrolls (figure 8.1). The center was equally reckless. Table 8.1 shows deficits in the budgets of the central, state, and municipal governments during 1995–97 ranging from 1.6 to 2.3 percent of GDP in the former two levels. Every government borrowed and incurred interest payments in the process that shot up to 7.4 percent of GDP in the aggregate budget when the central bank raised the basic lending rate to 43 1/2 percent (noted earlier) to stem the outflow of capital in 1997. The consolidated primary budget balance (net of interest payment liabilities) in 1998 was zero.

Balancing these deficits that spilled into current account imbalances required net foreign inflows that rendered the economy and the *real* vulnerable to panic-driven outflows despite the fact that, in contrast to the Crisis Five of East Asia, the Brazilian foreign debt structure was not excessively short term.

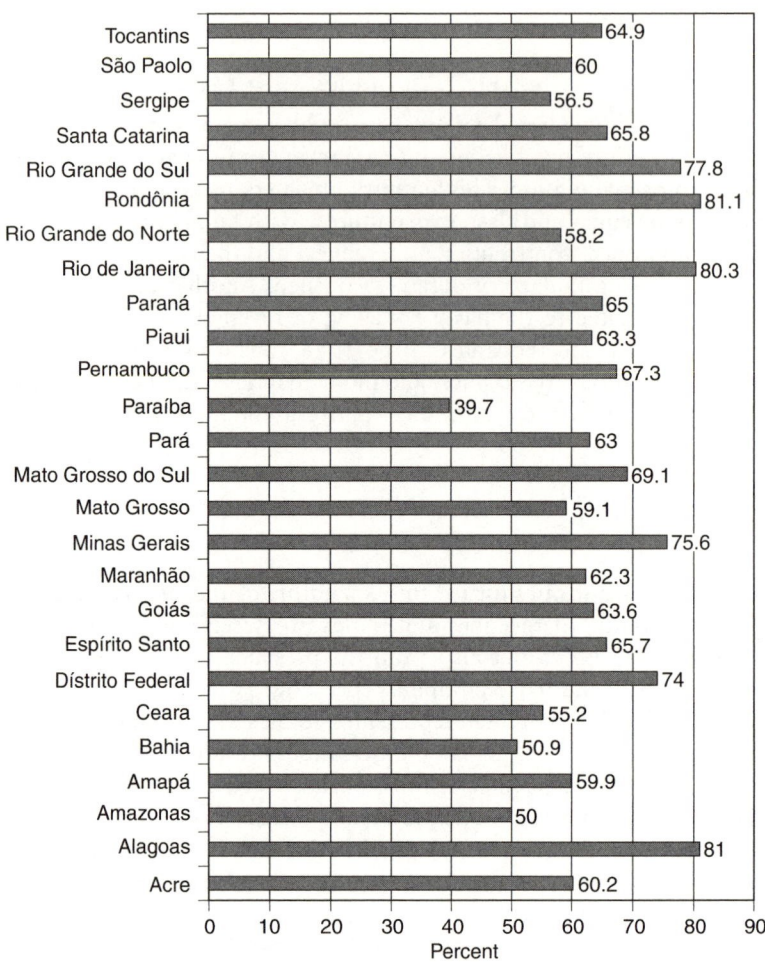

Figure 8.1. Brazilian states' payroll costs as a percentage of revenues, 1995.
Source: Fundação Instituto Brasileiro de Geografia e Estatística; Nyambi, 1999.

The Structure of Brazil's Foreign Debt on the Run-up to the 1998 Financial Crisis

Brazil's foreign debt fluctuated in the range of 25 to 28 percent of its GDP during 1994–97, a low steady range in contrast to the foreign indebtedness of the crisis-prone Asian economies, each of which registered increasing foreign indebtedness (relative to GDP) during 1991–96 (see table 5.2). During this time South Korea was the least indebted at a ratio of 28 percent in 1996, which was higher than Brazil's 25 percent in 1997. Brazil's indebtedness relative to GDP was more manageable than in the East Asian group when it was further broken into its short- and long-term components. Brazil's short-term foreign indebtedness as a fraction of the total during 1994–97 fluctuated between 17 and 21 percent (table 8.1), performing better than the rising relative share of short-term debt, which climbed to 25 percent in 1996 for Indonesia, the least vulnerable in that regard (see table 5.2). Finally, Brazil's short-term debt as a fraction of its international foreign exchange reserves, fluctuating between 59 and 82 percent during 1994–97, was worse than Malaysia's, highest at 41 percent in 1996, but vastly superior to the remaining three crisis-prone economies exhibiting triple digit ratios by 1996.

All in all, Brazil was less vulnerable in terms of its overall foreign indebtedness and less exposed to destabilizing speculative capital outflows than the crisis-prone Asian economies. During the opening up of the economy mandated by the *Real* Plan, Brazil had managed to attract long-term foreign direct investment of $1.3 billion in 1993, reaching a substantial $19.6 billion in 1997.

As a result, the structure of Brazil's external liabilities reflected in its negative current account deficits was relatively less geared to short-term capital inflows. However, these inflows, unlike in the Crisis Five of East Asia with solid public sector finances and balanced or surplus budgets, supported net public sector overspending right up to the collapse of the *real* in February 1999.

The Consequences of Lagging Fiscal Discipline

Budgetary management in Brazil was thus marked by a history of lack of concern for making ends meet at all levels and of an effective reining in of deficits via negotiated settlements before the East-Asian, crisis-driven capital outflows toward the end of 1997 set the stage for a worsening financial malaise ultimately leading to the sharp decline of the *real* in January 1999. The enhanced debt service payments on federal loans in state budgets, resulting from higher interest rates in 1995, could not be negotiated despite frequent attempts from the center to reschedule the state loans over a longer period with a view to restoring state debts to manageable levels and restoring their creditworthiness. At the end of prolonged negotiations, only a few states had signed restructuring contracts with the center. The attempts to plug capital flight in 1997 (triggered by the East Asian financial debacle) and in 1998 (following the fall of the ruble) via a program backed by IMF support of interest rate hikes and fiscal tightening only temporarily halted capital outflows. The situation called for a permanent lowering of fiscal imbalances at all levels via a cutback of public sector wage bills, overhaul of the social security system, and transparent budget balancing. The IMF revised package of March 1999, mandating low inflation targeting under a regime of strict monetary discipline and managed float of the *real,* also called for speedy structural reforms without which the IMF agenda would flounder despite visible signs of economic recovery in late 1999 continuing into 2000. Brazil's public finances needed to be cleaned of their imbalances for the recovery to be stable and sustained.

Following the February 1999 devaluation of the *real* and an IMF-mandated fiscal austerity, Brazil met its budget deficit targets in each quarter in 1999 and 2000 via spending cuts and higher tax receipts. The real economy grew by 4.2 percent in 2000, unemployment climbed to a high 7.1 percent of the labor force, and inflation measured by the consumer price index was a low 7 percent. The performance going into 2001 was worse with a growth rate of 1.5 percent with virtually unchanged unemployment and inflation rates. The long-standing fiscal problem spilling into current account deficits continued to demand attention of policy makers. The tax, pension, and administrative reforms moved slowly. High taxes, a third of GDP, contributed to budgetary revenues, but the unreformed tax system penalized businesses and constrained economic growth and potential tax receipts. Pensions consumed a significant 5 percent of GDP. Salaries of state employees were frozen but their numbers remained almost unchanged. More critically, the *real* devaluation pushed the public debt from 25 percent of GDP in 1997 to 47 percent in 2001. With 70 percent of the debt linked to the dollar or the overnight interest rate, each subsequent drop of the *real* and every interest rate hike to arrest it added to outlays from the budget so that interest payments exceeded the primary budget surplus. At the same time, low export earnings despite the *real* devaluation resulted in significant current account deficit at 4.7 percent of the GDP and low foreign exchange reserves of $32 billion in 2001. These numbers were grossly inadequate to service a foreign debt of $235 billion, requiring estimated payment obligations of $50 billion! Almost a third of the debt was to be paid back in a year.

Events at home and in neighboring Argentina further undermined growth prospects and investor confidence in 2001. A severe power shortage, the result of low rainfall in the hydroelectric reservoirs that drove the energy system and lagging progress in building gas-fired power stations, required rationing of energy use by households and industry. Threats of congressional investigation into alleged corruption by government officials damaged investor confidence. The recurring worries about a possible debt default by neighboring Argentina caused the *real* to slide by 30 percent by September, requiring five consecutive interest rate increases of 375 basis points by the central bank. At the microeconomic level, individual sectors were hit with varying severity. Electricity companies took revenue loss from rationing; telecommunication and steel companies faced soaring debt burden on their dollar debts as the *real* depreciated. Households worried about job losses as the economic slowdown deepened.

The terrorist attacks on the U.S. threatened to destabilize the currency further by halting capital inflows and damaging exports to the U.S. market that took 23 percent of Brazilian exports. The central bank tightened monetary policy by raising commercial bank reserve requirements and drew $4.7 billion of the $15 billion IMF funding of August 2001 for intervening in the foreign exchange market. As 2002 unfolded, the Cardoso team of policy makers managed to contain the economic fallout from the events of 9/11 and from the Argentine debt default (that I analyze in the next chapter); foreign investors picked up bonds floated by Brazilian companies, and Brazilian exports revived with the emergence of the U.S. economy from the recession at the start of 2002. But the government's commitment to control the budget deficit and inflation and arrest the *real's* decline under the IMF August funding r was a delicate act requiring a balance on its part between imposing fiscal austerity and retaining the support of the electorate as Brazil faced a presidential election in October 2002. The likely victory of a presidential candidate from the left-wing Workers Party, Luiz Inancio Lula da Silva, raised fears of the emergence of populist programs that could damage fiscal performance and inflation targeting, destabilize the *real*, and endanger the economic stability gained during the Cardoso presidency. The IMF's package calculated to stabilize the *real* until the October elections and prop up the candidacy of Jose Serra, the candidate of the ruling coalition led by Cardoso, was a risky gamble. The chances of the economy doubling the growth rates in 2002 from a low of 1.5 percent in 2001 in the midst of a real interest rate of 14 percent in August and generating the IMF-mandated primary budget surplus of 3.75 percent of GDP were uncertain. Brazil's economy was heading toward an unpredictable financial situation, raising doubts about the success of the IMF's standard bailout strategy and prompting suggestions for restructuring its foreign and domestic debt so that a default could be prevented.

Notes

1. Russia's budgetary management was plagued by similar structural imbalances between the federal center and the constituent regional and local authorities during the Yeltsin years. The tax codes passed by the Duma in 2000 and early 2001 streamlined the arrangements.

9

Beyond Bangkok: Crisis Erupts in Buenos Aires and in the Bosphorus

THE ECONOMIES OF the Crisis Five in East Asia and of Russia and Brazil revived in 1999 and 2000 leaving behind them the worst consequences of capital outflows and plunging currencies. Toward the end of 2000, the circumstances marking a financial crisis emerged elsewhere in debt-ridden Argentina and Turkey, raising fears about the collapse of their currencies, testing once again the firefighting skills of the International Monetary Fund (IMF), and setting off speculation about the likelihood of a new financial contagion. These concerns intensified after the terrorist attacks on U.S. territory on 9/11.

The origins of the crisis in each country were financial. In Argentina, fears in November 2000 about the government defaulting on its accumulated foreign debt of $125 billion, half of Argentine gross domestic product (GDP), created a panic among investors and raised concerns about the stability of the peso. The situation was brought under control with an IMF-backed support package of $40 billion in December but the economic recession continued. The budget deficit in the first quarter of 2001 exceeded IMF norms, and disagreement in the ruling coalition on the spending cuts proposed by the economy minister, Lopez Murphy, triggered a political crisis in the ruling alliance and union-led strikes on the streets of Buenos Aires, culminating in the installation in March of a new economy minister, Domingo Cavallo, the third in two weeks. The bond swap of $30 billion in June enabled Argentine borrowers to postpone their debt obligations but failed to stave off fears among international lenders of an eventual Argentine default of its debt obligations that had reached $130 billion by mid-2001. Capital outflows, and dwindling deposits in Argentine banks that the holders converted into dollars, threatened the peso-dollar peg. This once again activated the IMF to announce an emergency bailout of $8 billion in August. It imposed a zero-deficit budget on the government, and pushed it to work up debt restructuring plans moving into 2002. The inability of the treasury to persuade a hostile Congress and free-spending provinces to deliver a balanced budget by further spending cuts toward the end of 2001 led to withholding of a credit tranche by the IMF in December, a unilateral debt default by the government, the freezing of bank deposits—*corralito*—by the central bank to prevent capital flight, bloody street protests, and government changes in quick succession. The new team of policy makers under President Eduardo Duhalde floated the peso in February 2002. The central bank spent foreign exchange to support the peso and printed currency to pump liquidity in the banking system. It also introduced exchange controls to prevent the peso's further fall from 3.5 pesos to a dollar in early April. In the midst of an emerging scenario of more pell-mell controls, rising prices, declining GDP and growing unemployment, bank collapses and street rioting, the IMF insisted on further budget cutting and strict conditions for the unfreezing of bank deposits before it would release funding to the new government.

The crisis in Turkey was unrelated, less challenging but similar in its financial origin. The ballooning current account deficit put pressure on the lira in November 2000, and several Turkish banks that had borrowed heavily in foreign markets collapsed when their investors withdrew funds. In February 2001, President Ahmet Necdet Sezer openly criticized Prime Minister Bulent Ecevit for his soft pedaling on banking reform implying that the prime minister was protecting his political cronies. As a result of this public feud, investors got panicky, the stock market lost about a third of its value, and interest rates shot up to 7,500 percent as the drop in interbank credit lines and withdrawal of foreign funds got magnified into an unprecedented liquidity crunch. The government put together an IMF-backed stabilization plan and allowed the lira to float, which resulted in it dropping by 30 percent in a day. In the following months, the Turkish authorities struggled to rein in the budget deficit and curb inflation that ran ahead of the government's target of 61 percent for 2001. This in turn weakened the currency that had tumbled by 55 percent in six months from its February level despite high interest rates that averaged 90 percent on Turkish bonds. These pressing economic problems were overtaken by political turmoil in August 2002 when the governing coalition of Prime Minister Ecevit ended over acrimonious debates relating to the controversial issue of Turkey's candidacy in the European Union. It was doubtful if the early elections voted by the parliament, eighteen months ahead of schedule, would result in a stable government capable of steering the economy out of its stagnation.

The escalating Argentine and Turkish financial troubles did not create a global crisis—panicky investors did not flee from emerging markets causing their currencies to tumble. The fallout was contained in neighboring Brazil, which had run up a significant current account deficit financed by capital flows, and Uruguay, which was threatened with a banking sector collapse when cash-strapped Argentines withdrew their cash from Uruguayan banks.

In this chapter, I link the weak economic fundamentals of Argentina and Turkey (beginning with Argentina) to their policy and structural inadequacies, and raise doubts about their governments' ability to enforce the required fiscal discipline and structural changes in pursuit of economic stability. In this context, the burden of history weighs heavily on Argentina's prospects.

Argentina: The Burden of History

From a historical perspective, Argentina's crisis seemed to represent an episode in the country's century-old script of political and economic turmoil. An article in the *New York Times* stated, "Most of Argentina's presidents in the past seven decades have either resigned or have been overthrown in military coups. Their demises have often come in the midst of economic crises, and after the discontented filled Buenos Aires' broad, Parisian-style boulevards to battle the police" (December 22, 2001, p. A8). The latest chapter in the new millennium prompted assessments from several directions. From the viewing of a social scientist, the crisis represented a sordid case of out-of-control aspirations of people wanting to live beyond their means. The profligacy was fed by the extravagant populism of General Juan Domingo Perón in the forties who took from the rich and gave to the poor. It established a culture of automatic entitlements for the public to most services from free higher education to health benefits. For a non-IMF economist it symbolized the futility of implanting market-oriented policies in an institutional vacuum. The tax authorities could not collect adequate taxes, the judiciary lacked independence to enforce laws, and businesses failed to maintain transparent corporate practices and social accountability. The political scientist was likely to explain the debt default and the currency's collapse in terms of shifting alliances among politicians given to populist rhetoric devoid of tough decisions targeted at raising resources to repay debts. A Wall Street analyst would attribute the problem to Argentina's business class lacking in ability to perform under the rigors of strict market discipline and global competition. A scientist could only feel baffled at the country's inability to create a semblance of order out of anarchy. "How can so disorganized a country progress?" Albert Einstein was reported to have remarked in 1925 during a visit (*New York Times*, February 8, 2002, p. A6). A middle-class resident of Buenos Aires expressed his bewilderment amidst the relentless deterioration. "To start off with such abundance and end up this poor, that, my friend, takes a very special talent." (*New York Times*, December 22, 2001, p. A1). How could a country endowed with abundant natural resources and educated people and "an economy comparable to that of the United States" at the turn of the last century become bankrupt? (ibid.).

Argentina seemed to have gotten on top of this agglomeration of handicaps during the nineties when the government of President Carlos Menem and his energetic economy minister Domingo Cavallo brought quadruple-digit inflation under control, deregulated the economy, initiated privatization of industry, and invited foreign investors. The convertibility law of March 1991 linked the peso to the dollar, required that the pesos in circulation be backed by dollars and permitted citizens to exchange pesos for dollars in state-owned banks. But the chickens did come to roost. The arrangements backed by a currency board[1] failed to instill the necessary discipline among governments at the center and the provinces, which accumulated a massive debt burden. The improving economic performance of the nineties, which I describe subsequently, was overtaken by the collective burden of the inherent weaknesses, making a mockery of the IMF's short-sighted engagement in Argentina.

Argentina: The Fundamentals

In the three to five years prior to the onset of the crisis in November 2000, Argentina's fundamentals of GDP growth and inflation rates and its budget and current account deficits were unstable, and decidedly weaker than in the East Asian Crisis Five described in chapter 5. Overall, its foreign-debt exposure in terms of debt-to-GDP ratio and its relative short-term component compared favorably with the situation in the East Asian economies but the policy makers' ability to clear repayment obligations and import needs via the available foreign exchange reserves were no better than those in the worst East Asian group; it had steadily worsened since 1995.

GDP Growth and Inflation Rates

Figure 9.1 illustrates the growth of the Argentine economy for three years, from 1996–98, at average annual rates of 6 percent; it then shows a recession registering negative growth rates of 3.1 percent in 1999, 0.2 percent in 2000, and the negative trend continuing in 2001. The inflation rate shown in figure 9.2, measured via the consumer price index (CPI), fell sharply from a peak of 3,000 percent in 1991 after the adoption of the currency board that linked the Argentine peso to the dollar at the rate of one peso to a dollar. The drastic discipline of the monetary straightjacket

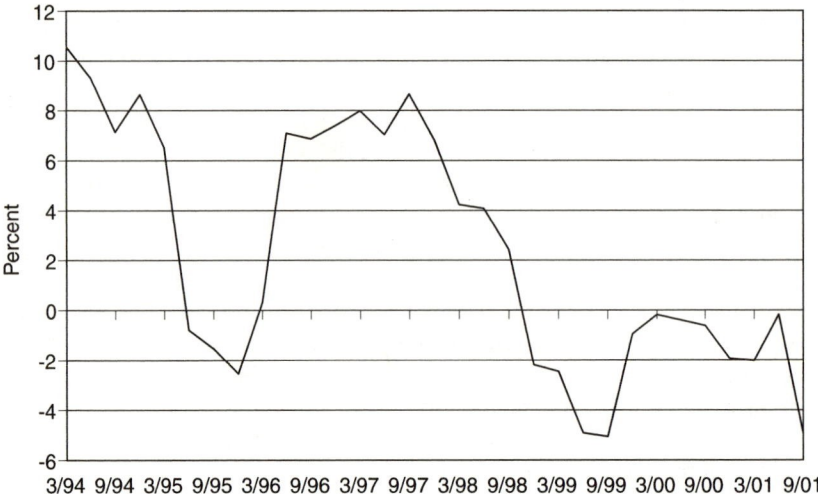

Figure 9.1. Argentina: Annualized percentage change in real gross domestic product. Quarterly data, first quarter 1994–third quarter 2001. *Source:* Economist Intelligence Unit.

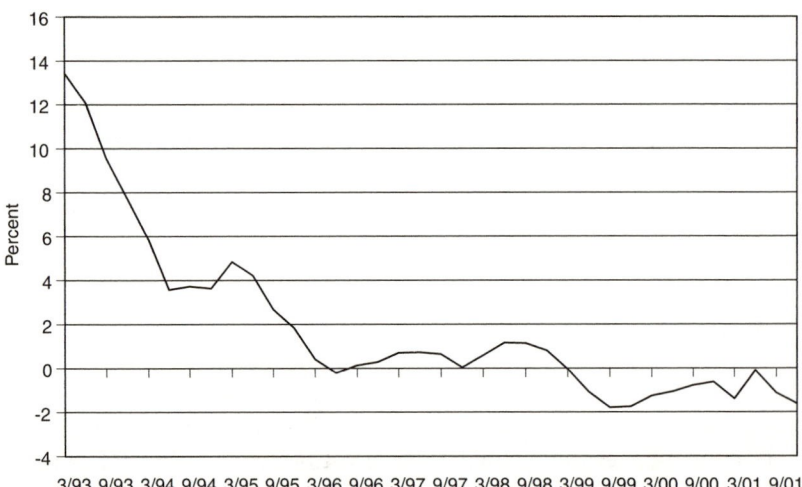

Figure 9.2. Argentina: Annualized percentage change in consumer price index. Quarterly data, first quarter 1993–fourth quarter 2001. *Source:* Economist Intelligence Unit.

linking the growth of money supply to foreign exchange earnings imposed a disinflation on the economy with negative CPI growth rates during 1999–2001.

The currency board arrangement however did not spare Argentina from the financial crisis for a variety of reasons. First, the one-to-one link of the peso to the dollar contributed to the overvaluation of the peso relative to the currencies of Latin American countries that are Argentina's trading partners. The overvaluation arose not only because the dollar remained strong with respect to these currencies but also because inflation inertia and wage rigidity in Argentina contributed to the appreciation of the fixed peso. (This connection was discussed in block 2.) In addition to the appreciation resulting from a strong anchor and wage-price rigidity, the peso lost its competitive edge in Latin American markets when Brazil devalued the *real* in January 1999. The lost exports (supplemented by other factors discussed subsequently) contributed to three years of negative GDP growth rates.

The currency board failed to impose fiscal discipline on Argentine policy makers. In the absence of the central bank acting as a lender of the last resort, the federal treasury, including the provinces, borrowed from abroad for meeting its budgetary needs, adding to the sovereign debt of the government and crowding out private investment.

Fiscal and Current Account Deficits and Foreign Debt

The government budget balance (figure 9.3) steadily worsened from a small positive surplus of 1 percent of GDP in 1993 to a negative 3.8 percent in 2001. At the same time, two consequences followed from the adoption of the currency board arrangement that deprived the financial system of the discretionary lender of the last resort role of a central bank. Interest rates could not be varied to counter the GDP growth-rate cycles shown in figure 9.1. In 1996–97, the Argentine economy averaged 7 percent growth rate and required higher interest rates. From 1999 to 2001, it needed a cutback in the rates to recover from the deflation. Second, the currency board arrangement tied money-supply growth to foreign exchange earnings that suffered from the overvalued peso linked to the U.S. dollar. The resulting low liquidity in the banking system created an artificial wedge between commercial bank lending rates to businesses and borrowing rates from depositors. As a result, it discouraged saving and investment activity in the private sector and lowered the economy's growth performance. Figure 9.4 graphs the saving rate as a percent of GDP from 1985 to 2000 as it hovered around 15 percent and the investment rate

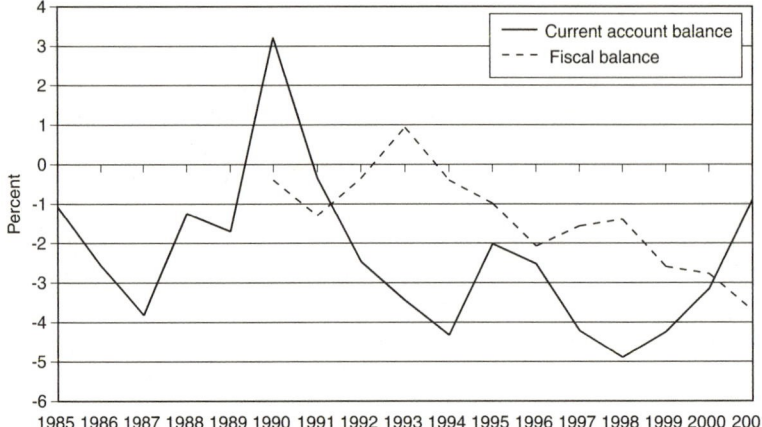

Figure 9.3. Argentina: fiscal and current account balances as percentages of gross domestic product. Annual data, 1985–2001. *Source:* Economist Intelligence Unit.

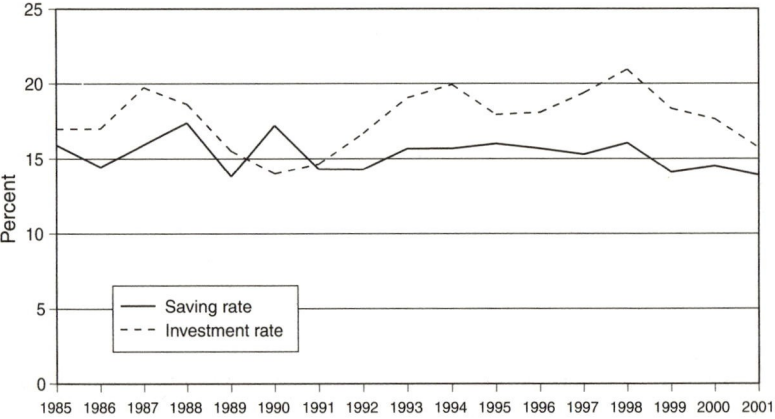

Figure 9.4. Argentina: national saving and investment rates as percentages of gross domestic product. Annual data, 1985–2001. *Source:* Economist Intelligence Unit.

ranged between 17 and 19 percent. These rates were significantly lower than the 30 percent saving and 33 percent investment rates of the East Asian economies (excluding Philippines).

The current account deficit of the economy shown in figure 9.3, reflecting the widening gap between investment and aggregate saving in the 1990s, gyrated from –4.2 percent of GDP in 1994 to a critical, –5 percent

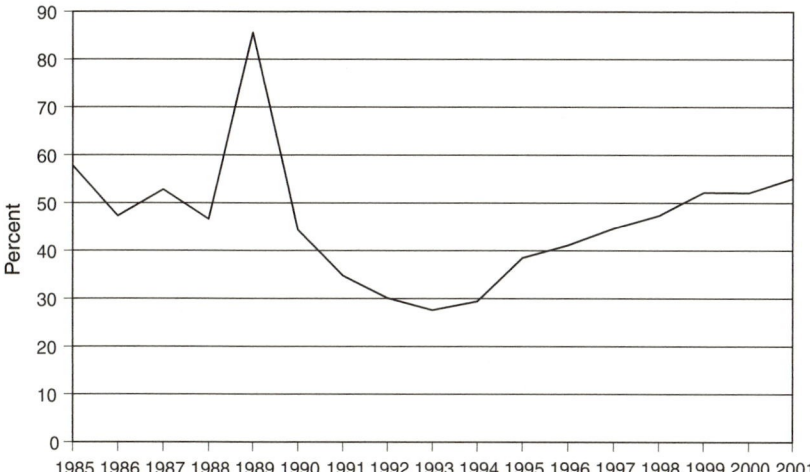

Figure 9.5. Argentina: foreign debt as a percentage of gross domestic product. Annual data, 1985–2001. *Source:* Economist Intelligence Unit.

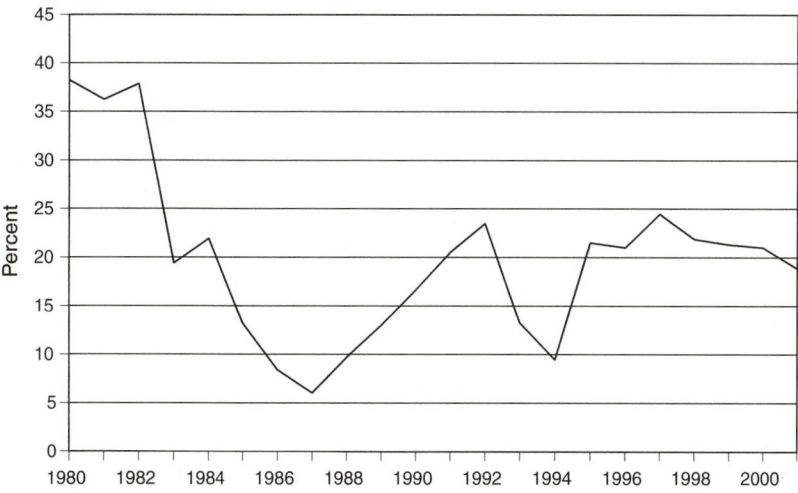

Figure 9.6. Argentina: short-term foreign debt as a percentage of total debt. Annual data, 1980–2001. *Source:* Economist Intelligence Unit.

in 1998 and a high, –4 percent in 2000 and 2001. This deficit was filled by foreign borrowing, which steadily increased (figure 9.5) from 28 percent of GDP in 1993 to 55 percent in 2001. Short-term borrowing as a share of the total (figure 9.6) was still low at 21 percent of the total in 2000 (in sharp contrast to the rising and high shares of short-term debt

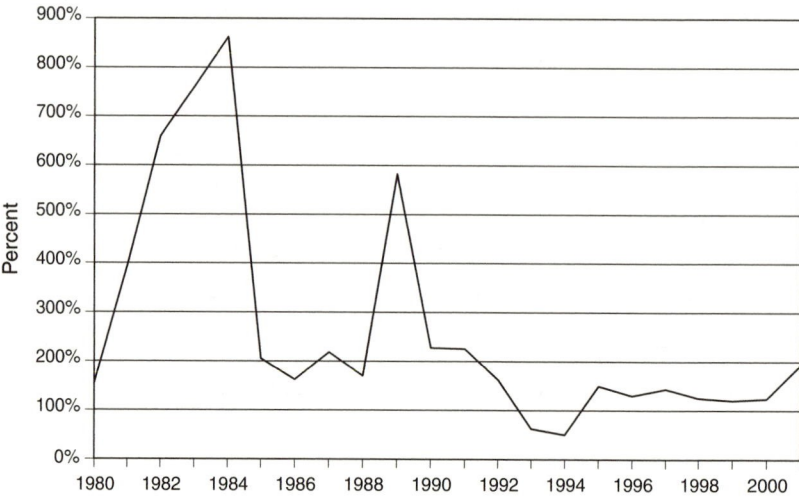

Figure 9.7. Argentina: foreign short-term debt as a percentage of foreign exchange reserves. Annual data, 1980–2001. *Source:* Economist Intelligence Unit.

in the East Asian economies at 50 percent for South Korea and 57 percent for Thailand in 1996). The risk to investors, however, arose from the fact that short-term debt as a fraction of foreign exchange reserves (figure 9.7) was as high as 110 percent in 2000 and reached almost 300 percent at its worst in 2001. Finally, these reserves (figure 9.8) could finance less than a month of Argentine imports in 1999 and 2000, down from 2.87 months in 1989, an alarmingly low figure compared to the lowest for South Korea in 1996 at 2.34 months.

In conclusion, the appreciating peso damaged the export competitiveness of Argentine exports. The discipline of the currency board, however lax, deprived policy makers of discretionary monetary policy choices to counter the cyclical ups and downs of GDP growth rates. The lack of liquidity in the financial system discouraged private investment and saving and curtailed growth. Low growth reduced tax flows in the treasury and raised budget deficits. High current account deficits required growing borrowings from abroad in relation to GDP. The share of short-term debt in the total was much lower than in the troubled East Asian economies, but this debt was unsustainable in relation to the foreign exchange reserves and the economy's import needs. The combination of the weak fundamentals and the growing foreign debt liabilities, especially since 1995, provided the ingredients for the crisis in late 2000. Reflecting the extreme financial vulnerability, the stock market index (figure 9.9)

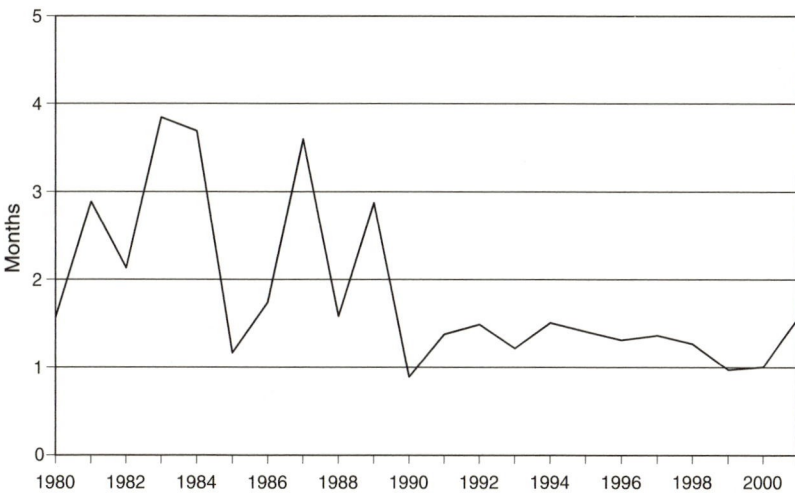

Figure 9.8. Argentina: average foreign exchange reserves in months of imports. Annual data, 1980–2001. *Source:* Economist Intelligence Unit.

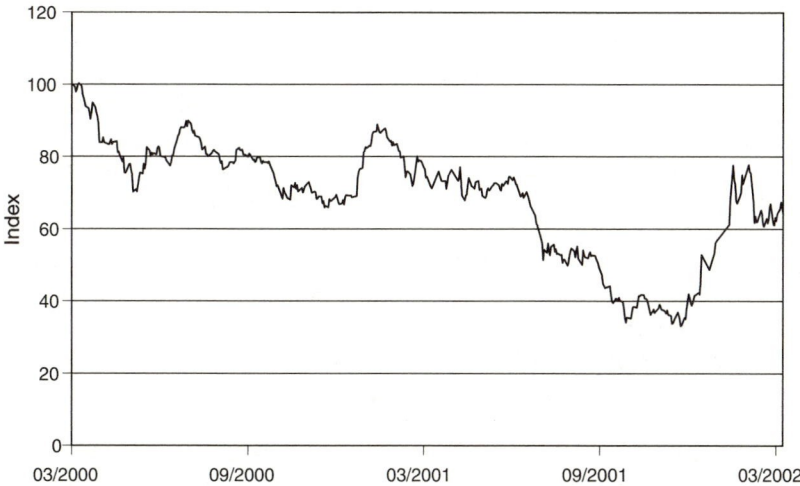

Figure 9.9. Argentina: Merval stock market index. Rebased: 3/17/2000 = 100. *Source:* Internet Securities, Inc.

dropped in November to about two-thirds of its level earlier in the year, gained strength in December, and January 2001, but continued plunging thereafter until the end of the year in reaction to investors' pessimism about the government's ability for avoiding a debt default.

On top of weak fundamentals and growing foreign indebtedness in the run-up to the crisis, Argentina had structural problems as well.

Argentina: Structural Issues

Structural instability arose from bloated government expenditures financed with foreign borrowing, pervasive tax evasion and corruption, and a penalizing tax and regulatory network that curbed investment.

The Bloated Government

The federal government was unable to slash populist spending set by former president Juan Perón in the fifties which gave generous medical insurance and unemployment benefits to Argentine workers. Nor could it regulate spending by the provinces and relinquish its practice of bailing them out from payment obligations. Argentina's volatile politics marked by weak democratic institution building, interrupted by military juntas and the prolonged populist rule of Juan Perón, deprived the country of sound fiscal management based on give and take among layers of the government and between the government and trade unions. High taxes contributed to tax evasion but it was doubtful if the Laffer curve could be triggered resulting in higher revenue flows from lower taxes in the absence of an efficient tax-collecting system and automatic tax payments by the public in response to lower tax rates. The government's policy options with respect to lowering pension payments or tightening its fiscal rein over provincial authorities were stretched to the limit on the eve of the congressional elections of October 2001.

The special powers legislated by Congress in March 2001, enabling the new economy minister, Domingo Cavallo, to pull the economy out of its 33-month recession, barred the government from removing a single employee from its payroll or privatizing any state-managed enterprise without congressional approval. President Fernando de la Rua promised labor leaders that the union-run, mandatory health insurance schemes and retirement benefits would be kept intact. Realizing this insurmountable hurdle, the Cavallo plan focused on raising tax revenues via new taxes and curbing tax evasion.

Battling Tax Evasion and Corruption

Habitual tax evasion to the tune of $35 billion a year reduced re
flows in the budget. A fraction could be recovered by a crackdown on
defaulters but the Cavallo plan offered an amnesty to tax dodgers who
would be allowed to buy bonds in the amounts of the tax liabilities they
owed to the treasury. A politically destabilizing scandal involving Argentine banks that laundered drug money and implicating several key political figures, among them the former head of the central bank, Pedro Pou,
erupted in late February 2001. The currency board regime lacked tax-
collecting muscle and banking sector regulation. The prevailing tax system coupled with ill-conceived regulatory safeguards smothered investment activity and productivity growth requiring rapid policy initiatives.

The Policy Initiatives

The Cavallo initiatives focused on reviving investment and generating
economic competition by streamlining regulations and reducing taxes
that were levied in 2000 with the aim of boosting tax revenues.

The president signed an emergency decree in early April 2001 aimed at
simplifying Argentina's antitrust law. Under existing law a multinational
corporation with global business of more than $2.5 billion could not ac-
quire an Argentine company without undergoing a six-month authorization procedure. That requirement was eliminated, inducing foreign investors to step into Argentine industry. Taxes on interest paid on loans taken
out by businesses to finance new investments were targeted for removal.
Taxes on incomes earned and assets employed in exporting activity would
be eliminated. The value-added 21 percent tax on capital goods would be
reimbursed. Import duties on capital goods were slashed from the prevailing 14 percent to zero and those on consumer goods were raised to 35
percent to selectively counter the overvaluation of the peso.

The measures were calculated to spur economic growth, raise tax revenues, and bring the budget deficit in line with the IMF target of $6.5
billion for 2001 that was part of the December 2000 support package of
$40 billion in loans and credit guarantees designed to stave off debt de-
fault. The business tax incentives (previously outlined) were designed to
promote growth, enhance the tax base, and bring in revenues as the year
advanced. A new tax of 0.25 percent on all bank inflows and outflows,
modeled after Brazil's successful financial transactions tax, was calculated, via automatic receipts, to bring in additional revenues. At the same
time, prompted by a 13 percent drop in tax revenues in March 2001

(compared with March 2000), Cavallo successfully negotiated a $500-million-a-year cut in budget outlays that were later raised to $900 million. Under the emergency powers granted to him, he proposed another stimulant to the economy and persuaded the central bank and its new governor, Roque Maccarone, to inject liquidity in the economy by reducing the reserves that commercial banks must deposit with it. He thus gained policy maneuvering by stretching the cash-pumping limits of the currency board arrangement.

The Cavallo plan thus relied on supply-side incentives via lower and fewer business taxes for reviving the economy and augmenting government tax revenues, and postponed for future consideration the politically controversial chores of streamlining government bureaucracies, revising the labor laws, and streamlining pension and other entitlement benefits to the workforce. Cavallo also ruled out enforced debt restructuring but proposed a change in the country's dollar-linked currency by pegging it to a 50:50 basket of euro and dollar at a future date when the euro, exchanging at 0.90 cents in early 2001, reached parity with the dollar.

Why No Enforced Debt Restructuring?

The new policy maker defined the challenge of pulling the Argentine economy out of its 33-month-old recession without involuntarily restructuring the debt because he believed that an enforced debt restructuring would imply a breach of contract with foreign creditors, damage long-term borrower-lender relations, curtail potential long-term investment flows, and prolong the economic recession. Besides, Argentina's debt problem, in Cavallo's view, was exaggerated: there were some pressing, short-term repayment obligations but most of the debt had an average maturity of eight years. Short-term liabilities in the amount of $30 billion in domestic and foreign bonds were due for repayment later in 2002 and 2003 (*Wall Street Journal*, April 27, 2001, p. A15). However, this lopsided assessment ignored the fact that the 2001 debt liabilities were as high as 250 to 300 percent of the foreign exchange reserves.

Having ruled out involuntary debt restructuring, Cavallo launched plans in early May for a substantial, market-friendly debt swap of $20 to $30 billion promising local and foreign investors new, long-term bonds backed by higher interest rates and attractive collateral. A well- planned rollover of the short-term debt was calculated to stabilize financial markets, narrow the interest rate spread between Argentine and U.S. treasury bonds, and spur investment and consumer spending. However, the $30 billion debt restructuring of June failed to restore investor confidence or curb deposit withdrawals from Argentine banks by nervous depositors as they converted their holdings into dollars and placed them in foreign banks. The IMF announced an emergency bailout of $8 billion on August 21, mandated a zero-deficit budget requirement, and prodded the government to implement debt swap belatedly pushing the process into involuntary negotiations between lenders and borrowers. (Details are in chapter 11.)

The policy measures excluded an immediate change in the peso-dollar link.

Why No Immediate Change in the Peso-Dollar Link?

An immediate and outright devaluation of the peso would spell disaster for the financial viability of Argentine banks and businesses that were burdened with dollar-denominated debts. However, on April 17, 2001, Cavallo sought to redefine the peso's tie to the strong dollar by pegging the peso to a 50:50 link with the euro and the dollar when and if the euro achieved parity with the dollar.

THE PESO'S MODIFIED PEG

An expected appreciation of the euro against the dollar would reduce the debt burden and the likelihood of its default in the future. It would also smooth the impact of a fluctuating dollar and better reflect Argentina's relative export shares at 20 percent with the EU and 11 percent with the U.S. But, as I argued in chapter 3, the chances of the euro regaining parity with the dollar in the near future were slim despite the U.S. economic slowdown in 2001 followed by a slower than expected recovery in 2002. The European and Monetary Union was expected to trail behind the U.S. in its growth performance. At the same time, the Cavallo proposal to change the peso's parity shook investor confidence and widened the interest rate spread between the benchmark Argentine government bond and comparable U.S. treasury bond that later narrowed in reaction to the proposals for a debt swap in early May that materialized in June.

The danger of Argentine debt default and currency collapse persisted despite the IMF August funding of $8 billion. Avoiding a default and maintaining the currency link to the dollar required a return of the government budget to a positive primary surplus based on sustained political consensus and public support so that the government continued repaying its debt obligations as they came up for clearance. The economy, however, was caught in a grim vicious circle: it needed to grow so that tax revenues could materialize but toward the end of 2001, low consumer confidence and a benchmark interest rate for 180-day peso loans fluctuating around 37 percent dampened industrial production and construction activity. Further budget cuts on top of the slashing of state salaries and pensions and reduced transfers to the provinces from the federal budget were politically unmanageable as the unemployment rate hit 16 percent of the workforce.

On December 5, 2001, the IMF suspended its support to the de la Rua government by withholding $1.36 billion, precipitating a debt default of $155 billion and removal of five leaders in less than two weeks, including temporary caretakers. Eduardo Duhalde, a Perónist former governor of Buenos Aires province, elected on January 1, 2002 as the interim president, was caught between a rock and a hard place, between meeting the demands of the IMF so that it would release the much-needed funding and preventing the social unrest on the streets from descending into unmanageable chaos. The 30 percent devaluation of the peso on January ended its ten-year, one-to-one link with the dollar. The adoption of the budget for 2002 representing a 14 percent cut in outlays from 2001 and belt-tightening agreement with the provinces, however, failed to meet IMF approval. Continuing central bank controls on free conversion of dollar holdings into pesos, an economy-wide cash shortage associated with a partial freeze on bank deposits, and a recession stretching over four years prevented a free fall of the peso in the weeks following its devaluation. But increasing currency emission by the central bank and proliferation of scrip issued by provincial governments as parallel money contributed to the peso's weakening. A more austere budget, strict disciplining of provincial authorities, and a revamping of bankruptcy laws designed to liquidate deadbeat companies could release IMF cash and prop up the banking system. But this package was not guaranteed to prevent street protests as the public faced shortages of essential items and developed a deep distrust of its leaders. The moment was long past for the successful imposition of such austerity required by the release of IMF funding on a desperate public. The IMF had an opportunity in December 2000 to depart from its standard approach, initiate an orderly and early debt restructuring of Argentine debt, and link it with its funding support (as accomplished in South Korea in 1998 on a smaller scale). A fresh start that also involved the scrapping of the outdated currency board and the peso-dollar link and the setting of credible budget deficit targets as part of the debt restructuring under IMF initiative was then possible. The IMF's bailout for Argentina backfired signaling that it had failed to devise fresh initiatives based on its handling of past crises.

The IMF and Turkey's policy makers initially faced a less demanding challenge in managing a financial crisis which began in late 2000, but which escalated into a government collapse and political uncertainties two years later.

Figure 9.10. Turkey: annualized percentage change in real gross domestic product. Quarterly data, first quarter 1994–third quarter 2001. *Source:* Economist Intelligence Unit.

Turkey: The Fundamentals

In the years prior to the onset of the crisis in late 2000, economic fundamentals in Turkey were unstable and weaker than comparable norms in the East Asian crisis-prone economies. Figure 9.10 shows that Turkey, like Argentina, had periods of positive and negative growth in the years from 1993 to 2000. The economy had crawled out of four quarters of negative growth in 1999 to a low 2 percent growth in 2000 but was precariously poised for a negative 8 percent in 2001. However, unlike in Argentina and the troubled East Asian region, inflation in Turkey, measured via a change in the CPI (figure 9.11), was consistently high and in the double and triple digits in the past decade and half. It ranged from an annualized triple-digit rate of 100 percent in the first quarter of 1998 to a still high double-digit 40 percent in 2000 and a higher 61 percent in 2001. The excessively high budget deficits (figure 9.12), whose monetization resulted in high inflation rates, set Turkey apart from all countries analyzed in this book: the budget deficit rose from a little over 2 percent of GDP in 1986 to a staggering 15 percent in 2000. At the same time, the substantial negative saving on government account weakened national saving shown in figure 9.13, and contributed to current account deficits that jumped to 5 percent of GDP in 2000 (figure 9.12). (This is reflected

Figure 9.11. Turkey: annualized percentage change in consumer price index. Quarterly data, first quarter 1993–fourth quarter 2001. *Source:* Economist Intelligence Unit.

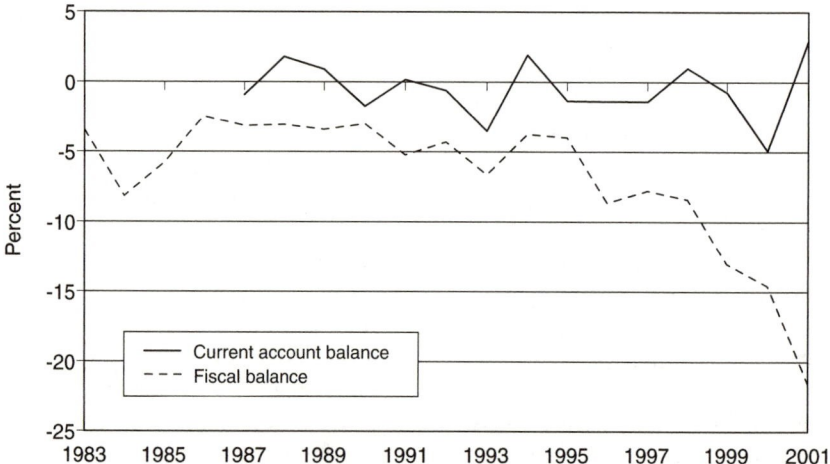

Figure 9.12. Turkey: fiscal and current account balances as percentages of gross domestic product. Annual data, 1983–2001. *Source:* Economist Intelligence Unit.

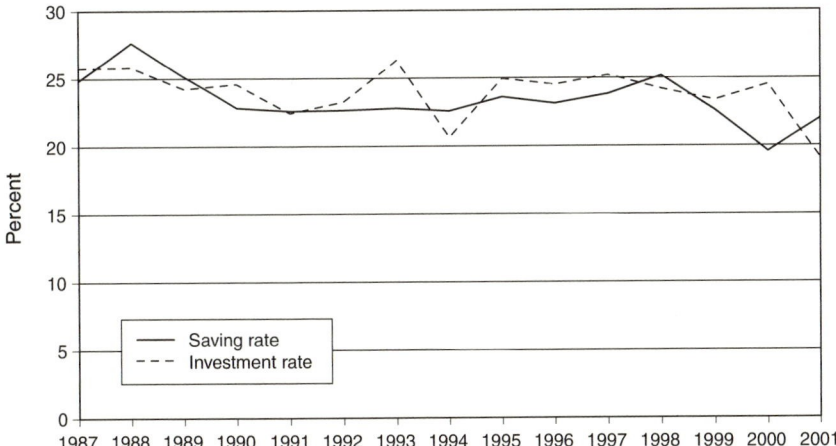

Figure 9.13. Turkey: national saving and investment rates as percentages of gross domestic product. Annual data, 1987–2001. *Source:* Economist Intelligence Unit.

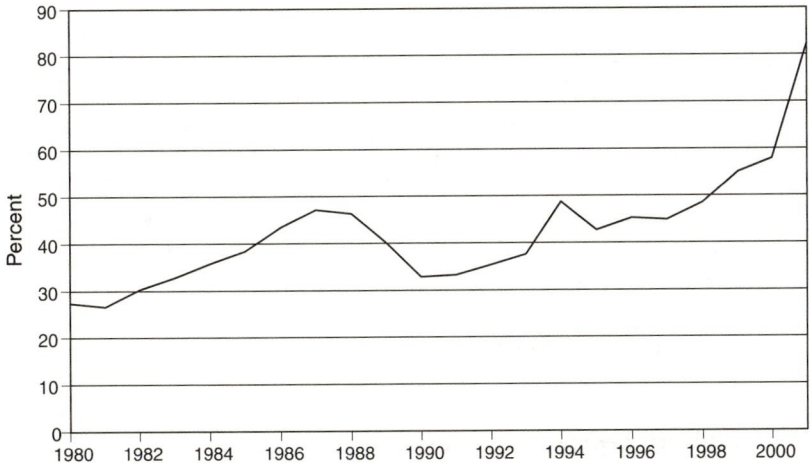

Figure 9.14. Turkey: foreign debt as percentage of gross domestic product. Annual data, 1980–2001. *Source:* Economist Intelligence Unit.

in a similar investment-saving gap for the year, shown in figure 9.13). This sharp rise triggered the crisis by putting pressure on the lira. For most of the years in the past decade and half, Turkey's current account balance, as shown in figure 9.12, was in the red, requiring foreign borrowing that had steadily moved from 28 percent of GDP in 1980 to over 80 percent in 2001 (figure 9.14). When the government abandoned the crawling peg

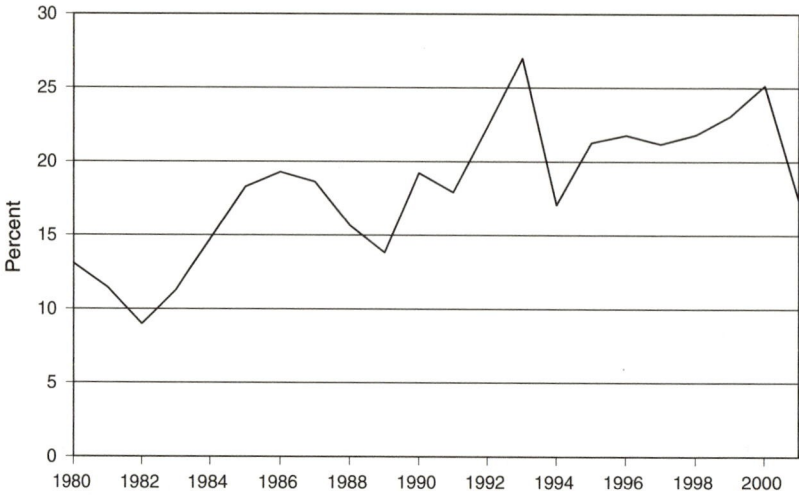

Figure 9.15. Turkey: short-term debt as a percentage of total debt. Annual data, 1980–2001. *Source:* Economist Intelligence Unit.

of the lira on February 22, 2001, the economy's foreign debt stood at $110 billion. Short-term debt as a fraction of the total had also risen to 25 percent of the total by 2000 (figure 9.15). A low number by the standard of the East Asian economies, the short-term debt, however, as in Argentina, was over 125 percent of the available foreign exchange reserves shown in figure 9.16. Again, these reserves, as also illustrated in figure 9.17, could meet about two months of imports for the Turkish economy in 2001 compared to 11 months in 1985.

Argentina and Turkey were both headed toward a debt repayment problem that threatened the stability of their currencies toward the end of 2001. There was however a major difference.

Argentina and Turkey: The Difference

In the absence of countervailing measures, the overvalued peso linked to the dollar depressed Argentine exports. Furthermore, the tight discipline of the currency board discouraged domestic saving and investment. The resulting low growth rates affected revenue flows in the budget that, along with continuing high outlays, resulted in significant budget deficits. The major achievement of the policy framework however was the conquest of inflation, which ran at quadruple-digit levels in 1991 when the peso-dollar link was established by Cavallo. In Turkey, by contrast, the IMF-imposed, crawling peg exchange-rate arrangement led to a real apprecia-

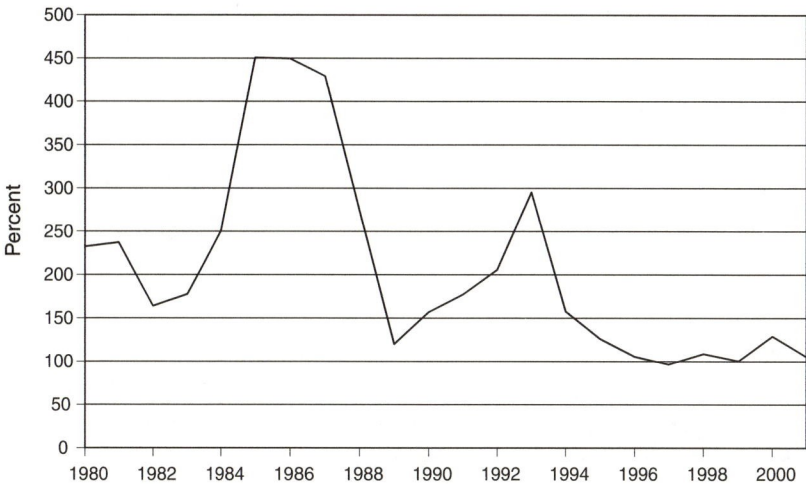

Figure 9.16. Turkey: foreign short-term debt as a percentage of foreign exchange reserves. Annual data, 1980–2001. *Source:* Economist Intelligence Unit.

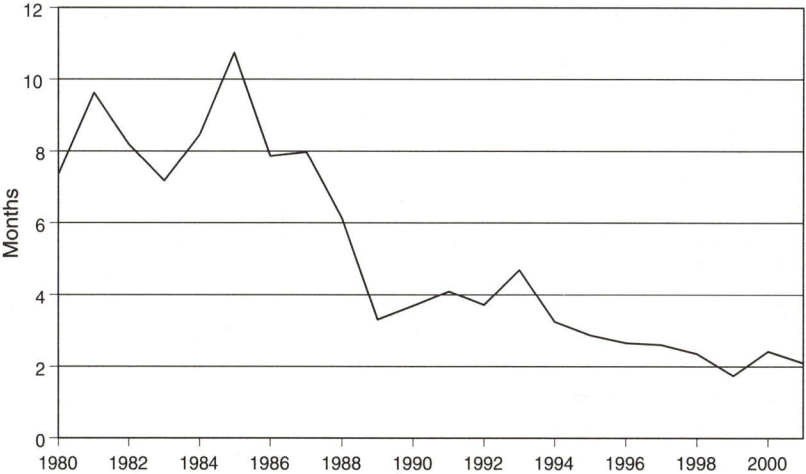

Figure 9.17. Turkey: foreign exchange reserves in months of imports. Annual data, 1980–2001. *Source:* Based on data from Economist Intelligence Unit.

tion of the lira but failed to tame inflation because of lax fiscal discipline. The high inflation-volatile-growth performance failed to convince foreign investors that the Turkish economy had moved into a low-inflation-steady-growth trajectory. On February 22, 2001, the Turkish authorities in agreement with the IMF floated the lira, which sank 36 percent within

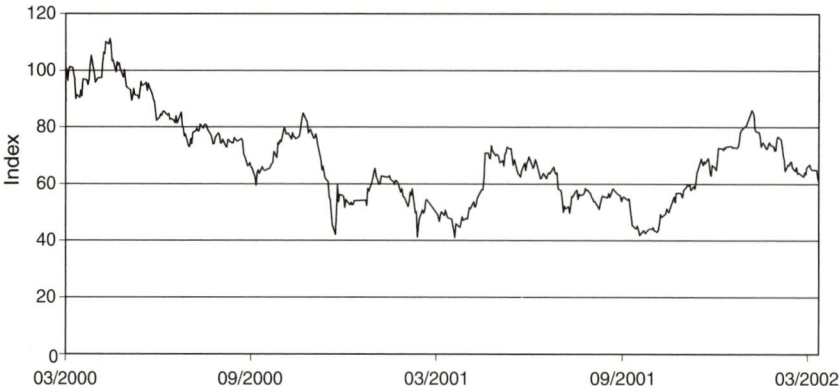

Figure 9.18.Turkey: Istanbul Stock Exchange-100 stock market index. Rebased, 3/20/2000 = 100. *Source:* Internet Securities, Inc.

two days, bringing the exchange rate to a million lira to the dollar. The Istanbul Stock Exchange (ISE) 100 index (figure 9.18) fell by 20 percent in a single day.

Financial and banking sector weaknesses and irregularities, reflecting the indecisive and fractured political arrangements, affected Turkey's reform momentum and economic performance.

Turkey: Structural Issues

On the eve of the November 2000 crisis, Turkey's banking sector was undercapitalized, poorly regulated, bifurcated between private and non-private asset ownership, and riddled with interference by politicians. At the same time, the fragmented politics deprived policy makers of the necessary political will to bring budget deficits under control and undertake rapid overhaul of the troubled banking system. Without fiscal discipline and banking reform, the crawling-peg disinflationary exchange-rate system remained dysfunctional.

Banking Sector Maladies

The November crisis was triggered by the collapse of ten commercial banks and panic-driven withdrawal of funds by foreign investors who sold Turkish financial instruments, pushing the overnight interbank lending rates to 2,000 percent. In February 2001, an Islamic "finance house," weighed down by years of mismanagement, abuse of depositors' funds, and generous extension of interest-free loans to questionable borrowers, collapsed (*Economist*, February 17, 2001). "The problem, simply put is: No one in the system is accountable. Turkey's needs for responsive, transparent banking and taxation systems have grown. But who would establish them?" (*New York Times*, February 27, 2001).

In September 2000, approximately 53 percent of banking sector assets were owned by fifty-four private banks of which the four largest had capital/asset ratio of 20 percent, far exceeding the required 8 percent recommended by the Bank of International Settlement. These four banks held 75 percent of the banking sector's $10 billion equity. However, the rest had variable rating in terms of risk management and borrowing/lending practices. Like Russian banks in the late nineties, they had borrowed short-term at low interest rates in foreign markets and invested in high-yielding government bonds. The double mismatch, borrowing short term in foreign currency and lending long term to local borrowers, rendered them vulnerable to foreign fund outflows by jittery investors in the fall of 2000 when the current account deficit (discussed earlier) approached 5 percent of GDP, putting downward pressure on the lira and upward pressure on the interest rates. The injection of liquidity to ease interest rates backfired because the banks used the cash to shift into foreign exchange. The scene was repeated on a bigger scale in February 2001, when the president and the prime minister openly quarreled, freezing interbank movement of funds in a panic-driven environment.

The absence of strict licensing procedures for setting up banks and the lack of enforcement of rules for regulating banking activity laid the groundwork for Turkey's financial crisis. A number of bank charters were granted to big campaign contributors as favors. The highly leveraged state banks and the weak private banks, in need of continuously rolling over their massive debts by borrowing from the market, kept interest rates high and affected the financial viability of healthy banks. The former needed to be taken over and recapitalized or folded, an arrangement that featured in the program announced by Kemal Dervis, the new economy minister. In his judgment, the cost of clearing the short-term debt of the three debt-ridden state banks would amount to $13 billion and their recapitalization needs to an additional $3 billion.

The rampant irregularities and lax supervision of the banking system resulted from weak political authority. At the same time, continuing, high and volatile double-digit inflation resulted from the government's inability to control budget deficits by trimming the vast bureaucracy and slashing extra-budgetary outlays. Turkey had failed to build viable political arrangements that could devise and maintain a reform momentum via effective consensus building on the major issues.

Turkey's Fractured Politics

In the more than seven decades since Mustafa Kemal Ataturk, the soldier-cum-statesman, salvaged Turkey from the ruins of the crumbling Ottoman Empire and declared it a modern republic in 1923, the country had failed to evolve into a mature, stable democracy. A prolonged war with Greece over Cyprus, followed by martial law and military rule, led to the installation of a government of technocrats supported by the military. In the midst of the continuing internal disorder and ethnic fighting with the Kurdish minority, Turkey's weak political institutions failed to impose the necessary fiscal discipline or reform the banking system, both of which were necessary for the economy to move into a stable, inflation-free growth path.

In the midst of the continuing political uncertainty, the IMF and the World Bank sought to impose financial discipline and structural reforms with little success. Following the November 2000 crisis, the IMF announced a $10.4 billion support package for Turkey, of which $7.5 billion was in the form of new loans. The government was expected to clean up its banking system and to speed up its slow privatization process as conditions for the loan. Immediately, the markets responded positively to the loan announcement—the stock market index rose, and interest rates fell. The loan infusion provided a temporary relief until February 2001, when panic struck again from the high-level political brawl: interest rates jumped to 7,200 percent, making the crawling-peg arrangement unsustainable, the devaluation of the lira inevitable, and the announcement of a fresh start for the economy by Kemal Dervis, the new economy minister.

Turkey, One More Reform Push

The new program put banking sector reform at the top of the agenda. Banks, strong and weak, were battered by the twin shocks of the lira's depreciation and the high interest rates: the former because of higher, local currency costs of clearing foreign liabilities and the latter because of higher borrowing charges. Marketable bonds in the amount of $16 billion would help meet the restructuring needs of the highly indebted state banks and fend off their immediate collapse. Insolvent banks would be liquidated. This process would be supervised by a common board of directors consisting of independent bankers. New legislation would ensure the independence of the central bank.

The major policy shift was the adoption on February 22, 2001 of a floating lira in place of the earlier managed crawl of the currency. The objectives of the earlier IMF program of fiscal discipline backed by tax reforms, rapid privatization, and spending cutbacks were to be pursued more aggressively. The program also proposed sale of 51 percent of state-owned Turk Telecom, rapid privatization of Turkish Airlines, and breakup of alcohol, tobacco, and sugar monopolies. The switch of public sector enterprises to private ownership and management and the shakeup of entrenched monopolies raised the specter of job loss among workers who, supported by unions, small and mid-sized businesses, and opposition parties, protested in Ankara, Izmir, and Konya in early April. The government, a shaky three-party coalition, immediately responded by re-scheduling shopkeepers' tax debts and subsidizing interest charges.

At the same time, output and employment continued contracting in 2001 from the high interest rates that were necessary for restoring investor confidence and containing inflation. In April, the IMF promised an early release of $7.5 billion and the World Bank of $5 billion to support the restructuring program and ease the cost. But the U.S. and other industrialized countries declined to augment the IMF-World Bank funding with additional bilateral support. By mid-August, the lira was 54 percent of its February value, interest rates hovered around 90 percent, unemployment mounted, and GDP was slated to fall by 8 percent in 2001 marking Turkey's worst recession since the Second World War. The IMF released a further $1.5 billion in August, allowing part of it to be used for the government's domestic outlays. The primary budget surplus of 5.5 percent of GDP (net of interest charges) was inadequate for the Treasury to clear its debt obligations earmarked in foreign currency as the lira lost its value. Domestic banks were unwilling to lend to the government, which could not borrow in foreign markets after the events of 9/11 because risk-averse investors turned away from emerging markets.

As 2002 advanced, Turkey was headed toward economic and political uncertainties that neither the resolve of Kemal Dervis nor the standard remedies of the IMF were geared to overcome. The political crisis following Prime Minister Ecevit's illness in May escalated into bitter divisions over the controversial issues of economic and human rights requirements that Turkey must fulfill in order to qualify for European Union membership. The governing coalition fell and parliament voted on July 31 to hold elections 18 months ahead of schedule. Politicians with pro- and anti-EU sentiment, the press, and the public energetically debated the issue of Turkey's loss of national identity and religious values upon the country becoming an EU member. Irrespective of the election's outcome and the economic prospects, Turkey will in all likelihood continue to be supported by IMF funding. As a NATO member, an antiterrorism alliance partner, and a possible launching pad for military action against Iraq, it cannot be allowed to flounder.

Like dead cats responding to a stimulus, Argentina and Turkey revived momentarily in response to the frequent IMF bailouts but lapsed back to economic rigor mortis. Their prospects for sustained recovery depended on budget deficit cutbacks by fragile coalition governments in the midst of chaotic domestic politics and a depressed global environment. The standard prescriptions employed by the IMF in the crisis-ridden economies of East Asia held little promise of stabilizing Argentina and Turkey.

Even as their economic outlooks at the end of 2001 remained precarious, the financial and currency contagion from the Argentine and Turkish crises was contained in Latin America, unlike the impact of the Asian turmoil which hit Russia and Brazil. In the next chapter, I analyze this contrasting pattern by introducing the contagion models that have evolved from the traditional trade-induced transmission from the center to the periphery to the more recent financial-flow-generated disturbances across national borders.

Notes

1. The peso was tied to the dollar by law, but the arrangements in practice lacked the strict monetary disciplining of an orthodox currency board defined on page 265.

10

The Contagion

THE ASIAN CRISIS originating in Thailand in July 1997 hit Brazil in November 1998, devastating Russia's fragile finances in August 1998 along the way. The crisis originating in Asia became global. By contrast, the financial and currency problems of Argentina, unrelated to those in Turkey, remained largely confined to the neighboring economies of Latin America. The conceptual and empirical analysis of this chapter provides three important insights with regard to crisis transmission.

First, excessive and indiscriminate short-term capital inflows from financial institutions of the developed center, including banks as well as mutual and hedge funds with linked global operations, not only created the financial and currency turmoil in the Crisis Five of Asia (analyzed in chapters 5 and 6), but also transmitted it beyond their borders via the domino effect. The common lender not only withdrew from the original source of financial trouble but from all around. By contrast, the risk-averse, quality-conscious approach of these lenders, the result of their Asian experience of concentrating in the high-return, safe havens of China and Mexico in emerging markets and of the U.S. and the European Union, prevented the Argentine financial turmoil from becoming worldwide. For the same reason, a possible debt default by Brazil was likely to contaminate other indiscriminate borrowers in Latin America, bypassing the Asian emerging markets. Second, the debt default of Argentina, unlike the August 1998 Russian debacle, was anticipated by creditors who had managed to adjust their balance sheets over time preempting an extensive turbulence. Third, the financial transmission mechanism of the East Asian crisis differed from the earlier trade-related fallout from the developed center that affected the peripheral emerging markets. For example, the negative impact of the oil shock of 1973 on the U.S. economy set off a trade-induced chain reaction, although a manageable one, among a group of countries. This first-generation contagion model reappeared in 2000 and 2001 as the synchronized slowdown, which turned into a post-9/11 recession in the world's three largest areas, the U.S., the European Union, and Japan, affected the economic growth of several emerging market economies via their reduced exports (including tourism).. While the developed center spared them a financial knockdown, it hit them instead with a trade-related downturn.

Source: Wonsoo, *Seoul Shimbun*, Seoul, Korea. Cartoonists and Writers Syndicate.

I begin with an analysis of the global contagion that resulted from the financial crisis of 1997–98.

The East Asian Crisis and the Contagion

On August 27, 1998, the stock markets tumbled at varying rates in every major economy in the world, except for Hong Kong (figure 10.1). Despite this *one-day* stock market contagion reflecting the August 17 collapse of the ruble, the U.S. and European stock indexes registered positive gains on *a year-to- year basis*. This suggested that markets in the developed economies had overcome the negative impact and moved up since the August 27, 1997 East Asian crisis fallout: their one-day, ruble-related turmoil was a dip in markets that were moving up. By contrast, stock markets of all emerging market economies, and of Hong Kong and Australia (physically close to East Asia) failed to crawl out of the financial turmoil of East Asia during the year.

The European Exchange Rate Mechanism (ERM) breakdown of 1992–93 and the Mexican peso crisis of 1994–95 were confined to their respective regions. By contrast, the East Asian financial and currency meltdowns swept across continents knocking currency values, threatening high inflation, and imposing severe economic decline from one country to another.

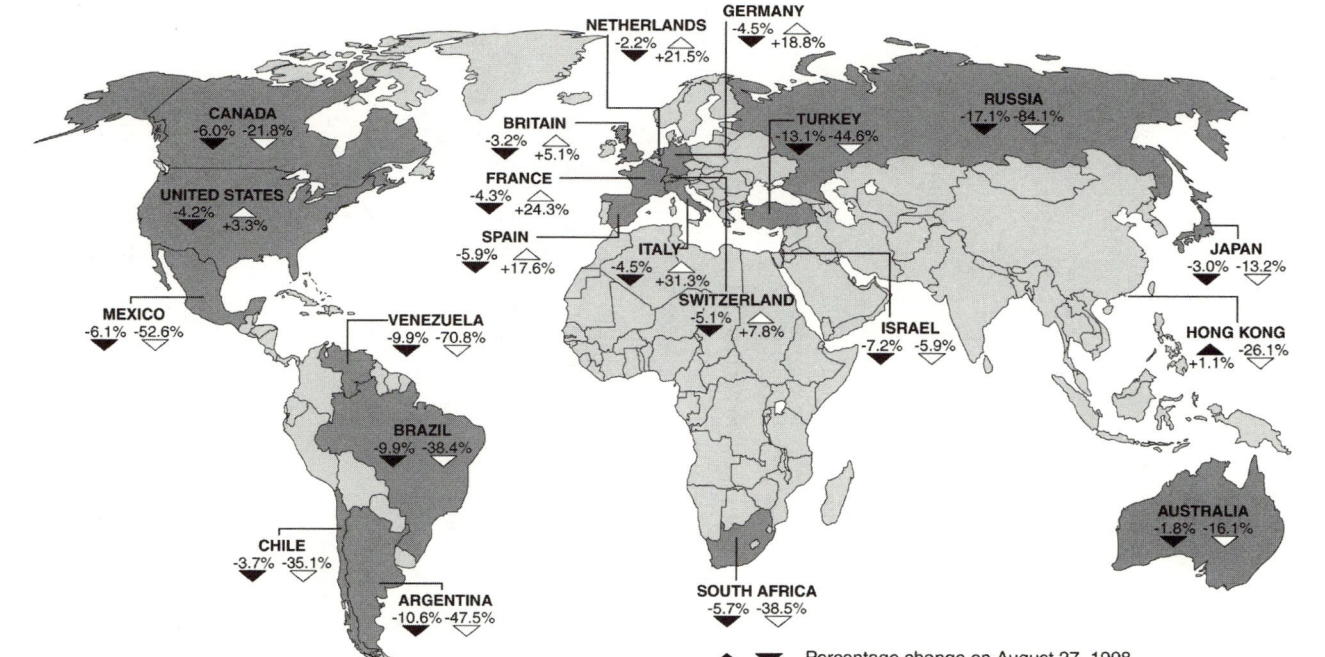

NETHERLANDS
-2.2%
+21.5%

GERMANY
-4.5%
+18.8%

CANADA
-6.0% -21.8%

BRITAIN
-3.2%
+5.1%

RUSSIA
-17.1% -84.1%

TURKEY
-13.1% -44.6%

FRANCE
-4.3%
+24.3%

UNITED STATES
-4.2%
+3.3%

SPAIN
-5.9%
+17.6%

ITALY
-4.5%
+31.3%

JAPAN
-3.0% -13.2%

SWITZERLAND
-5.1%
+7.8%

MEXICO
-6.1% -52.6%

VENEZUELA
-9.9% -70.8%

ISRAEL
-7.2% -5.9%

HONG KONG
-26.1%
+1.1%

BRAZIL
-9.9% -38.4%

CHILE
-3.7% -35.1%

AUSTRALIA
-1.8% -16.1%

ARGENTINA
-10.6% -47.5%

SOUTH AFRICA
-5.7% -38.5%

▲ ▼ Percentage change on August 27, 1998
△ ▽ Year-to-date percentage change, as of August 28, 1998

Figure 10.1. The crisis spreads. Stock markets around the world closed broadly lower on August 27, 1998, as financial crises in Russia, Asia, and Latin America unnerved investors around the world. All of the year-to-date percentage changes are in dollar terms. *Source: New York Times,* August 28, 1998, p. D7.

Contagion arises because modern economies are linked via trade and finance. A group of countries may have strong bilateral trade or they may compete in a third market by dominating in the sale of common items; they also manage trade flows via financial arrangements with suppliers and commercial banks. Often regional trade is facilitated by banks of a single dominating creditor: Japanese banks dominate in East Asia just as American banks prevail in Latin America. Common lenders can not only transmit a crisis but aggravate it as well. Banks, compelled to reassess their overall asset risk and strengthen their capital position following initial losses will not only call back loans and curtail credit lines in the original country but also all around. The appearance of excessive nonperforming loans in one country thus sets off a chain reaction with several banks pulling out of other affected countries spreading the financial contagion (Kaminsky and Reinhart, 1998, p. 15).

Banks however do not concentrate on trade financing alone nor are they the only actors in financial markets. Hedge funds that channel financial flows in diverse economies by acquiring their currencies, and mutual funds and institutional investors that invest in cross-border bonds and equities react the same way as banks when signs of financial trouble appear in one country. Brazilian asset prices fell in reaction to a crash in South Korean asset prices. Countries with internationally traded financial assets and liquid markets that allow investors to move in and out of their holdings are likely to be more vulnerable to contagion.[1] Countries providing limited opportunities for readily disposable financial assets and therefore claiming minor representation in international portfolios are shielded from such contagion (ibid., p. 6).

The changing patterns of intercountry links expanding from trade transactions to the far-flung multinational financial activities of investment and hedge funds influenced the formulation and empirical examination of contagion models (briefly discussed below).

Theories of Contagion

When can spillovers be defined as a contagion? The oil shock of 1973 was absorbed by oil importing countries including the U.S. at a cost that did not transpire into a global contagion. The resulting decline in the U.S. economy affected the exports of partner countries without creating an unmanageable chain reaction in the world trading and financial system. In this instance of a first-generation contagion model, the spillover, the result of an oil shock, operated via weakened fundamentals and foreign trade transmission among a group of countries.

With the Latin American debt crisis of the eighties, the contagion mechanism expanded from spillovers via goods and services into those involving financial assets, among them Latin American debt instruments. The second-generation models took on extra features relating to the behavior of financial agents and the market information at their disposal, the costs of gathering and evaluating the information in a target country, and the expanding cluster of potential financial markets at the disposal of a single investor. Analysts faced new questions: Do investors act rationally? As rational actors, do they act in herds? Do financial asset returns move together across countries resulting from or inducing cross-market hedging by fund managers? What is the role of common lenders—U.S. banks in Latin America and Japanese Banks in East Asia—in triggering and spreading a crisis? How does one separate the impact on contagion of these financial factors from the standard, macroeconomic, foreign trade ripples?

From an empirical perspective, the financial and currency crises of East Asia and Latin America signaled new channels of contagion on top of the standard, foreign trade-induced transmission.

Transmission Channels: Empirical Evidence

Since a cluster of countries with high trade participation with one another or a high share of exports in third markets are contagion-prone, a screening of the relevant foreign trade information will provide prima facie evidence leading to a measure of contagion outcome. Similarly, borrowing banks' relative liabilities to a common creditor and their liabilities in relation to the common creditor's total exposure will suggest a potential contagion when banks in an infected country are targeted for fund withdrawal by the common creditor. Finally, concentrated financial sector linkages through liquid holdings and cross-hedging by mutual funds in a group of countries and their walkout from the financially vulnerable debtor would create a likely stampede engulfing the entire region.

Did the Asian financial crisis spread across the region and hit Brazil through trade channels?

Contagion through Trade, the First-Generation Transmission

Transmission via trade can occur from an economic downturn resulting in reduced purchases of a partner country's goods or via a devaluing currency conferring a competitive advantage to one country at the cost of a rival trading partner in third markets. For example, Thailand, the infected country, could transmit the crisis by slashing its demand for Indonesian, Malaysian, and South Korean goods as evidenced by the exports of these countries (relative to their total exports) to Thailand. The Malaysian ringgit, declining earlier and more rapidly than the Korean won, could push

No strong trade etiology *NOT trade contagion* *little intra trade (not to Russia)*

up Malaysian semiconductor exports at the cost of Korean semiconductor exports in third markets. The relevant trade data rule out a critical role for foreign trade via these two channels in the contagion.

For example, Thailand, Indonesia, Malaysia, and South Korea, each exported a small fraction of its total exports to the remaining three partners during 1990–97. Indonesian exports to the three intraregional partners averaged 12 percent of its total exports. Each of the remaining three exported a smaller fraction, averaging 8 to 9 percent, to the intragroup trading partners. At the same time, the East Asian contagion did not hit Russia via trade knocking down Russia's exports to the four countries of the region, which averaged less than 1 percent of Russia's total exports. Nor did Brazil catch the contagion via a diminished demand for its products by the East Asian four. Its exports to the region were a small 4 percent of its exports during 1990–97. Its exports to Russia were even lower, averaging 1 percent of its total exports.

By contrast, the East Asian four exported a significant fraction, individually averaging 35 to 40 percent of their total exports to Japan, and 25 to 30 percent to the U.S., suggesting the likelihood of their experiencing a recession as a result of a downturn in the two dominant economies, in the U.S. beginning in mid-2000 and in Japan continuing in the nineties and beyond.

Next, did significant trade in a given commodity in a third market transmit the contagion in the East Asian cluster and beyond? Did South Korea manage to outperform Malaysia in the Japanese and other markets with respect to exports of semiconductors thereby worsening Malaysian trade balance? In 1996, semiconductors made up 15 percent of South Korea's total third market exports and 18 percent of Malaysia's total third market exports (Kaminsky and Reinhart, 1998, table 14). In 1998, the share of each had diminished with no reversal of their relative export performance. The evidence supportive of South Korea (Malaysia) replacing Malaysia's (South Korea's) share of semiconductor trade in third markets and thereby contributing to Malaysian (South Korean) recession was missing.

The evidence in support of the contagion spreading through trade channels was absent, but the indications of crisis transmission in the region via potential activities of a dominating single creditor, namely Japanese banks in East Asia, were strong.

Contagion via Fund Withdrawal by a Single Creditor, the Second-Generation Transmission Model

On the eve of the Asian crisis, Japanese banks were highly exposed in terms of their lending to the four East Asian economies relative to their total lending activity. These economies, in turn, were heavily indebted to Japanese banks.

As of December 1996, the exposure of Japanese banks in terms of the loans extended by them, relative to their total lending, to the four crisis-swept East Asian economies was 54 percent. As the crisis unfolded in Thailand, the banks recalled their loans, mostly short term, from the region as a whole accentuating the crisis. Their exposure had declined sharply a year later. At the same time, East Asian banks had borrowed heavily from Japanese banks. Banks in each country showed substantial liabilities relative to their total liabilities to Japanese banks. More than half of Thai banks' total borrowing, at 54.5 percent on the eve of the December 1996 crisis was from Japanese banks. The liabilities of South Korean banks to the Japanese banking sector, as a fraction of their total at 24 percent, was again significant, although lower than Indonesia's 39.7 percent and Malaysia's 36.9 percent. As Japanese banks recalled their loans, the banking industry in the region was thrown into a massive liquidity crunch. A year later, bank exposure in each country to Japanese banks had slumped to single digit numbers.[2]

But banks were not the only lenders in emerging markets. The dominating presence and activities of mutual funds stretching from East Asia to Latin America set the stage for the start and spread of crisis as they withdrew funds from collapsing banks and businesses and liquidated their equity holdings. With the removal of capital account controls in East Asian economies (narrated in block 3), the assets of these countries found a place in the portfolios of developed country mutual funds that invested across national frontiers and carried out cross-market hedging worldwide. These funds moved into Asian bonds and stocks in their ascending phase pulling them up, and moved out en masse as the markets began their decline in Thailand. On June 30, 1997, mutual funds registered in developed countries and operating in emerging market economies carried 2.68 percent of their holdings in Thailand, 4.35 percent in Indonesia, 5.88 percent in Malaysia, and 6.16 percent in South Korea. Their stake in China, that discouraged such entry, was 2.44 percent. Brazil had a 13 percent share of the funds' emerging market holdings. The funds were not only active in the crisis-prone Asian, Russian, and Brazilian markets; they also moved their holdings in and out in locked steps contributing to synchronized and volatile stock markets (reported in figure 10.6 later in the chapter).

The crisis spread as a result of the destabilizing activities of dominating Japanese creditor banks in East Asia and of developed country mutual funds with liquid holdings in the sampled countries rather than through the traditional channel of trade links. Therefore, it is not surprising that the financial and currency market pointers, among them interest and exchange rates and stock market indexes, each moved to-

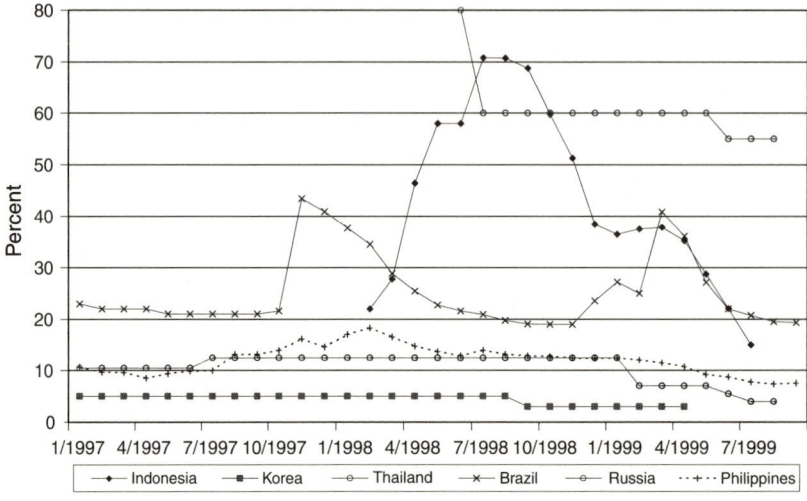

Figure 10.2. Central bank discount rates: crisis-prone economies. *Notes:* End-of-month values. The central bank discount rate is the rate at which central banks lend or discount eligible paper for deposit. *Source:* International Monetary Fund, Banco Central do Brasil.

gether across countries from Thailand to Malaysia, Indonesia and South Korea, Russia and Brazil.

Indicators Moving in Sync

The monthly interest rates, real exchange rates, and stock market indexes shown in figures 10.2–10.7 illustrate the synchronized (rising and falling) movements in each indicator in East Asia, Russia, and Brazil. The contagion, measured in terms of these financial flash points, stalked the East Asian group, Russia, and Brazil in locked steps excluding China, Hong Kong, Singapore, and Taiwan.[3]

The July 1997 interest rate hike in Thailand, calculated to moderate the pressure on the currency from withdrawal of foreign funds by speculators, was followed by the one in Philippines and the remaining sampled countries. Figure 10.2 shows that interest rates remained generally much higher in Brazil, Indonesia (in continuing financial and political turmoil), and Russia than in Thailand, Philippines, and South Korea which had an edge in their economic fundamentals on the eve of crisis onset. Interest rates began their decline as the financial crisis was brought under control at different points in time in each country. Figure 10.3 shows that interest rates in crisis-immune China, Hong Kong, and Taiwan were low, below

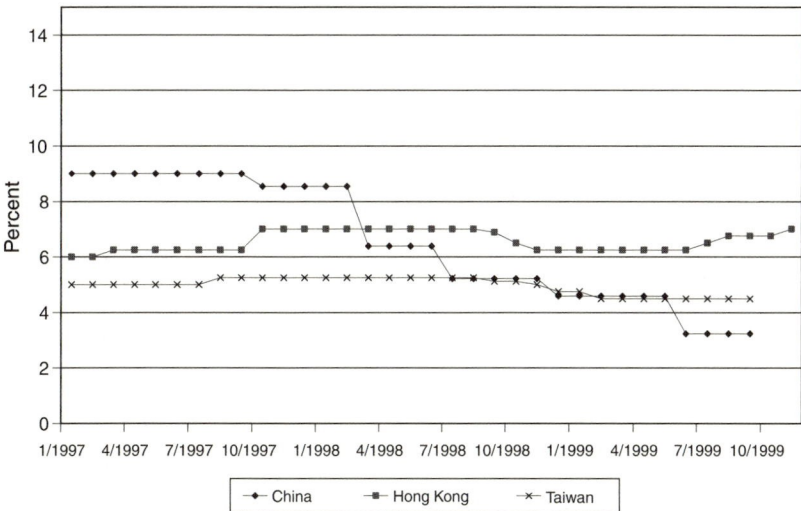

Figure 10.3. Central bank discount rates: crisis-immune economies. *Notes:* End-of-month values. The central bank discount rate is the rate at which central banks lend or discount eligible paper for deposit. *Source:* International Monetary Fund, Central Bank of China (Taiwan).

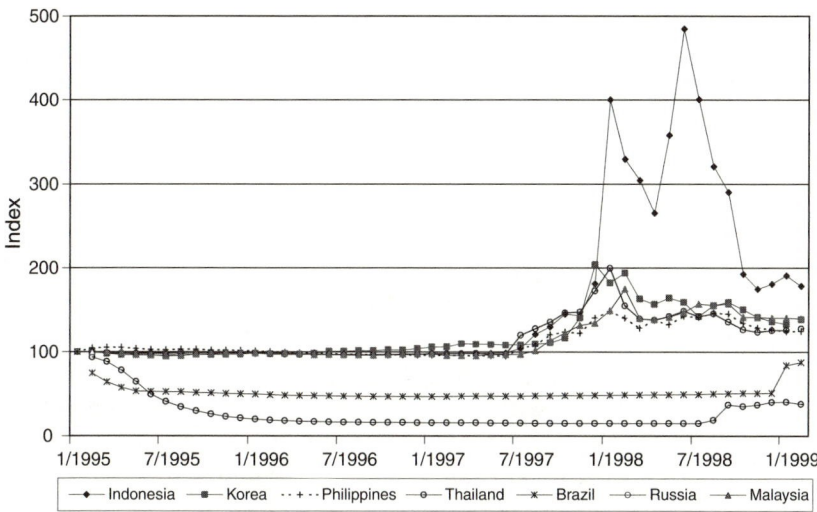

Figure 10.4. Real exchange rates: crisis-prone economies. *Notes:* A downward movement represents real appreciation. January 1995 = 100. *Source:* International Monetary Fund.

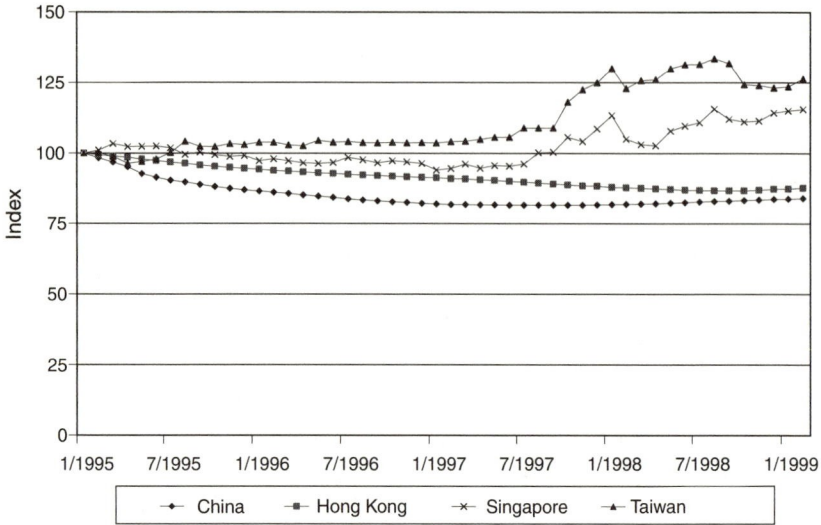

Figure 10.5. Real exchange rates: crisis-immune and crisis-safe economies. *Notes:* A downward movement represents real appreciation. January 1995 = 100. *Source:* International Monetary Fund, Central Bank of China (Taiwan).

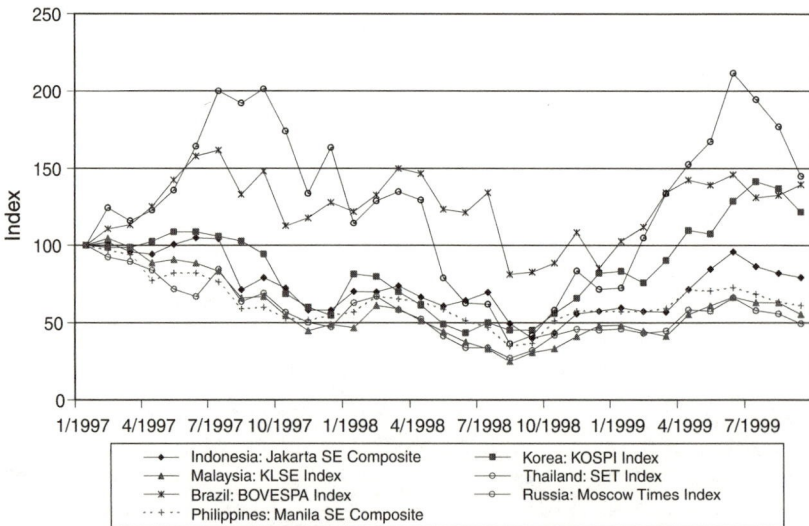

Figure 10.6. Stock exchange indexes: crisis-prone economies. *Notes:* End-of-month values; rebased, January 1997 = 100. *Source:* Dow Jones & Company.

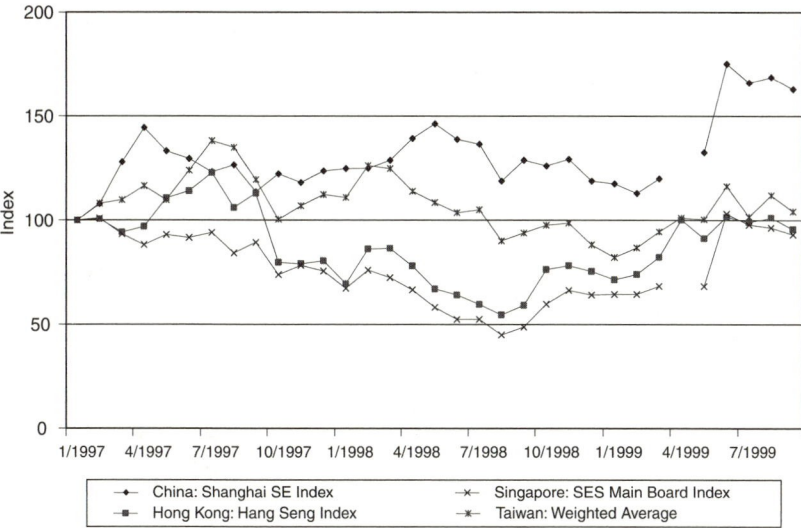

Figure 10.7. Stock exchange indexes: crisis-immune and crisis-safe economies. *Notes:* End-of-month values; rebased, January 1997 = 100. *Source:* Dow Jones & Company.

annual 10 percent, and stable (except in China where they were brought steadily down to 3 percent by mid-1999) in contrast to their high levels and up-and-down movements in the economies displayed in figure 10.2.

Figure 10.4 shows that real exchange rates in the crisis-prone Asian economies were stable and overvalued from 1995 to mid-1997. As noted earlier (in note 5 of chapter 5 and block 2), the combination of high short-term foreign debt, low foreign exchange reserves, and overvalued real exchange rates contributed to the crisis onset. They depreciated together after July 1997 as the Thai baht came under attack, and began appreciating together in early 1998 as the impact of the crisis on the exchange rates moderated. Indonesia, although volatile, reflected this pattern. The exchange rate movements in Russia and Brazil have a similar pattern although they depreciated later than the Asian set because the currencies came under pressure with a lag. The Russian ruble began appreciating in early 1995 and remained high between July 1996 and July 1998 until its collapse and real depreciation thereafter. (The International Monetary Fund[IMF]-supported, exchange-rate-based stabilization policy in Russia is discussed in chapter 7.) The Brazilian *real* also appreciated in the first half of 1995 and remained steady until its January 1999 devaluation. Such synchronized real exchange rate movements of these financially troubled economies were absent in the crisis-immune economies of China and Hong Kong shown in figure 10.5. China (following systematic and gradual relaxation of exchange controls) and Hong Kong (under a fixed exchange rate regime of the currency board) had strong currencies marked by slight real appreciation throughout the period from January 1995 to January 1999. The exchange rates in (crisis-safe) Singapore and (crisis-immune) Taiwan also deviated from the pattern of the Asian Crisis Five. They were stable until mid-1997, but continued declining thereafter, evidently correcting the earlier overvaluation.

Finally, the stock market indexes shown in figure 10.6 in the crisis-prone economies moved in synchronized steps. They declined from January 1997 to July–August 1998, then climbed up until July 1999. Russia and Brazil had a similar down and up movement with greater volatility. Figure 10.7 shows how Singapore, Hong Kong, and Taiwan followed the down and up pattern of the stock indexes of the crisis-prone economies but the deviation was less pronounced. China's stock market, more regulated than the rest, was the least affected during the two years from January 1997 to January 1999.

In the Asian group, contagion measured impressionistically by these indexes, linked Thailand, Philippines, Malaysia, Indonesia, and South Korea because of speculative capital outflows. China, Taiwan, Hong Kong, and Singapore were less affected by the transmission process because their speculative exposure was either manageable (in Taiwan and Hong Kong) or minimal (as in Singapore) or practically nonexistent (as in China).

Why did the later Argentine and Turkish financial and currency problems create a limited contagion?

The Twin Crises and Their Limited Fallout

Unlike in the East Asian crisis, the financial turmoil in Turkey remained localized with minimum impact on neighboring emerging markets.

Crisis Containment within Turkey: Minimum Trade and Financial Linkages

In February 2001, some emerging bond markets dipped in reaction to Turkey's financial and currency problems, and Moscow's stocks dropped 9 percent, but they bounced back the next day. Turkey's crisis did not spread because it was Turkey-specific. It originated from a combination of political, institutional, and policy weaknesses in Turkey: the coalition government was fragmented, the banking system was weak, and the crawling peg exchange rate regime was under constant pressure from fiscal abandon. At the same time, Turkey's trade links with other emerging markets were limited and the exposure of foreign institutional asset holders in Turkey was marginal. Measured by their share in the J. P. Morgan emerging market bond index, Turkish bonds had a minuscule weight of 2 percent. No major U.S. banks are known to hold more than 1% of their assets in Turkey. No major investment fund is thought to have Turkey among its top-five country weightings, and many had slimmed down holdings in recent months (*Wall Street Journal*, February 26, 2001, p. 13).

By contrast, Argentina's trade and financial links with Latin American neighbors rendered them susceptible to a fallout from a threat of debt default or currency collapse in Argentina. Argentina's financial troubles affected Brazil, the *real* slipped to low levels in 2001, and Brazilian recovery was stopped in its tracks. The withdrawal by cash-strapped Argentines of their deposits in Uruguayan banks threatened a banking crisis in Uruguay requiring a temporary closure of banks and a U.S. Treasury-financed support of $1.8 billion in August 2002. However, the domino effect of a serious crisis spreading worldwide was absent.

Argentina: Contagion via Trade Links

The continuing Argentine recession resulted in declining imports from Latin American neighbors and threatened an economic slowdown among Argentina's trading partners. Again, this impact affected Brazil, which sold 10 percent of its total exports to Argentina, more severely than Chile and Mexico, which shipped less than 5 percent of their exports to Buenos Aires.

Argentina: Contagion via Financial Links

Argentine bonds had a weight of 23 to 24 percent in the J. P. Morgan emerging market bond index in contrast to Turkey's minuscule weight of 2 percent. When high interest charges prompted Economy Minister Domingo Cavallo to cancel an auction of $350 million in treasury bills scheduled for April 24, 2001 to cover the maturing debt held by local banks and companies, the spread between the Argentine floating rate bond and the U.S. Treasury bond widened to a high 16.9 percentage points. Argentine bond prices plunged reflecting concerns by creditors that the government might default on its debt obligations or the peso might be devalued. The cancellation of the bond auction sent negative signals to Latin American bond markets and put pressure on their currencies. However, the up and down impact of Argentine bond prices on neighboring country debt instruments varied with their exposure. For example, Brazilian investors were among the leading speculators in the Argentine bond market and the exchange of the short-term Argentine assets into long-term instruments concerned them more than Mexican investors who were increasingly active in the U.S. financial sector in the post-North American Free Trade Agreement era.

A marked change in foreign investors' attitude, following the East Asian global meltdown and the Russian debt default, contained the financial impact of the crisis even after the Argentine debt default of December 2001, and the uncertainties surrounding the peso's value after it was delinked from the dollar. Unlike the Russian debt default of August 1998, which was sudden in its timing, the Argentine default was anticipated. The escalating risk of holding on to Argentine bonds was reflected in the spread between their returns and the yields on U.S. Treasury bonds which had widened to 35 percent in December 2001 from 7 percent the previous year. Foreign holders had appropriately adjusted these bond valuations in their balance sheets, removed these bonds from their assets, and replenished their portfolios by acquiring other emerging market bonds. Again, foreign lenders had become quality conscious since their Asian experience, preferring to invest in more stable emerging markets that were less risk-prone, such as China and Mexico. They had acquired multiple emerging market assets in the speculative binge of the nineties that were financed by excessive bank loans exposing them to forced asset sale in one market to recoup losses in another. In the new millennium, they were smaller, more selective, less leveraged, and better poised to handle the fallout from the Argentine debt default except those that had switched to Brazilian debt instruments.

Although the second wave of the financial and currency crises of 2000–02 in Turkey, Argentina, and Brazil lacked a global reach—an outcome to which creditors' risk aversion contributed—these crises originated from the unsustainable borrowing and high spending by these economies that were financed by the gung-ho capital flows of the nineties from the developed economies. The economic costs of the risky "debt-growth" strategy spilled into serious political uncertainties in these countries in late 2002 as they faced national elections.

The ripples of the post-9/11 contagion transmitted via trade and investment channels into emerging markets were short-lived, but nevertheless global as the U.S. recession in the third quarter of 2001, followed by the slow recovery in 2002, synchronized with poor economic performance in Europe and negative growth in Japan.

The Post-9/11 Contagion

This contagion originated in the industrialized world and spread via trade and investment links in emerging markets. Emerging market businesses could not float new equity or bonds for subscription by foreign investors.

Overall, Latin American stock market indexes declined more sharply within a week of 9/11 than their counterparts in Asia. Investors lost their appetite for overseas investment putting off plans for acquiring emerging market assets via mergers and acquisitions or new greenfield ventures. Such investment in electronics in some Asian economies, among them Singapore, Taiwan, and Malaysia, ground to a halt as investors became risk-averse in the midst of prolonged uncertainty, damaging the export potential of these economies. Again, trade-linked contagion via reduced demand for exports spread in East Asian economies, among them South Korea, Taiwan, Singapore, and Malaysia as their exports of electronics and components slumped. Mexico, in Latin America, with 90 percent of its exports targeted for the U.S. market, was most severely affected. Declining tourism affected hotel and airline industries across Latin America. A rapid and robust U.S. recovery in 2002 was necessary for arresting this trade and investment decline and restoring growth optimism in these economies.

The East Asian and Latin American economies, swept by financial and currency turmoil, received IMF financial support that was tied with structural and institutional reforms in recipient countries. The size of the funding and the intrusiveness of the needed changes varied from country to country. However, as I argue in the next chapter, the policy approach requiring monetary and fiscal austerity in these recession-prone economies for restoring investor confidence was, without exception, standardized and severe.

Notes

1. Frankel and Schmukler (1998) employ data on closed-end country funds to test contagion and show how shocks from the Mexican devaluation crisis of December 1994 may have been transmitted to other emerging markets.

2. According to Kaminsky and Reinhart (1998, p. 16), the share of U.S. bank lending in Mexico relative to total lending in emerging markets in June 1994 on the eve of the Tequila crisis was 22 percent; the relative indebtedness of Mexican banks to U.S. banks was again a significant 34 percent. A similar disaster-prone pattern emerged in Asia three years later.

3. The purpose here is to show coordinated movements in each indicator across countries rather than suggest leads and lags. For example, the initial rise of interest rate in Thailand can be argued to lead to subsequent rate increases in other countries. Nor do I explore cause and effect among the three indicators in a given economy. For example, interest rate hikes were calculated to control plummeting currencies and stock markets (as argued in chapter 6) and therefore preceded them in their declining phases; but as currencies and stock markets began firming up (as a result of IMF bailout going into action), it is not clear if the declining interest rates preceded or followed such improving performance in the sampled countries.

11

International Monetary Fund to the Rescue:
How Did It Fare? Badly

As THE ASIAN financial crisis spread from Thailand to the neighboring countries and beyond to Russia and Brazil with a speed and on a scale not encountered before, the International Monetary Fund (IMF) found its financial resources and negotiating skills, its technical expertise and public posturing, and above all, its policy relevance tested to the hilt. Three years later in late 2000, the IMF faced a debt and currency turmoil in Argentina in the midst of a recession that arose from an antiquated policy framework tying the peso to the dollar under a currency board straightjacket. After the debt default of December 2001, the economy resembled a tired beast in chains, which the IMF sought to tame with its standard offering of financial support coupled with fiscal tightening. The Fund also faced the prospects of the unraveling of its stabilization programs in Brazil and Turkey as voters in both countries signaled uncertain election outcomes in the fall of 2002. As I argue in this chapter, the IMF's policy record from Bangkok to Buenos Aires was colored by its ideological policy preference in favor of capital mobility; marked by its standard procyclical response of fiscal disciplining of recession-prone economies with a view to restoring investor confidence; and occasionally influenced by pressure from the U.S. Treasury motivated by non-economic considerations. Itself a slow, inflexible bureaucracy, the IMF failed to carry out timely and innovative solutions differentiated by the circumstances of member countries seeking its support.

The crisis in East Asia created an unprecedented challenge. It was starkly different from the run-of-the-mill situations in which member countries in the past had sought IMF support for handling imbalances resulting from excessive public sector outlays leading to monetary expansion or from economy-wide overspending spilling into current account deficits. The new supplicants in East Asia did not have fiscal imbalances nor did they have significant current account deficits, except Thailand. Rather, they faced a liquidity crisis triggered by outflows of foreign short-term capital.

Russia, by contrast, had hardly anything right. As I argued in chapter 7, its fundamentals were out of joint; it lacked the necessary institutions of a functioning market system; and its politics were fractured. More than anywhere else, the G-7 under U.S. leadership desired the Fund's continuing engagement in Russia, a disintegrating nuclear power, whose destabilization carried a high security risk and heavy political costs. The IMF's long association with Russia's reformist band of policy makers dating back to mid-1992 had become a contentious issue by the end of the millennium.

Brazil was crisis-prone: its long record of budgetary weakness and unsustainable borrowing interacted with exogenously triggered capital outflows in 1998 and political uncertainties in mid-2002 that shook investor confidence, weakened the *real*, and raised speculations about an Argentine-style default of the country's $250 billion debt.

The financial crises in Argentina and Turkey, unrelated to each other, intensified in late 2000 as a result of weak fundamentals in each that pressured their currencies. Argentina's declining economy hobbled by the peso's link to the strong dollar, dwindling tax revenues, unsustainable budget and current account deficits, and escalating foreign debt kept international lenders of its $132 billion debt nervous about a default or a currency devaluation, both of which occurred in December 2001. Turkey's crisis in November 2000, continuing into late 2002, originated from its rising budget and current account deficits that pressured the lira and led to capital outflows. In both countries, the IMF responded with its worn-out recipe of financial support coupled with budget deficit slashing in the midst of declining economic growth and escalating political uncertainties.

I analyze IMF engagement in Thailand, Indonesia, and South Korea in East Asia, Russia, Brazil, Argentina, and Turkey, omitting Malaysia because it did not seek IMF support.

IMF Support in East Asia: The Details

On August 20, 1997, the IMF Executive Board approved a loan of $4 billion for Thailand, the first country to seek IMF assistance, in a three-year standby arrangement, part of an $18 billion package with additional funds from the World Bank, the Asian Development Bank, and Japan. Indonesia turned to the IMF following a massive depreciation of the rupiah in late October. The IMF approved $10 billion for Indonesia in November as part of a three-year standby arrangement, followed by $8 billion from the World Bank and the Asian Development Bank, and a pledge of $18 billion from bilateral sources as additional support. Korea approached the IMF in December, receiving the largest package, a total of $21 billion from the IMF, $14 billion from the World Bank and the Asian Development Bank, and a pledge of $23 billion from bilateral sources as a second line of defense.

The support was unprecedented. A member's access to IMF funding depends on its quota in the organization. Financial support for Thailand amounted to 505 percent of its quota. Indonesia's package was 490 percent. The figure for South Korea was a staggering 1,939 percent!

The IMF's commitment to these countries amounted to over $36 billion. The World Bank and the Asian Development Bank contributed almost $27 billion, and bilateral sources pledged about $54 billion, bringing the total to $118 billion. By the beginning of 1999, a year after the third country had turned to the IMF for assistance, the Fund had distributed $30.9 billion, almost all the promised support (IMF, 1999, p.3). The funding provided foreign exchange to each country's central bank, enabling them to repay debts falling due.

The Fund loan program, similar in design for the three countries, reflected its diagnosis of the crisis.

IMF Diagnosis of the East Asian Crisis

The IMF diagnosis focused on four features.

First, massive short-term funds had moved into the countries because their exchange rates prior to the crisis were more or less stable and their interest rates were higher relative to those in potential lenders. Implicit or explicit government guarantees also encouraged such borrowing (ibid., p. 12). (I discuss the moral hazard consequences of the presumed automatic bailout flowing from such guarantees for borrowers in block 6.) Second, the foreign currency debt, private and short term, was largely unhedged. Assuming that exchange rates would remain stable, South Korean and Thai institutional and corporate borrowers, who borrowed from abroad, ignored the risk of foreign currency exposure and avoided the cost of hedging it. Lenders overlooked the fact that the risk to their borrowers arising from a currency drop translated into a credit risk for them. (I analyze the implications of the Fund's policy switch from these managed exchange rates to floating arrangements for emerging market economies in the next chapter.) Third, short-term foreign borrowings were lent long term to finance risky and dubious investments, for example, in the property sector at home. In hindsight, the Fund acknowledged that "the inflows were to a considerable extent financing asset price inflation and an accumulation of poor quality loans in the portfolios of banks and other financial institutions" modifying its earlier, mistaken perception that the inflows arose mainly "from favorable investment prospects associated with a stable macroeconomic environment and high growth" (ibid., 1999, p.10). Finally, the currency and maturity mismatches in the portfolios of banks and financial institutions, in the IMF view, arose from structural weaknesses and lack of prudential and regulatory environment. Governments had traditionally encouraged investments via policy loans and corporate debt guarantees, overlooking the need for risk assessment. Depositors or creditors did not monitor banks because their liabilities carried implicit guarantees. Close links between banks and borrowers encouraged excessive lending. (I address the issues of the connection between such links and corruption, and between corruption and the growth performance of the East Asian economies in block 7.) As a result, bank balance sheets showed substantial nonperforming loans, big exposure to the property sector, large holdings of corporate stock, and low capital/asset ratios. "In Korea and Thailand, large corporations were highly leveraged, aided among other things, by a complex system of debt guaranteed within *chaebol* (Korea) and a relatively generous tax treatment of corporate debt compared to equity" (ibid.,).

The "root cause" of the crisis and its distinguishing feature from earlier episodes, in the Fund's assessment, were structural. "The programs therefore featured structural reforms that had few precedents in depth and breadth" (ibid., p.18).

The Rescue Strategy

The immediate concern of the IMF was to commit its financial resources to Thailand, Indonesia, and South Korea with a view to stemming capital outflows, exchange rate collapses, and inflation spirals. Its related goal was to initiate and enforce structural reforms for restoring investor confidence, capital inflows, and economic growth. The resource commitment noted above was conditioned on the adoption by the recipient countries of swift macroeconomic adjustment via monetary and fiscal tightening under a floating exchange rate regime.

Monetary Tightening

Without a monetary squeeze, the nominal exchange rate could fall unchecked and, in turn, induce a wage-price spiral, impose massive burden on banks and corporations struggling with their overexposure to foreign-currency-denominated liabilities, and lead to competitive devaluations. The IMF adopted interest rates rather than credit or monetary aggregates as de facto instruments of monetary tightening.

Fiscal Trimming

Initially, the IMF did not see the need for massive fiscal belt tightening to offset current account imbalances because these were not problematic except in Thailand. The budgets however were expected to cover the costs of financial sector overhauls. For example, they must set aside resources to recapitalize viable banks.

Exchange Rate Arrangement

The country policy makers could be advised to opt for a new currency peg consistent with medium-term fundamentals or to let the currency float.
    Each option had pluses and minuses.
    Pegging in the midst of a crisis was impractical and inadvisable. To start with, how does one locate an ideal peg? A level fixed in the heat of the crisis may turn out later to be over-depreciated. The option would require raising interest rates to ruinous levels in order to defend the peg. Foreign exchange reserves in any case were inadequate for the purpose. The peg may have to be abandoned later if market pressures resurfaced. Floating also had its negatives. Countries could start competitive adjustments following the downward slide of one currency for protecting their market share in third countries. A depreciated currency would lead to increased money supply because banks had foreign currency deposits. It would weaken the budget by raising debt-servicing and food subsidy costs. Companies battling foreign currency debts would cut back their tax payment to the treasury. Ultimately, the decision to let the currencies float was predicated on the provision of financial support for the currency combined with monetary policy solidly leaning against the wind: it was calculated to dampen the overshooting of nominal exchange rates and avert depreciation-led inflation spirals. No specific targets however were assigned to the floats.
    The IMF rescue packages raised energetic debates.

The Debates

Was the IMF diagnosis of the crisis correct? Not in my view.
    The diagnosis was lopsided because the IMF overemphasized structural lapses and inadequate financial sector supervision and regulation in the Asian economies as the "root cause" of the crisis to the neglect of the premature opening up of these economies to short-term speculative capital inflows.

Lopsided Diagnosis and the Intrusive Mandate of Structural Reforms

Was the "root cause" of the crisis structural? These economies had solid and stable growth records despite these shortcomings in the years before short-term capital inflows inundated their banks and businesses. At the same time, the IMF encouraged a disaster-prone policy gamble of capital account liberalization in these economies before they had put their "structural house" in order.[1] The Fund did not signal anywhere in advance that the volatile mix of near-stable exchange-rate regimes and premature short-term capital inflows was guaranteed to bring in its trail the "financial vulnerabilities" and "maturity mismatches" it *subsequently* discovered. Finally, in identifying structural factors as the primary source of the crisis, the Fund laid itself open to the charge of being inordinately demanding in its structural reform requirements, and of simultaneously failing in implementing them in recipient countries despite the intrusiveness because of political constraints, traditional corporate practices, and well-established cultural norms.

The premature capital account liberalization and the short-term capital inflows complicated policy initiatives for authorities in Thailand where the crisis began in mid-1997. The IMF had warned them of an impending crisis. "In the case of Thailand, the crisis, if not its exact timing, was predicted. Beginning in early 1996, a confluence of domestic and external shocks revealed vulnerabilities in the Thai economy that, until then, had been masked by rapid economic growth and weakness of the U.S. dollar to which the Thai baht was pegged. But in the following 18 months leading up to the floating of the Thai baht in July 1997, neither the IMF in its continuous dialogue with the Thai authorities, nor increasing market pressure, could overcome their sense of denial about the severity of their country's economic problems . . . but action was not taken" (Fischer, 1998a, p. 8). The Fund staff also "warned about financial sector weaknesses in several of the countries badly hit by the crisis" (ibid., p. 3). The financial sector weaknesses however could not have been repaired overnight. If the Fund desired that the Bank of Thailand promptly lift interest rates to retain foreign investor confidence, the measure could have drained funds from the neighboring countries requiring similar action by their policy makers which they all undertook eventually and failed in relieving the pressure on their currencies. The Fund not only misjudged the severity of the capital-outflow–led crisis in individual countries but also the impending contagion in the region.

The hasty opening up of the Asian economies to significant capital flows was predicated on the belief that they would absorb them productively to the advantage of borrowers and lenders. The advocates of capital

Source: Cartoonists and Writers Syndicate.

mobility assumed that these economies had the necessary institutional and regulatory safeguards enabling them to function resiliently like the U.S. economy, for example. Having realized that these safeguards did not exist, the IMF sought to generate them in the region by incorporating them in its funding packages. This approach had negative repercussions. First, the Fund, according to the Meltzer Commission, went beyond its traditional role of managing macroeconomic stability in troubled economies. Feldstein (1998) raised the issue of the encroachment imposed by the Fund's structural reforms on sovereign governments' autonomy. Next, the external pressure was not necessarily successful in implanting the desired institutional and regulatory changes. Emerging market policy makers encountered problems in implanting the reforms during an economic downturn, and thought they were unnecessary during an economic upturn. (I provided the details in block 1.) Finally, the global hedge funds destabilized emerging market economies by imposing an exogenous crisis on them. The catalytic potential of short-term capital flows, which according to Fischer (1998c, p. 6) were undertaken by global hedge fund and some investment banks, was to continue because proposals to impose transparency on their activities invoked fierce opposition from the industry (as I discuss in the next chapter). The IMF's structural reform agenda therefore placed the reform burden of crisis prevention on emerging market economies and contributed to the center-periphery tensions in the continuing debate on reforming the global financial system.

The IMF's policies, emphasizing fiscal and monetary contraction in the crisis-swept economies that were sliding into severe slowdown, prompted serious criticism as well.

Misguided Fiscal Policy

The fiscal health of the East Asian economies noted in chapter 5 prior to the crisis gave no cause for concern. Actually, strong growth and budgetary positions over time had contributed to a decline in their ratios of public debt to gross domestic product (GDP). Why then did fiscal pruning constitute an important part of IMF conditionality? Evidently, the Fund was only "mirroring market sentiment. If a country like Brazil [to be discussed below] were to respond to slower economic growth by cutting taxes and increasing public spending, investors would flee, the currency would crash and the resulting financial distress would only make the recession worse. Thus, market discipline is perverse. As Paul Krugman put it: 'Brazil, we are informed, must suffer a recession because of its unresolved budget deficit. Since when does a budget deficit require a recession?'" (Eichengreen, 1999b, p. 35).

The IMF fiscal stance thus violated the received Keynesian wisdom of expansionary fiscal policies to deal with economic downturns. Wasn't fiscal contraction egregious in the presence of withdrawal of foreign funds? asked Radelet and Sachs (1998). Not so fast according to Lane and colleagues (Lane et al., 1999), who argued that the measures were taken to assuage the concern raised by their critics: since domestic private agents were expected to scramble for funds as foreign capital withdrew, allowing the government to expand the budget deficit would squeeze the available funds. These IMF economists overlooked two alternative possibilities. Since monetary brakes were activated to stem capital outflows, an overly stringent fiscal tightening aggravated output decline, revenue flows, and budgetary management. A less austere fiscal stance was possible and advisable. Second, country-specific, temporary capital control measures could have arrested capital outflows as in Malaysia, and prevented the "crowding out" of private activity from enhanced government spending feared by Lane and associates.

The IMF's fiscal policy stance in the targeted countries was subsequently revised and softened, not with a view however to increasing liquidity in the economies but because the Fund's growth and revenue projections and social safety net requirements for the economies turned out to be wrong.

Source: "IMF conditionality in the crisis," Nop's World, *Bangkok Post*, July 31, 1997.

Revised Fiscal Targets

In Thailand the original plan, calculated to turn a fiscal deficit of 3 percent of GDP into a surplus of 1 percent, was scuttled in February 1998 (Lane et al.,1999 and IMF, 1999). The target was lowered to a *deficit* of 2 percent, the result of the lower-than-expected improvement in the economy. Increased social spending contributed to the emergence of projected deficit. Similar belt tightening was built into the original letter of intent for Indonesia yielding a budget surplus of 1 percent of GDP. The target was reduced by mid-January 1998 to a fiscal deficit of 1 percent of GDP. As economic turmoil intensified, government outlays to cover increased social spending were revised upward, resulting in a projected deficit of 8.5 percent of GDP by June! South Korea saw similar target revisions. Initial capping of fiscal outlays was reversed by February 1998, allowing a projected deficit of 1 percent of GDP to cover the increased social safety net expenditures; the deficit target was revised to 2 percent in May, reaching 5 percent by July.

Having applied monetary and fiscal brakes, the IMF relied on unrealistically positive growth projections, and underestimated the need for social safety nets via budgetary provisions. The IMF's macroeconomic packaging could have been less draconian if it was combined with controls on capital outflows which could have moderated such outflows and the recessionary drag in these economies. Financial support from non-Fund official contributors was inadequate. The massive and fast-paced capital outflows that threatened financial havoc, economic downturns, and worker layoffs, far exceeded the official inflows; again, these had to be phased to ensure fulfillment of IMF conditionality by the recipients. Besides, the promised cash from the rest of the official contributors was uncertain and, at best, slow to materialize. The IMF resources were hopelessly inadequate to meet the formidable financial requirements of the hour. "The plain fact is that capital flows have become so large that the official sector often does not have enough resources to stabilize an economy without private sector participation" (Fischer, 1998c, p. 9). Having encouraged the wild beast of capital inflows to freely step into the Asian markets, the Fund tried trapping it on its outward flight in a mousetrap.

The IMF thus administered the bitter pill of austerity in the East Asian economies in the midst of their downturn contributing to their further decline. By contrast, it bit more than it could chew in its five-year policy-making venture in Russia and, in effect, stepped aside from the scene after the collapse of the ruble in August 1998.

The IMF and Russia

The goals of the West under U.S. leadership in post-Soviet Russia have been strategic and political as well as economic. They required that Russia's nuclear weapons be kept under a unified and effective control; its disintegrating military be prevented from descending into further chaos; its authoritarian political past be remodeled into a democratic alternative; and its planned economy be converted into a market system.

This multifaceted program raised questions about the means and the resources for its implementation. Two decisions guided the process from day one that began in 1992. First, direct channeling of aid via individual Western governments was excluded although some, including the U.S., pursued bilateral programs. The collective decision was that financial support for transforming Russia into a democratic market economy must essentially be multilateral and routed via the multilateral financial institutions drawing in the G-7 governments in the process through their presence in these institutions. Second, the overall resource commitment was limited despite Russia's enormous needs and despite earlier calls by some to mount "Grand Bargains" for rescuing Russia in exchange for its commitment to wind down as a nuclear superpower. The big-bucks promoters overlooked the fact that Russia lacked the institutional infrastructure to absorb massive aid flows.[2] However, the involvement of the multilateral institutions helped Russia reschedule and restructure its substantial debt including its sovereign obligations from the Soviet period (negotiated from time to time by the Paris club of creditors) and its commercial debt (negotiated by the London club of creditors). The multilateral institutional commitment to the reform process also kept foreign investor interest alive in Russia.

The decisions to multilateralize the resource inflow and cap it at relatively low levels with adequate monitoring were in my view sensible. From both perspectives, the IMF was perceived as ideally suited for navigating the reform agenda for Russia, disbursing the financial support, monitoring its use under its performance criteria, and moving Russia forward into a market economy. From 1992, the year of Russia's membership to the Fund with a stake of 2.8 percent (in contrast to 17.7 percent for the U.S.) to the August 17, 1998 collapse of the ruble, the Fund steered the policy agenda for Russia analyzed at length in chapter 7.

Where did it go wrong? The questions were posed from four directions.

First, did the IMF concentrate excessively on inflation control to the neglect of structural reforms in Russia? Second, while it operated in a volatile political environment, did it ignore the political reality by enforcing unsustainable inflation control targets, in the process inviting the financial debacle of August 1998? Third, was the July 1998 funding of $4.8 billion to stave off the ruble collapse mishandled by the Central Bank of Russia raising doubts about the Fund's monitoring clout? Finally, was a fraction of other IMF funds concealed by the central bank via offshore accounts raising charges that it misused IMF credits?

Macroeconomic Stabilization versus Structural Reforms

The IMF faced formidable realities in crafting a policy blueprint for Russia in interaction with the reformist groups in the government. The economy emerging from the Communist command straightjacket totally lacked the basic institutions of a market system, among them a functioning central bank. The 1991 budget deficit was estimated at a staggering 17 to 21 percent of GDP. Wages had been freed and most prices were freed by the government on January 2, 1992, threatening a wage-price spiral. Out-of-control inflation, fed by mounting growth rates of money supply in the second half of 1992, hit 2,500 percent by the end of the year.

Given this scenario, the Fund's choice of inflation control as the top priority with a view to stabilizing the ruble made sense. At the same time, market economy institutions could not be expected to emerge except in reaction to and interaction with appropriate, market-oriented policies. For example, money-supply growth rate could not be controlled without a central bank in charge; budget deficit targets could not be implemented without a tax code. The decision to implement a managed float of the ruble from mid-1992 required a functioning currency exchange as well. Market economy institutions in my view do not emerge automatically except in response to an acute need for them created by appropriate policies.

However, the IMF miscalculated the constraint on the *speed* of macroeconomic stabilization imposed by the lack of the necessary institutions, such as a crackerjack central bank, a simplified tax code, and a functioning tax collection agency. As a result, Russian inflation was tamed via monetary control rather than decisive budget- deficit trimming. Faced with inadequate tax collection and bound by IMF budget deficit targets, the government resorted to a variety of tactics: It turned to the banker-oligarchs who provided cash infusion into the budget in exchange for government stake in lucrative companies as collateral which they eventually captured. It borrowed from the public including from foreign sources, that in turn required hasty and premature removal of exchange controls on capital inflows. (Details are in chapter 7.) Premature capital account mobility turned out to be destabilizing for the East Asian economies that had sound government accounts. It was a disaster for Russia that had a bankrupt treasury. In fact, Russia fulfilled the criteria for the imposition of market-based capital account controls that the IMF did not consider. According to Fischer (2001, p. 6): "The typical instance [for the adoption of a temporary tax on short-term capital inflows] occurs when a country is trying to reduce inflation using an exchange rate anchor [as Russia did], and for anti-inflationary purposes needs interest rates higher than those implied by the sum of foreign interest rate and the expected rate of currency depreciation [as in Russia]. A tax on capital inflows can in principle help maintain a wedge between the interest rates. In addition, by taxing short-term capital inflows more than longer term inflows, capital inflow controls can also in principle influence the composition of inflows."

Finally, the unsustainable stabilization of the ruble under a managed float (replaced in mid-1995 with a crawling band) required a sustained appreciation of the real exchange rate that damaged the trade competitiveness of Russian goods. Seized with the mantra of leveling inflation to single-digit numbers, the IMF failed to distinguish between desirable and feasible speeds of macroeconomic stabilization. By contrast, Fischer (1999, p. 2) suggests that the speed of fiscal discipline was woefully inadequate: "Russia is a vivid example of the cost of gradualism on the fiscal front. The failure to bring the budget deficit under control was responsible for the increases in the government debt that increased the vulnerability of the economy to external economic developments, and that set off the unsustainable debt dynamics that culminated in the crisis of August 1998." Rapid macroeconomic stabilization on the fiscal front, however desirable, turned out to be the IMF's Russian pipe dream because legisla-

Source: "Bailout claimants from Asia to Russia," Heng, *Lianhe Zaobao*, Singapore. Cartoonists and Writers Sndicate.

tive decisions on a simplified tax code and adequate tax collection by the tax agencies, both of which required political will and institutional capacity, were sorely missing. The IMF overlooked this gradualist structural roadblock in its misguided enthusiasm in favor of fast-paced inflation control.

A serious impediment en route to rapid stabilization was therefore political. As late as 1997, four years into the Fund's entry into Russia, the Communist-dominated intransigent legislature refused to pass measures relating to reform of the pension system and the Soviet era across-the-board housing and utility subsidies that were a huge burden on the budget.

The IMF in the Midst of Continuing Political Turbulence

The IMF cannot be faulted for supporting Russia's reformist governments that continued to be formed with a tolerable mixture of constitutional legitimacy and backroom string pulling by assorted "cabinet makers." That support, starting in early 1993, made sense: it was necessary to identify and shore up several pro-reform groups in a situation rife with anti-reform sentiments and Communist agendas. But instead of positioning itself and the reformist governments to build a slow but firm macroeconomic stability, the Fund allowed itself to be overwhelmed by a policy agenda that flew in the face of Russia's political reality.

Veteran Russia watchers were aware of the predicament learned the hard way by the IMF and U.S. decision makers *after* their hasty policy agenda had collapsed with the meltdown of the ruble in August 1998. According to Treasury Secretary Lawrence Summers cited by Stanley Fischer, First Deputy Managing Director of the IMF (*Financial Times,* September 27, 1999, p. 12): "We cannot want reform in Russia more than Russia's government and people do." In other words, external pressure did not produce the intended economic outcomes or the desired institutional changes. The Russian electorate's verdict in the December 1999 Duma elections brought forth a centrist, pragmatic Duma with a vastly reduced, 25 percent representation of the Communists among the elected deputies. The disappearance of Boris Yeltsin, confrontational in style, deteriorating in health, and unpredictable in decision making, the election of Vladimir Putin as his successor, counted on by the voters to bring order and stability, and the virtual withdrawal of the IMF from an active policy-making role in Russia set the stage for the adoption of a homegrown reform orientation.

Yet another lesson of the nuts-and-bolts variety related to the presumed misuse of IMF loans by Russian authorities to which I turn below beginning with the July 1998 disbursement of $4.8 billion by the Fund to shore up the Russian ruble as it came under speculative attack.

Where Did the $4.8 Billion Go?

Having received the funds, the Russian central bank sold some of it on the Moscow Interbank Currency Exchange with a view to supporting the sinking ruble by acquiring rubles; it also lent rubles to banks enabling them to stave off bankruptcies and pay off depositors; it loaned them dollars so that they could pay off their foreign creditors. In the process, the central bank may have channeled some cash to its preferred bank clients. However, the disposal of the IMF cash among various users could not be verified by Pricewaterhouse Coopers, the firm hired by the central bank to review these transactions, because it prepared a report on the basis of information supplied by the bank. In any case, IMF dollars, having found their way into the coffers of the Central Bank of Russia, could not be distinguished in practice from the hard currency already available with the bank.

Despite the fungibility of such cash, several questions arose: Did the banks that acquired rubles convert them into dollars and deposit them in foreign banks rather than pay their depositors? Since depositors' cash was not guaranteed, their loss was unfair but not illegal. Since the foreign exchange rules allowed designated banks to transfer dollars abroad, no law was broken. In fact, contrary to charges of corruption leveled against them, such transfers were policy-induced (as I argued in block 5). Again, these banks might have deposited the dollars abroad rather than paid their foreign creditors. The proof to that effect was missing. Did the banks acquire dollars at varying rates favorable to some? But the rate, in fact, fluctuated from day to day. Did some insiders anticipating the impending ruble devaluation convert their government short-term bills (GKOs) into rubles and convert the rubles into dollars before the ruble was actually devalued? According to Russian oligarch Mikhail Khodorkovsky, government bureaucrats rather than businessmen were the ones to cut their losses. According to IMF sources, the devaluation decision was taken on Friday, August 14, and the government signed it on Saturday when the market was closed. Ergo, insiders could not have profited from the devaluation decision. Short of the Russian central bank completely revealing its balance sheet involving these transactions to an independent auditor, the disposal of funds at the command of the bank among various users could not be verified accurately.

It was clear that the IMF funding of $4.8 billion was too small in relation to the need of the hour. The government actually defaulted on $40 billion worth of ruble-denominated bills and bonds, and declared a moratorium on payment of foreign debt by commercial banks. Indiscriminate rationing by the central bank of the available IMF funding to preferred commercial bank clients was therefore inevitable.

In contrast to its disposal of $4.8 billion in July 1998, the Central Bank of Russia violated IMF conditionality in 1996 when it transferred $1.2 billion of its reserves to Fimaco, an offshore company located on the Channel Island of Jersey.

The IMF and Fimaco

Having transferred the cash to Fimaco, its offshore subsidiary, the central bank used the cash to buy Russian government bonds for supporting the budget, which it was prohibited from doing. It thus concealed its reserves from the IMF and used them for an illegal purpose. The IMF reaction to the clear misuse of Fund support by the central bank via the Fimaco subsidiary and to its inability to track down the disposal by the bank of the later (July 1998) $4.8 billion was threefold. The IMF released its next credit installment by moving it from one account to another without transferring a cent directly to the Russian central bank. It also required that several central bank overseas affiliates be closed before it would loan more money to Russia. Finally, the IMF would check Russian central bank balance sheets before releasing cash to the government of President Putin.

Its exceptionally long Russian engagement left the IMF increasingly leaner in its material support to Russia, unusually drawn into political controversies, and occasionally subject to arm twisting by the U.S. Treasury. The withholding of the post-meltdown second tranche of $342 million in the midst of the Chechen war, despite the Fund's acknowledgment of an improving economy, was timed to convey the U.S. Administration's displeasure over the war. With the restoration of political stability under Vladimir Putin, the revival of the economy in 2000, and the disappearance of the overarching Western goal of not letting Russia go adrift, the IMF assumed a peripheral policy-making stance in Russia.

Brazil, whose authorities turned to the IMF for support in November 1998, was different from Russia, although the crisis symptoms of capital flight brought on by an unsustainable public sector–deficit spilling into a current account deficit and pressuring the currency resembled Russia's. An emerging market economy under an elected president, Brazil had tamed inflation from a quadruple-digit 1,927 percent in 1993 to a low 7 percent in 1997, and posted an annual GDP growth rate of over 3 percent during the period with a reasonably low unemployment rate of 5 to 6 percent. Again, its current account deficit was financed with relatively less contribution from short-term foreign financing (in terms of the norms stated in chapter 5) than in the East Asian economies on the eve of the onset of their payments crisis. However, Brazilian government deficits posed significant problems requiring the overhaul of public sector finances long accustomed to bloated salary and social security payments and federal-provincial differences in containing traditional overspending practices.

The IMF and Brazil

The IMF policy stance in Brazil in late 1998 was based on the short-term goal of stemming capital outflow from the economy and the medium-term goal of restoring credibility in the management of its public finances. The former called for higher interest rates and the latter for fiscal tightening via improved revenue collection and reduced outlays combined with fast-paced approval of spending cutbacks targeted at permanently restoring fiscal balances.

IMF Support Program of November 13, 1998

The IMF three-year standby credit of $18.1 billion approved on November 13, 1998 was supplemented by support from the Inter-American Development Bank (IDB) and the World Bank, raising the aid package to $41 billion. The prompt approval of the disbursement of $4.5 billion in IDB and World Bank funding was designed to ease the impact of monetary tightening and decline in economic activity via support to small and medium businesses and to lower-income groups. Monetary control exercised through a rise in interest rates was to be joined by fiscal discipline, defined in public sector primary budget surpluses that were targeted to go up from 0.1 percent of GDP in 1998 to 2.6 percent in 1999 and 3 percent in 2001, stabilizing the ratio of public sector indebtedness to GDP at 45 percent. The policies and the support package, in the Fund's view, would restore investor confidence thus ruling out a change in the prevailing exchange-rate arrangement pegging the *real* to the dollar. Despite the support, capital outflows continued forcing the authorities to switch from the regime of "managed" devaluation to the *real* float of January 18. It slumped from R$1.32 per dollar to R$2.14 per dollar on January 29, requiring a revised policy framework and program.

Revised IMF Program of March 8, 1999

A major policy shift letting the *real* float (as with the East Asian currencies and later in 2001 with the Turkish lira and Argentine peso) was linked with inflation targeting: it was to be brought down from its annualized monthly rate of 45 percent to single-digit range by the end of the year. The Fund's attachment to single-digit inflation rates in Brazil (as in the case of Russia and later of Turkey) flew in the face of Brazil's weak public sector finances. Fiscal improvement and monetary tightening via flexible interest rates were to contain the inflationary impact of the currency depreciation of 40 percent since January. The revised targets of public sector primary surpluses were moved up to 3 to 3.5 percent of GDP for 1999–2001. Interest rates were expected to come down at levels below 30 percent by the end of the year thus easing the burden of public debt relative to GDP.

The program anticipated extensive structural reforms designed to lower social security payments, enhance fiscal transparency, and speed up privatization of state assets. The social security payment reforms were to build further on the November 4, 1998 law approved by the Brazilian Congress after four years of debate. The law banned retired civil servants from returning to work in the public sector; raised employee and retiree contributions to social security funds; capped pension benefits, forcing potential retirees to join private social insurance plans; and laid down new eligibility criteria by linking the retirement ages and benefits for men and women to their employment lengths and benefit contributions. The law on fiscal accountability was designed to remove loopholes in budget preparation and implementation at every government level by setting norms for budget deficits and permissible debt ceilings. Automatic trigger mechanisms would slash budget outlays if the norms were violated. Yet another proposed amendment to the 1988 Constitution would empower federal and state governments to legally remove redundant employees with a view to lowering the public sector wage bill. Most of these structural reforms were calculated to reduce and stabilize budget outlays in the long run.

The austerity measures coupled with diminished interest payments produced a surprise gain to the budget in March 2000 resulting in the biggest monthly federal budget surplus since 1991. The government successfully overcame political pressures for wage hikes by allowing a modest minimum increase of 11 percent. The central bank, set to lean against a strong *real* and promote export competitiveness, cut its benchmark lending rate to 18.5 percent from a steady 19 percent since September 1999 and a peak of 45 percent toward the end of 1998.

The authorities however struggled with tax, pension, and banking sector reforms, and the fulfillment of inflation and budget surplus norms in 2000. Despite the 40 percent devaluation of the *real* in January 1999 and the lowering of interest rates (noted previously), Brazilian export performance remained inadequate resulting in a current account deficit of 4.7 percent of GDP in 2001. Moreover, the further impact on Brazilian exports of a slowing U.S. economy and the fallout from Argentina's likely debt default, interacting with domestic problems of a government corruption scandal and the imposition of rationed energy use by households and industry, weakened the *real*. As foreign investment flows from risk-averse investors slipped from $33 billion in 2000 to an anticipated half the amount in 2001, the *real* depreciated by 20 percent from January 2001 to August 2001. The depreciating currency added to inflationary pressures and debt burden threatening to wipe out the modest gains of price stability and improved fiscal management as the debt burden mounted from 25 percent of GDP in 1997 to 47 percent in 2001. The IMF announced a $15 billion financial support to Brazil in August calculated to arrest a further decline of the *real*. The September 11 terrorist attacks on the U.S. raised prospects of the *real's* further fall by turning away nervous investors, denting Brazilian exports further as the U.S. economy headed toward a recession, and setting off a damaging ripple effect in Brazil of reduced tourism, hotel occupancy, and airlines activity. Voter discontent, political uncertainty, and the resurgence of fiscal free spending threatened to wipe out the economic gains of price stability as the Brazilian electorate faced presidential elections in October 2002.

Having failed to resolutely clean up its structural budgetary problems and raise its export earnings, and bring its debt burden under control, Brazil, the last to be hit by the Asian payments crisis, had failed to move rapidly to a sure-footed growth path like South Korea, Thailand, and Malaysia, all three of which had sustained records of healthy public sector finances, robust export performance, and high saving rates. The institutional reforms (which I narrated earlier) moved too slowly for the government to generate a primary budget surplus large enough to maintain a resolute repayment schedule of its debt liabilities. Public sector domestic debt as a share of GDP had climbed from 34 percent in 1997 to 55 percent by mid-2002. The cost of repaying the fraction of this debt denominated in dollars (at 20 percent of the total) had steadily risen with the continuing depreciation of the *real*. Brazil's foreign debt, mostly private, was less than 50 percent of GDP, but with foreign exchange earnings having failed to rise sufficiently, the debt service ratio had jumped from a minuscule 0.59 percent of GDP in 1990 to 8.20 percent in 2001 (see table 8.1). In fact, the overall saving rate was 16 to 17 percent of GDP (almost half of South Korea, Thailand, and Malaysia when they were hit by the crisis). It had lagged behind aggregate investment by almost 5 percent; reflecting itself in the current account deficit (see table 8.1).

With the deepening political uncertainties of the October 2002 presidential elections, Brazil found itself in a predicament that was marked by low growth, high spending, and unsustainable borrowing. It was doubtful if the dangers posed by the "debt-growth" model encouraged by unsustainable borrowing could be successfully averted by the Fund rescue package of $30 billion on August 7 of which $6 billion was promised for immediate use upon approval by the Fund management. The Fund needed to set in motion the option of an orderly restructuring of Brazil's nearly $250 billion debt. Otherwise an Argentine-style default was likely. The cow, to paraphrase the words of presidential candidate José Serra, could walk into the swamp.

The IMF and Argentina

With each successive financial package, which began with a release of nearly $14 billion from the IMF out of $40 billion worked up multilaterally in December 2000, and was followed by an additional $8 billion in August 2001 to support the peso-dollar peg and ward off debt default, the IMF conditionality became stricter and its policy stance tilted toward debt swaps by Argentine authorities. The zero budget deficit prescription necessitated state salary and pension cuts from the 2001 budget, and required more slashing of payments to individual recipients and provincial administrations from the 2002 budget. At the same time, monetary tightening raised the benchmark interest rate for 180-day peso loans to 37 percent in early October 2001. The government desperately needed to continuously roll over short-term debt in the final quarter of 2001 so that the remaining debt could be paid from the (primary) budget surplus, keeping the IMF program on track. It negotiated lower transfers to provincial governments in the 2002 budget and scaled back their debt obligations to the federal treasury by converting them into lower interest and longer period instruments. It arranged a similar swap of government debt of $60 billion with *local* banks and pension funds. Despite these frantic efforts, financial markets remained skeptical of the government's ability to prevent a default of the government's short-term debt of $35 billion to *foreign* creditors.

The $40 billion multilateral support of December 2000 under the Clinton administration and the subsequent IMF funding of $8 billion of August 2001 under the Bush administration failed to confront the grim reality of the Argentine crisis and depart from the worn-out IMF policy agendas of monetary and fiscal tightening. The signals from Washington from the new presidential administration pointed to reduced Fund handouts and more self-help and house cleaning by Argentine policy makers. Underlining its opposition to the Clinton administration's megabuck IMF rescues, the U.S. Treasury preferred a less generous bailout stance by the Fund. The new treasury secretary, Paul O'Neill, famously remarked: "We're working to find a way to create a sustainable Argentina, not just one that continues to consume the money of the plumbers and carpenters in the United States who make $50,000 a year and wonder what in the world we're doing with their money" (*Wall Street Journal*, August 20, 2001, p. A10). As if to initiate a novel policy departure, $3 billion of the $8 billion August IMF funding was tied to "a voluntary and market-based" debt rescheduling by Argentine authorities. This policy wrinkle, a fly swatter aimed at trapping an out-of-control stallion, came too late. From the start of Argentina's financial problems, the Fund had three options.

Backed by the U.S. Treasury, the IMF could have proposed a debt rescheduling plan[3] for consideration of all parties and tied the budget targets and a floating peso to its acceptance. If the proposal was turned down by Argentine authorities, it could have refused Fund support. Or, it could adopt its standard funding package and fiscal austerity, and watch the Argentine authorities implement it via pell-mell debt restructuring and escalating budget tightening in the midst of the destructive peso-dollar link. It chose the third option, which was least likely to succeed, most damaging to its policy record, and ominous in its consequences for Argentina's economy. An early debt-restructuring alternative initiated by the Fund and supported by the Treasury, would have figured

Source: "A brutal view of IMF bailouts," Nop's World, *Bangkok Post*, August 11, 1997.

in the agenda if the Argentine debt liabilities heavily affected the balance sheets of U.S. banks (as did South Korean debts), if they threatened the stability of the global or even Latin American financial system (which they did not), or if Argentina were a strategic partner (as Turkey was in the antiterrorism alliance).

What were the problems of an early restructuring of Argentina's debt?

Problems of Restructuring Argentina's Debt

Argentina's debt, approximately $133 billion by the end of 2001, had moved up in relation to its GDP from about 50 percent in mid-2000 to 60 percent a year later as the economy continued declining and interest charges accumulated. The debt, on federal government account, was $95 billion in bonds (of which $60 billion were held by local financial institutions including banks and pension funds), $4 billion in treasury bills, and $34 billion in credits from multilateral and other sources. The debt was a significant 23 to 24 percent of the emerging market bond index, and market analysts feared that its swap at less-than-market valuation would create a precedent for similar reductions for investors of Brazilian bonds. The debt was also held by far-flung financial institutions, mutual funds and insurance companies, domestic and foreign, involving complicated negotiations.

Given the complexity of the problem, the debt settlement formula required multiple features and a bold departure from the Fund's standard policy approach.

- Since most of the debt was sovereign (unlike the Korean debt which was private), the government had to be brought into early negotiations and acceptance of the restructuring option.

- In view of the wealth losses that the debt clearing was bound to entail, the foreign bondholders had the option of facing some losses earlier for their miscalculations on investments gone sour or risking bigger losses later.

- In order for the IMF program to remain on track, the formula also required that the restructuring losses of local holders of the debt be limited so that they remained financially viable, and the fiscal pressures on lower levels of government and the citizens be minimized. A further belt tightening of Argentine voters threatened the emergence of populist left-wing politicians who could undo the gains of the successful inflation battles of the early nineties.

- The Fund had information at its disposal relating to the emerging fiscal imbalance in Argentina, the formidable difficulties of improving it quickly via the government's ability to raise taxes or slash outlays, and maintaining a steady progress in meeting debt repayment obligations from budget surpluses.

- In order, however, to convince all parties of the urgency for early negotiated debt settlement, the IMF itself needed to bite the bullet of mounting an initiative for an early settlement of a member's sovereign debt. Although a precedent did not exist, the signal for such an unusual step existed in a communiqué of the IMF International Monetary and Finance Committee issued at its ministerial meeting on September 24, 2000 in Prague. For countries facing possible disruptions in their payments to private creditors, the communiqué's approach ranged from the most desirable, involving speedy and successful access by the debtors to the financial markets, to the least palatable of debt restructuring. If early restoration of full market access was unrealistic "a broader spectrum of actions by private creditors, including comprehensive debt restructuring, may be warranted to provide for an adequately financed program and a viable medium-term payments profile. This includes the possibility that, in certain cases, a temporary payments suspension or standstill may be unavoidable." (Details are in Mussa, 2002, pp. 32–33.) Finally, an orderly, timely, and total debt settlement under an IMF initiative could have paved the way for the removal of the peso's link with the dollar and the depressing discipline of the currency board. Argentina called for a bold policy move from the Fund at the very start of its bailout in December 2000.

Following the debt default, the peso's break from its eleven-year link with the dollar, and its switch from a three-week dual exchange rate to a free float in the market, the Argentine government and the IMF indulged in a chicken-and-egg routine. The former demanded reliable budget and growth numbers before extending a fresh round of funding, and the latter asked for new credits so that a credible plan could be devised. The peso did not crash in its first week of float in early February because of restrictions on banks to convert it into dollars and transfer them abroad, and a widespread shortage of cash in the economy. In Argentina, the IMF faced the indispensable policy trinity of a negotiated, orderly restructuring of all debts, viable budgets, and a floating peso before and after the debt default of December 2001. Debt restructuring was essential in order for the banks, businesses, and pension funds to start operating normally and for the Argentine treasury to begin formulating credible budgets across the governmental hierarchy, and to avoid the temptation of bridging the gap between revenues and outlays via monetary expansion that could send the peso spiraling downward.

Like Argentina but on a less formidable scale, Turkey remained a funding drain and a policy challenge for the IMF in 2001 stretching into 2002.

Turkey and the IMF

The IMF and the World Bank put together a support package of $15.7 billion in November 2000 when the Turkish lira came under pressure as a result of a large current account deficit which resulted from the unsustainable public sector deficit. The lira, which was allowed to appreciate under a crawling-peg regime, failed however to rein in inflation that exceeded 50 percent in 2000. The financial crisis of February 2001, the result of a public brawl between the president and the prime minister, required a policy change from the IMF: the lira was allowed to float, the central bank targeted inflation, and the government agreed to create primary budget surpluses with relief provided to the budget from IMF funding.

By September 11, the authorities had used up most of the IMF credits without generating the intended results. The inflation rate ran at an annual 60 percent, the average interest rates ranged between 90 and 100 percent, the economy was expected to contract by 8 percent for the year, and the lira had failed to arrest its decline. By mid-year, the IMF had revised its forecast of growth rate down to 3 percent and year-end inflation up to 58 percent. The primary budget surplus (before interest payments), 5.5 percent of GDP, was inadequate for meeting the government's payment obligations on its accumulated debts, requiring it to borrow up to \$2 billion at the end of the year and in early 2002. Domestic banks, which borrowed in foreign markets at lower interest rates, were hesitant to invest in lira-denominated government bonds of dubious future worth especially because banking sector reform imposed tighter asset valuation rules. As foreign lending from risk averse investors dried up after the terrorist attacks on the U.S. of 9/11, the government received \$16.3 billion in funding from the IMF for 2002, and promised to simplify the bureaucratic procedures facing domestic and foreign investors. Steady fulfillment of Fund targets and progress in structural reforms were stopped in their tracks in mid-2002 when Turkey was caught in a political crisis and awaited parliamentary elections. The economy again moved from the operating table to intensive care as the IMF medical team watched for signs of recovery.

The Turkish economy suffered from thirty years of high inflation despite a long association with the IMF, which had launched seventeen rescue programs since 1958 to stabilize it. The IMF targets and policies had proved unmanageable because of a combination of factors that included political divisiveness, weak banks, a faltering tax system, and an unsustainable debt burden. In view of these glaring handicaps, the IMF agenda of driving the inflation rate to its frequently favored, single-digit rate by 2003 was highly unrealistic. On the other hand, manageable inflation, monetary growth, and budget deficit targets supported by orderly debt restructuring over a longer period held out better chances for a successful stabilization.

The IMF, judged by the size of its funding programs, its inappropriate policy strategizing, and lack of innovative sequencing proved inadequate to the challenges it faced, from East Asia to Argentina over a period of five years.

Summing Up

Was IMF funding for the crisis-ridden economies inadequate?

The Size of the Funding

IMF credits were "megabucks" in contrast to its Bretton Woods era, balance-of-payments relief for member countries in need; as noted earlier, they were also substantial in relation to the quota entitlements of the crisis-ridden East Asian recipients. However, the funds were grossly inadequate to counter the recessionary liquidity crunch imposed by the actual and potential speculative capital outflows from the crisis-swept countries analyzed here from Thailand in 1997 to Argentina in 2001. IMF funding also materialized slowly; some from bilateral sources was unlikely to appear, in time or at all. Faced with the actual resource constraint, the Fund imposed severe austerity via fiscal and monetary tightening in countries that were recession-prone (in East Asia and later Brazil and Turkey) or in the midst of severe recession (Russia throughout the Fund's engagement; and more recently Argentina). The renewed imposition of the earlier, vigorous procyclical policies of the Asian global crisis, five years later for Argentina raised credible charges against its role, such as: What did the Fund learn from its Asian bailout experience? Will it go from crisis to crisis with a recipe that was not only stale but also brutal in its recessionary impact? Will the Fund leadership, dominated by quota holders from the G-7 center, continue imposing it on the emerging market periphery in financial crisis?

The IMF can handle these charges by following one of two alternatives. It can increase the amount of financial support with a view to softening the fiscal-cum-monetary pressure on a country in financial trouble and, in the process become a genuine lender of the last resort. Alternatively, it can change its standardized outdated recipe by introducing policy innovations to suit the individual needs of a financially troubled emerging market economy, revive it with less economic cost, and become a genuine multilateral agency with a diversified policy agenda.

The IMF as a Possible Lender of Last Resort?

According to Allan Meltzer (1986, p.83),

> "The central bank is called the lender of last resort because it is capable of lending—and to prevent failure of solvent banks must lend—in periods when no other lender is either capable or willing to lend in *sufficient volumes* [emphasis added] to prevent or end a financial panic."

Replenishing the IMF quota with a view to providing it with adequate funding for preventing or ending a financial crisis would be problematic in view of the political battles in the U.S. Congress that preceded its augmentation by $17 billion in 1999. More to the point, the IMF funding targeted to prevent or contain a crisis, which might spill into the neighborhood and across the globe, did not necessarily follow the objective criteria of an independent central bank of a given country. Political imperatives, security concerns, and economic importance tilted the size, timing, and type of bailouts. Thus, the Soviet-planned arrangements had to be converted into a market system with active participation by the IMF (and the World Bank) so that Russia, a nuclear power, did not descend into anarchy. Turkey, a NATO member and a partner in the antiterrorist alliance, could not be allowed to go under. Brazil, the largest economy in the Latin American backyard of the U.S. with sizable investments by U.S. banks and companies, must also be kept afloat. The dominant share of U.S. private banks in South Korea's debt prompted its rescheduling and a revised IMF rescue plan in 1998. These pulls and pressures, involving closed-door networking and negotiating, can provoke charges of double standards with respect to the Fund's bailout procedures when it insists that a Fund recipient get rid of deals among cronies in its financial sector.

It is advisable then for the IMF, which cannot be an effective and neutral lender of the last resort, to diversify its policy prescriptions by adding fresh arrows in its quiver. Three suggestions emerge from the Fund's bailout record in the countries considered here. First, they relate to the Fund's inflation control and budget deficit targeting for a recipient country. Next, the need for an occasional departure in practice from the Fund's hidebound ideological insistence on free capital mobility be established to match its pronouncements in favor of market-based capital account controls. And, finally, a preemptive initiative needs to be orchestrated by the Fund for sequencing orderly debt settlement for a heavily indebted recipient in financial crisis ahead of and along with the standard macroeconomic agenda to be implemented by the recipient's policy makers. By reducing debt repayment burden and promoting effective fiscal management, such debt restructuring can promote investor confidence without requiring explicit capital account controls.

The IMF and Macroeconomic Targeting

Economic targeting, less precise and more painful in its consequences than dartboard shooting, can be improved with practice. From this perspective, the Fund failed to distinguish between desirable and feasible monetary and budget deficit targets for the troubled economies. All of the countries discussed in this book borrowed heavily in the nineties following their capital account liberalization drives. However, the East Asian group differed from the rest in having a sustained record of balanced government budgets and high saving rates before they were hit by the financial crisis. By contrast, Russia (before August 1998), Brazil, Turkey, and Argentina were marked by low or declining economic growth rates, lagging tax revenues, and substantial debt burdens at the onset of crisis. As part of the IMF bailout, all recipients, despite differences in their economic fundamentals, were required to maintain high interest rates for retaining investor confidence and at the same time generate sufficient primary budget surpluses through tax revenues for meeting their debt repayment obligations. Fiscal prudence through expenditure cutbacks was politically unmanageable and through increased tax revenues was difficult because of high interest rates that curtailed economic growth. Ultimately, the uniformly severe and unrealistic policy contributed to the damaged credibility of the IMF rather than a substantiation of the pressure theory that stricter monetary and budget deficit targets elicited better follow-through and greater effort at institutional cleanup by recipient country governments.

Despite the pre-crisis macroeconomic differences in the two groups, the IMF prescriptions thus carried a monotonous policy imposition on the recipient countries. Of course, the timing and amount of support varied and involved critical judgments, but the policy program was strictly uniform. This uniformity raises the critical issue of the role of the Fund's research staff in working up diverse macroeconomic policy tools for member countries in trouble. A deluge of annual reports and macroeconomic models by the Fund economists, having first-rate expertise and access to vast information, has failed to preempt, or minimize, the costs of financial crises when they arose. Is it possible that Brazil, Argentina, and Turkey could have benefited from the policy experiences of Chile in the nineties (discussed in block 8) and Malaysia in 1998 (detailed in chapter 6), both of which temporarily departed from the Fund's policy orthodoxy? Or is it possible that the party line from the IMF top, firmly wedded to free capital mobility and free market ideology, rules out the design and implementation of alternative policy scenarios from the Fund research department for emerging market economies? While claiming to be a multilateral organization, the IMF remains a top-heavy agency with an entrenched and nonreformable policy ideology.

The budget deficit and inflation control targets, supported with inadequate funding by the IMF, could arguably have been less severe if they were combined with temporary controls on capital outflows for countries that in fact were overwhelmed with financial chaos resulting from unsustainable short-term inflows. These targets could also have been less stringent if they were linked with a systematic and timely reduction in debt repayment obligations under IMF initiative.

The IMF and Capital Account Controls

Russia plunged into a financial meltdown in August 1998 under IMF watch because the Central Bank of Russia with IMF acquiescence lifted restrictions on foreigners in 1997, allowing them to buy Russian government treasury bills and in the process enabling the government to meet its budget deficit target. This ultimate step, a colossal mistake, came on top of a series of earlier hasty measures that allowed citizens to freely convert their rubles into dollars (for deposits at home), and designated banks to engage in foreign-exchange transactions. Neither the speculative inflows that moved in to take advantage of the phenomenal yields on short-term government bonds nor the panic-driven outflows (that began in November 1997 when the Asian financial panic hit investors in Russian government paper) were sought to be regulated by capital account controls.

Controls on *outflows*, in the absence of strong institutional and supervisory mechanisms, can contribute to black markets, dual or multiple exchange rates, and illegal capital flight. IMF economist Andrew Berg (2001) attributed the success of Malaysia's temporary controls on outflows to its infrastructural robustness in implementing them without the emergence of corruption or a currency black market. The case for such controls on outflows, in the Fund view, is therefore predicated on the existence of solid institutional and supervisory mechanisms. In the absence of such mechanisms, capital must be allowed to move out because the outflow saves the economy from the scourge of illegal currency transactions and exchange rate distortions. On the other hand, capital, in Fund practice, must be encouraged to step into an economy devoid of such safeguards even though it can result in far greater costs of financial destabilization bordering on economic ruin!

The IMF record of minimizing losses to crisis-prone borrowers, and creditors who scrambled to unload their holdings of currencies under pressure, also lacked preemptive action.

Poor Performance of Debt Resolution under IMF Initiative

From the IMF perspective, timely and orderly restructuring of debts, be they private (as in South Korea) or sovereign (as in Russia and Argentina), raises complicated issues.

- The IMF cannot undertake such an initiative because the necessary procedures are not embedded in its Articles of Agreement enabling it to impose temporary debt suspension under internationally legislated bankruptcy laws.[4] Indeed, more than four years into the August 1998 Russian debt default, the G-7 architects of the new financial order had not devised formal procedures for "bailing in" private lenders in order for them to bear the costs of debt overhaul. Prospects for their adoption are not promising either. (I discuss these issues in the next chapter.)

- The IMF will refrain from persuading the parties to begin a dialogue because, in its view, borrowers bear the responsibility of debt management and clearance. Such an attitude can degenerate into passing the buck and sharing the blame and subject the Fund to charges of inflexible policy posturing. In the nineties, emerging markets were coaxed by the IMF, the U.S. Treasury, and Wall Street investors to throw open their economies to capital inflows. They fell for the temptation in the same way as they welcomed McDonald's, Madonna's music, Snicker bars, and T-shirts. Only the big players, among them India and China, saw the difference and refrained from hasty capital account liberalization (I discuss the Chinese and Indian records in block 9). Besides, the Fund's surveillance mechanism failed when some emerging markets borrowed excessively. If the IMF walks away from the destabilizing consequences of these inflows for the peripheral economies, it can be seen as an emissary of the G-7 center rather than a multilateral institution. Besides South Korea's debt restructuring of 1998 followed by a revised IMF program provides a precedent for a link between debt settlement and Fund policy packaging. In the next chapter I argue in favor of a case-by-case debt renegotiating role for the Fund supported by the U.S. Treasury when necessary rather than a formal incorporation of bankruptcy-type provisions in its mandate.

Perhaps a coordinated, preemptive debt restructuring of Argentina's sovereign debt could not have saved the Fund's macroeconomic blueprint for Argentina. Without such an initiative, however, the funding turned out to be money down the drain. A similar possibility awaited the Fund's role in Brazil following the country's presidential elections of October 2002. Instead of chalking up a new policy innovation in resolving debt crises in emerging markets, the IMF remained committed to its policy orthodoxy of fiscal and monetary austerity, recently supplemented by a switch from a managed to a floating exchange-rate arrangement. The Fund's inability to shake its bureaucratic lethargy and unwillingness to modify its policy stance has damaged its credibility as a bona fide instrument of change prompting physician-heal-thyself doubts among observers. The proposals and policy changes aimed at reconstructing the global financial system (which I analyze in the next chapter) do not provide hope for speedy and effective adoption of the necessary reforms.

Notes

1. Contrary to the Fund's pronouncements in favor of an orderly opening up of emerging market economies to global flows moderated by market-based measures, such as the Chilean capital inflow tax, the actual policies ran contrary to such a sequenced liberalization. I provide the details in the next chapter.

2. These issues are discussed at length in Desai (1992).

3. In May 2001, Allan Meltzer and Adam Lerrick recommended that the IMF restructure all of Argentina's public debt owed to private creditors. Details of their proposal are in Price (2001).

4. As I pointed out earlier, the IMF's International Monetary and Finance Committee had suggested in a communiqué dated September 24, 2000, that "in certain extreme cases," a temporary suspension or standstill may be an unavoidable policy option.

Block 6

Was There Moral Hazard in the Asian Financial Crisis?

MORAL HAZARD is invoked in situations involving human responses that tend to be reckless if their consequences are guaranteed not to be penalized.

If divorce were automatic, people might choose to get married at the drop of a hat. Since 911 has no more than a minimal charge for individual callers to seek help in emergencies, they tend to use it in seemingly trivial situations. American teenagers behave recklessly because they expect to be bailed out by parents. In other words, if people have a guarantee that they will not bear the costs of the outcomes of an activity that they find gainful or pleasurable, they might act in a morally reprehensible fashion.

The argument has been applied in the analysis of the Asian financial crisis.

Moral Hazard and the Asian Financial Crisis

According to the moral hazard proponents, foreign financial agents made excessive short-term portfolio investments in emerging markets because they believed that they would be rescued if they incurred losses. Host-country borrowers lent this readily available cash to businesses that invested it in risky ventures, including real estate, because they also expected to be bailed out if the investments went sour. The safeguards may be implicit or explicit and may originate from foreign guarantors for foreign lenders and from domestic sources for the domestic players.

Paul Krugman (1998) modeled moral hazard by assuming that domestic banks and financial companies, spurred by implicit guarantees based on political connections, fueled investment booms in their economies by extending excessive credits in wrong activities.

Defenders and detractors of the moral hazard scenario have found it difficult to support the bailout-of-reckless-speculators-via-guarantees argument or refute it for lack of a smoking gun at various stages of the activity from the opening up of financial markets by host countries to the financial meltdown that overtook them.

Moral Hazard: Pro and Con

In the very first step, was the original sin of opening up the financial markets undertaken by decision makers in host countries prematurely *and* under pressure from external policy makers, strong believers in the virtues of free flow of capital in promoting global growth? More to the point, was pressure from outside sweetened via offers of special deals for recipient- country policy makers and promises of protective bailouts to foreign lenders?

Next, did recipient insiders act recklessly in their borrowing and lending activities, hoping to be bailed out from the consequences of an inevitable boom and bust? To what extent were they actually rescued by their governments?

Finally, did the actual IMF-financed rescue programs favor the financial outsiders to the neglect of the local insiders?

The evidence that can be dredged up in answering these questions is presented below.

Policy Choices and Decisions on Capital Account Decontrol by Recipient-Country Policy Makers

Regarding the first phase of financial sector opening up in the East Asian emerging markets, the decisions of domestic policy makers were influenced by their desire to attract foreign funds. In hindsight, these turned out to be reckless judgment calls. China, by contrast, tilted its policies toward attracting foreign direct investment while imposing capital account controls with a view to discouraging short-term, destabilizing inflows. Indian policy makers selectively operated capital account controls and kept a more or less tight lid on long-term direct investment flows as well. Even within Asia, therefore, the East Asian decision makers could choose from a wide menu with regard to the type, timing, and speed of financial flows from outside.

On the other hand, the preference of creditor-country decision makers was, and continues to be, distinctly in favor of a speedy open-door policy by recipient countries. According to Bhagwati (2000a), the Wall Street-Treasury Complex, in its ideological championing of free capital flows, failed to distinguish between trade in capital and trade in goods. Wade (1998a) provides a blow-by-blow account of the deliberate prying open of East Asian capital markets by the Wall Street-Treasury-IMF Complex.

Did the preference for openness from outsiders spill over into pressure on insider policy makers? Thus, South Korea's policy makers orchestrated rapid financial decontrol of short-term capital inflows ahead of long-term foreign investments in response to the Organisation for Economic Co-operation & Development membership bait. Developing-country finance ministry officials blithely narrate episodes of pressure from IMF and World Bank missions for open-door policies.

Generally, host-country authorities displayed a scramble for opening up with occasional backtracking (details are in block 3), hoping that the efficiency gains from short-term capital inflows would outweigh the losses from their unpredictable movements. Most were caught up in the false belief, China's success story to the contrary, that long-term direct investment would flow only if capital were completely free to march in. In distinguishing between short-term speculative and long-term foreign direct investment, Malaysia's mercurial prime minister, Mahathir Mohamad, got carried away when he denounced foreign short-term lenders as "racist speculators" (*Financial Times*, September 4, 1997, p. 1) while cooing to foreign fund managers a week later, describing them as "serious investors" rather than manipulators of the local stock market (*Financial Times*, September 8, 1997, p. 4).

As for bailout guarantees, the case is hard to prove, especially with regard to explicit guarantees of rescue operations for investors who were threatened with losses.

Bailout Guarantees for Foreign Creditors?

Turning first to such guarantees for outsiders, it is possible that, having perceived Mexico's big-money bailout by the combined IMF-U.S. Treasury cash infusion, foreign creditors elsewhere acted on the assumption that they would be rescued next time around. On the other hand, they may have stepped into East Asian capital markets on the basis of interest rate differentials and informed guesses about the currency stability of their target economy. Opinion polls on decision making by foreign creditors with regard to their timing and exposure in a given country are hard to come by. They may all have been shooting in the dark. Hans Teitmeyer reportedly told a conference in New York that "he had talked to Western bankers who clearly knew 'nothing' about some of the Asian countries in which they were lending." (Phelps, 1999, p. 3).

Next, I turn to bailout guarantees for host-country financial inter-mediaries and businesses that created the web of extensive bor-rowing and lending activity.

Bailout Guarantees in Borrowing Countries?

Banks and financial institutions of borrowing countries incurred massive nonperforming loans. Their corporations were highly lever-aged with unfavorable debt/equity ratios. Flushed with cheap, liquid funds from abroad and seized with an irrational casino fever, finan-ciers and investors became susceptible to "cognitive dissonance" blocking out "negative, or dissonant, information and focus[ing] only on the positive aspects of their position" (*New York Times*, July 13, 1999). The compulsive attraction of money making rather than calculated assessment of bailouts drove the process that rapidly crossed the credible limits of bailout possibilities by governments of these countries.

The actual record of governmental rescue of struggling banks, financial companies, and corporate entities to the run-up of the crisis was one of confusion, delayed action, fudged inquiries, ministerial resignations, government toppling, and ultimate capitulation to IMF requirements. (Details are in block 7.) While a few insiders may have successfully minimized losses by moving funds to safe havens, bailout of insiders en masse, caught up in political maneuverings, was impossible as the crisis became systemic.

Asian financial markets were soon taken over by the "casino ele-ment" as they began recovering from the financial turmoil of 1997. From Thailand to Indonesia, the 1999 stock markets had climbed, by mid-1999, by 61 percent in Indonesia, 51 percent in Singapore, 43 percent in Malaysia, 40 percent in Thailand, and 34 percent in Hong Kong. Although foreign investors were holding back, local banks and small investors, flushed with funds from domestic savers, had begun aggressively moving into the stock market "eager to make a quick profit on the surge in stocks. Trading in Kuala Lumpur has nearly quadrupled, compared with its level at the start of the crisis. At the same time, the market is twice as volatile as it was two years ago. Bangkok's stock market is almost as turbulent now as it was in the uncertain days before the Thai baht was devalued in July 1997. And Jakarta's stock market yo-yo's more than any of the oth-ers." (*New York Times*, July 22, 1999, p. C3). Was anyone among the fever-seized herd banking on bailout guarantees?

Evidence supporting moral hazard, that is financial actors, insiders and outsiders, having acted hazardously in anticipation of bailout guarantees or having been rescued in large numbers from financial ruin during the East Asian crisis, is therefore not decisive.

However, the perception that outsider creditors were deliberately rescued by IMF-arranged packages has persisted. According to confidential remarks by finance ministry officials, the conditionality of IMF letters of intent required that IMF credits be used to pay off foreign creditors first. This impression continued to cast its shadow in the region's electoral politics, and drove East Asian leaders led by China, South Korea, and Japan into designing regional currency swap, trade, and cooperation arrangements. Collapsing properties, factory closures, bank failures, and job losses—all features of the 1997 financial crisis—, the 1998 recession, and the slow recovery could not be absorbed by voters without a feeling that the outsiders got away while they got burnt.

Block 7

How Much Corruption?
Does Corruption Matter?

CORRUPTION, LIKE ADULTERY, exists across cultures but is difficult to measure.

It is equally difficult to define. Recently several French chefs, some of the best in the culinary profession, were fined in amounts ranging from $10,000 to $12,000 for having "bribed" their wholesale fish suppliers. But according to Manuel Martinez, one of the best chefs in the business, "nobody got rich. We spread it around among the staff. It was a kind of tradition in the business to create good will. It's not as if it was public money and these were kickbacks" (*New York Times*, July 14, 1999, p. A5). The magistrate thought differently.

Vladimir Rushaylo, the former Russian interior minister, provided another perspective on defining corruption when he flatly denied the allegation that seven out of ten Russian officials were corrupt. Such statements, he said, were "based on expert opinions that have no common criteria for a definition of corruption." He explained that "numerous bribe-takers are also usually seen as corrupted." But that overstated matters, in his view, because "only those who have links with the organised criminal gangs can be regarded as corrupted officials" (*Financial Times,* March 20, 2001, p. 15.).

Despite the problems, there have been attempts at defining and measuring corruption.

Definition

Thus, Shang-Jin Wei (1999, p. 3) focuses on "corruption in the economic sphere involving government officials. Corruption here is defined as government officials abusing their power to extract/accept bribes from the private sector for personal benefit. This is to be distinguished from political corruption (e.g., vote-buying in an election, legal or illegal campaign contributions by the wealthy and other special interest groups to influence laws and regulations), and bribes among private sector parties."

Wei also presents corruption indexes for a set of countries, reproduced in the table below, from three sources.

Corruption Ratings for Selected Countries

	BI (1–10 scale)	TI97 (1–10 scale)	GCR97 (1–10 scale)
Asian Countries			
Singapore	1	2.34	1.84
Hong Kong	3	3.72	2.31
Japan	2.25	4.43	2.50
Taiwan	4.25	5.98	3.43
Malaysia	5	5.99	5.01
South Korea	5.25	6.71	5.50
Thailand	9.5	7.94	7.98
Philippines	6.5	7.95	6.73
China	n.a.	8.12	6.73
India	5.75	8.25	7.32
Indonesia	9.5	8.28	8.40
Pakistan	7	8.47	n.a.
Bangladesh	7	9.20	n.a.
Non-Asian countries			
Canada	1	1.90	1.84
United Kingdom	1.75	2.72	1.71
Germany	1.5	2.77	1.92
United States	1	3.39	2.11
France	1	4.34	2.77
Mexico	7.75	8.34	5.83
Kenya	6.5	8.70	7.08
Colombia	6.5	8.77	6.81
Russia	n.a.	8.73	7.08
Nigeria	8	9.24	7.83

Notes: Higher numbers imply more corruption. BI (Business International) Index, based on surveys of experts/consultants (typically one consultant per country) and conducted during 1980–83 ranks countries "according to the degree to which business transactions involve corruption or questionable payments" (Wei, 1999, p.3). TI (Transparency International) Index, carried out annually since 1995, is based on "weighted average of approximately ten surveys of varying coverage" (ibid., p. 4). GCR (Global Competitiveness Report) Index, based on a 1996 survey of managers of 2,381 firms in fifty-eight countries, captures the level of corruption via their responses to questions on "irregular, additional payments connected with import and export permits, business licenses, exchange controls, tax assessments, police protection or loan applications" (ibid., p.4).

Measures of Corruption

Two features are apparent from the table. First, the country rankings across the three measures move together, giving high pair-wise correlation values. Second, among countries included in the book, Malaysia, South Korea, Thailand, and Philippines, with increasing corruption, are listed in the middle, and Indonesia is ranked almost at the bottom among Asian countries.

Despite middling to high corruption, the countries considered here grew rapidly in their heyday; and they recovered at varying speeds in the post-crisis years of 1999 and 2000 despite the culture of cronyism which could not have vanished overnight.

This raises the question of the connection between corruption and economic growth.

The Link between Corruption and Economic Growth

Several studies suggest that corruption retards growth by reducing domestic investment (Mauro, 1995) and by discouraging foreign investment (Wei, 1997). The evidence provided by the practitioners of econometrics is striking. "If Bangladesh were able to reduce its corruption to the Singapore level, its average annual per capita GDP growth rate over 1960–1985 would have been higher by 1.8 percentage points" (Wei, 1999, p. 9). According to this argument, the Asian tigers, in the absence of corruption, could have grown even faster. On the other hand, some corruption might grease the wheels of economic progress.

Bhagwati's distinction (2000c, pp. 61–63) between Washington and Asian cronies and between rent-seeking and profit-maximizing cronies provides the necessary analytical link between corruption and growth. First, the rewards to Washington cronies are constrained by the institutional bounds of the rule of law in a democratic environment marked by a vigilant press. A Clinton crony is rewarded by a stay in the Lincoln bedroom whereas a Suharto crony gets the monopoly rights of manufacturing autos in Indonesia. The economic costs of such corrupt cronyism tend to be limited in law-based societies.

Next, corruption can be rent seeking or profit seeking. The former arises when cronies are given exclusive rights in production or distribution activity resulting in efficiency losses and growth impairment. On the other hand, cronies may capture shares in profit-making enterprises, siphon off the profits abroad, and invest less at home, the whole process affecting economic growth as has happened in Russia. In such cases, efficiency and growth are set back. However, profit-seeking corruption will enhance growth if the favored cronies are spurred to enlarge the size of the pie in joint ventures with foreign partners as the economy is opened up to foreign investment and trade. Economic growth in the expansion phase of the East Asian economies considered here may have gained from the prevalence of such profit-seeking corruption.

But how do cronies manage their fortunes in an economic downturn which escalates into a full-blown crisis?

Corruption and Financial Crisis

According to Wei and Sievers (2000), "corrupt countries are more likely to have inadequate government supervision of the financial system, and are also more likely to have vulnerable banks." Their politicians may bail out their cronies in the private sector instead of cleaning up the financial malaise on time.

Such targeted rescues, feasible in a normal or slowing economy, become impossible in a financial crisis, as is supported by conflicting evidence of bank bailouts in Indonesia, which I provide below. Again, the pattern of bailouts during a deepening crisis depends on the networking connection between the political benefactor and the bailout beneficiary. The latter may form a decentralized group as distinct from a favored band of benefit recipients. Indonesian bailouts in the early nineties were focused on rescuing the president's cronies whereas Thai bailouts in the early phases of the financial troubles in 1997 were directed toward supporting the viability of the banking sector which had political connections.

Indonesia

When Bank Duta, a private bank holding deposits of "shadowy" Suharto political foundations, lost nearly half a billion dollars in financial speculation in 1990, it was "promptly rescued by two other large corporate groups with very close financial ties to Suharto, which in turn were quickly rewarded with other forms of state largesse" (Haggard and MacIntyre, 2001, p. 15). By contrast, Bank Summa, owned by the Astra group (the second largest industrial conglomerate in Indonesia) was forced into liquidation as a result of massive mismanagement because it lacked a Suharto connection (ibid.).

However, a few years later in 1997, as the situation escalated from a financial to a full-blown currency crisis, private businesses failed to continue successfully manipulating their links with the country's supreme political boss. As cronies fought to safeguard their nest eggs, "the policy backsliding and outright policy reversals" in the midst of the launching of IMF reform package in 1997, brought out Suharto's vacillation between outright financial rescuing of family and friends and commitment to reforms. His indecisiveness ultimately damaged the interests of cronies and noncronies alike. Cronies doubting the guarantees of effective protection from the boss, and noncronies sensing deteriorating business environment, withheld investment and moved liquid assets abroad.

The bailout operation worked differently in crisis-prone Thailand where the networking alliances between private business and political decision makers were decentralized and involved scattered groups of individuals rather than a select band of presidential favorites. In other words, the rescue was aimed at saving a major part of the banking sector rather than a few favorites.

Thailand

Indonesia's political framework under Suharto was massively centralized and corruption-prone, creating possibilities of economic gains to the president's closed circle. By contrast, such opportunities in Thailand through privileged connections involved a wider set of political operatives and financial players. "Political links between members of the government and financial institutions" provided "opportunities for failing financial institutions to protect themselves and to delay the process of financial restructuring. Where outright corruption was not implicated—and it frequently was—political forbearance towards the interests of the financial sector was. Broader constitutional weaknesses compounded these problems. With some important differences, all of the democratically-elected governments prior to the crisis—Chaitichai, Chuan, Banharn and Chavalit—rested upon shaky multiparty coalitions, made up of internally weak and fragmented parties that . . . provided opportunities for private interests to gain access to the policy process" (Haggard and MacIntyre, 2001).

Thus, the Bangkok Bank of Commerce (BBC), which had extended loans to several politicians within Prime Minister Banharn's

Chart Thai Party, was bailed out by the Bank of Thailand, the central bank, with a capital infusion of up to $7 billion in the early nineties. In March 1997 the central bank also shored up financial companies in which members of Chart Pattana, the second largest party in the government coalition, had controlling interest. In July, in the midst of negotiations with the IMF, the party managed to persuade the central bank to pour liquidity into sixteen additional financial companies in amounts "that exceeded the total capital of the finance companies and equaled 10 percent of GDP" (ibid.).

As financial problems mounted, the pressures brought by private business and banks on policy makers prevented the systematic initiation of financial sector cleanup via closure of bankrupt businesses and banks, not only in Thailand, but across the region. Policy makers feared that widespread restructuring and closure of the nonviable units would precipitate the onset of the financial crisis and deepen its severity. Timely cleanup of the mess through restructuring was perhaps constrained more by fears of an economy-wide collapse that would ensue than by the deliberate desire to save the financial fortunes of friends and family. Indeed, the process was caught in massive political uncertainties en route and toppling of governments everywhere except in Malaysia. If there were implicit guarantees to potential beneficiaries, they could not be implemented quietly through negotiations on the golf course or string pulling in the boardroom. Because of the scale of restructuring and the lack of adequate institutional underpinning amidst political uncertainties, the process lacked the systematic deal making in a settled political environment similar to the U.S. Savings and Loan and Long Term Capital Management bailouts.

Block 8

Chilean Capital Inflow Tax

EMERGING MARKET economies tend to have poor credit rating because creditors find it difficult to assess their loan risks. The necessary information about the viability of banks and corporate businesses for the purpose is missing; often, the information is misleading because the accounting system is different. Again, managers are still coping with problems of risk management. The supervisory system is lax. Governments often rush in to bail out failing banks and corporate units. Above all, a loan contract may not be enforced. Creditors therefore prefer to loan short term, choosing to move their cash in and out speedily in order to minimize losses. Borrowers, on the other hand, would prefer to lock the funds for a longer period for minimizing the destabilizing impact of financial volatility.

Some financial architecture innovators have accepted the view that borrowers should be allowed to launch initiatives aimed at curbing short-term capital inflows provided they conform to market economy norms and last for a short period during which the recipients put their financial house in order. In other words, they must avoid direct controls on such inflows and abolish the measures when they succeed in purging their financial and banking system of the inhospitable attributes.

The Chilean capital inflow tax, in the view of several proposals, meets these requirements. (Details are in Eichengreen, 1999a, pp. 51–55 and Edwards, 1998.)

Features of the Chilean Tax

The Chilean tax evolved over a period of seven years from December 1990 to January 1998 during which the authorities meticulously plugged several loopholes and adjusted the implicit tax rate to curb excessive flows (in 1995) and attract funds that had dried up in 1998.

Its hallmark was the requirement that foreign lenders deposit non-interest-bearing amounts that varied with the length of the credits: the shorter the loan duration, the higher the deposit and the implicit tax. Initially, inflows of less than $10,000 were exempt, encouraging investors to break up large transactions into small, tax-free amounts (Eichengreen, 1999a, p. 54). Over time, the nonremunerative deposit requirement covered all foreign lending except foreign direct investment and American Depository Receipts with high ratings that would be picked up by foreign investors.

In 1995, the rule required that deposits be made in dollars rather than in yen that carried lower interest costs (ibid., p. 53).

What did the tax accomplish? According to a variety of assessments (cited in Eichengreen, 1999a, pp. 52–53), the tax did shift lending into long-term maturity deals without curtailing the overall fund inflow into Chile. That should be chalked up as an intended outcome of the measure.

The counter-cyclical adjustment of the implicit tax rate, raised in 1995 when inflows were plentiful and slashed to zero when they dried up, was deliberate. According to Valdes-Prieto (cited in Eichengreen, 1999a, p. 53): "Our tax on capital inflows is like an umbrella: you use it when it rains and close it when the rain stops."

Such a calculated policy stance suggests that the Chilean capital tax may not yet be dead. As short-term capital flows to emerging markets pick up, it may be revived, although Chile's banking sector is fairly well regulated and supervised, its foreign exchange regime remains flexible, and its financial system has avoided the fallout from the crises in Argentina and Brazil.

The tax raises concerns however from yet another perspective.

Problem with the Capital Inflow Tax: When Can the Tax Be Dispensed With?

A major reservation arises from the fact that the process of upgrading prudential regulation and supervision of banks, of refining their risk management practices, of modernizing their accounting procedures, in fact of bringing their financial system up to the level of developed market economies, is complex and time consuming. "Even under the best circumstances and with the best technical assistance—upgrading risk measurement practices, adopting new regulations, and putting in place new supervisory procedures can take no less than five years" (Calomiris, 1998, cited in Eichengreen, 1999a, p. 52).

But there is a deeper problem. Would central banks and supervisory agencies really expose the financial vulnerabilities of the banks that they supervise? How stringently will the monitoring authorities ensure that the banks have adequate capital reserves in line with the Basel Accord of 1998, or that their asset risks are accurately measured, or that their balance sheets carry reliable numbers?

With the best supervisory, asset-rating, and accounting guidelines in place, their actual enforcement in emerging markets may lag behind because the supervisors share a common goal with banks and other financial institutions they supervise. They want to shield them in good times and bail them out in bad times in the interest of minimizing systematic volatility. Obfuscation may be practiced in the interest of fulfilling a mutually shared goal.

It would seem that Chilean-style capital inflow taxes may last longer and may be invoked more often than is warranted by progress on reform of banking and financial infrastructure in emerging markets. This calls for strict monitoring by the IMF over a period during which the financial infrastructure in the countries receiving fund support is reformed. As a supervised emergency measure, the Chilean capital inflow tax is superior to direct controls of such inflows or a completely open, speculative attack-prone regime.

A famous proposal by Tobin (1978; also discussed in Frankel, 1996a; 1996b) consisted of imposing a small, uniform tax on all foreign exchange transactions, buying and selling, irrespective of their purpose. These transactions might occur in pursuit of short-term speculative gain electronically in sophisticated foreign exchange markets or for financing trade in goods and services. The tax would not discourage the former if speculators expected to make substantial gains, despite flexible exchange rates, arising from large interest rate differentials. Again, the tax would need to be imposed in all financial centers worldwide. As a result, it generated much discussion but remained impractical.

Capital Account Convertibility in China and India: A Cautionary Tale of Two Countries

CHINA AND INDIA fitfully progressed from exceedingly regulated and painstakingly bureaucratized arrangements of direct controls of activities (involving foreign exchange transactions by residents and nonresidents) to current account convertibility of their currencies. They have however quite a distance to travel in order to reach full capital account convertibility. Policy makers in both countries implemented a liberalization progression marked by encouragement of foreign direct investment inflows followed by their outflows by resident companies culminating in the final phase of regulated freeing of inflows of private equity and bonds and their outflows by residents. (I outlined the steps relating to a desirable progression from a controlled regime to full capital account convertibility in block 3.) Chinese decisions, timed earlier, were fast paced and decisive in contrast to the ones in India which were slow and lacked clear signals. As a result, China's direct investment flows—in and out—in the nineties massively outdistanced India's.

China

Strict rules governing foreign exchange and investment transactions made large sections of the Chinese economy impenetrable to foreigners for several decades. The authorities began relaxing the system in measured steps only recently, and its membership in the World Trade Organization (WTO) as of December 11, 2001 is expected to quicken the process.

The Dual Currency System

A payment instrument, known as a foreign exchange certificate (FEC), was introduced on April 1, 1980 so that foreign tourists entering and leaving China could exchange their money into Chinese renminbi, "the people's currency," also known as the yuan. Officially, only foreign firms and visitors were allowed to use the FECs at designated places and for specific goods. Upon leaving the country, they had to convert the remaining FECs into their home currency. Chinese residents were only permitted to use yuan. A black market emerged for goods that could only be obtained with FECs. This two-tier currency system existed until the government abolished the FECs on January 1, 1994, allowing foreigners to convert their currency into yuan, which had a more favorable exchange rate than the certificates. The unification also allowed Chinese residents to purchase goods previously available only through FECs. The central bank however purchased foreign exchange earnings of firms and placed them under the management of State Administration of Foreign Exchange (SAFE). This arrangement implied that although the currency was unified, it was not freely convertible on current account. Resident importers had to also get an import license before they could buy the required foreign exchange from SAFE. SAFE currently manages China's foreign exchange reserves.

Current Account Convertibility of the Yuan

China introduced current account convertibility of the yuan in December 1996 by accepting Article VIII of the International Monetary Fund (IMF) with a view to simplifying payments for foreign goods and services. At around the same time, the government announced plans to achieve capital account convertibility by the year 2000. However, the Asian financial crisis of 1997–98 pushed back the target date and led to a resurrection of controls which continued into 2000. The yuan came under pressure from the currencies of the region in1998 prompting rumors of its devaluation and activating currency speculators to take advantage of loopholes in the system that were already being used to divert their foreign exchange earnings abroad. Importers over-invoiced import bills with a view to obtaining larger than the required amounts of foreign exchange from SAFE, and exporters under-invoiced their export earnings with a view to concealing them from the agency. Illegal currency trading became widespread. In response, the government announced harsh penalties for currency traders who failed to return all illegally acquired foreign exchange by October 1998. Beginning in July 1999, foreign banks were prohibited from purchasing yuan from overseas branches of the Bank of China, the country's primary foreign exchange bank, with a view to minimize currency smuggling: in other words, they were required to buy the necessary yuan from the domestic branches of SAFE in exchange for foreign currency which accumulated in its coffers. The following month, the government introduced permits enabling residents and nonresidents to carry foreign currency out of China. A Chinese resident wishing to take out over US$ 4,000 (US$ 10,000 for nonresidents) would need prior approval directly from SAFE. However, foreign-funded firms were now allowed to use foreign exchange settlement accounts as time deposits with a view to encourage foreign direct investment. But in March 2000, SAFE again tightened foreign exchange purchases by importers. It introduced three categories of importers, divided by the type of product they imported, and allowed foreign exchange dealing on the basis of these categories. It was not until 2001 that the authorities allowed foreign banks to undertake banking operations in China.

Entry of Foreign Banks

SAFE announced in December 2001 that foreign banks would be allowed to open branches and undertake foreign exchange services and limited yuan transactions for Chinese customers, starting in the cities of Shenzen, Shanghai, Dalian, and Tianjin. Four additional cities were to be added every year until all geographical restrictions and limits on foreign banks were removed in five years. Soon after, HSBC became the first foreign bank since the 1949 revolution to have gained entry in a Chinese bank when it acquired an 8 percent stake in the Bank of Shanghai on December 28, 2001 (*Financial Times*, December 28, p.5). Although capital account convertibility has yet to materialize, China is currently considering expanding its foreign exchange operations in Hong Kong.

Foreign Direct Investment: From a Trickle to a Flood

Foreign direct investment flows increased from $4.4 billion in 1991 to $37.5 billion in 1995 and averaged at $40 billion thereafter until 2000.

The growth not only resulted from a bold policy decision to invite long-term investment but also from special circumstances. Foreign investors are allowed to remit profits, dividends, and interest earnings from their foreign currency accounts and convert their yuan earnings into hard currency at designated banks before sending them out. Provinces and cities along the East Coast granted tax incentives and import duty exemptions to foreign affiliated businesses. The flows, however, were concentrated at 90 percent in twelve coastal provinces and municipalities and in manufactured items for foreign markets claiming an export share of 31.3 percent in 1995. Finally, 60 percent of these investment flows came from overseas Chinese businesses (*World Bank,* 1997, p. 22). In the post-WTO years, the leadership was expected to diversify the flows by source, location (into the interior of the country), sector (into infrastructure), and uniform incentives (to domestic and foreign businesses by abolishing the differential tax advantages to the latter).

By contrast, foreign flows into stocks and bonds of Chinese enterprises have been paltry. The stock market is not only thin and occasionally marked by trading frauds but also bifurcated into class A and B shares. The B shares in which foreigners are allowed to invest were introduced in the newly opened Chinese securities markets in 1992. Significant price discrepancy persists between these and the domestic A shares which foreigners cannot own. Select Chinese companies are allowed to issue American and Global Depository Receipts. Officially permitted outflows of portfolio and direct investment at $17 billion in 1995 were 2 percent of global flows (ibid, p. 26).

China's liberalization policies, therefore, have been dominated by encouragement to inflows of foreign direct investment followed by such outflows and disincentives relating to inward and outward flows of bonds and equity capital. Although China is set to liberalize its policies as a member of the WTO, full capital account convertibility is still a distant goal.

India

India, like China, had extensive restrictions on foreign exchange transactions implemented by regulations which, in their extensive crossing of every t and dotting of every i, displayed the strangulating talent of Indian bureaucracy to its fullest. The Foreign Exchange Regulations Act (FERA) went into effect in 1973.

Foreign Exchange Regulations, Indian Style

Harsh penalties were imposed on those who broke FERA's stringent regulations. The act controlled all foreign currency transactions. Its formulation was designed to close all loopholes via a liberal sprinkling of "to," "from," and "with": "No person other than an authorized dealer shall in India, and no person resident in India other than an authorized dealer shall outside India, purchase or otherwise acquire or borrow from, or sell, or otherwise transfer or lend to or exchange with, any person not being an authorized dealer, any foreign exchange" (Foreign Exchange Regulations Act, 1993). At the same time, the placing of Indian securities abroad, and the owning of foreign securities in India were prohibited without special permission of the Reserve Bank of India. That implied that foreigners could not own Indian securities and Indians could not own foreign securities. Special controls were also imposed on companies with foreign ownership exceeding 40 percent, limiting their investment activity. In short, foreign exchange transactions required explicit permission from the Reserve Bank, directly or through FERA. Otherwise they were illegal.

This steel-plated armor of regulations began to be loosened two decades later.

Article VIII of IMF and Measured Steps toward Capital Account Convertibility

The government ended its restrictions in March 1993 on companies that were more than 40 percent foreign-owned, and allowed residents to deposit up to 25 percent of their foreign exchange earnings in foreign currency bank accounts. The next major liberalization occurred in August 1994, when the rupee was made fully convertible on current account under Article VIII of the IMF. The Reserve Bank's capital account controls, however, remained in place. The rupee's peg to a basket of currencies was also removed in 1993, so the currency floats and its value is now determined by the market. In 1998, the Reserve Bank permitted foreign institutional investors to invest in government bonds and in unlisted debt securities. Foreign investors were next allowed to trade in derivatives starting in August 2000 and commercial paper starting February 2001.

In December 1999, the Indian government replaced FERA with the Foreign Exchange Management Act (FEMA). Whereas the aim of FERA was to "consolidate the law regarding certain payments, dealings in foreign exchange and securities, transactions indirectly affecting foreign exchange and import of foreign currency, for conservation of the foreign exchange resources and proper utilization thereof," the preamble of FEMA states its goal as the consolidation and amendment of "the law relating to foreign exchange, so as to facilitate foreign trade and payments and for promoting the orderly development and maintenance of the foreign exchange markets in India" (Banking India Update, 1999). The shift in the purpose of the foreign exchange law from a negative to a positive stance was also evidenced in the treatment of foreign exchange violations under FEMA as civil offenses subject to less severe punishment than under FERA. FEMA also allows Indian residents to sell or draw foreign exchange to or from an authorized person for a capital account transaction. In addition, all companies incorporated in India are currently governed by the same rules irrespective of their level of foreign ownership.

As with the Chinese liberalizing process, the incremental steps distinguished among three categories of inward flows of foreign direct investment, portfolio capital, and their outward flows. Ratios of foreign investment participation multiplied depending on the sector of entry, the amount offered, and its share in the sector. Some sectors are allowed 51 percent foreign share, others 74 percent, and a few are allowed 100 percent ownership. Over time more sectors have been freed and higher foreign shares have been allowed obviating the need for approval by the central cabinet. Portfolio investment by foreign holders in Indian companies is restricted at 24 percent. They are free to repatriate profits, capital gains, and their original capital. Foreign direct investment by Indian companies abroad has also been gradually freed up involving larger amounts and more sectors including some software companies. The government has begun to allow Indian citizens to participate in mutual funds, which can invest a part of their holdings abroad.

In all these respects, Indian performance has lagged behind the Chinese, especially with regard to foreign direct investment inflows that amounted to $4 billion in the twelve months ending on March 31, 2002. Foreign portfolio investment of $2.2 billion and bank deposits by nonresident Indians settled abroad of $2.8 billion lifted the total to $9 billion during the period. By contrast, China's spectacular advance, the result of a decisive and early political decision by its leadership, was also helped by the greater political muscle of a "strong state" and the economy's macroeconomic fundamentals. The Indian process was halting, marked by conflicting signals to foreign investors of "we want you but we can do without you" in the midst of the fragile consensus building of a "soft state." The economy registered lower growth rates, poor export performance, and lower accumulated foreign exchange earnings at $60 billion in mid-2002 in contrast to China's $250 billion.

Although full capital convertibility has yet to materialize in China and India, the liberalization has picked up speed in the last decade.

The currency regulations have not prevented illegal outflows of foreign exchange especially in China, but they have certainly spared the two economies from the fallout of the Mexican, Asian, and the latest Argentine currency crises. Both have registered strong growth and low inflation rates in the nineties and manageable debt to gross domestic product ratios. But most important, the two countries have retained their policy-making autonomy by avoiding fast-paced, destabilizing opening up of their economies to volatile capital flows.

12

Crisis Prevention and Containment: The Next Steps in Financial Reform

THE AFTERMATH OF the East Asian financial turmoil was followed by calls for redesigning the international financial architecture with a view to preventing and containing future debacles.[1] The Argentine and Turkish economic turmoil resurrected the pressure for reforming the global financial system in 2001. It became acute after 9/11 as the synchronization of economic recession in the U.S., the eurozone, and Japan threatened the economic prospects of emerging markets via reduced trade and capital flows.

Despite the new urgency, analysts and policy makers disagree on measures for preempting the recurrence and containing the impact of financial crisis. The advisability of imposing capital controls on hot money inflows in emerging market economies that lack the institutional and regulatory underpinning in their financial sectors continues to be a contentious issue. The protagonists in favor of capital controls in borrowing countries acknowledge the desirability of international capital flows in principle but argue in favor of market-based, temporary measures for steering capital inflows toward more long-term direct investment. Other issues relate to the adoption of an ideal exchange rate regime that can promote currency stability, private sector burden sharing for preempting the occurrence and softening the impact of financial meltdowns, and a revised role for the international financial institutions, especially the International Monetary Fund (IMF) and the World Bank. The issue of the participation of private bondholders in rescheduling the debt burden of an emerging market economy in the midst of a severe shortage of foreign exchange revived after Argentina's pell-mell efforts to restructure its debt and its unilateral default in December 2001. The prospects for the formal incorporation of such burden sharing in debt contracts that can work to the advantage of borrowing countries have so far been limited. At the same time, the standards devised by the Financial Stability Forum for remedying the inadequacies of the global financial arrangements have not departed from the orthodoxy of financial liberalization. The forum, launched by the G-7 finance ministers and central bank governors, has focused on safeguarding the stability of the international financial system rather than promoting stable capital flows from the center to the periphery. The calls for reforming the

IMF have also been long on ideas and short on their implementation. Indeed, more than four years into the emergence of the Asian financial crisis, the IMF has remained active in crafting bailouts and imposing unrealistic fiscal discipline in Argentina and Turkey. Its hermetic policy focus has been devoid of a fresh initiative aimed at systematically restructuring debt repayment obligations without which the post-default budget formulation and implementation for Argentina will remain ineffective.

I analyze these proposals below beginning with suggestions for an ideal exchange rate regime.

Which Exchange Rate Regime?

The economies analyzed here followed intermediate exchange rate arrangements[2] (that were neither firmly fixed nor freely floating) except the Argentine peso that was fixed to the dollar on a one-to-one basis. Again, each country's policy makers allowed capital mobility in and out of their borders.

The Failure of Intermediate Exchange Rate Regimes in the Presence of Free Capital Mobility

As a result, before the financial crisis unfolded in the East Asian economies, their banks and businesses had been receiving capital inflows from outside, even as their exchange rates were kept more or less stable without being formally and legally fixed with the dollar. Their central banks maintained monetary discipline in the interest of avoiding excessive exchange rate instability. Having thus compromised their monetary policy independence, they could not provide liquidity to the commercial banks when they developed maturity and currency mismatches in their balance sheets. Financial bailouts arranged by the IMF came late and were inadequate to prevent the inevitable currency collapses. Russia (in August 1998) and Turkey (in January 2001), each following an intermediate exchange rate regime, also could not avoid similar outcomes. Their central banks followed exchange rate-based stabilization agendas and allowed the Russian ruble and the Turkish lira to devalue nominally, with respect to the country inflation rates (relative to the outside world), such that the real exchange rates appreciated. In both countries, however, the macroeconomic stabilization targets turned out to be unsustainable in view of shaky budgetary management and government overspending.

The failure of the intermediate exchange rate system opened the choice in favor of either a fixed or a floating exchange rate as part of the post-crisis arrangements.

Is a Fixed Peg a Feasible Choice for Emerging Market Economies?

A fixed peg consigns the central bank to a monetary straightjacket for defending the peg at the risk of losing its foreign exchange reserves and ultimately abandoning the peg. It can work for a small open economy with high labor mobility, cyclical ups and downs of business activity linked with a large neighbor whose currency is likely to be chosen for the peg, and fiscal muscle to manage economic downturns because discretionary monetary policy is ruled out. Estonia (in 1992) and Lithuania (in 1994) fixed their currencies respectively to the D-mark and the SDR (IMF Special Drawing Rights) under arrangements resembling a currency board with a view to ultimately link their small, open economies with the larger European Union. The adoption of a pure currency board, sold as "credibility in a bottle" (Frankel, 1999e, p. 2), represents a stricter confinement: the peg must be fixed by law and maintained; the monetary base (currency in circulation plus commercial bank reserves with the central bank) must be fully backed by foreign exchange reserves; balance of payments deficits (surpluses) must lead to tighter (expansionary) monetary policy resulting in automatic adjustment of spending in the economy.

Was the adoption of the currency board by Argentina in 1991, a large economy whose peso was fixed to the dollar, a successful exception to the small country rule? It did kill the quadruple-digit inflation providing a growth stimulus to the economy until 1998. But in the absence of a discretionary central bank acting as a lender of the last resort, the Argentine treasury and provincial governments borrowed for their liquidity needs, ultimately creating an unsustainable sovereign debt liability to the tune of $95 billion by mid-2001. This could not be repaid in time from inadequate growth in export earnings because of the peso's link to the strong dollar. Perhaps an economy, large or small, would not need a currency board in the first place if it could swing the rigorous legal and monetary strictures of the arrangement! The equally radical conversion of the monetary unit into the U.S. dollar involves the surrender of monetary policy to the Federal Reserve and raises political roadblocks for decision makers except for small, open economies such as Panama with close ties and proximity to the U.S., and Ecuador, with similar features, that discarded a worthless currency in favor of the dollar in 2000.

Will floating exchange rates that fluctuate with the demand for and supply of a currency suit the needs of emerging markets better?

Are Floating Exchange Rates a Credible Choice?

Floating exchange rates allow monetary policy discretion to central bankers. "When exchange rates float, there is no target that needs defending" (Frankel, 1999a, p. 1). The U.S. qualifies fully for a freely floating exchange rate that does not require regular intervention by the Federal Reserve in the foreign exchange market. It is a large economy. "The states of the union are more highly integrated with each other than they are with the rest of the world: There is more movement of trade, labor, and fiscal transfers within our borders, and a higher correlation of the business cycle within our border, than across our borders. Fluctuations in the exchange rate are simply not as important to us as they are to most countries. Furthermore we have a strong and well-functioning central bank, and the confidence of international investors. We do not have to subordinate our monetary policy to conditions abroad. Thus the advantages of floating overwhelm the advantages of fixing" (Frankel, 1999b, p. 9). Therefore (as I noted in chapter 2), economic growth with price stability can be pursued by the Federal Reserve within the policy triad of monetary policy independence, capital mobility, and a freely floating exchange rate. By contrast, the eurozone, having adopted a similar triple policy framework, has found it difficult to implement inflation-free growth for the zone (as I analyzed in chapter 3) because of halting zone-wide integration and deregulation. Finally, the Japanese authorities' choices to maneuver the economy out of a recession by pursuing a credible monetary policy under a floating currency regime for the yen with free capital mobility have been limited as well (as I argued chapter 4) by the massive nonperforming loans of Japanese banks.

Can emerging markets succeed in adopting floating exchange rates, pursue independent monetary policies, and maintain stable growth if Japan and the eurozone, relatively advanced market systems with institutional capabilities and open economy adaptability, face problems in designing appropriate monetary policies with the floating yen and euro? Do floating exchange rates represent a genuine choice for them in a global economy with fully liberalized capital markets? Fully floating exchange rates will imply a policy switch from the old impossible trinity of capital mobility, fixed exchange rates, and monetary autonomy (which I explain below) to the new, presumably possible trinity of capital mobility, floating exchange rates, and monetary autonomy.

The Alternative Policy Trinities

According to the old impossible trinity, a country that chooses to fix its exchange rate with free capital mobility can manage two features out of three. It can fix the exchange rate and allow capital mobility but cannot pursue an autonomous monetary policy. If its exchange rate comes under pressure, the central bank must spend its foreign exchange reserves to protect the fixed peg to which it is committed, but in so doing, it can lose all its reserves if foreign lenders, alarmed at the prospect of an impending devaluation, dump the local currency and bring about its collapse. The IMF concluded from the Asian financial debacle that the managed exchange rates prevailing in the economies contributed to the downfall of their currencies. Foreign speculators, hoping to profit from the substantial interest rate differentials in the midst of stable exchange rates, bought the currencies but discarded them when they came under pressure. In the IMF's view, the situation called for a switch from pegged to floating exchange rates including arrangements with a wide band.[3] Committed to the orthodoxy of global capital markets, it assumed that such a switch would afford greater flexibility and monetary policy discretion to emerging market policy makers.

However, the adoption of the alternative policy triad of floating exchange rates in the midst of free capital mobility is unlikely to result in monetary policy autonomy in emerging markets. Most of them lack the monetary policy independence that is automatically associated with floating exchange rate regimes. They must move their interest rates in tandem with those in the capital exporting center in order to regulate capital flows. Again, monetary easing, aimed at reviving the domestic economy, might prompt a sudden reversal of capital flows. On the other hand, monetary tightening via higher interest rates aimed at reining in domestic inflation will attract inflows. These will appreciate the exchange rate which policy makers may find difficult to counter via costly sterilization (because domestic interest rates are higher than foreign rates) or through fiscal cutbacks (because political dissension renders them impractical). Equally daunting problems arise because of institutional bottlenecks: emerging market banks may not react promptly to monetary signals because of poor lending practices reflected in inadequate backing of assets with available capital. The moratorium on debt repayment by Russia's highly leveraged commercial banks resulted from their inability to raise cash to repay foreign debts. Emerging market financial institutions also lack depth, experience, and electronic transmission capability. Few of them have extensive bond markets or a treasury bond rate that can serve as a benchmark for their capital markets.

Thailand provides a suitable example of an economy struggling with monetary policy decision making. In early June 2001, Thai policy makers were embroiled in controversies about lifting the interest rate to stem capital outflows as they faced falling exports and foreign exchange reserves, a widening trade deficit, and a declining baht. The finance minister's policy pronouncement reflected a painful choice devoid of genuine monetary policy autonomy: "We want an appropriate interest rate level: not so low that it creates capital outflow and not so high that it disrupts the investment environment." (*Financial Times*, June 7, 2001, p. 7). The government also planned a campaign under the slogan *Palang Paen Ding*—the Power of the Nation—to encourage Thais to curb unnecessary imports. Again, a regime of free capital flows and floating exchange rates, suitable for economies with low and stable single- digit inflation rates, can create problems for a central bank battling high and unstable inflation. According to Fischer (1996, p. 37): "Once a country has achieved low inflation, and provided it can keep fiscal discipline without the constraint of the fixed exchange rate, it can move to a more flexible [exchange rate] system." However, it is doubtful if Brazil, Colombia, Indonesia, Russia, and Thailand, out of the thirteen emerging economies which have adopted "independently floating" exchange rates (in Fischer, 2001. p. 17), can confidently combine autonomous monetary policies with free capital mobility in view of their unsteady record of containing inflation.

It would be prudent therefore for some emerging market economies to link floating exchange rates with market-based temporary capital account controls and, in effect, combine the advantages of floating with monetary policy autonomy. IMF principles and practice with regard to capital account controls fall into two categories. They relate specifically to transitional arrangements for members in temporary balance of payments difficulties that do not seek IMF support and alternatively for countries in the midst of severe financial problems that do seek Fund support.

Capital Account Controls from the IMF Perspective

Temporary Controls on Capital Transfers

"Members may exercise such controls as are necessary to regulate international capital movements, but no member may exercise these controls in a manner which will restrict payments for current transactions [in violation of current account convertibility] or which will unduly delay transfers of funds in settlement of commitments . . ." (IMF Articles of Agreement, 1992, p. 19). . . . members shall withdraw restrictions . . . as soon as they are satisfied that they will be able, in the absence of such restrictions, to settle their balance of payments in a manner which will not unduly encumber their access to the general resources of the Fund (ibid., p. 31). "If the Fund finds that the member persists in maintaining restrictions which are inconsistent with the purposes of the Fund, . . . the Fund may declare the member ineligible to use the general resources of the Fund . . . . If, after the expiration of a reasonable period following a decision [to suspend the voting rights of the member], the member persists in its failure to fulfill any of its obligations under this Agreement, that member may be required to withdraw from membership in the Fund by a decision of the Board of Governors . . . (ibid., pp. 43–44). As originally stipulated, these strictures clearly apply to violations of current account convertibility and evidently to capital account controls which "unduly delay transfers of funds in settlement of commitments" by a member.

Interpreting the IMF approach to capital account controls, Fischer (1998c, pp. 4–5) states: "The IMF's attitude to controls on outflows has been that these should be removed gradually, as a country's macro economy, balance of payments, and financial system strengthen. The most advanced countries have fully liberalized capital flows, and that is where all countries should ultimately be heading—but not prematurely. With regard to inflows, we see no case for controlling long-term inflows, particularly of foreign direct investment, but can see the disadvantages of surges of short-term capital, both inflows and outflows, and therefore can support market-based controls, along Chilean lines, that are intended to discourage short-term inflows." Again, the Fund attitude toward such destabilizing hot money is borne out by the following pronouncement from its chief former economist: "High openness to international capital flows, especially short-term credit flows, can be dangerous for countries with weak or inconsistent macro-economic policies or inadequately capitalized and regulated financial systems" (Mussa, 2000, p. 23).

The IMF therefore sees the need for temporary market-oriented controls for economies that are inadequately prepared to benefit from capital account liberalization. However, emerging market economies, which get into severe liquidity crisis because of hasty opening up of capital accounts, cannot invoke the argument of insufficient readiness and revoke capital account liberalization measures as part of Fund bailout.[4] Once the horses of capital account controls have been let loose from the stables, they cannot be brought back, even if needed!

Capital Account Controls for Emerging Markets in Crisis Seeking Fund Bailout

Thus, according to Fischer (1998b, p. 2), IMF lending is needed because " . . . from time to time, for whatever reason, countries get into trouble, frequently because of mistakes in their own policies. But the tendency in those situations is to take measures that would be destructive of their own prosperity or of their neighbors. What measures would be destructive of their own prosperity? It would be to close down the system, to increase tariffs, *to impose capital controls* [emphasis added]." Evidently, the imposition of temporary, market-based controls by borrowers seeking Fund support violates the IMF's purpose, which is "to give confidence to members by making the general resources of the Fund temporarily available to them under adequate safeguard, thus providing them with opportunity to correct maladjustments in their balance of payments without resorting to measures destructive of national or international prosperity" (IMF, Articles of Agreement, 1992, p. 3).

In effect, the Fund conveys the following signal to an emerging market member: "We think it is positively beneficial for you to opt for arrangements marked by free flow of cash from outsiders. You and your partners will reap a string of benefits and prosper. However, should you fail to profit from the arrangement because of your inexperience and inadequacies and seek our help, we will give you cash combined with a series of mandatory do's and don'ts which will eventually break you into accepting the consequences of the invitation to predatory outsiders." By the end of 1996, 134 out of 181 Fund members had eliminated controls on current account transactions and over 50 countries had removed capital account controls. "Careful progress in this direction is attracting increased attention in our policy dialogue" (Camdessus, 1996, p. 1). As the liberalization strategy promoted via "policy dialogue" and subtle pressure pulls in more emerging market economies into the global capital network, and forces them to seek Fund support when they encounter financial problems, the opening up becomes irreversible!

The IMF practice of denying selective choice of capital account controls to member countries in crisis which seek its support runs contrary to its positive nod in favor of temporary capital account controls. Its mandate of correcting crisis-induced maladjustments without "resorting to measures destructive of national or international prosperity" rules out the option. The East-Asian economies prematurely opened up their capital accounts under the Fund's watch even as the Fund was warning Thai policy makers about a worsening financial situation. A simultaneous imposition of temporary controls on outflows during the Asian crisis could have moderated the recession in each and halted the contagion all around, both of which were arguably more "destructive of national and international prosperity" than the rejected alternative of coordinated restrictions on capital outflows! Commenting on the adoption of controls by Malaysia to moderate capital outflows, Fischer (1998c, p. 4) states: "This approach has been taken by Malaysia, and has had support from leading academics. But it is surprising how few countries have intensified capital controls *in the present crisis* [emphasis added]." They did not because the IMF would not allow them to "regress" into such controls whereas

Malaysia went ahead because it did not seek Fund bailout! Subsequently, the Fund gave a qualified nod of recognition to the Malaysian selective capital account controls without endorsing them as a crisis-resolution strategy. In the view of the Fund (noted in chapter 11), the fixed exchange rate of the ringgit operated successfully in the controlled regime without a currency black market and illegal outflows because Malaysia already possessed a solid regulatory system and strong financial institutions.

In effect, therefore, the IMF promoted full capital mobility, in and out, for emerging markets by conveying the following signal to their policy makers: "You must allow capital to move in for you to benefit from its welfare improving gains although your economies may lack the necessary institutional and structural underpinning. And you must allow capital to move out because capital controls, in the absence of such underpinning, will lead to criminal activity in your foreign exchange markets and illegal capital flight from your borders." With respect to inflows, the Fund in effect ignores emerging market economies' inadequate preparedness, which it invokes, however, in support of outflows! The approach is asymmetric at best and self-serving at worst and carries enormous costs for the peripheral borrowers from speculative inflows and their sudden reversals.

Can the costs be shared and partially passed on to the lenders? Is it possible to curtail inordinate short-term lending by investors and design equitable burden-sharing schemes? The cycle of excessive speculative flows leading to frequent crises and massive IMF bailouts, it is argued, can be broken if investors are forced to bear the costs of their recklessness. The automatic penalty will also remove the presumed moral hazard protection afforded by Fund lending: private investors assume that Fund credits will materialize during financial turmoil enabling them to minimize the losses from their excessive risk taking. (I discussed the implications of the moral hazard safeguard in block 7.) The proposed rearrangements involve formulation and implementation of appropriate norms and standards; taxation on currency flows from centers dealing in foreign exchange; and creditor participation via IMF intermediation requiring an incorporation, in the Fund Articles of Agreement, of internationally accepted bankruptcy provisions when reversals are threatened. Discussions surrounding these issues (which I address immediately below) became increasingly vocal in 2001, as Argentina, despite IMF-supported funding, headed toward an inevitable debt default.

Standards, Norms, and Tax Proposals for Regulating Speculative Flows

Ideally, the standards devised to moderate the flow of short-term funds from their origin can *preempt* a financial crisis which would otherwise overwhelm a recipient. From emerging market economies' perspective, however, these norms must also ensure their access to international capital markets, tilt the available funds from speculative flows to more long-term provision, and ensure an equitable burden sharing for borrowing and lending countries alike in their implementation.

Hedge Funds and Destabilizing Flows

The activities of hedge funds, which invest in securities and currency markets with a view to earning high returns from anticipating their movements, can destabilize these markets because they can engage in massive cross-border operations, liquidate their holdings swiftly, and add to market volatility by damaging investor confidence. The systemic impact of their activities arises from their lack of transparency and their ability to borrow extravagantly from banks of their origin. They operate from offshore financial centers offering them special tax benefits without requiring them to disclose the size of their investments often financed with unsustainable bank borrowing. The concerns of the Financial Stability Forum regarding the lack of transparency and excessive leverage of these funds cannot actually promote stable financial flows in emerging markets unless G-7 governments improve their own bank lending appraisal, and promote information sharing among borrowing and lending regulatory agencies. Without such exchange of information and even technical support, most borrowers will fail to assess the risks to their financial sector from hedge fund activities.[5] The call by Hans Eichel, the German finance minister, for coordinating the supervision of hedge fund activities, for temporarily banning their short selling of shares, and for enforcing greater transparency in their activities was fiercely opposed by the industry (*Financial Times*, February 15, 2002, p. 24).

Numerous handicaps from the perspective of emerging market borrowers prevailed in the proposed codes of the international Financial Stability Forum ranging from "transparency in monetary and fiscal policies, to codes on accounting, corporate governance, and banking" (see Rodrik, 2001 for full details). The actual implementation in emerging markets of the codes proposed by the relevant issuing agency was bound to vary with the institutional receptivity of a given country (Will an African country with poor institutional underpinning be more geared than a Central American one?), the resources devoted for the purpose (Should Bangladesh concentrate more on rewarding its primary school teachers than training its accountants in the modern practices of Anglo-American accounting?), and the cultural resistance of its managerial elite to the invasion of Western norms (Why should the profit motive take precedence over employees' welfare?).

The Basel Committee on Banking Supervision, the watchdog arm of the Bank for International Settlements, proposed new, legally nonbinding rules in 2001 that also put the adjustment burden for ensuring the soundness of global banking business on emerging market borrowers.

Basel Committee Standards

Banks will continue to hold capital at 8 percent of their risk-adjusted loans as before, but these loans will be classified into separate "buckets" according to their default likelihood. Riskier assets will require larger backing. External rating agencies will assess the risks associated with loans, and banks will disclose their internal assessment rules to regulators. The application of the proposed rules was aimed at promoting credits to sound borrowers and discouraging them to unreliable ones. Failure to meet the rules can preempt access to global funds by emerging market borrowers: regulators can penalize lenders by requiring higher capital/asset ratios if they lend to emerging market banks that fail to meet the norms. The standards will therefore exclude borrowers who are less geared in terms of their technical, financial, and supervisory capabilities for fulfilling them and will impose the restructuring burden on marginalized emerging markets. In the end, the norms will be implemented for promoting the stability of the global capital markets rather than encouraging adequate or long-term capital flows from the center to the periphery.

Can a tax be levied to discourage short-term flows emanating from centers that engage in currency transactions?

The Tobin Tax

The tax on transactions in currency markets proposed by Nobel Laureate James Tobin in 1971 was intended to provide monetary policy discretion to emerging market central banks by curtailing the impact of destabilizing speculative inflows in their financial markets. The tax, in his view, could not be imposed because the currency transaction centers would escape it by swiftly moving their deals via electronic transfers to offshore tax havens. French and German leaders revived it in September 2001 and set up a working group to examine it with a view to appease antiglobalization protestors who wanted the tax revenue to be used for alleviating world poverty even though it could not be enforced in practice. In any case, Wall Street and the U.S. Treasury are positively against it.

Can lenders be made to bear some costs of *resolving* a financial crisis via temporary suspension of debt obligations by borrowers?

Crisis Resolution via Temporary Debt Repayment Suspension

This idea, an international variant of the Chapter 11 bankruptcy proceedings in U.S. corporate practice, will allow an orderly resolution of the debt obligations in a cooperative framework by enabling borrowers to gradually raise the necessary cash and by preventing lenders from asset grabbing and launching disruptive litigation against borrowers. Currently, borrowers cannot invoke such temporary suspensions and enforce them on bondholders via their domestic bankruptcy procedures because these are not binding on foreign creditors. Borrowers may be unwilling to suspend payments unilaterally because their credit rating can collapse. A mandatory adoption of debt suspension can also contribute to moderating the frequency of financial crises in emerging markets by placing the burden of debt restructuring on potential investors. A change in IMF Articles of Agreement for members can allow it to mandate a temporary suspension. In November 2001, IMF Deputy Managing Director Anne Krueger proposed that emerging market economies with serious repayment problems be allowed suspension of their sovereign debt obligations to foreign creditors.[6] By contrast, the U.S. Treasury indicated its preference in April 2002 for the adoption of voluntary standstill clauses, presumably similar to collective action clauses (which I discuss subsequently), in bond contracts of emerging market economies.

Mandatory debt suspension under an IMF program for an economy in financial trouble will give it an effective breathing spell if it is handicapped by a temporary liquidity crunch rather than a solvency crisis. It may not work for a heavily debt-ridden economy such as Argentina if it cannot eventually clear its negotiated obligations with adequate financial resources. In such extreme cases, the debt burden can be resolved without temporary suspension via the inclusion of collective action clauses in bond contracts for lenders and borrowers. Bondholders will agree to restructure the debt, take some losses, and abide by the terms of the agreement. The unilateral debt default by Argentine authorities brought to the forefront the issue of the adoption of collective action clauses in bond contracts that might help promote amicable debt settlement in future crises without such an abrogation which damages a borrower's credit rating.

Collective Action Clauses in Bond Contracts

These clauses introduce transparency and resolution procedures by enabling all creditors to share information on debts already paid; by allowing a majority to speak for all; and by permitting bondholder meetings for voicing opinions. Their inclusion can minimize disputes and pre-empt litigation but can also raise costs for borrowers with low credit rating because lenders will be required to share the costs of debt restructuring if the contracts include such clauses. The question arises if these clauses should be incorporated only in new bond contracts or if existing bond contracts of emerging market debtors should be reformulated to include them. Emerging market borrowers could be persuaded to revise their contracts via an offer of lower indirect interest rate payments by them on IMF loans. Borrowing country regulators are not enthusiastic about the adoption of collective action clauses or of international bankruptcy provisions because both, in their view, stigmatize their borrowers by signaling their low creditworthiness to potential lenders. In fact, potential borrowers qualify for IMF Contingent Credit Line facility only if their contracts include such clauses. On balance, emerging market borrowers will end up by paying higher interest charges if they include them, and by being left out of borrowing altogether from the private market and from the IMF if they exclude them. The responsibility for upgrading their credit rating therefore rests squarely on their shoulders.

The prospects for the adoption of bankruptcy-style provisions in IMF Articles of Agreement or of collective action clauses in bond contracts, in my view, are not encouraging. It is doubtful if the U.S. Congress will readily delegate authority on bankruptcy rulings to an international institution and subject potential U.S. creditors to such extraterritorial jurisdiction. Collective action clauses, which prevail in U.K. business arrangements, are excluded from U.S. corporate practice, which requires agreement by all bondholders. The inclusion of mandatory bankruptcy provisions and collective action clauses will not preempt a crisis if creditors, foreseeing signs of financial problems with borrowers, promptly sell their assets and actually hasten the onset of a crisis! The best policy option is for the IMF to monitor the debt burden of an emerging market economy under its surveillance system, encourage a preemptive shift to long-term bonds as short-term instruments are redeemed, and link its stabilization policy packaging with debt rescheduling on a case-by-case basis, if a crisis does occur, by arranging negotiated debt settlement among borrowers and lenders.[7]

By contrast, the Meltzer Commission placed an undue adjustment burden for creating an investor-friendly environment on emerging market economy policy makers with a view to preempting altogether such debt settlement complications. It was appointed by the U.S. Congress to reform the IMF following the meltdown of Russia's finances in August 1998 and the money laundering scandal of the Bank of New York. Congress was ready to radically redefine the role of the international financial institutions (IFIs). Having approved, in November 1998, $18 billion in additional funding for the IMF, vigorously lobbied by the Clinton administration, Congress sought to address the "growing frequency, severity and cost of financial disturbances, the fragility of the international monetary system, the ineffectiveness of development banks," and "the expanding mandate of the IFI, their new facilities and programs" (Meltzer, 2001, p. 1). More specifically, an International Financial Institution Advisory Commission (IFIAC) was appointed by Congress under the chairmanship of Allan Meltzer. The commission focused on redefining the role of the multilateral institutions so that they would extend effectively and efficiently the services that private markets would not provide, and develop infrastructure that would permit market solutions where feasible and nonmarket solutions elsewhere (ibid., p. 2). The commission recommended that potential borrowers should clean up their financial sectors to qualify as recipients of capital inflows, adopt floating, market-determined exchange rates (which the likely investor could look up from the Internet or the *Wall Street Journal*), and maintain abundant foreign exchange reserves in order to be able to absorb unexpected capital account shocks. In the commission's view, emerging markets must categorically avoid controls on capital mobility. A departure from this set of commandments would increase the cost of borrowing for the nonperformers or keep foreign creditors from stepping in. "March in step to the tune of the market or remain on the sidelines" was the commission's signal to emerging market borrowers.

The Meltzer Commission Recommendations

The majority of the commission members went about their chores in the fashion of scalpel-wielding surgeons, cutting back funding and advisory fat in the institutions, removing its overlap, and proposing to relocate the residual in a manner that would promote its efficient use. The recommendations covered the future role of the IMF, the World Bank, and the regional development banks. I focus on the suggestions that sought to reshape IMF activity.

The IMF Overhaul

The majority's overriding premise was that the IMF practice of bailing out most countries reduced their incentive to reform despite imposition of fund conditionality. The IMF, in its view, had failed as a Skinnerian watchdog. On the other hand, if the Fund were to adopt an incentive-cum-punishment mandate and accept some countries as deserving of automatic assistance and reject others in terms of some preconditions, financial markets, which provided 95 percent of world capital flows, would be able to distinguish between countries with proper and improper policies and standards. "IMF acceptance of the country as qualified for automatic assistance would serve as a seal of approval and reduce expected losses. The market would have a list of countries that qualified, and a list of those that did not. The latter would get fewer loans [from the market] and would pay higher interest rates to compensate for the additional risk. Thus, preconditions redirect private sector flows away from high-risk borrowers toward those that pursue stabilizing policies. This reduces the risk in the entire system" (ibid., pp. 5–6). Also, "there would be fewer crises if the pre-conditions were met. Financial sectors would be solvent and open to competition from foreign banks, governments would be prudent, and exchange rates would either float, even if not freely, or be firmly fixed and supported by adequate reserves and appropriate policies. Lenders to countries that did not adopt the pre-conditions would bear the losses they undertook. Hence, they would limit loans to non-qualifying countries increasing incentives for reform" (ibid., p. 6).

The commission's proposals for IMF reform were intended to kill several birds with one stone. The compulsion to impose a Washington consensus will disappear because the insistence on preconditions for Fund aid will induce countries to reform on their own volition. Second, the IMF will lend less because there will be fewer crises. Third, moral hazard will cease to be an issue because foolhardy creditors who lent to countries that failed to satisfy preconditions would bear the losses in a crisis if they did not price their loans and assets correctly to compensate them for the expected losses. Finally, private lenders should not be forced to share the cost of a financial meltdown in a crisis-swept country by being prevented from withdrawing from its financial market (as Malaysia did). Exchange controls on capital flows were to be forbidden in the majority view. The IMF should not help a country support a pegged exchange rate by lending enough to allow creditors to leave. Instead, the reliance on a floating exchange rate will allow the exchange rate to fall "until those who chose to exit were matched by private investors willing to lend or acquire assets at what they think are bargain prices" (ibid., p. 9). The bondholders and lenders will then be free to negotiate their remaining outstanding claims.

The proposed role of the IMF would reduce it to a quasi-lender of last resort, providing liquidity to members that met preconditions. These include financial norms as well as structural reforms. The World Bank should not lend to middle-income countries with investment-grade rating, sending them instead to the marketplace for financing economic development. The bank should directly transfer resources via grants to Africa where the majority of the world's poorest countries are located. It should continue giving technical advice to all member countries but give up its programs for institutional reforms and the relevant funding to the Inter-

American, Asian, and African Development Banks that are more attuned to local needs and diverse cultures.

The commission's recommendations, driven by the market ideology of free capital mobility, put the adjustment burden on emerging market borrowers (the same standards were applied by the Financial Stability Forum and the proposed rules of the Basel Committee). Its diagnosis of the IMF's emergence as a multibillion-dollar rescuer and the failure of its conditions in crisis-ridden economies were lopsided. The commission failed to acknowledge that the IMF's original role as a problem solver of temporary, mini-size balance of payments deficits in member countries in the Bretton Woods world of restricted capital mobility with fixed exchange rates expanded into mega-size bailouts in the financially open global economy because the IMF actively, indiscriminately, and prematurely promoted that. Nor could the structural reform conditions work even as the Fund programs imposed massive recessionary costs via fiscal and monetary austerity on crisis-afflicted borrowers because such changes could not spring forth readily in peripheral economies like Athena from the brow of Zeus. (I discussed the problems encountered by South Korean policy makers in initiating such reforms in block 1.) The commission's recommendation that the IMF work up a list of borrowers with inadequate qualifying preconditions would render the IMF less than evenhanded if it failed to also create a list of leveraged private lenders who speculate in volatile capital flows destabilizing these borrowers.

The IMF's emergence as an active troubleshooter for putting out financial storms that occurred with habitual frequency and the collapse of the Russian ruble following the tumbling of East Asian currencies prompted calls that ranged from rolling back its funding activities to closing its credit windows. The former have proved difficult to implement whereas the latter were unrealistic to begin with.[8] Complaints about the overarching role of the U.S. Treasury in steering the direction and scale of IMF's funding activity became commonplace as well.

How Much Pressure from the U.S.?

As the largest shareholder in the IMF with a 17 percent quota holding, the U.S. has a dominating voice and an arsenal of choices at its disposal. It can veto a proposed loan. It can persuade private banks to reschedule a leveraged debtor's loan obligations as it managed, somewhat belatedly, in the Korean rescue operation in 1998. It can steer IMF-managed policy in a market-oriented direction as it did with Russia while pursuing its own foreign policy agenda financed by the Nunn-Lugar program for collecting Soviet-era nuclear warheads in Russia and systematically defusing them according to a mutually agreed schedule. It can convince the remaining G-7 members to approve IMF funding for a member that has been warned earlier with a "no more" signal as was Argentina, which nevertheless managed to get a $40 billion IMF-sponsored package despite having been told by the Clinton administration in late 2000 to put its house in order. It can withhold bilateral contribution from a package proposed by the IMF as it did when Turkey was provided with $10 billion in May 2001 by the Fund, again with a futile, "this is your last-chance with us" notification. The IMF's inability, under pressure from a leading quota contributor, to deny support to a member in financial crisis despite a failing policy record, brings out the impracticality of the Meltzer Commission's suggestions (considered previously) that the Fund deny financial lifeline to a member that has failed to meet preconditions. The evidence on the imposition of U.S. strategic or foreign policy interests on the Fund activity, however, is circumstantial because the decision-making process is confidential, making it impossible for an outsider to track down details of "who said what" in a particular meeting or in a telephone conversation from the U.S. Treasury to the Fund.

The IMF, chastened by its East Asian experience and pressured all around by the need to change, responded in a standard bureaucratic fashion by adding an additional borrowing facility, the Contingent Credit Line, which imposed higher interest charges for borrowers and required qualifying preconditions for eligibility. It set up a new capital markets group that would communicate with bankers and traders for identifying crisis symptoms. It started a pilot project with the World Bank for assessing the stability of members' financial institutions. Based on its privileged access to information in member countries, the Fund has increased its surveillance of their economic and financial conditions. These plans, designed to forestall the need for multibillion-dollar rescue packages, failed to provide early warning signals of the impending financial storm in Argentina. The Fund has in effect continued imposing its "one- rule-fits-all-situations" prescriptions to borrowers in financial trouble.[9]

The Meltzer Commission's recommendation in favor of the IMF curtailing its financial bailouts and restricting its monitoring to the recipients' financial sectors has merit. The commission however approved the Fund's free market ideology of capital mobility but disapproved of its increasing intrusiveness in host countries without acknowledging that the latter resulted from the former. It failed to reformulate the question of how a leaner IMF agenda can be implemented fairly in emerging markets if the market-based, first-best arrangements of free capital mobility and floating exchange rates cannot work to their advantage in view of their structural and institutional weaknesses.

Can the IMF Be Leaner and Kinder in the Context
of a Fair Global Financial Order?

Four concluding comments are in order.

First, the IMF cannot function as an impartial lender of the last resort under current conditions of selective pressure from its leading quota holders led by the U.S. and of its adherence to free capital mobility despite pronouncements to the contrary. The former has influenced the frequency and size of its bailouts and the latter has required funding packages that in reality have proved insufficient for the needs of crisis-swept economies. The Fund can emerge as a lender of limited resort by cutting back potential funding either by extending preconditions similar to those outlined by the Meltzer Commission for more borrowers (already incorporated in the IMF Contingent Credit Line) or by selective adoption of market-based capital account controls for crisis-prone or crisis-swept emerging market economies. The former approach will divide emerging markets in two camps of financial haves and have-nots with the former set clubbing with the advanced economies and their creditors in the center. The latter approach will cast the Fund in a more cooperative and pragmatic role. As the U.S. revives and leads the global system into fresh economic resurgence, investors' exuberance to lend to emerging market economies will resurface, posing destabilizing dangers of excessive short-term capital flows from the center to the periphery. In other words, an emerging market, which seemed financially viable, such as Brazil in late 2002, may cease to be so, and its reversal into financial trouble will resurrect the familiar cycle of debates calling for a departure from the IMF's worn-out policy focus. The current arrangements of free capital flows and their negative impact on the finances and exchange rates of the emerging market periphery will confine the Fund to the continuing role of imposing fiscal austerity, intrusive conditionalities, and spectacular failures as in Russia and Argentina. By contrast, a flexible policy framework based on the Fund's monitoring of borrowers' financial sector shortcomings can be tailored, via the adoption of market-based measures, to long-term flows. The IMF faces that choice.

Second, the IMF policy preference for floating exchange rates will not endow borrowers with monetary policy independence in the presence of free capital flows. Floating exchange rate regimes supported by selective capital account controls will by contrast confer monetary policy autonomy to emerging market central banks.

Third, the inclusion of bankruptcy-type provisions, and collective action clauses in bond contracts to facilitate debt rescheduling, were these suggestions to be adopted, will not work to the advantage of emerging market borrowers: it will deter potential lending from the advanced center and stigmatize marginal borrowers in the periphery. It may even precipitate a crisis by early withdrawal of lenders from a crisis-prone economy. A case-by-case resolution of debt settlement with a formal engagement of the IMF in the bailout funding or informal backdoor negotiations is to be preferred.

Finally, the G-7 leadership's failure to multilateralize the discussions and negotiations relating to the designing of the new financial architecture is a serious shortcoming from the perspective of borrowing countries. The East Asian crisis-hit region's populations suffered from the severe social and political consequences of the radical recessionary brakes of the IMF rescue program for resolving the crisis. Its leadership felt left out from the subsequent financial reform agenda in which it had no defining voice or active role. The exclusion of the emerging market economies from the G-7 led discussions to reform the global financial system will result in the emergence of standards and procedures guaranteed to promote the stability of the international financial system rather than discourage the flow of short-term flows from hedge funds that destabilize these economies. This exclusionary decision making in the center has thus far ruled out alternative arrangements consisting of temporary adoption of suitable capital account controls and intermediate exchange rate systems during which the Financial Stability Forum norms could be systematically implanted in emerging markets with technical and financial support from the IMF. The alternative stick-wielding approach by G-7 architects, however, is unlikely to readily eliminate the deficiencies in the functioning of the financial systems that the early warning system of the IMF hopes to identify. The IMF-led external pressure embedded in the crisis bailout packaging with free capital mobility has not resulted in rapid reform of financial sector inadequacies in peripheral economies. These shortcomings will disappear at varying speed in different countries from their autonomous recognition that the new practices and institutions of the Anglo-American-style market economy are worth the modification and destruction of the traditional arrangements that constrain the collective gains from the free flow of global capital.

Notes

1. Eatwell and Taylor (2000); Eichengreen (1999a); Hills and Peterson (1999); *Rebuilding the International Financial Architecture* (2001); and Swoboda (1999).

2. Thus the East Asian economies and Brazil (before the *real* devaluation of January 1999) in effect followed adjustable pegs without their central banks openly committing themselves to devalue or revalue the currencies in the presence

of balance of payments deficits or surpluses. Russia followed a target band within which the Central Bank of Russia allowed the ruble to fluctuate before it collapsed in August 1998. Turkey, under IMF monitoring, allowed the lira to crawl on the basis of a pre-announced devaluation in relation to the inflation rate such that it appreciated slightly in real terms in the interest of inflation control.

3. According to Fischer (2001, p. 2): "In essence, the excluded arrangements are fixed, adjustable peg, and narrow band exchange rate systems." In the presence of free capital mobility, the preferred regimes are "free floating to a variety of crawling bands *with wide ranges* [emphasis added], and then very hard pegs sustained by a highly credible policy commitment, notably currency boards and the abandonment of a national currency. . . ." Fischer suggests that between 1991 and 1999, countries with free capital mobility have moved away from the old intermediate arrangements to either hard pegs or more flexible arrangements. I believe, along with Williamson (2000, cited in Fischer, 2001, p. 4) that the move from the intermediate arrangements of the adjustable pegs of the old days to the greater flexible arrangements in emerging markets has been associated with IMF conditionality attached to its bailout support for a number of these countries.

4. However, the IMF may spare a semi-liberalized economy the full burden of the Fund's policy orthodoxy by allowing its negotiators the selective *retention* of existing controls on capital flows if they make a sound case for them in terms of their limited preparedness for short-term flows. For instance, the IMF extended its $3 billion funding to help India overcome its foreign exchange liquidity shortage in the summer of 1991. It linked the funding to a decisive removal of the maze of direct controls in industry and trade but allowed the government to stick to IMF Article VIII relating to the current account convertibility of the Indian rupee that was devalued *without being made fully convertible on capital account*. The Indian situation, however, resembled the traditional balance of payments maladjustment rather than a serious liquidity crisis of the East Asian variety brought on by massive capital flows which resulted from the premature removal of capital account controls.

5. Fischer (1998c, p.6) underlines the difficulties of "regulating hedge fund activities—even if only by requiring them to provide more information about the positions they take—particularly given the existence of offshore banking and financial centers."

6. For an illuminating discussion of the economic implications of the Krueger proposal, see Cooper (2002).

7. A differentiated debt settlement approach depending on the circumstances of each country is also suggested by Fischer (1998c, p. 10).

8. Even before the collapse of Russia's finances, George P. Shultz, the former secretary of state; William E. Simon, the former secretary of the treasury; and Walter B. Wriston, the former chairman of Citicorp, had called the IMF "ineffective, unnecessary and obsolete" ("Who Needs the IMF?," *Wall Street Journal*, February 3, 1998, p. A22).

9. From an historical perspective "the Fund has evolved *during its history* [emphasis added]—shifting from the balance-of-payments problems of industrialized countries in the 1950s and 1960s, to the currency problems of developing coun-

tries post-1973 and their debt problems post-1982, and then adding the broader problems of the transition economies post-1989. Better that it continue to evolve post-1997, to address the financial and other structural problems in East Asia, than that (like some institutions) it fail to change with the times" (Frankel, 1998b, p. 11). In my view, the Fund cannot evolve in new, realistic directions if it regards even a market-oriented, temporary departure from its policy orthodoxy of fully free capital mobility as a reversal. In that basic sense, the Fund is nonreformable.

References

Alba, Pedro, Leonardo Hernandez, and Daniela Klingebiel. 1999. Financial liberalization and the capital account: Thailand 1988–1997. Washington, D.C.: World Bank—Country Economics Department. Working paper 2188.

Alexashenko, Sergey. 1999. Russian crisis: Was there an escape? Unpublished manuscript presented at a conference on Exchange Rate Regimes, Financial Markets, and Economic Stabilization in Emerging Market Economies, Columbia University. November.

Banking India Update. 1999. Foreign Exchange Management Act. *http://www.bankingindiaupdate.com/fema.html*. Accessed October 1, 2002.

Berg, Andrew. 2001. Comment. In *Annual World Bank Conference on Development Economics 2000*, edited by Boris Pleskovic and Nicholas Stern. Washington, D.C.: The World Bank.

Bhagwati, Jagdish. 1998. Why free mobility may be hazardous to your health: Lessons from the latest financial crisis. Prepared for the NBER Conference on Capital Controls in Cambridge, Mass. November 7.

———. 2000a. The capital myth: The difference between trade in widgets and dollars. In *The wind of the hundred days: How Washington mismanaged globalization*, Jagdish Bhagwati. Cambridge, Mass.: MIT Press, pp. 3–11.

———. 2000b. The 'miracle' that did happen: Understanding East Asia in comparative perspective. In *The wind of the hundred days: How Washington mismanaged globalization*, Jagdish Bhagwati. Cambridge, Mass.: MIT Press, pp. 27–49.

———. 2000c. A friend in the United States, but a crony in Asia. In *The wind of the hundred days: How Washington mismanaged globalization*, Jagdish Bhagwati. Cambridge, Mass.: MIT Press, pp. 61–64.

Camdessus, Michel. 1996. Promoting freer trade: The IMF's perspective. Remarks at the First Ministerial Conference of the World Trade Organization in Singapore, on December 9. *http://www.imf.org/external/np/sec/mds/1996/mds9621.htm*. Accessed October 1, 2002.

Coe, David, and Dennis Snower. 1997. Policy complementarities: The case for fundamental labor market reform. *IMF Staff Papers* 44(1):1–35.

Cooper, Richard. 1999. A tour of international financial reform. *Challenge* 42(4):5–28.

———. 2002. Chapter 11 for countries? *Foreign Affairs* 81(4):90–103.

Corden, W. M. 1984. Booming sector and Dutch disease economics: Survey and consolidation. *Oxford Economic Papers* 36(3):359–80.

Corsetti, Giancarlo, Paolo Pesenti, and Nouriel Roubini. 1998. What caused the Asian currency and financial crises? Part I: A macroeconomic overview. Cambridge, Mass.: NBER working paper 6833, December.

Desai, Padma. 1976. The production function and technical change in postwar Soviet industry: A reexamination. *American Economic Review* 66(3):372–381.

Desai, Padma. 1987. Total factor productivity in postwar Soviet industry and its branches. In *The Soviet economy: Problems and prospects*, Padma Desai. Oxford: Basil Blackwell.

———. 1992. From the Soviet Union to the Commonwealth of Independent States: The aid debate. *The Harriman Institute Forum* 5(8):1–15.

———. 1994. Aftershock in Russia's economy. *Current History* 93 (October): 320–23.

———. 1995a. Beyond shock therapy. In *Economic reform and democracy*, edited by Larry Diamond and Marc F. Plattner. Baltimore: John Hopkins University Press.

———. 1995b. Russian privatization: A comparative perspective. *The Harriman Review* 8(3):1–34.

———. 1997. Russia. In *Going global: Transition from plan to market in the world economy*, edited by Padma Desai. Cambridge, Mass.: MIT Press, pp. 317–351.

———. 1998. Macroeconomic fragility and exchange rate vulnerability: A cautionary record of transition economies. *Journal of Comparative Economics* 26(4):621–641.

———. 1999. Russian reform: What went wrong? *The Harriman Review* 11(4):5–8.

———. 2000. Why did the ruble collapse in August 1998? *American Economic Review* 90(2):48–52.

Eatwell, John and Lance Taylor. 2000. *Global finance at risk: The case for international regulation.* New York: New Press.

Edwards Sebastian. 1998. Capital flows, real exchange rates and capital controls: Some Latin American experiences. Cambridge, Mass.: NBER working paper 6370, November.

———. 1999. Crisis prevention: Lessons from Mexico and East Asia. Cambridge, Mass.: NBER working paper 7233, July.

Eichengreen, Barry. 1999a. *Toward a new international financial architecture: A practical post-Asia agenda.* Washington, D.C.: Institute for International Economics.

———. 1999b. Capital mobility: Ties need not bind. *Milken Institute Review* (first quarter): 29–37.

Feldstein, Martin S. 1998. Refocusing the IMF. *Foreign Affairs* 77(2):20–33.

Fischer, Stanley. 1996. Maintaining price stability. *Finance and Development.* December. *http://minneapolisfed.org/pubs/region/97–06/fisher.html*. Accessed October 1, 2002.

———. 1998a. IMF Deputy Stanley Fischer on the IMF and the East Asian Crisis. Paper prepared for delivery at the Forum Funds Lecture at UCLA, Los Angeles on March 20. *http://www.j-bradford-delong.net/Politics/Fischer_Asia.html*. Accessed October 1, 2002.

———. 1998b. Edited transcript of remarks by Stanley Fischer, First Deputy Managing Director of the IMF, at the World Economic Development Council in Washington, D.C. on October 1. *http://www.imf.org/external/np/tr/1998/tr981002.htm*. Accessed October 1, 2002.

———. 1998c. Reforming the international financial system. Paper prepared for delivery at the David Finch Lecture, Melbourne on November 9. *http:// www.imf.org/external/np/speeches/1998/110998.htm.* Accessed October 1, 2002.

———. 1999. The financial crisis in emerging markets: Some lessons. Outline of comments prepared for delivery at the Conference of the Economic Strategy Institute, Washington, D.C. on April 28. *http://www.imf.org/external/np/ speeches/1999/042899.htm.* Accessed October 1, 2002.

———. 2001. Exchange rate regimes: Is the bipolar view correct? Prepared for delivery at the Meetings of the American Economics Association in New Orleans, January 6. *http://www.imf.org/external/np/speeches/2001/010601a.htm.* Accessed October 1, 2002.

Flood, R. and P. Garber. 1984. Collapsing exchange rate regimes: some linear examples. *Journal of International Economics* no. 17:1–13.

Foreign Exchange Regulation Act (FERA), as amended by the Foreign Exchange Regulation (Amendment) Act. 1993. Section 8(1). *http://exim.indiamart.com/ act-regulations/fera-1993.html.* Accessed October 1, 2002.

Frankel, Jeffrey, 1996a. How well do foreign exchange markets function: Might a Tobin tax help? In *The Tobin tax: Coping with financial volatility,* edited by M. ul Haq, I. Kaul and I. Grungberg. New York: Oxford University Press, pp. 41–81.

———. 1996b. Recent exchange rate experience and proposals for reform. *American Economic Review Papers and Proceedings* 86(2):153–158.

———. 1998a. Asian economics in perspective. Keynote address, Fourth Asia Pacific Economic Cooperation Roundtable: Regional Cooperation and Asian Recovery. Boston, May 26. *http://ksghome.harvard.edu/~.jfrankel.academic .ksg/Apecbrds.PDF.* Accessed October 1, 2002.

———. 1998b. The Asian model, the miracle, the crisis, and the Fund. Delivered at the U.S. International Trade Commission. April 16. http:// ksghome.harvard.edu/ ~.jfrankel.academic.ksg/eacritc.pub.pdf. Accessed October 7, 2002.

———. 1999a. The international financial architecture. Brookings Institution. Policy Brief 51. June. *http://www.brook.edu/dybdocroot/comm/PolicyBriefs/ pb051/pb51.htm.* Accessed October 1, 2002.

———. 1999b. No single currency regime is right for all countries. Testimony before the Committee on Banking and Financial Services, U.S. House of Representatives. May 21. *http://ksghome.harvard.edu/~.jfrankel.academic.ksg/ TESTIMNY.HBC.PDF.* Accessed October 1, 2002.

———. 1999c. Proposals regarding restrictions on capital flows. *The African Finance Journal* 1(1). *http://ksghome.harvard.edu/~.jfrankel.academic.ksg/ proposalsregardingrestrictionsoncapitalflowsafj.pdf.* Accessed October 7, 2002.

Frankel, Jeffrey. 1999d. Asia: Opportunity or obstruction. Session of conference on Global Economics and Global Security: The Balance in the New Millennium. Kennedy School of Government, Cambridge, Mass. September 23. *http:// ksghome.harvard.edu/~.jfrankel.academic.ksg/AsiaNyenob.pdf.* Accessed October 7, 2002.

Frankel, Jeffrey. 1999e. Dollarization in Latin America: Solution of straitjacket? Remarks at the IMF. June 24. *http://ksghome.harvard.edu/~.jfrankel.academic.ksg/dollrztn%20imf.PDF*. Accessed October 1, 2002.

Frankel, Jeffrey, and Andrew K. Rose. 1996. Currency crashes in emerging markets: An empirical treatment. Washington, D.C.: Board of Governors of the Federal Reserve System, International Finance Discussion Papers, no. 534, January.

Frankel, Jeffrey, and Sergio L. Schmukler. 1998. Crisis, contagion, and country funds: Effects on East Asia and Latin America. In *Managing capital flows and exchange rates*, edited by R. Glick. Cambridge: Cambridge University Press, pp. 232–266.

Gordon, Robert. 2000. Does the new economy measure up to the great inventions of the past? *Journal of Economic Perspectives* 4(14):49–74.

Hall, Robert. 2001. Struggling to understand the stock market. Presented as the 2001 Ely Lecture, January 3. *http://www.stanford.edu/~rehall/Ely.pdf*. Accessed October 1, 2002.

Haggard, Stephan, and Andrew MacIntyre. 2001. The politics of moral hazard: The origins of financial crisis in Indonesia, Korea and Thailand. In *The political economy of the East Asian crisis and its aftermath: Tigers in distress*, edited by Arvid Lukauskas and Francisco Rivera-Batiz. Northampton, Mass.: Edward Elgar Publishing.

Hills, Carla and Peter Peterson, co-chairs. 1999. *Safeguarding prosperity in a global financial system: The future international financial architecture*. New York: Council on Foreign Relations.

Hooper, Peter, and Trevor Dinmore. 2000. What's behind the recent US productivity boom and why it will last. *Global Markets Research*. Deutsche Bank. September 5.

International Monetary Fund. 1992. *Articles of agreement of the International Monetary Fund. http://www.imf.org/external/pubs/ft/aa/index.htm*. Accessed October 1, 2002.

———. 1999. IMF-supported programs in Indonesia, Korea, and Thailand: A preliminary assessment. Washington, D.C.: International Monetary Fund. Occasional Paper 178.

Jorgenson, Dale. 2000. Information technology and the U.S. economy. Presidential address to the American Economics Association, New Orleans, Louisiana, January 6. *http://www.economics.harvard.edu/faculty/jorgenson/papers/NewAmerican.pdf*. Accessed October 1, 2002.

Kaminsky, Graciela and Carmen Reinhart. 1998. On crises, contagion, and confusion. Draft of paper prepared for the Duke University Conference Globalization, Capital Market Crises and Economic Reform. December 10. *http://www.puaf.umd.edu/faculty/papers/ reinhart/document.pdf*. Accessed October 1, 2002.

Kaplan, Idanna and Avery Tillet Ke. 1998. Malaysia. In *The Asian crisis: What has happened and why?*, edited by Kar-yiu Wong The Economics Research Group on Southeast and East Asia, University of Washington, Department of Economics.

Kindelberger, Charles P. (2000), *Manias, panics, and crashes: A history of financial crises*. 4th ed. Boston: John Wiley & Sons.

Krugman, Paul. 1979. A model of balance of payment crisis. *Journal of Money, Credit, and Banking* 11(8):311–325.

———. 1998. What happened to Asia? Unpublished manuscript from a conference in Japan, January. *http://web.mit.edu/krugman/www/DISINTER.html*. Accessed October 1, 2002.

Krugman, Paul and Richard Baldwin. 2001. Agglomeration, integration and tax harmonization. Working paper. *http://heiwww.unige.ch/~baldwin/papers/BKtax.PDF*. Accessed October 7, 2002.

Lane, Timothy, Atish Ghosh, Javier Hamann, Steven Phillips, Marianne Schulze-Ghattas, and Tsidi Tsikata. 1999. IMF-supported programs in Indonesia, Korea, and Thailand: A preliminary assessment. Washington, D.C.: International Monetary Fund. Occasional Paper 178.

Litan, Robert and Alice Rivlin. 2001. *Beyond the dot.coms: The economic promise of the Internet*. Washington, D.C.: Brookings Institution Press.

Mauro, Paolo. 1995. Corruption and growth. *The Quarterly Journal of Economics* 106(2):681–711.

Meltzer, Allan. 1998. Financial failures and financial policies. In *Deregulating financial services: Public policy flux*, edited by G.G. Kaufman and R.C. Kormendia, eds. Cambridge, Mass.: Ballinger.

———. 2001. The report of the International Financial Institution Advisory Commission: Comments on the critics. *http://www.gsia.cmu.edu/afs/andrew/gsia/meltzer/Spanishedition3.doc*. Accessed October 1, 2002.

Mussa, Michael. 2000. Factors driving global economic integration. Paper presented in Jackson Hole, Wyoming at a symposium sponsored by the Federal Reserve Bank of Kansas City on Global Opportunities and Challenges, August 25.

———. 2002. *Argentina and the Fund: From triumph to tragedy*. Washington, D.C.: Institute for International Economics.

Nyambi, Nelly. 1999. Brazil: The critical journey from macroeconomic instability to sustainable growth. Seminar paper. Department of Economics, Columbia University.

Obstfeld, Maurice. 1994. The logic of currency crises. *Cahiers Economiques et Monetaires* no. 43:189–213.

———. 1995. International currency experience. Brookings paper on economic activity. Number 1. Washington, D.C.: Brookings Institution.

Obstfeld, Maurice and Kenneth Rogoff. 1995. The mirage of fixed exchange rates. Cambridge, Mass.: NBER working paper 5191, July.

Organisation for Economic Cooperation & Development. 2000. *EMU one year on*. Paris. April.

Oliner, Stephen D. and Daniel E. Sichel. 2000. The resurgence of growth in the late 1990s: is information technology the story? Finance and Economics Discussion Series 2000–20, Board of Governors of the Federal Reserve System, Washington, D.C..

Petras, James and Steve Viewux. 1992. Myth and realities in Latin America. *Monthly Review* (April):9–20.

Phelps, Edmund. 1999. Lessons from the corporatist crisis in some Asian Nations. *Journal of Policy Modeling* (May) 21(3):331–339. (From the roundtable on the East Asian financial crisis, American Economic Association meetings, New York, January 4, 1999.)

Popov, Vladimir. 1999. Currency crisis in Russia in a wider context. Mimeograph. Institute of European and Russian Studies, Carleton University, Canada.

Price, Elizabeth. 2001. Meltzer-Lerrick plan would have IMF buy troubled debt. *Dow Jones International News.* May 10, electronic news feed.

Radelet, Steven and Jeffrey Sachs. 1998. The onset of the East Asian financial crisis. Cambridge, Mass.: NBER working paper 6680. August.

Rebuilding the international financial architecture. Emerging Markets Eminent Persons Group Report. 2001. Seoul: Institute for Global Economics.

Rodrik, Dani. 2001. The developing countries' hazardous obsession with global integration. Working paper. *http://ksghome.harvard.edu/~.drodrik.academic.ksg/obsession.pdf.* Accessed October 1, 2002.

———. 2000. Exchange rate regimes and institutional arrangements in the shadow of capital flows. Paper prepared for a conference on Central Banking and Sustainable Development, held in Kuala Lumpur, Malaysia, in honor of Tun Ismail Mohammed Ali. August 28–30.

———. 1998. "Who needs capital-account convertibility?" Contribution to a symposium, edited by Peter Kenen, published as part of a Princeton *Essay in International Finance* no. 207 (May–June). Princeton, NJ: Princeton University Press.

Rodrik, Dani and Andres Velasco. 1999. Short-term capital flows. Paper prepared for the 1999 ABCDE Conference at the World Bank. Cambridge, Mass.: NBER Working paper 7364.

Sazanami, Yoko and H. Kawai. 1999. An empirical analysis of Japanese multinational corporate strategies in Europe, Asia and North America. In *The global integration of Europe and East Asia*, edited by Sang-Gon Lee and Pierre-Bruno Ruffini, Cheltenham, U.K: Edward Elgar.

Sazanami, Yoko and Seiji Yoshimura. 1999. Restructuring East Asian exchange rate regimes. Paper presented at an international conference: International Trade and Capital Flows in Economic Restructuring and Growth—European and East Asia Experiences, organized by Inha University and University of Le Havre, October 5–6.

Shiller, Robert. 2000. *Irrational exuberance.* Princeton, N.J.: Princeton University Press.

Swoboda, Alexander. 1999. Reforming the international financial architecture. *Finance and Development* 36(3):2–4.

Tobin, James. 1978. A proposal for international monetary reform. *Eastern Economic Journal* no. 3–4:53–159.

Wade, Robert. 1998a. The Asian crisis: The high debt model versus the Wall Street-Treasury-IMF complex. *New Left Review* no. 228 (March-April): 3–23.

————. 1998b. The Asian debt-and-development crisis of 1997–?: Causes and consequences. *World Development* 26(8):1535–1553.

Wade, Robert and Frank Veneroso. 1998. The gathering world slump and the battle over capital controls. *New Left Review* no. 231 (September–October): 13–42.

Wang, Jabatan Kawalan Pertukaran. Exchange control policy. Bank Negara Malaysia from *http://www.bnm.gov.my/feature/ecm/overview.htm*. Accessed October 7, 2002.

Wei, Shang-Jin. 1997. How taxing is corruption on international investors? Cambridge, Mass.: NBER working paper 6030, May.

————. 1999. Corruption in economic development: Beneficial grease, minor annoyance, or major obstacle? Paper presented at the Sixth Mitsui Life Symposium on Economic Freedom and Development, Tokyo, June 17–18.

Wei, Shang-Jin and Sara Sievers. 2000. The cost of crony capitalism. In *The Asian financial crisis: Lessons for a resilient Asia*, edited by Wing Thye Woo, Jeffrey D. Sachs, and Klaus Schwab. Cambridge, Mass.: MIT Press, pp. 91–102.

Weitzman, Martin L. 1970. Soviet postwar economic growth and capital-labor substitution. *American Economic Review* 60(4):676–92.

Wong, Kar-yiu, ed. 1998. *The Asian crisis: What has happened and why?* The Economics Research Group on Southeast and East Asia, University of Washington, Department of Economics.

World Bank. 1997. *China engaged: Integration with the global economy.* Washington, D.C.: The World Bank.

Young, Alwyn. 1995 The tyranny of numbers: confronting the statistical realities of the East Asian growth experience. *Quarterly Journal of Economics* no. 110 (August): 641–680.

Index

trols, 269–71; characterized, 2, 6, 10–11; and credibility damage, 238; East-Asian, 84–85; and flexible exchange rates, 282n; and IMF-led external pressures, 281; in Indonesia, 213; and intermediate exchange rates, 264, 282n; and Meltzer Commission, 276–78; policy ideology questioned, 238; prescriptions monotonous, 238; recommendations for, 237; requirements for, 237–38; in Russia, 225; size of, 235–36; in South Korea, 125, 237; and Suharto cronyism, 251; in Thailand, 213, 214; in Turkey, 173, 194, 195, 196, 234–35; and World Bank, 214

IMF Contingent Credit Line, 279

India: and capital account controls, 243; and capital account convertibility, 260–62; and current account convertibility, 282n; and foreign exchange regulations, 259–60; and fundamentals, 261

Indonesia: banking sector of, 113, 114; capital account controls of, removed, 113–14; corruption in, 250–51; cronyism in, 250–51; economic indicators in, 89t, 90; and IMF, 125, 220; IMF bailout of, 213; political uncertainty of, 127

industrial production, in Japan, 73, 74f

inflation: in Argentina, 175, 176f, 177; in Brazil, 162, 163, 164; and Cavallo Plan, 190; in crisis-prone economies, 90; and euro stability, 60; in eurozone, 48, 49f; inertial, 108; and interest rates, 29–30; in Japan, 71, 72f, 73; pre-9/11, 33; and productivity, 29; in Russia, 140, 141f, 148, 151, 222–23; and Russian exchange rate, 147f, 147; in Turkey, 187, 188f, 234; in U.S., 16, 17f

information technology: and capital investment, 25; and debt impact, 35; and eurozone, 53; and giant hardware suppliers, 35; and labor productivity, 24–27; and total factor productivity, 26

intangible wealth, 23–24

Intel, 28

Inter-American Development Bank (IDB), 228

interest rates: and crisis-era movements, 204, 204f, 205f, 211n; post-9/11 turnaround of, 43; pre-9/11 cuts, 39; and ruble appreciation, 149; increase of, in U.S., 29

International Financial Institution Advisory Commission (IFIAC), 276

International Monetary Fund (IMF): and Argentina, 183, 185, 186, 230–34; and Argentina bailout, 172–73; and Argentina debt settlement, 233–34; and Argentina options outlined, 231–32; and Asian crisis recovery scenarios, 132; and Asian financial crisis, 101, 119–20; and Asian financial crisis as unprecedented, 212; bailouts characterized by, 2, 6, 10–11; and Brazil, 169–71; and Brazil policy stance, 227–30; and Brazil rescue package, 5; and capital account controls, 238–39, 268–71; capital account role of, 98n; characteristics of response of, 212; and Chinese current account convertibility, 257; and Communist resistance, 224; fiscal policy of, as misguided, 219; fiscal targets of, revised, 220–21; historical shift in focus of, 282n–83n; and Indonesia, 125, 127–28, 135n; and inflexible policy posturing, 240; and macroeconomic targeting, 237–38; and Meltzer Commission overhaul, 276–78; operating as G-7-led institution, 7; policy record of, assessed, 7–8, 212; as possible lender of last resort, 236–37, 280; as quasi-lender, 280; and recession resulting, 4; record of, questioned, ix–x; reform of, called for, 263–64; rescue packages of, 10–11; and Russia, 138, 161; and Russian financial crisis, 147–48; Russian membership in, 222; and Russian policy agenda, 222; and Russia's market reforms, 224–25; and solutions to crisis, 10; and South Korea, 125; and sovereignty issue, 218; unsatisfactory role of, 86; U.S. role in, 278–79

Internet Tax Freedom Act of 1998, 57

Internet technology, purchasing, 26–27

intervention, unsterilized, 85n

inventory control, 27

investment: and foreign holders in India, 261; and pre-9/11 monetary policy, 40–41

investment, domestic, in Japan, 71, 73f, 73

investment rates: in Argentina, 177–78, 178f; in Turkey, 189f, 189

Japan: ASEAN + 3 collective, 131; and bad loans, 2; borrowing patterns of, 1; and loans to East Asia, 202–203; origins of